estimated

good luck™

Good Luck Volume 2
Created by E-Jin Kang

Translation - Ellen Choi
English Adaptation - Darcy Lockman
Retouch and Lettering - Star Print Brokers
Production Artist - Jennifer Carbajal
Graphic Designer - Al-Insan Lashley

Editor - Carol Fox
Digital Imaging Manager - Chris Buford
Pre-Production Supervisor - Erika Terriquez
Art Director - Anne Marie Horne
Production Manager - Elisabeth Brizzi
VP of Production - Ron Klamert
Editor-in-Chief - Rob Tokar
Publisher - Mike Kiley
President and C.O.O. - John Parker
C.E.O. and Chief Creative Officer - Stuart Levy

A  Manga

TOKYOPOP and ⓦ are trademarks or registered trademarks of TOKYOPOP Inc.

TOKYOPOP Inc.
5900 Wilshire Blvd. Suite 2000
Los Angeles, CA 90036

E-mail: info@TOKYOPOP.com
Come visit us online at www.TOKYOPOP.com

ISBN: 978-1-59816-762-7

First TOKYOPOP printing: May 2007
10 9 8 7 6 5 4 3 2 1
Printed in the USA

good luck™

by
E-Jin Kang

Vol. 2

HAMBURG // LONDON // LOS ANGELES // TOKYO

good luck™

Shi-Hyun is pure bad luck. That's what everyone says...and in some ways, she believes it. So for their protection and her own, she maintains a hard shell that keeps people at bay.

Our story began when Shi-Hyun transferred to a new school and an array of new characters came into her life. The Queen Bee had a cool personality and the fighting skills to match. The Cold Prince had the good looks and cold demeanor to make all the girls swoon. And Shi-Hyun's reputation for being bad luck somehow traveled with her to her new school. Only one girl, Hee-Soo, was even willing to come near her.

But Hee-Soo was no friend. She was secretly plotting revenge against Shi-Hyun for breaking her sister's wrist in a kendo match. First Hee-Soo spread the rumor that Shi-Hyun was bad luck, to win allies for her cause. Then Hee-Soo sent one of these new allies to Shi-Hyun, with the message that Hee-Soo had been kidnapped by the Queen Bee's gang.

Now Shi-Hyun rushes to rescue Hee-Soo from an abandoned warehouse...where Hee-Soo waits to exact her final revenge.

CONTENTS

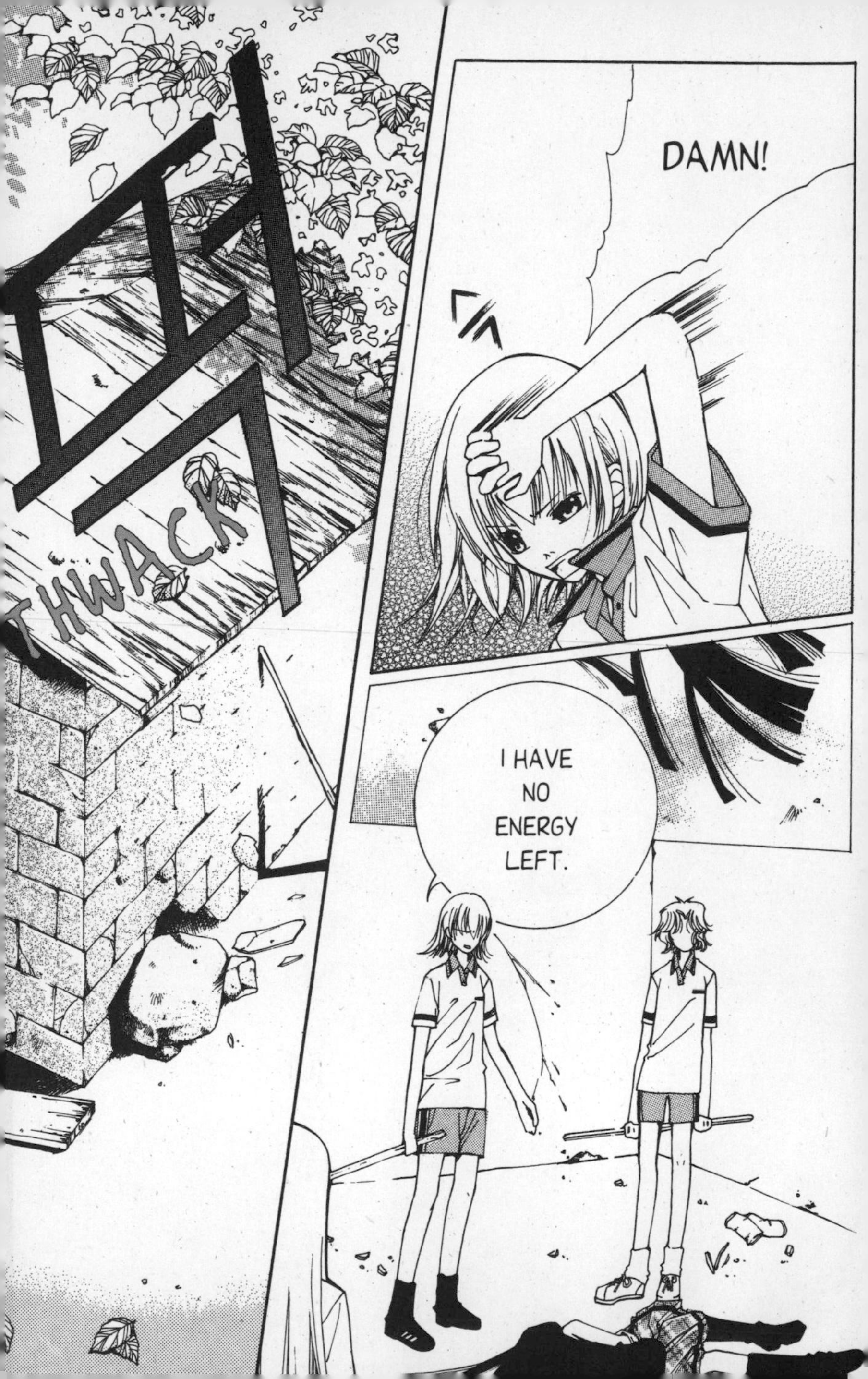
THWACK
DAMN!
I HAVE NO ENERGY LEFT.

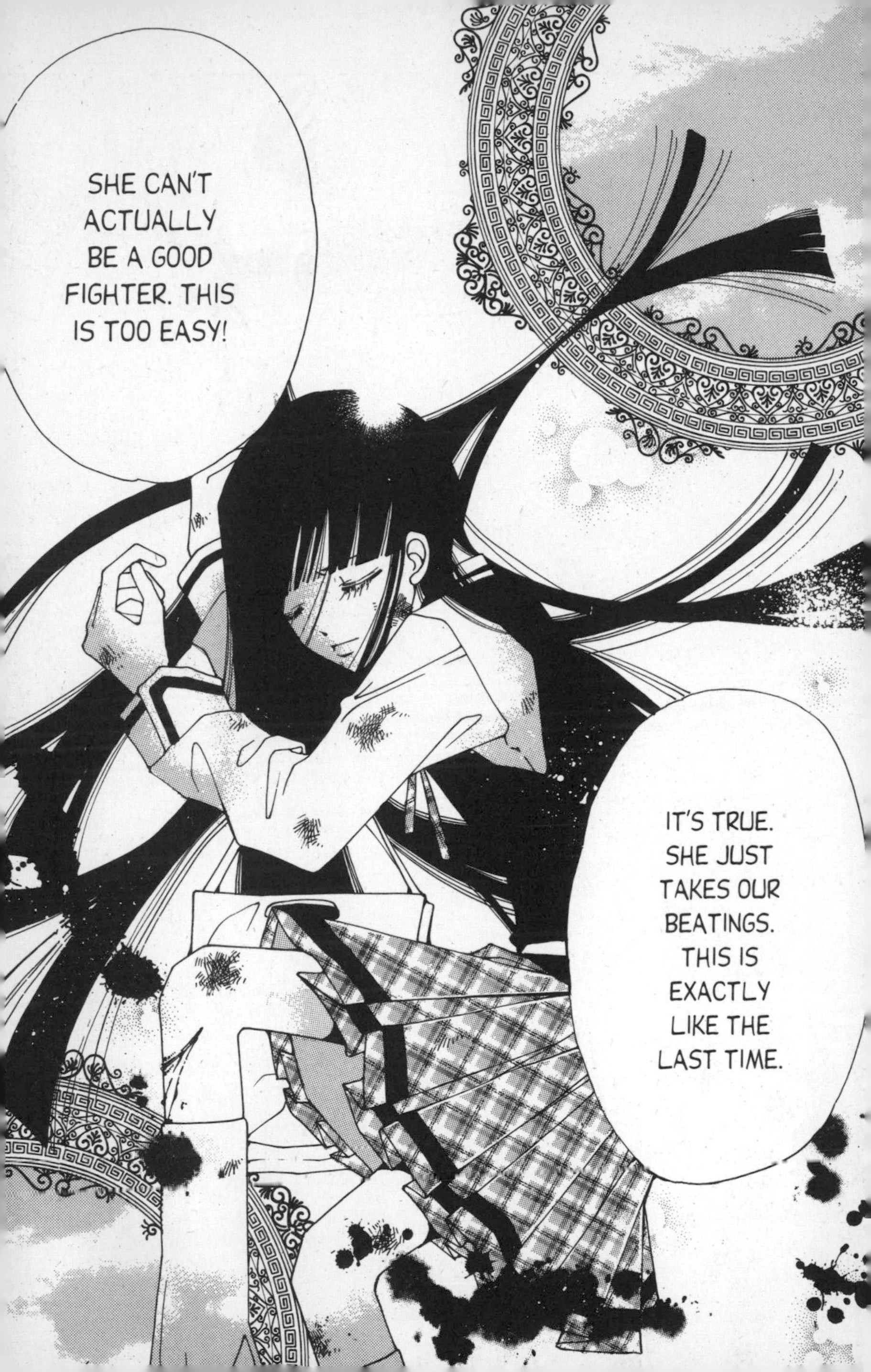
SHE CAN'T ACTUALLY BE A GOOD FIGHTER. THIS IS TOO EASY!
IT'S TRUE. SHE JUST TAKES OUR BEATINGS. THIS IS EXACTLY LIKE THE LAST TIME.

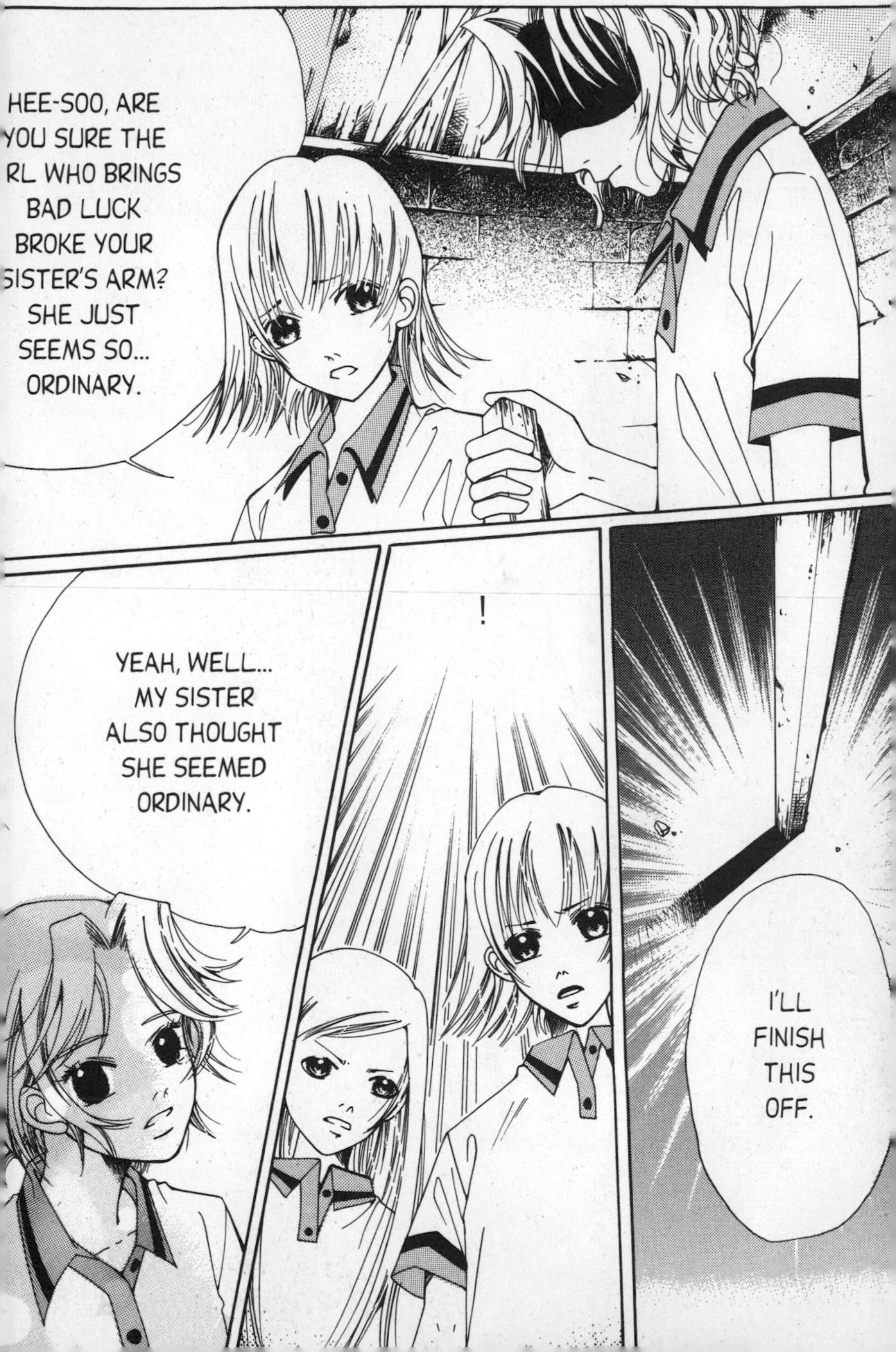
HEE-SOO, ARE YOU SURE THE RL WHO BRINGS BAD LUCK BROKE YOUR SISTER'S ARM? SHE JUST SEEMS SO... ORDINARY.
YEAH, WELL... MY SISTER ALSO THOUGHT SHE SEEMED ORDINARY.
!
I'LL FINISH THIS OFF.

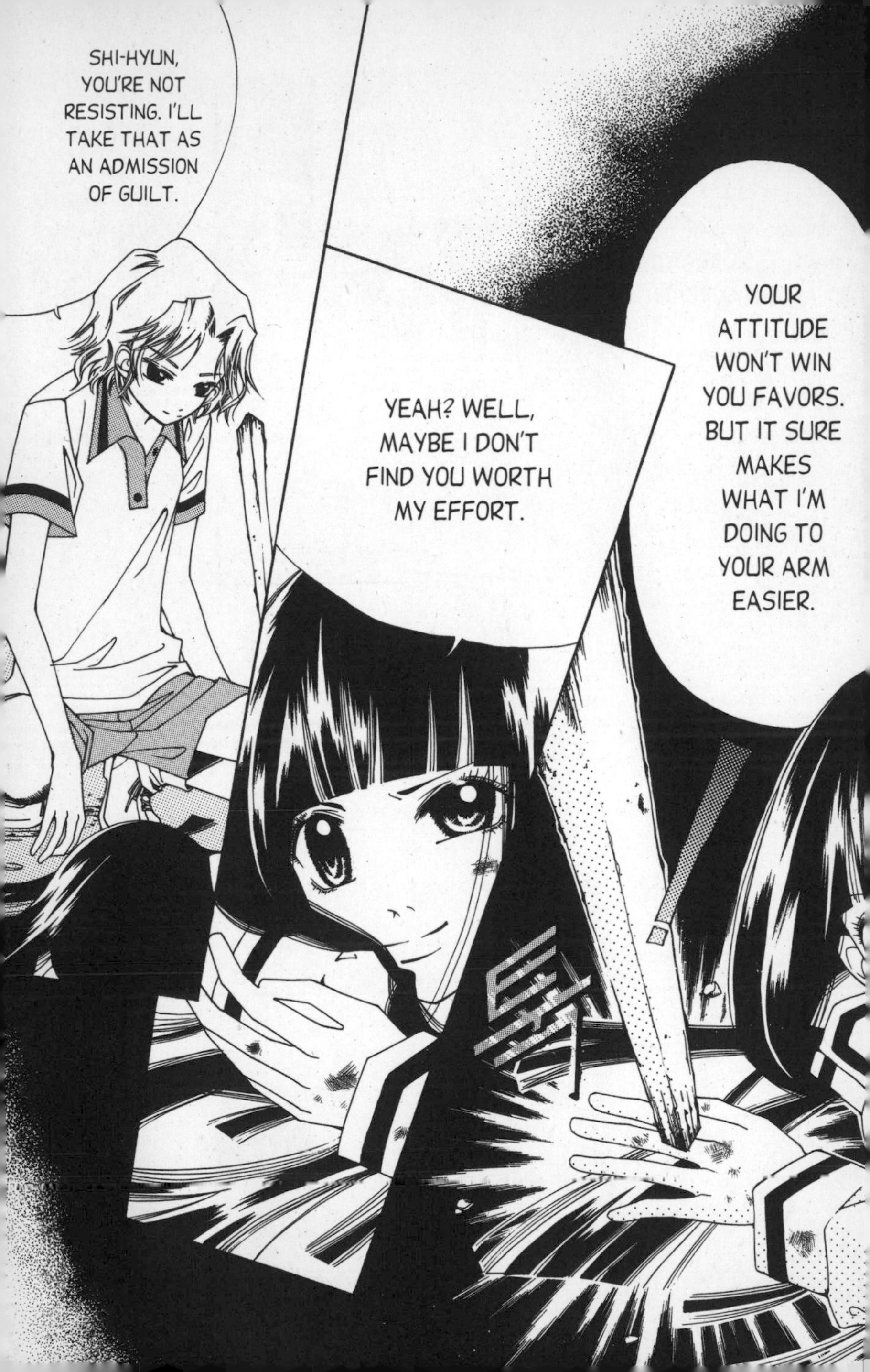
SHI-HYUN, YOU'RE NOT RESISTING. I'LL TAKE THAT AS AN ADMISSION OF GUILT.
YEAH? WELL, MAYBE I DON'T FIND YOU WORTH MY EFFORT.
YOUR ATTITUDE WON'T WIN YOU FAVORS. BUT IT SURE MAKES WHAT I'M DOING TO YOUR ARM EASIER.

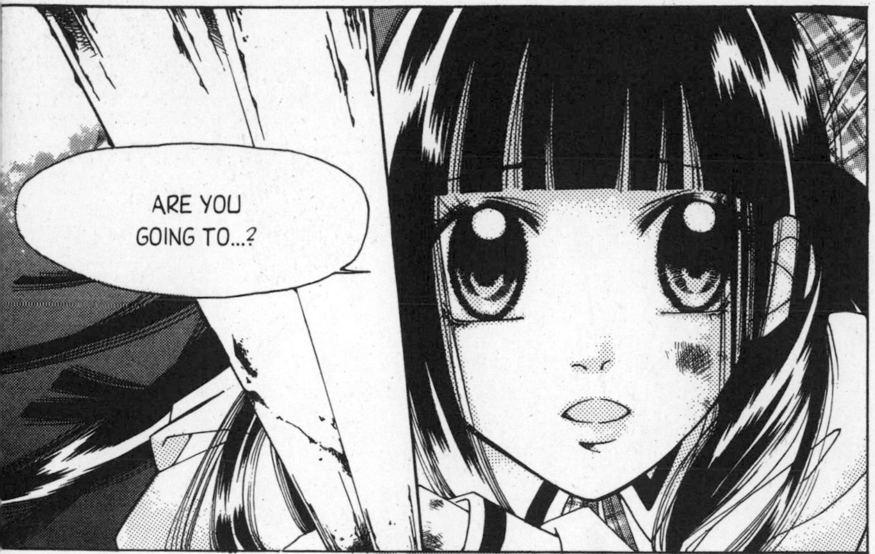
ARE YOU GOING TO...?
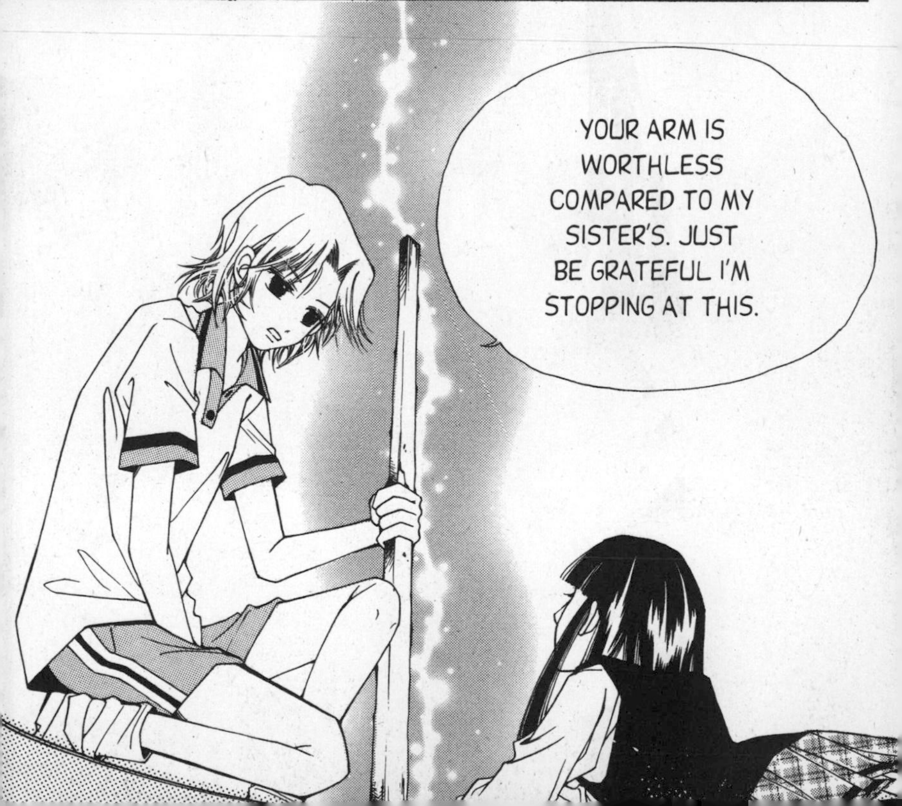
YOUR ARM IS WORTHLESS COMPARED TO MY SISTER'S. JUST BE GRATEFUL I'M STOPPING AT THIS.

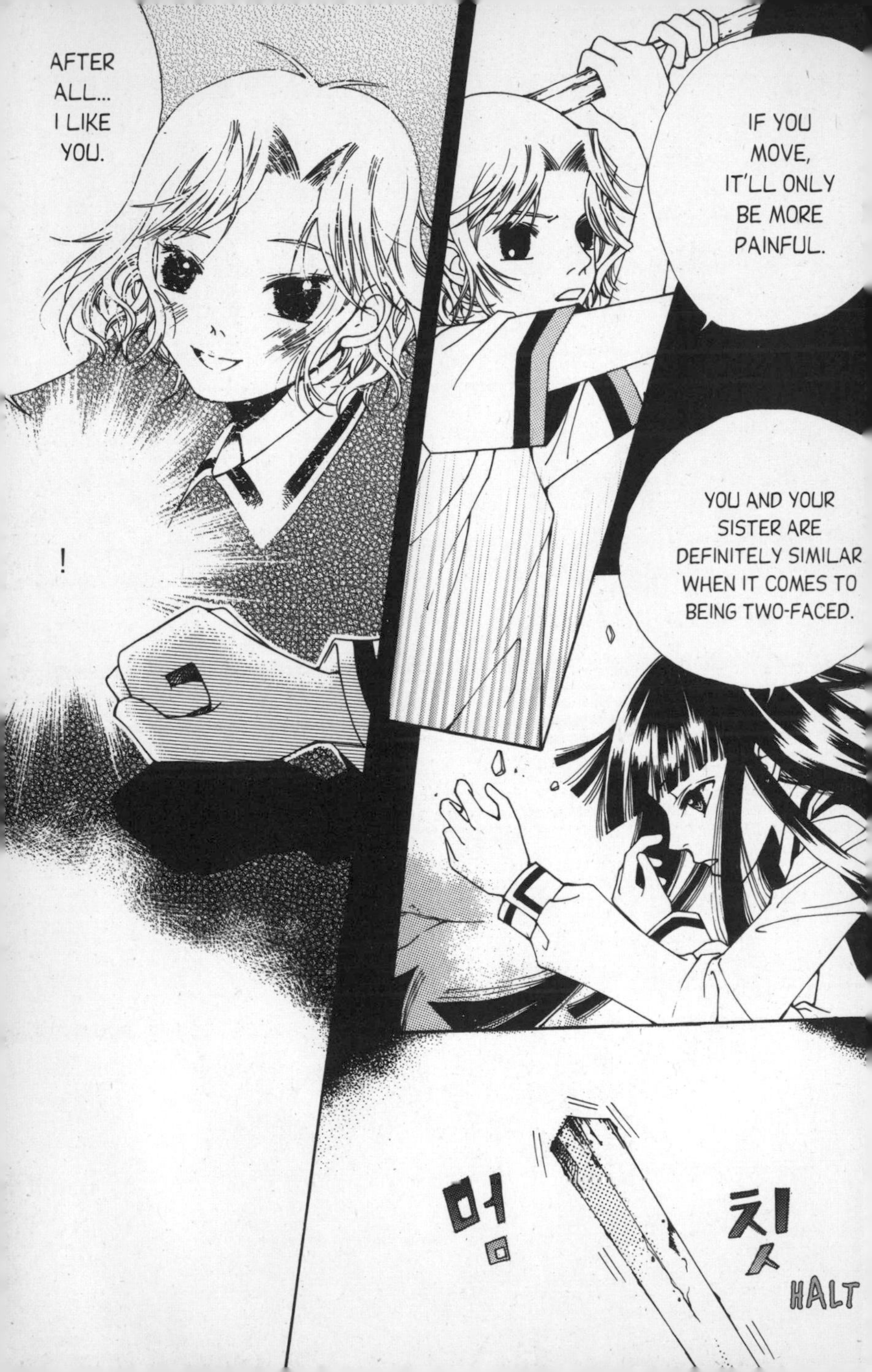
AFTER ALL... I LIKE YOU.
!
IF YOU MOVE, IT'LL ONLY BE MORE PAINFUL.
YOU AND YOUR SISTER ARE DEFINITELY SIMILAR WHEN IT COMES TO BEING TWO-FACED.
멈
칫
HALT

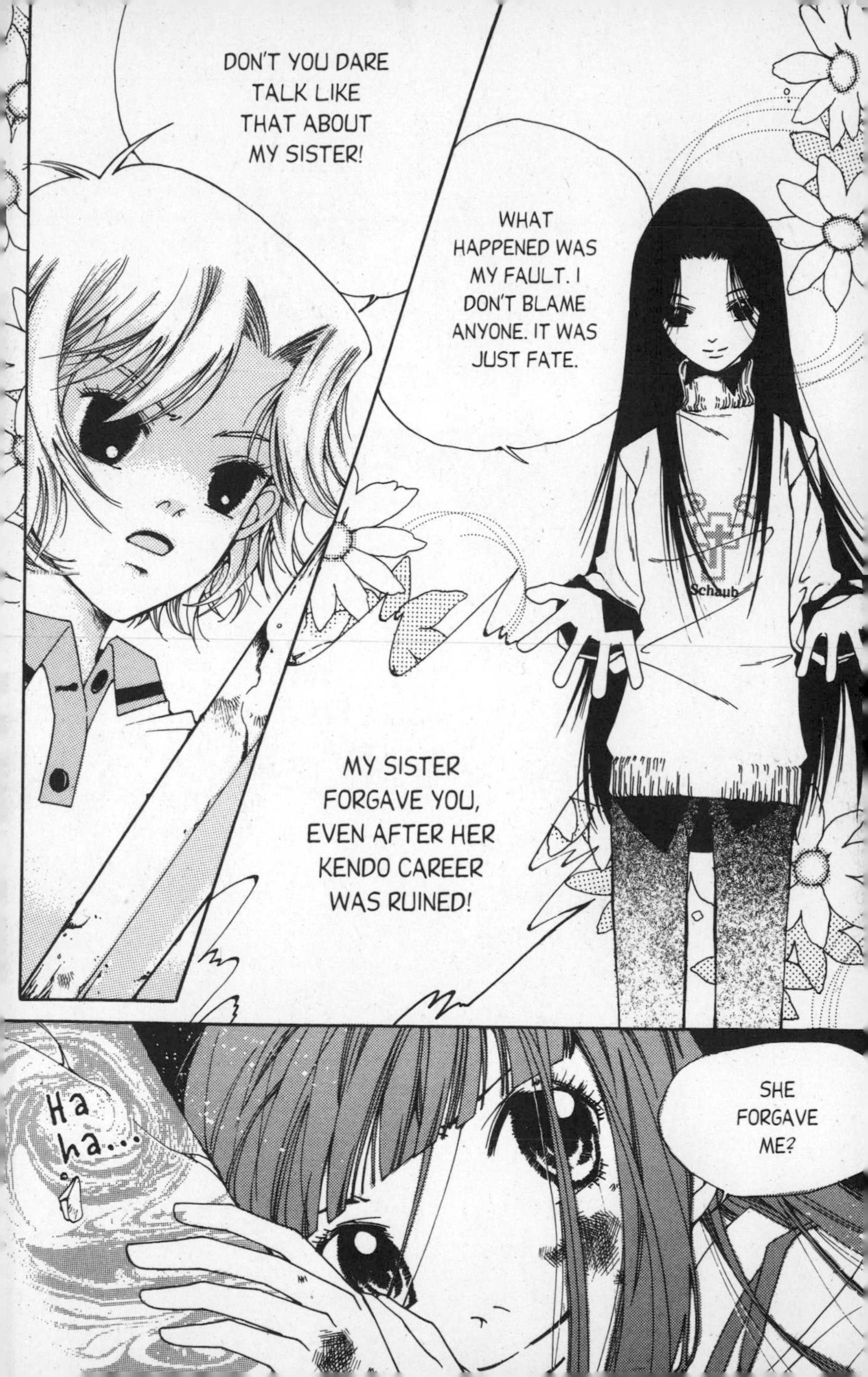
DON'T YOU DARE TALK LIKE THAT ABOUT MY SISTER!
WHAT HAPPENED WAS MY FAULT. I DON'T BLAME ANYONE. IT WAS JUST FATE.
Schaub
MY SISTER FORGAVE YOU, EVEN AFTER HER KENDO CAREER WAS RUINED!
Ha ha...
SHE FORGAVE ME?

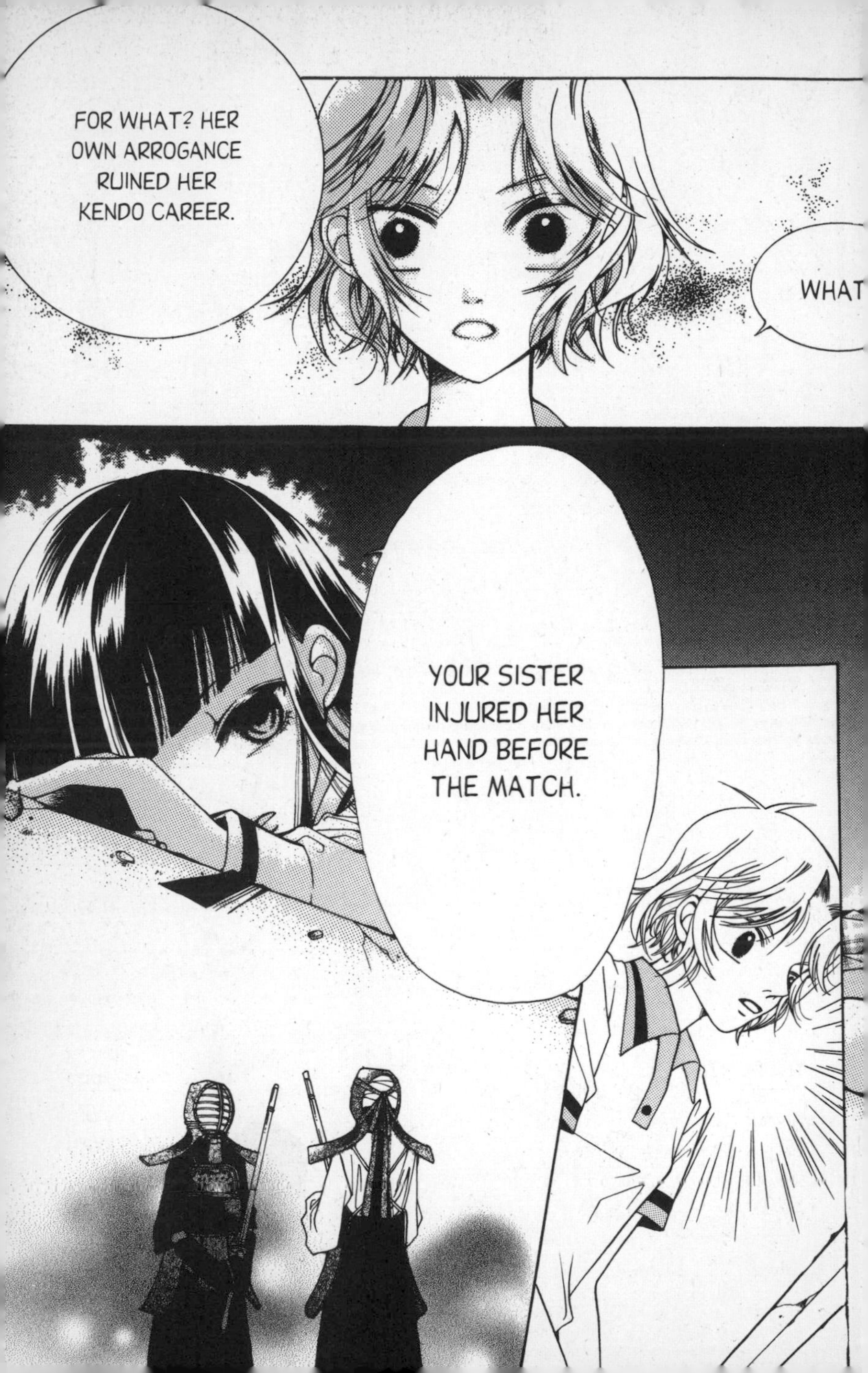
FOR WHAT? HER OWN ARROGANCE RUINED HER KENDO CAREER.
WHAT
YOUR SISTER INJURED HER HAND BEFORE THE MATCH.

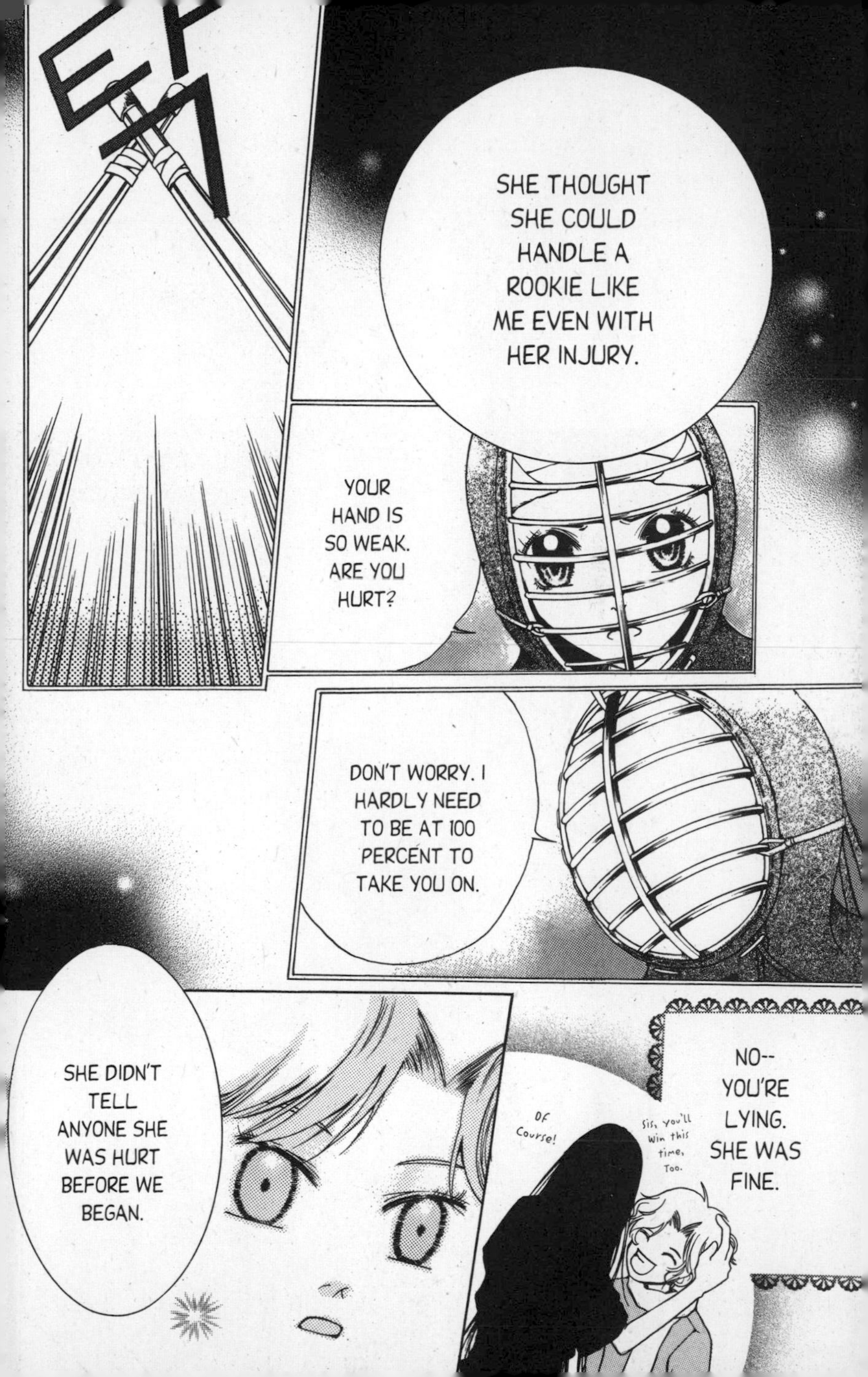
SHE THOUGHT SHE COULD HANDLE A ROOKIE LIKE ME EVEN WITH HER INJURY.
YOUR HAND IS SO WEAK. ARE YOU HURT?
DON'T WORRY. I HARDLY NEED TO BE AT 100 PERCENT TO TAKE YOU ON.
SHE DIDN'T TELL ANYONE SHE WAS HURT BEFORE WE BEGAN.
Of Course!
Sis, you'll win this time, Too.
NO-- YOU'RE LYING. SHE WAS FINE.

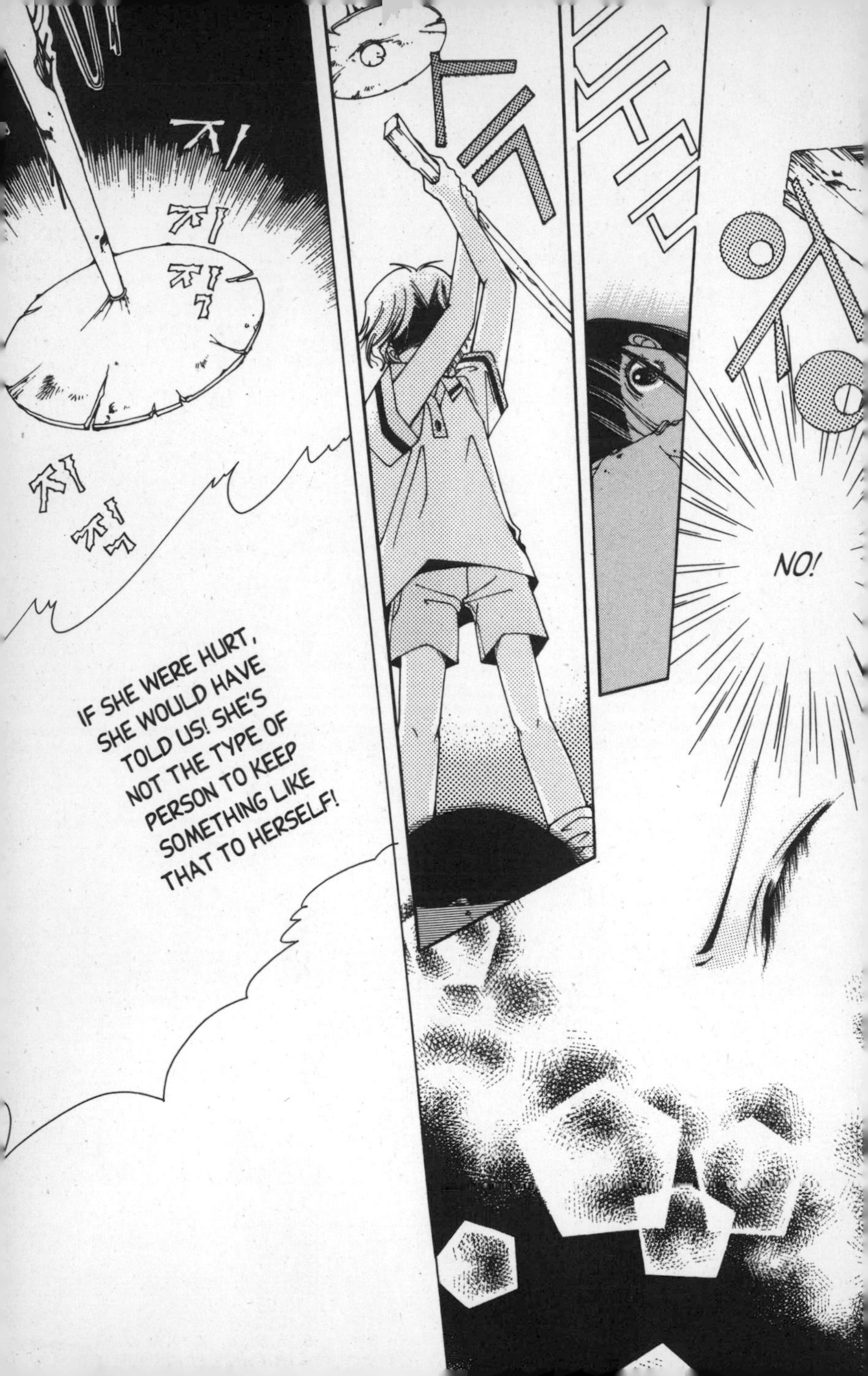
IF SHE WERE HURT, SHE WOULD HAVE TOLD US! SHE'S NOT THE TYPE OF PERSON TO KEEP SOMETHING LIKE THAT TO HERSELF!
NO!

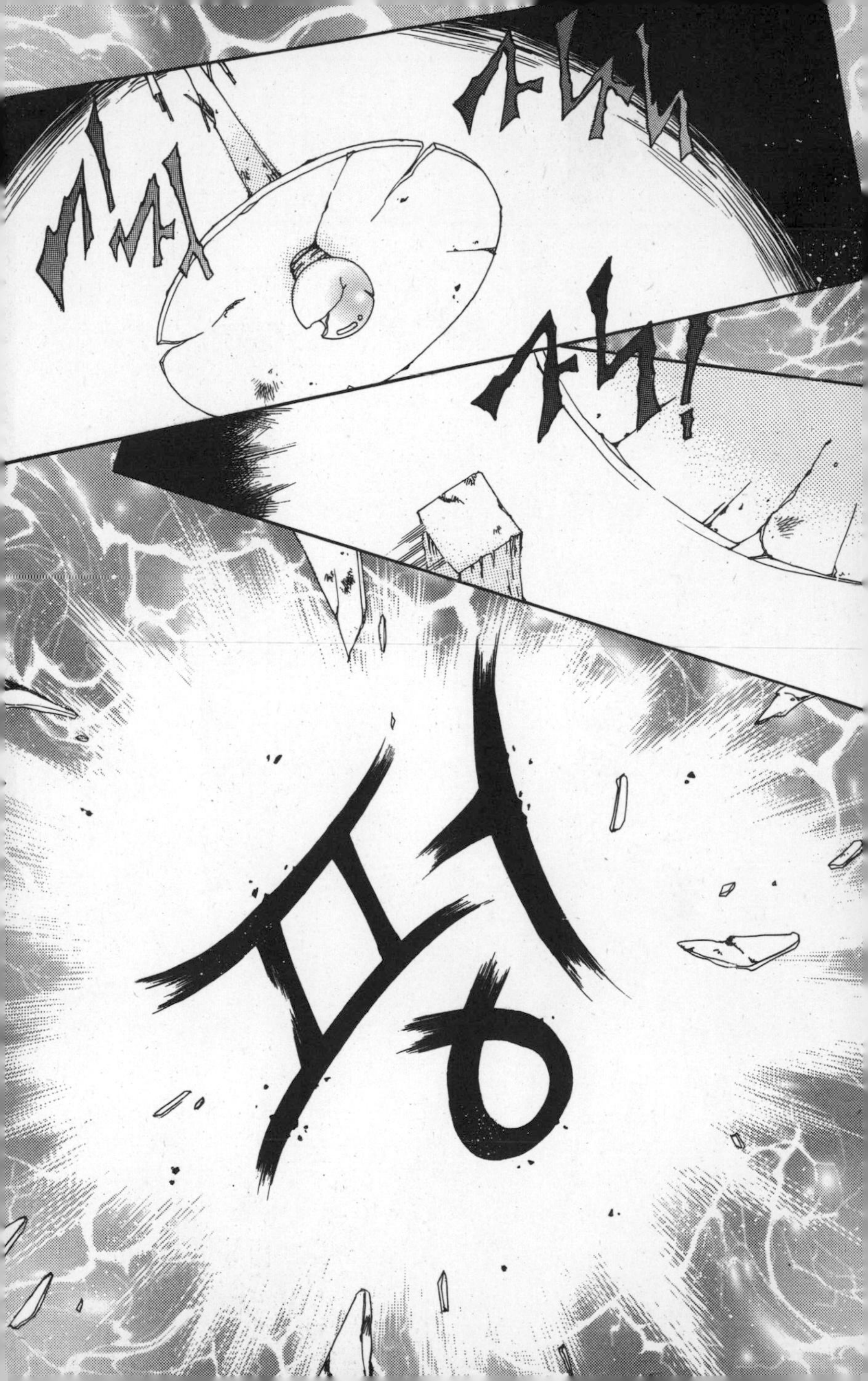

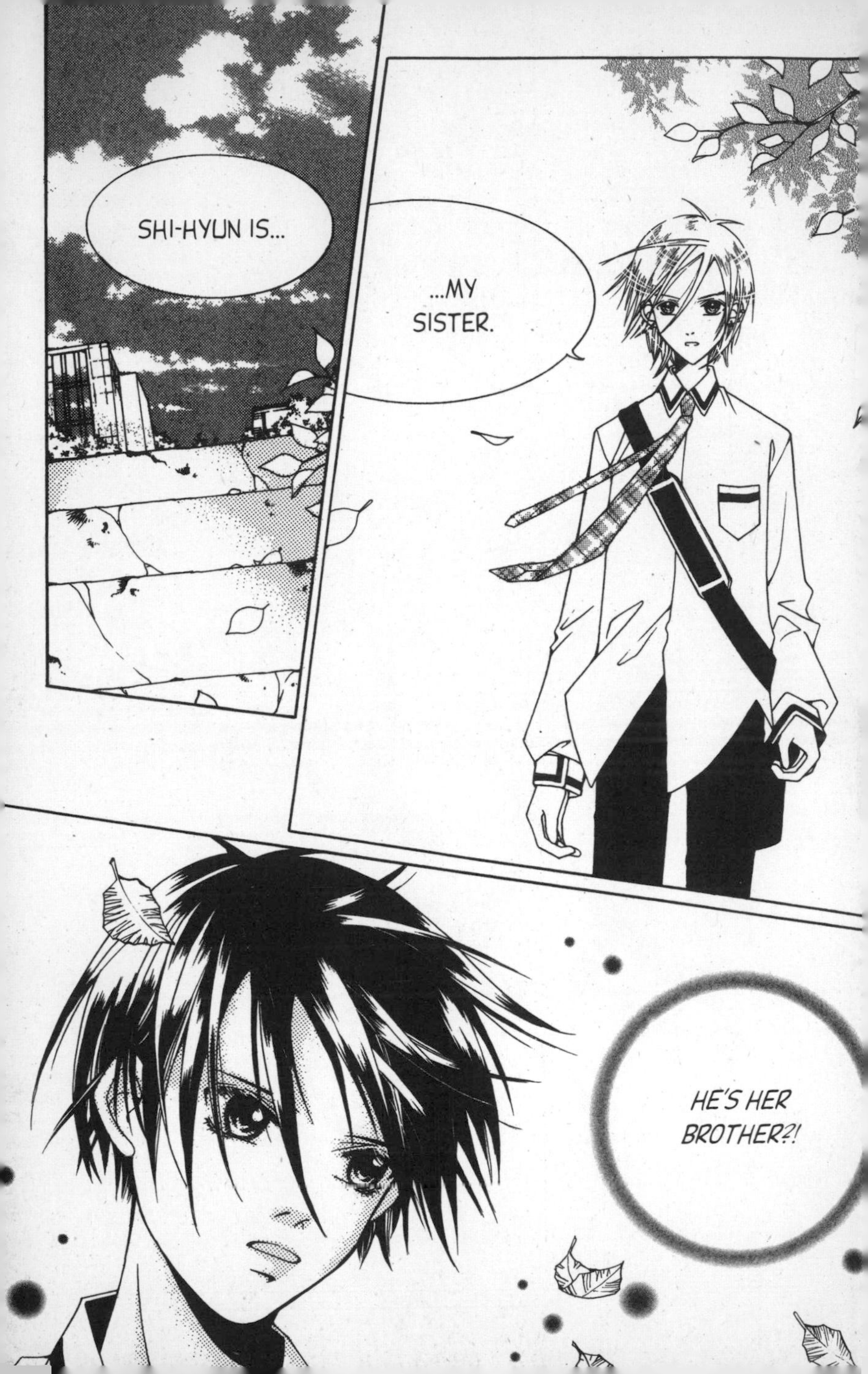
SHI-HYUN IS...
...MY SISTER.
HE'S HER BROTHER?!

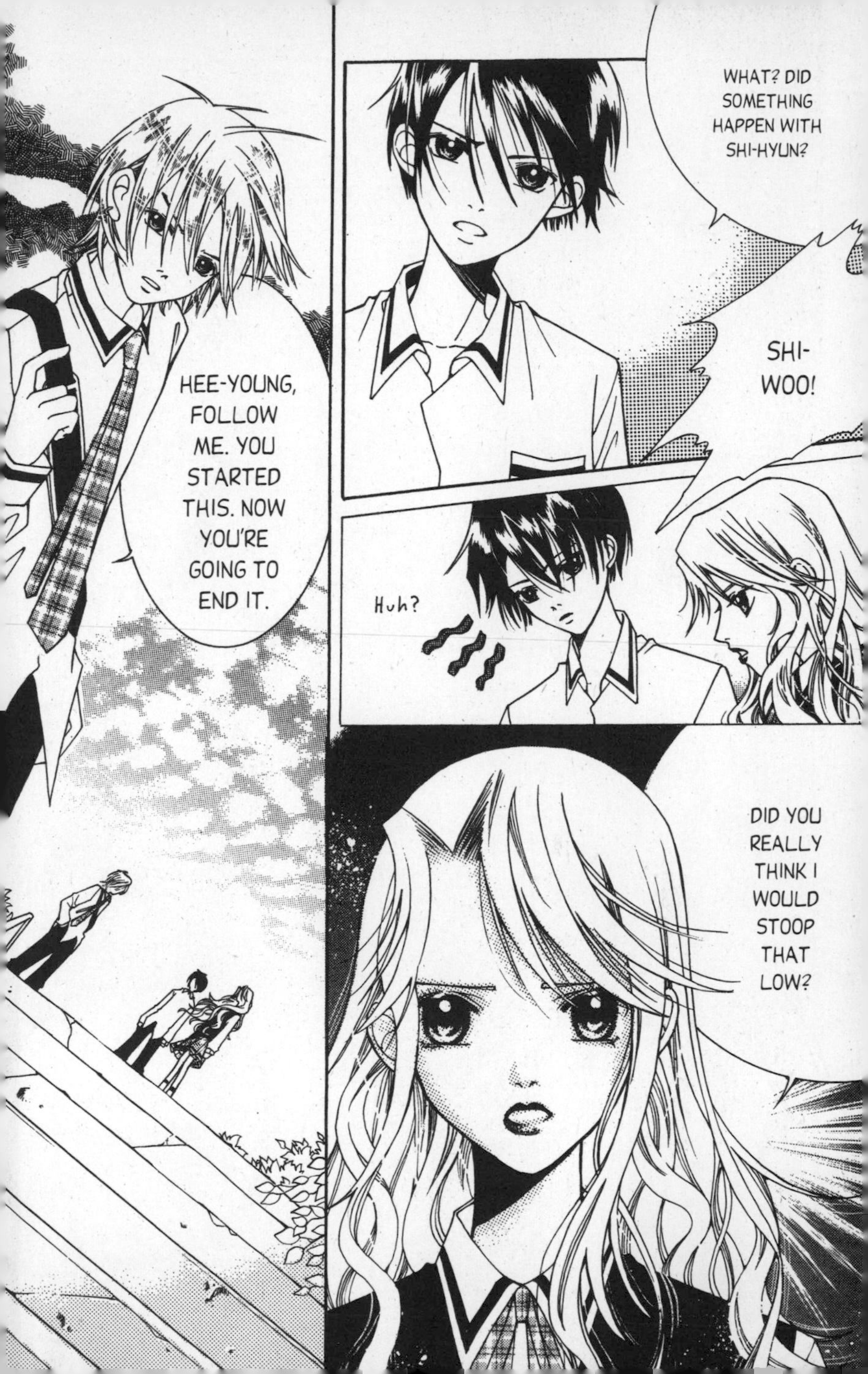
HEE-YOUNG, FOLLOW ME. YOU STARTED THIS. NOW YOU'RE GOING TO END IT.
WHAT? DID SOMETHING HAPPEN WITH SHI-HYUN?
SHI-WOO!
Huh?
DID YOU REALLY THINK I WOULD STOOP THAT LOW?

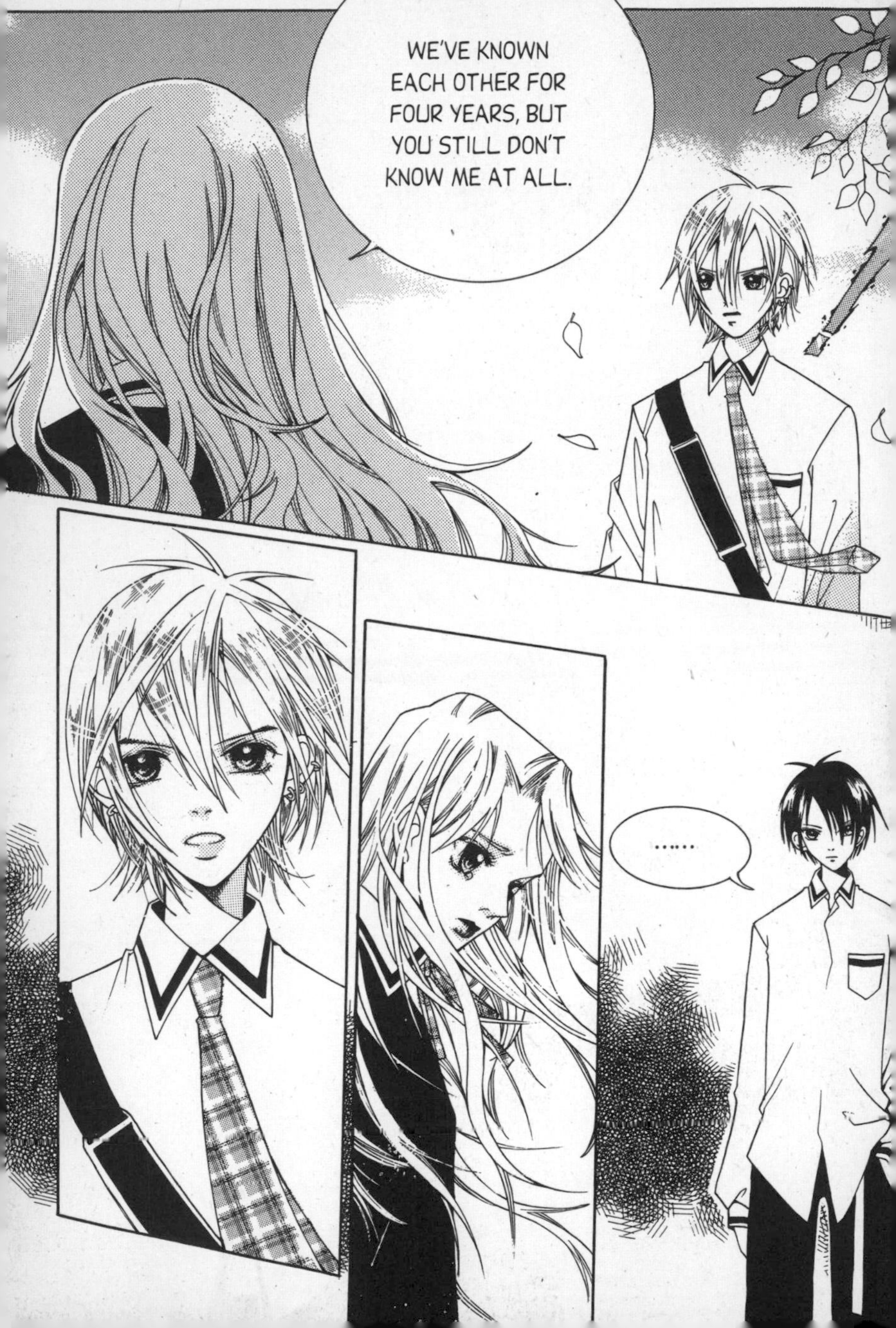
WE'VE KNOWN EACH OTHER FOR FOUR YEARS, BUT YOU STILL DON'T KNOW ME AT ALL.
......

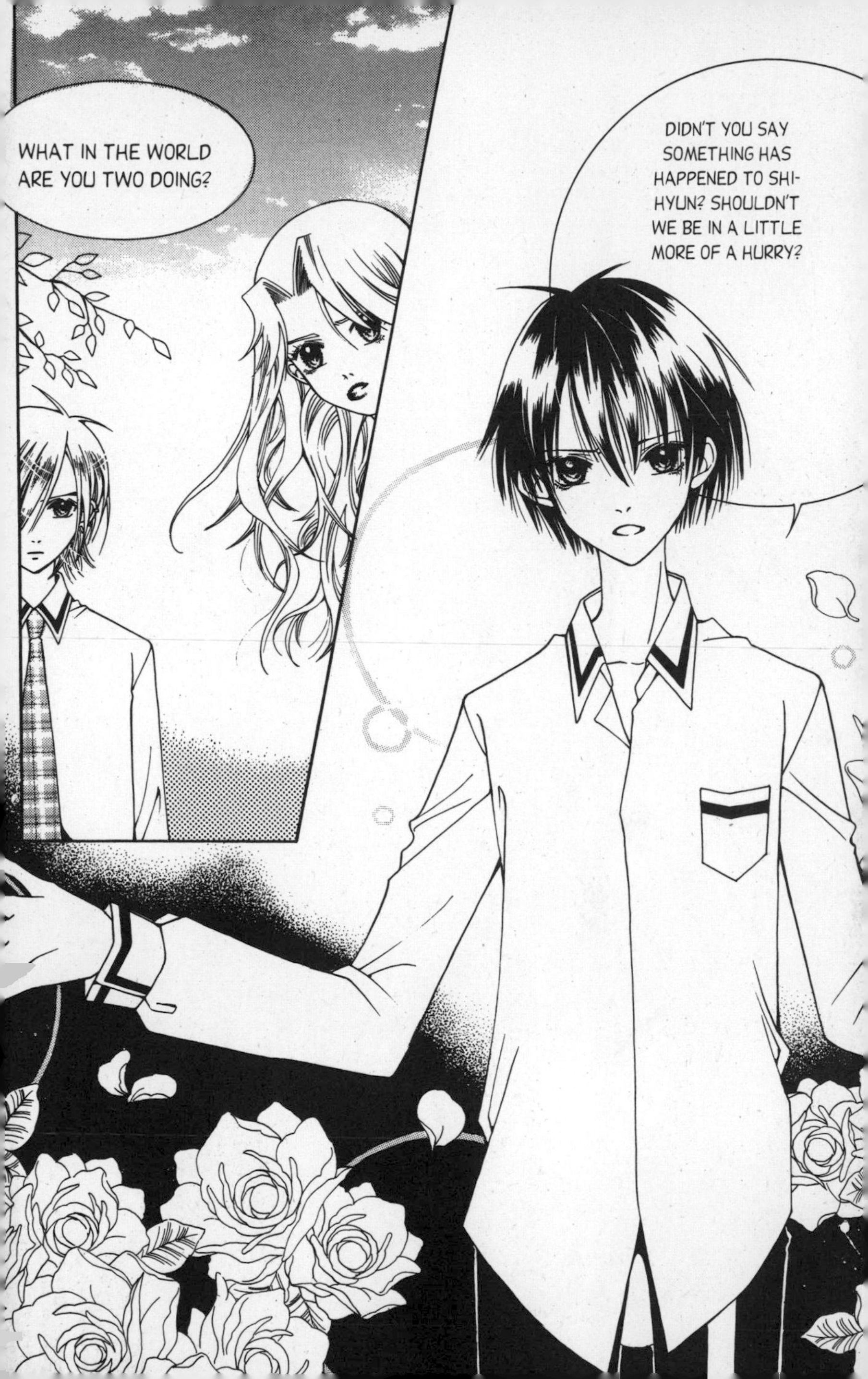
WHAT IN THE WORLD ARE YOU TWO DOING?
DIDN'T YOU SAY SOMETHING HAS HAPPENED TO SHI-HYUN? SHOULDN'T WE BE IN A LITTLE MORE OF A HURRY?

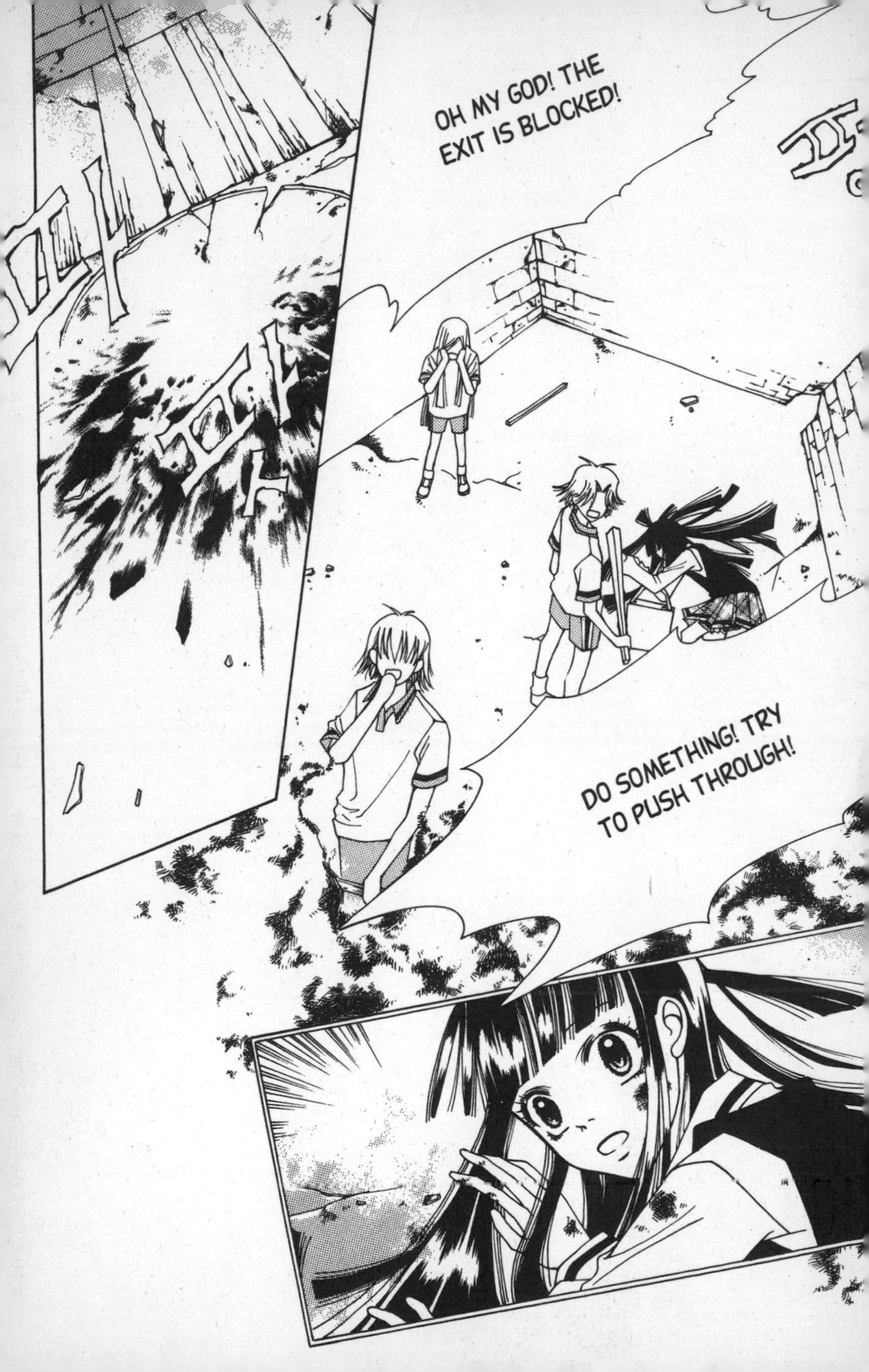
OH MY GOD! THE EXIT IS BLOCKED!
DO SOMETHING! TRY TO PUSH THROUGH!

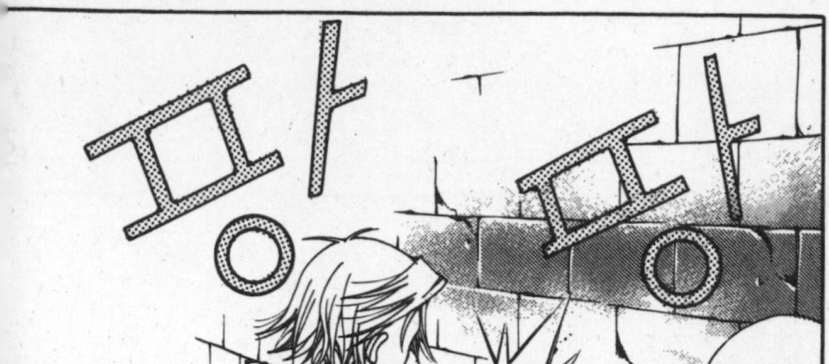
팡 팡
STOP IT! YOU'RE GOING TO KILL US ALL!

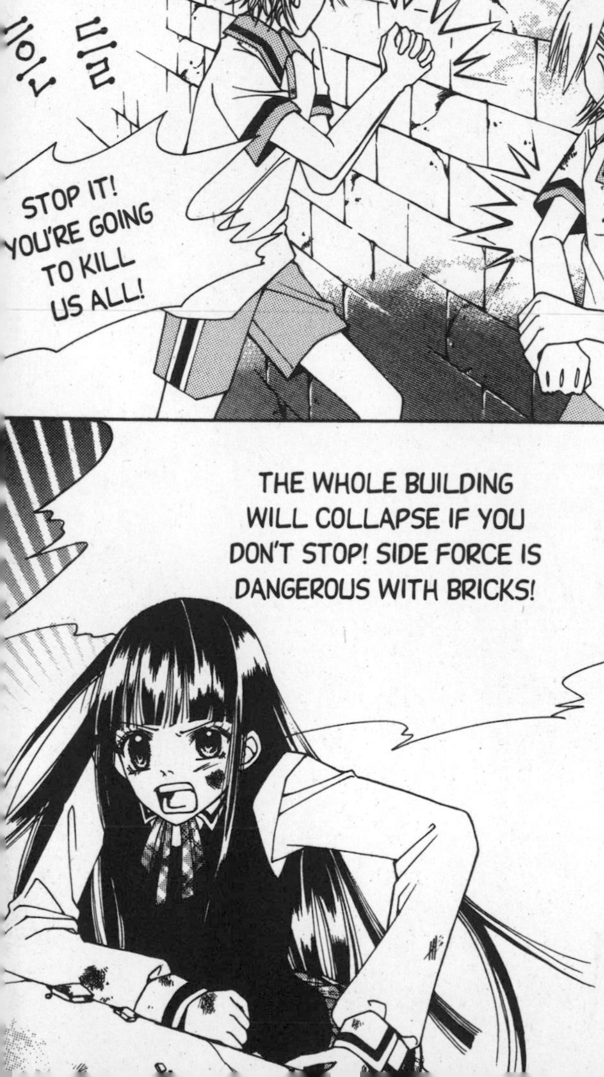
THE WHOLE BUILDING WILL COLLAPSE IF YOU DON'T STOP! SIDE FORCE IS DANGEROUS WITH BRICKS!

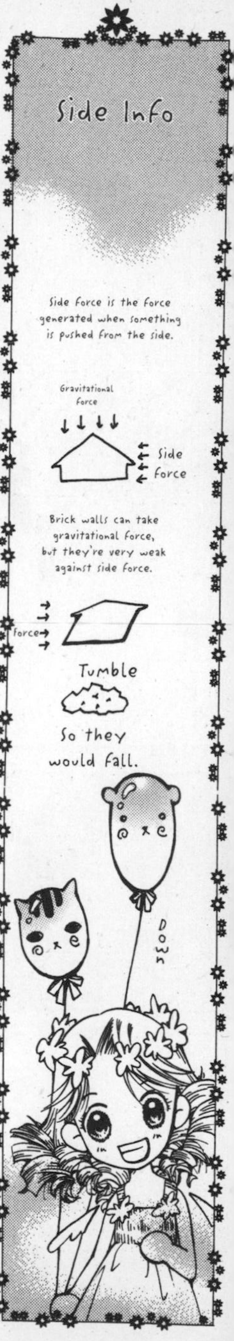
Side Info
Side force is the force generated when something is pushed from the side.
Gravitational force
Side force
Brick walls can take gravitational force, but they're very weak against side force.
force
Tumble
So they would fall.
Down

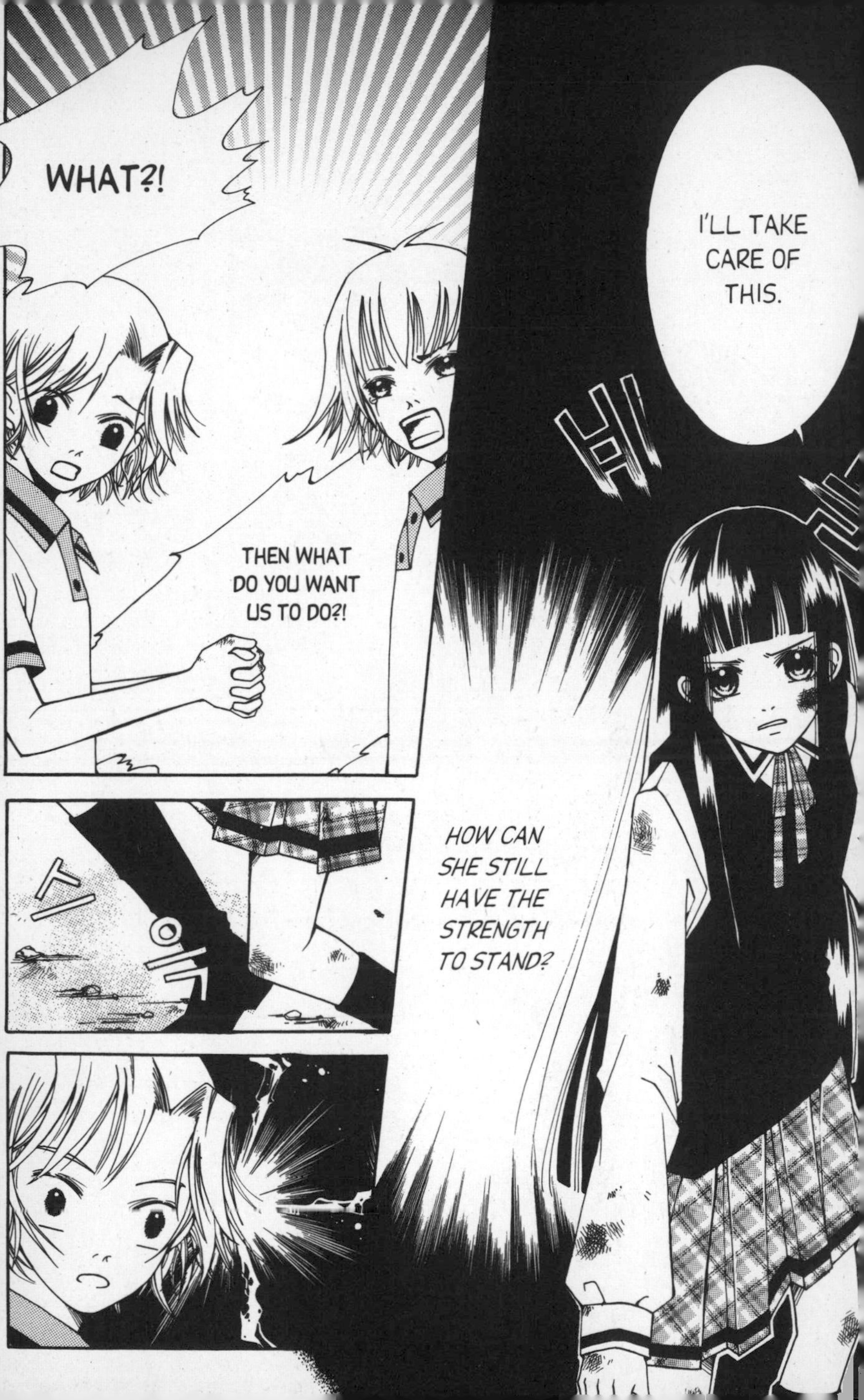
WHAT?!
THEN WHAT DO YOU WANT US TO DO?!
I'LL TAKE CARE OF THIS.
HOW CAN SHE STILL HAVE THE STRENGTH TO STAND?

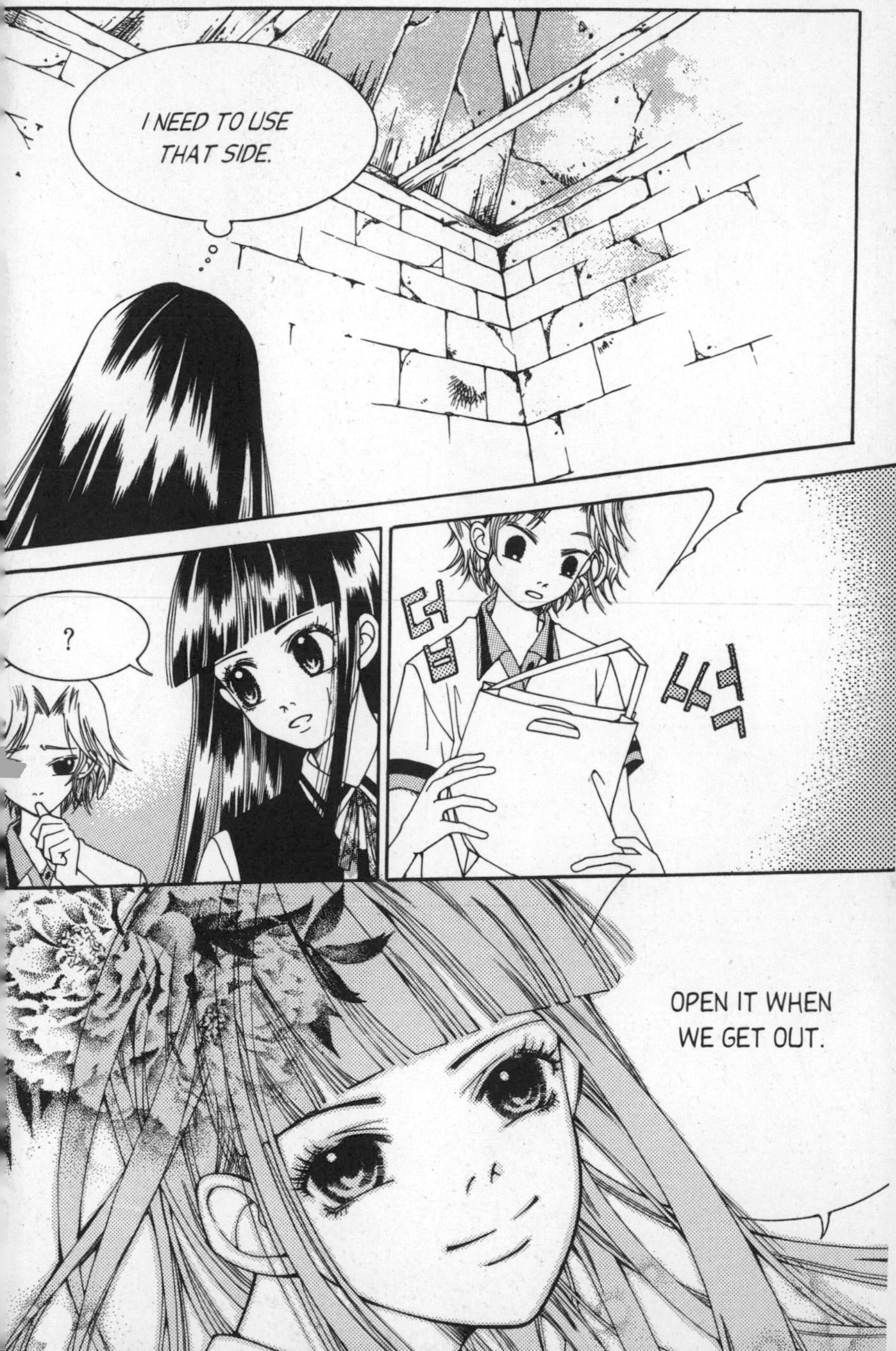
I NEED TO USE THAT SIDE.
?
덥썩
OPEN IT WHEN WE GET OUT.

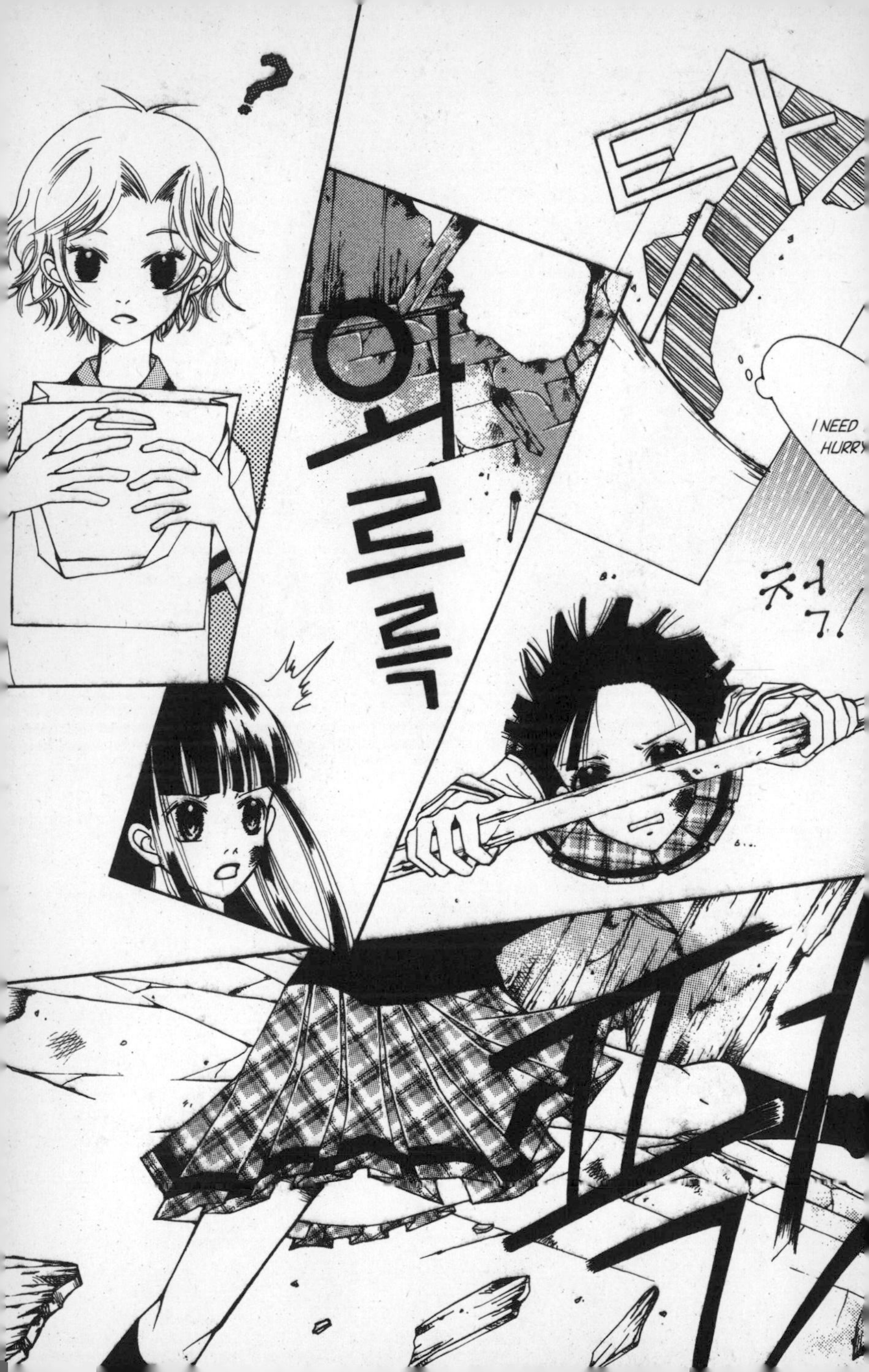
?
탁
와르륵
I NEED
HURR
척!
퍽

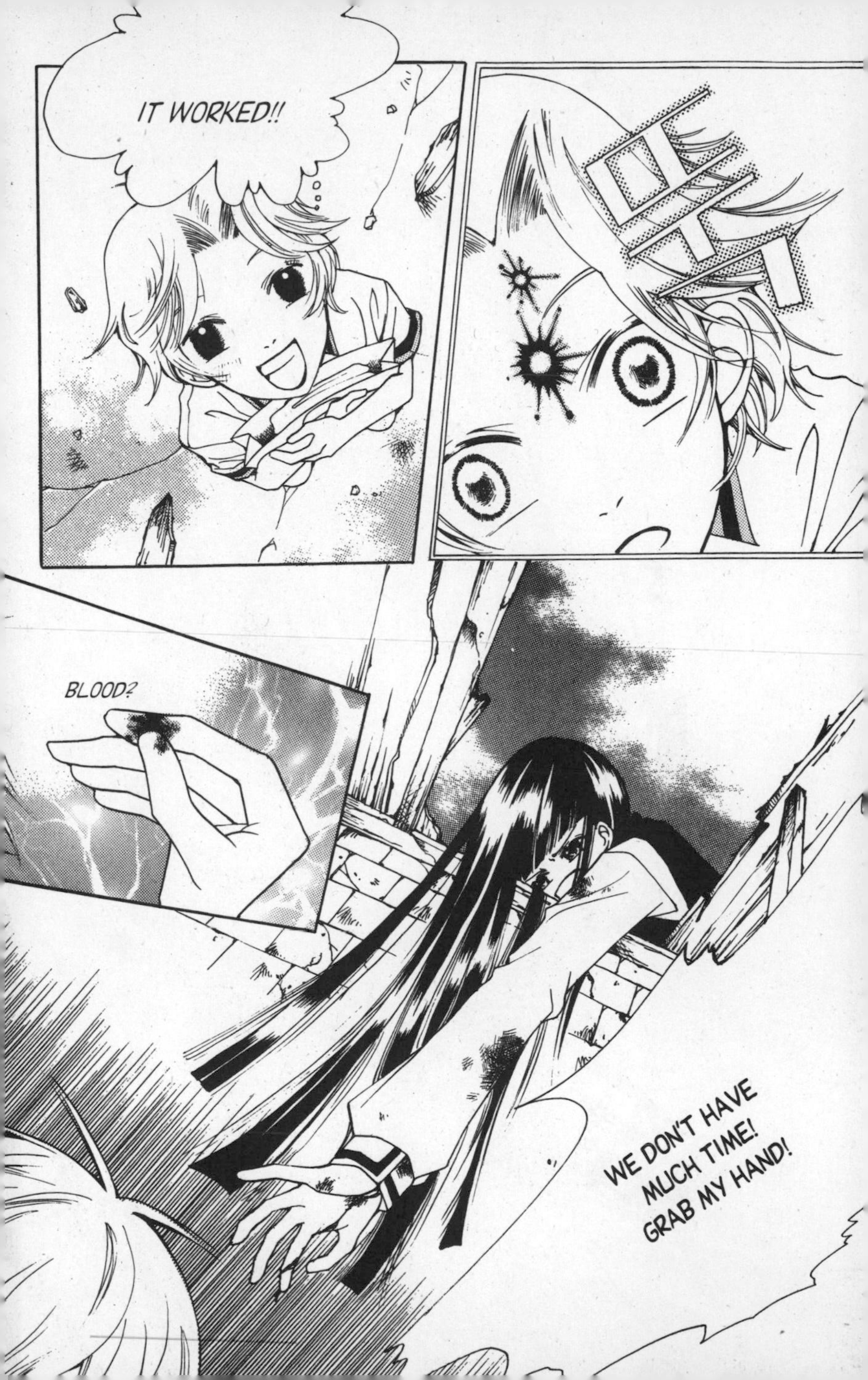
IT WORKED!!
BLOOD?
WE DON'T HAVE
MUCH TIME!
GRAB MY HAND!

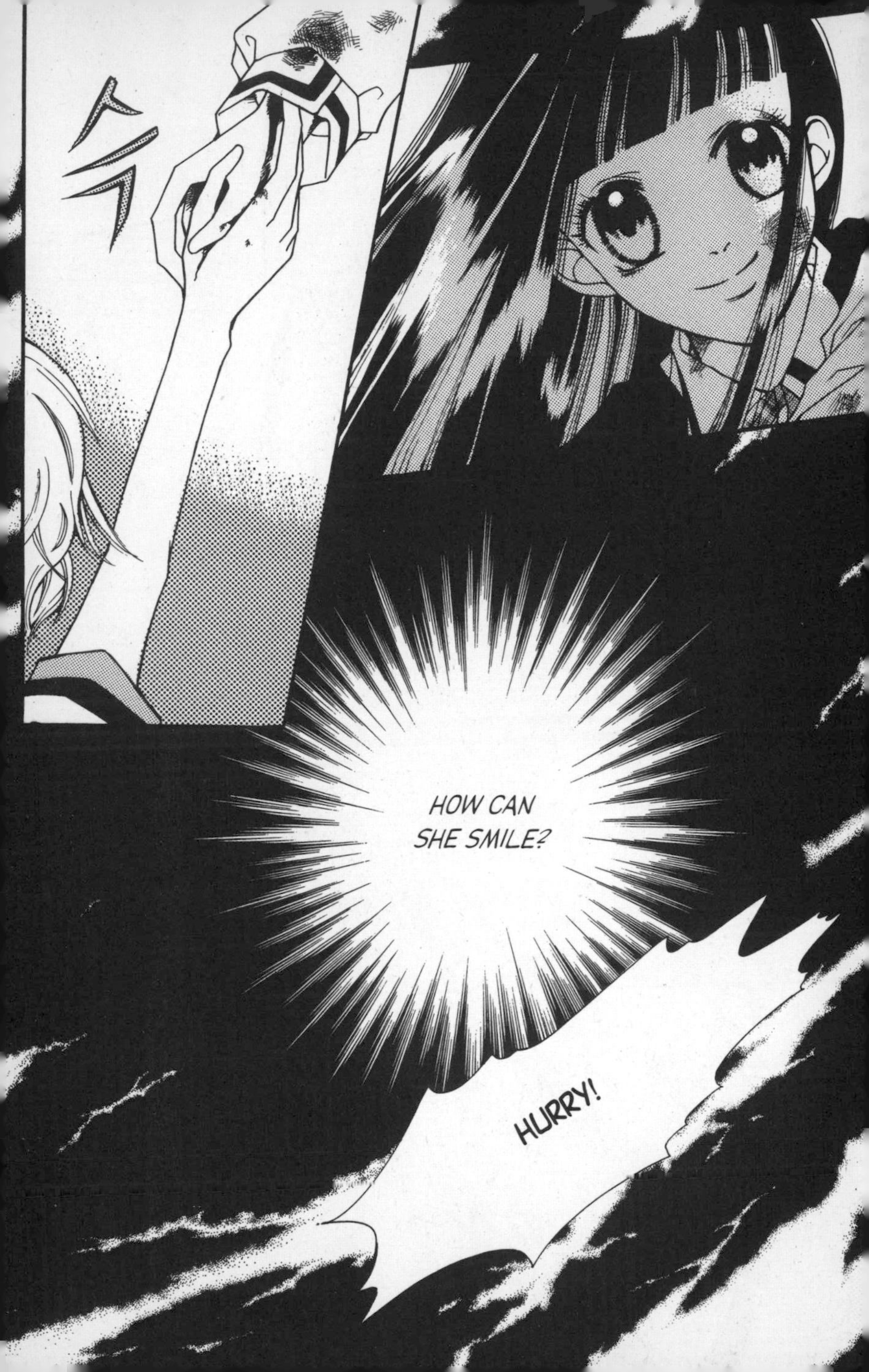
HOW CAN SHE SMILE?
HURRY!

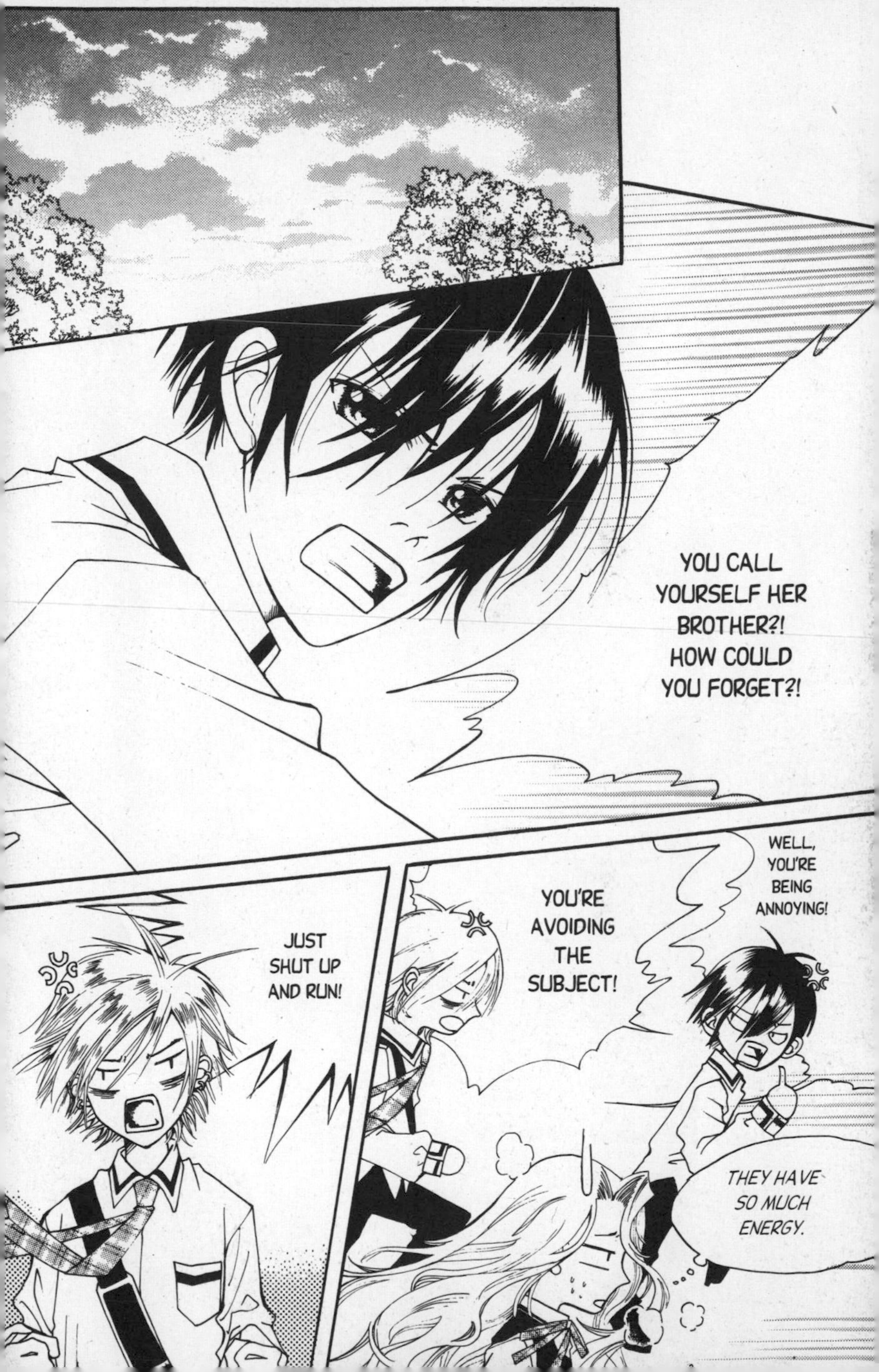
YOU CALL YOURSELF HER BROTHER?! HOW COULD YOU FORGET?!
JUST SHUT UP AND RUN!
YOU'RE AVOIDING THE SUBJECT!
WELL, YOU'RE BEING ANNOYING!
THEY HAVE SO MUCH ENERGY.

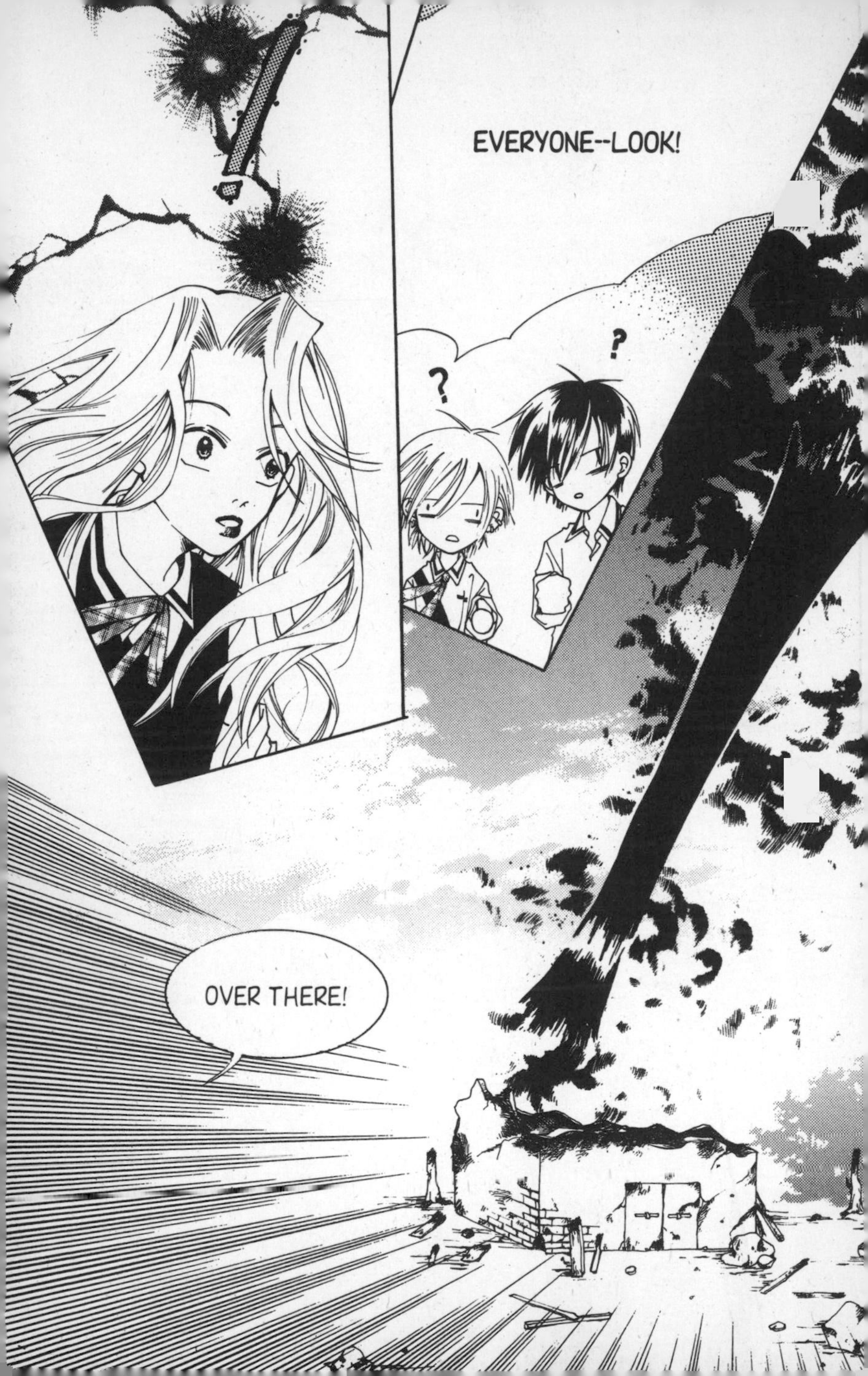
EVERYONE--LOOK!
?
?
OVER THERE!

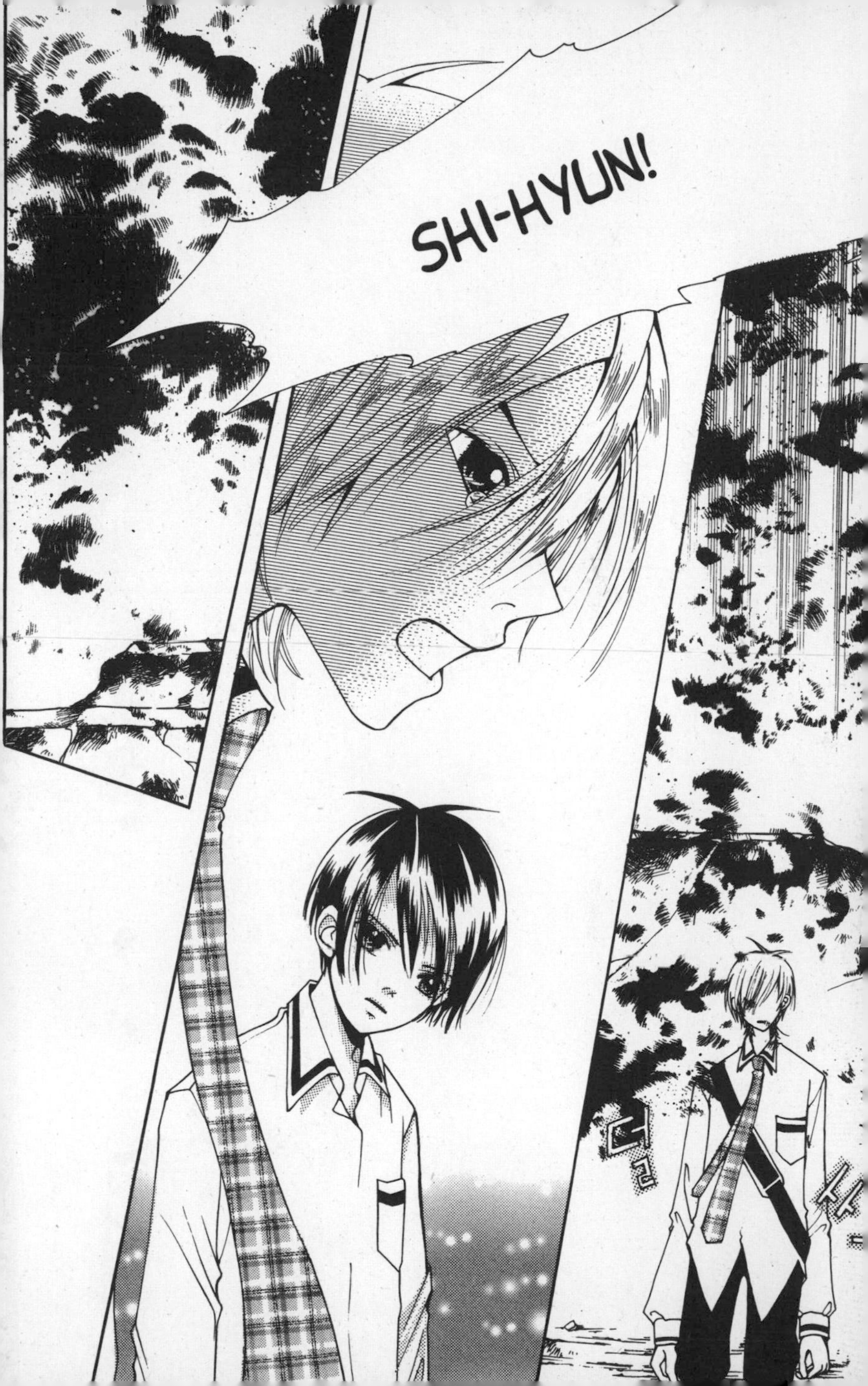
SHI-HYUN!

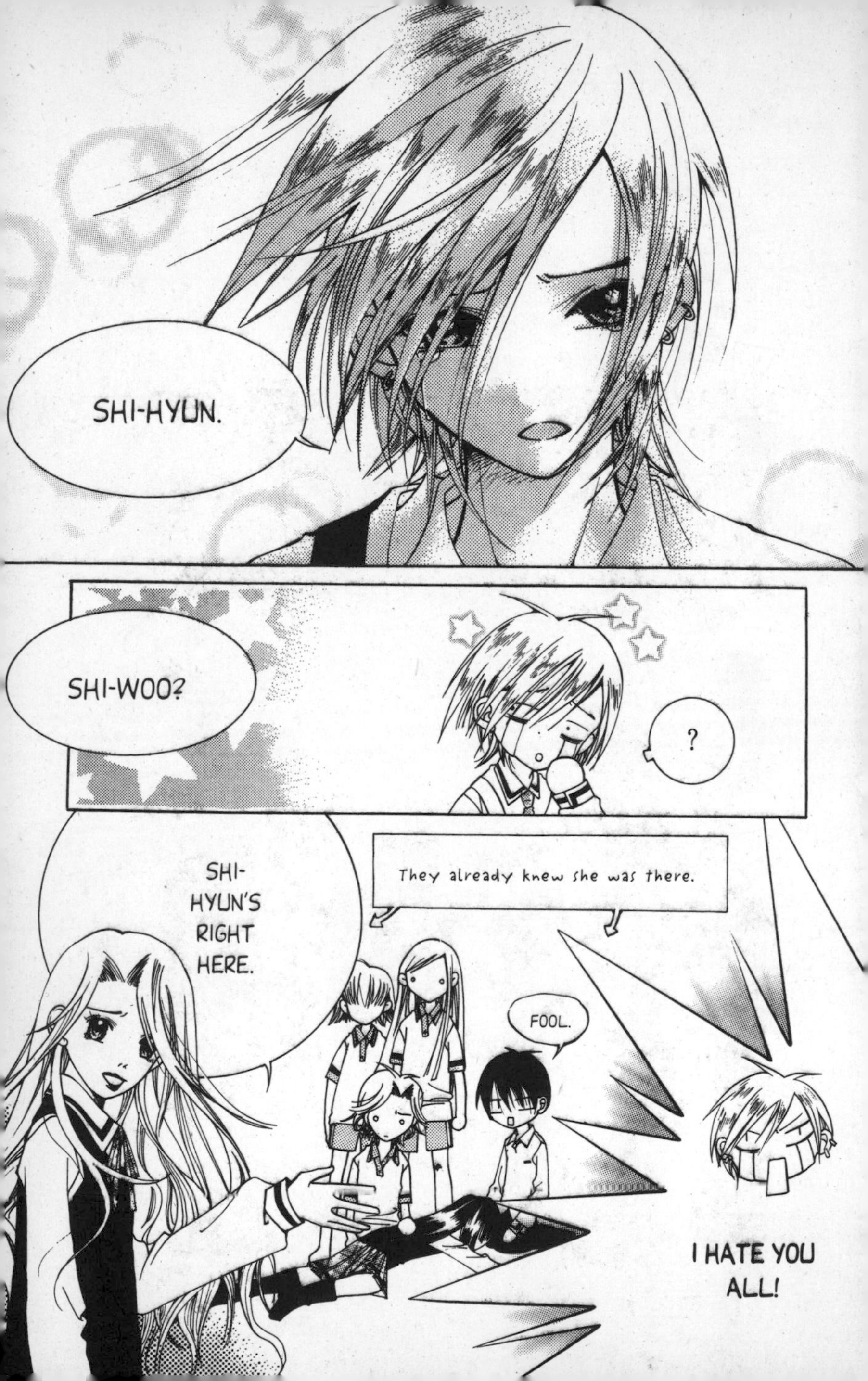
SHI-HYUN.
SHI-WOO?
?
SHI-HYUN'S RIGHT HERE.
They already knew she was there.
FOOL.
I HATE YOU ALL!

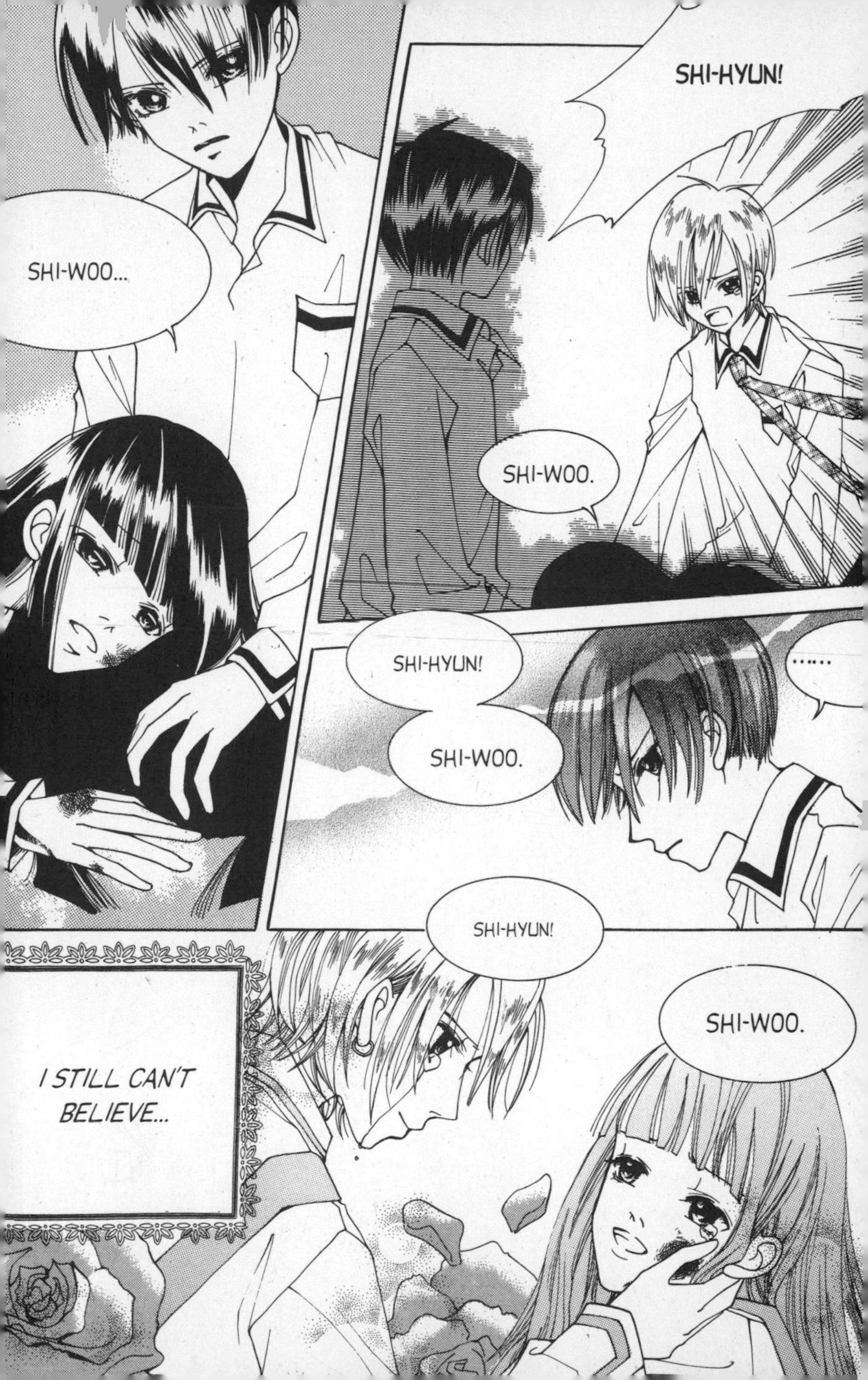
SHI-WOO...
SHI-HYUN!
SHI-WOO.
SHI-HYUN!
SHI-WOO.
......
I STILL CAN'T BELIEVE...
SHI-HYUN!
SHI-WOO.

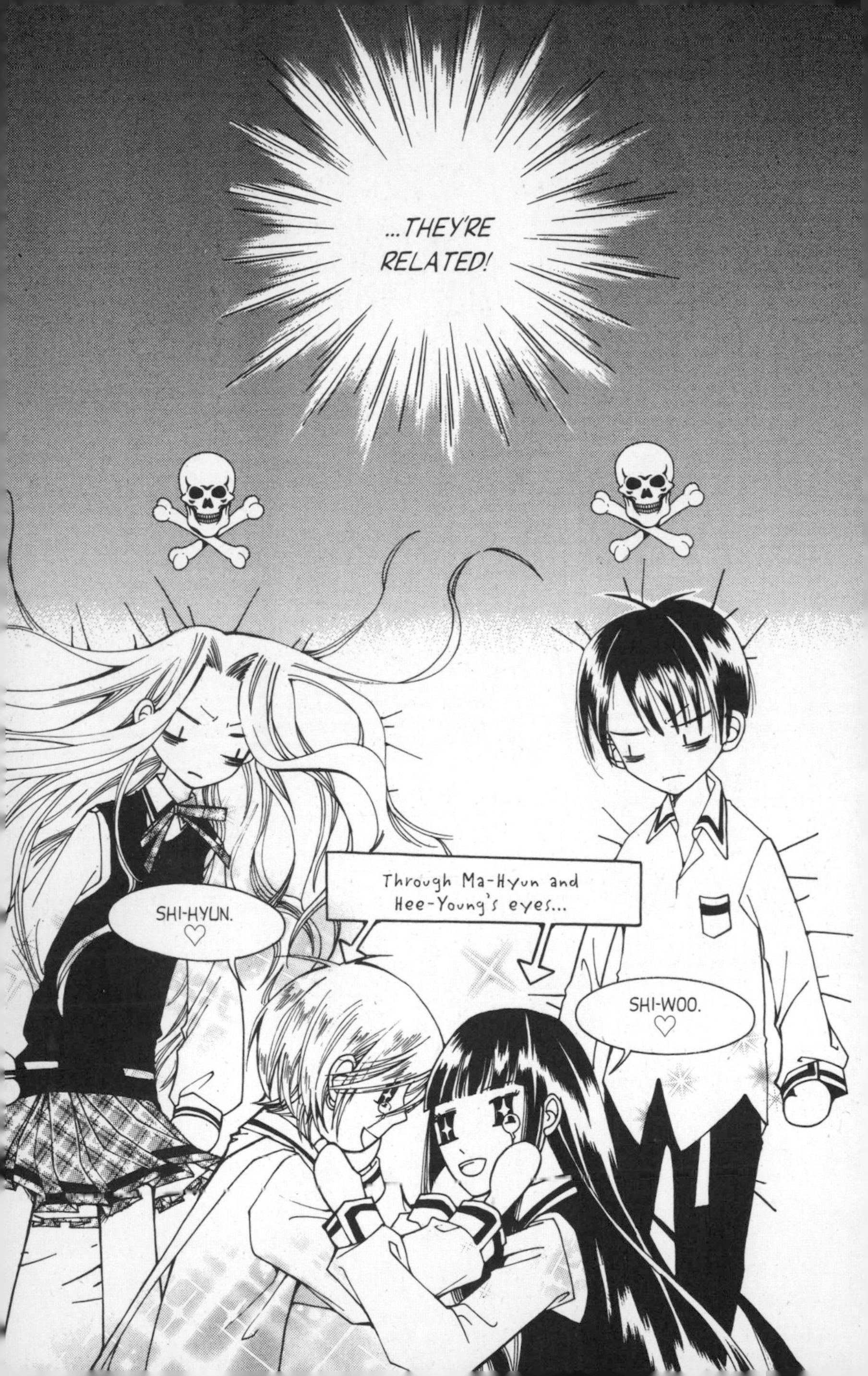
...THEY'RE RELATED!
SHI-HYUN. ♡
Through Ma-Hyun and Hee-Young's eyes...
SHI-WOO. ♡

good Luck™

stage6

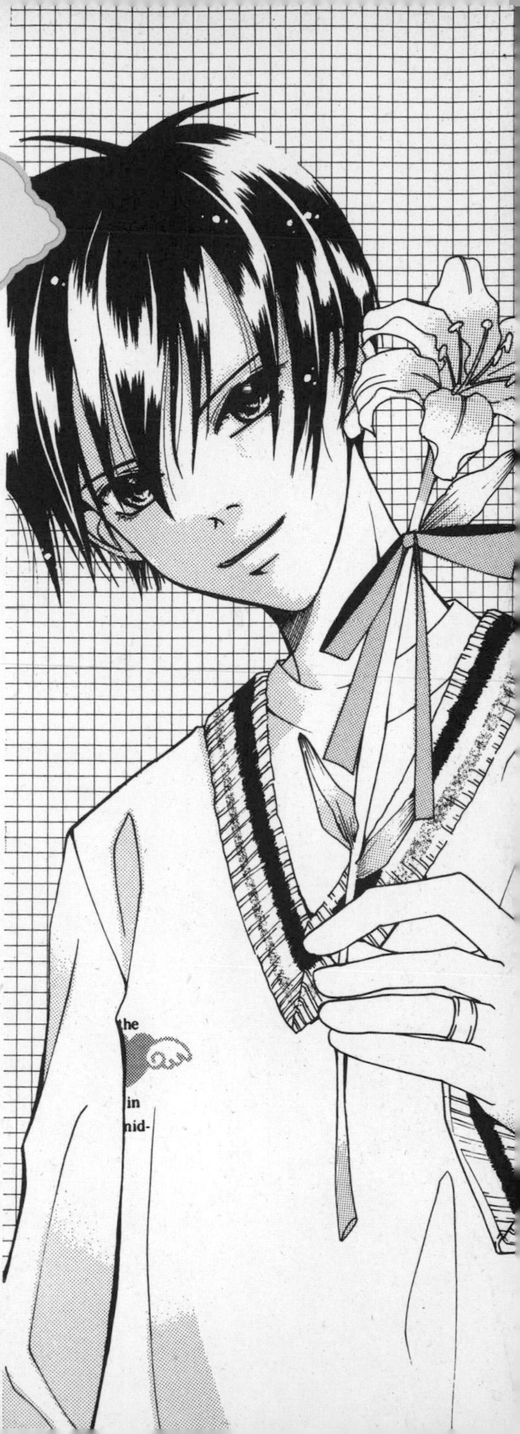

the
in
nid-

HTTP://cooky.anipy.com orange.2002.9.1

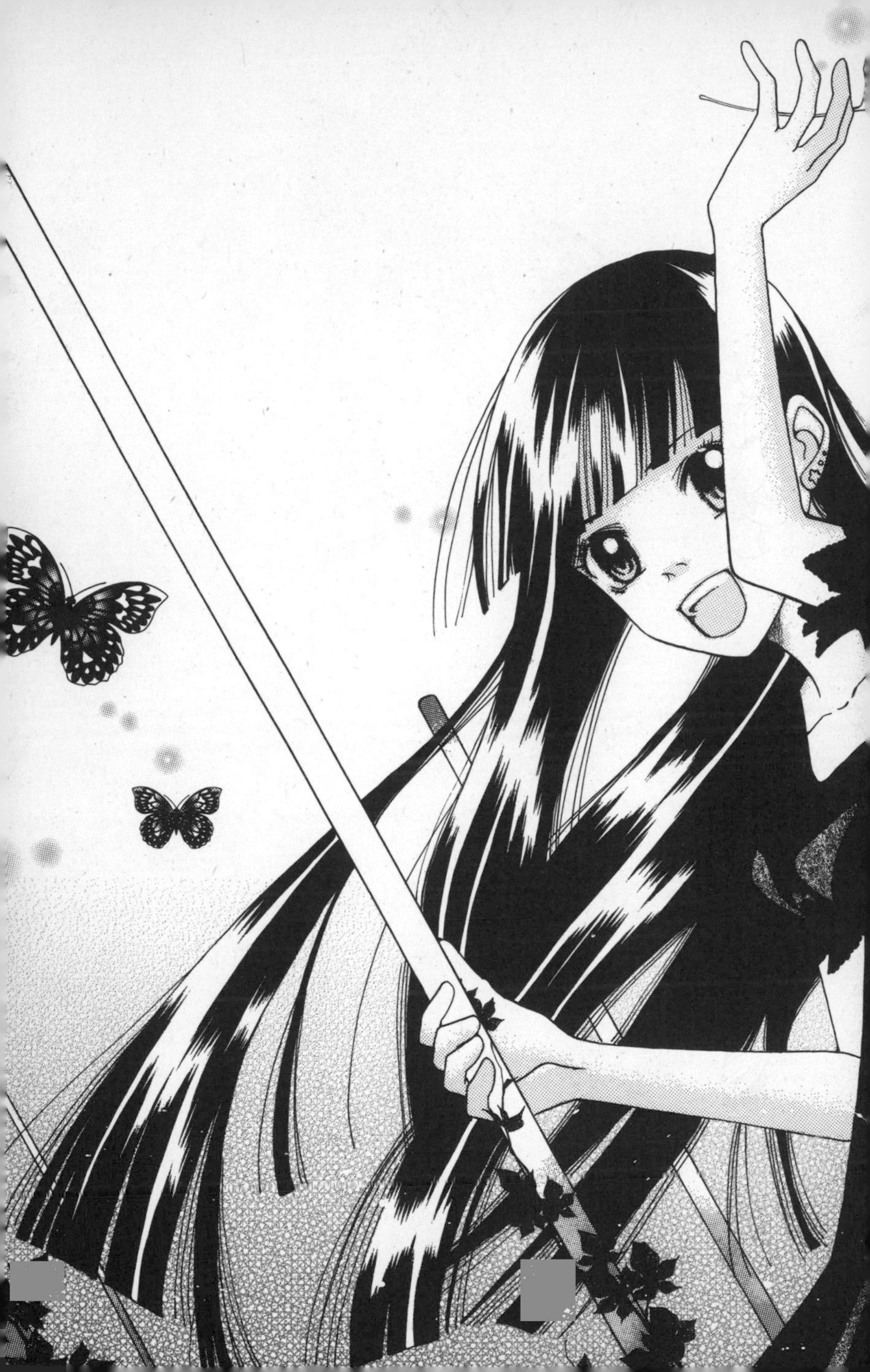

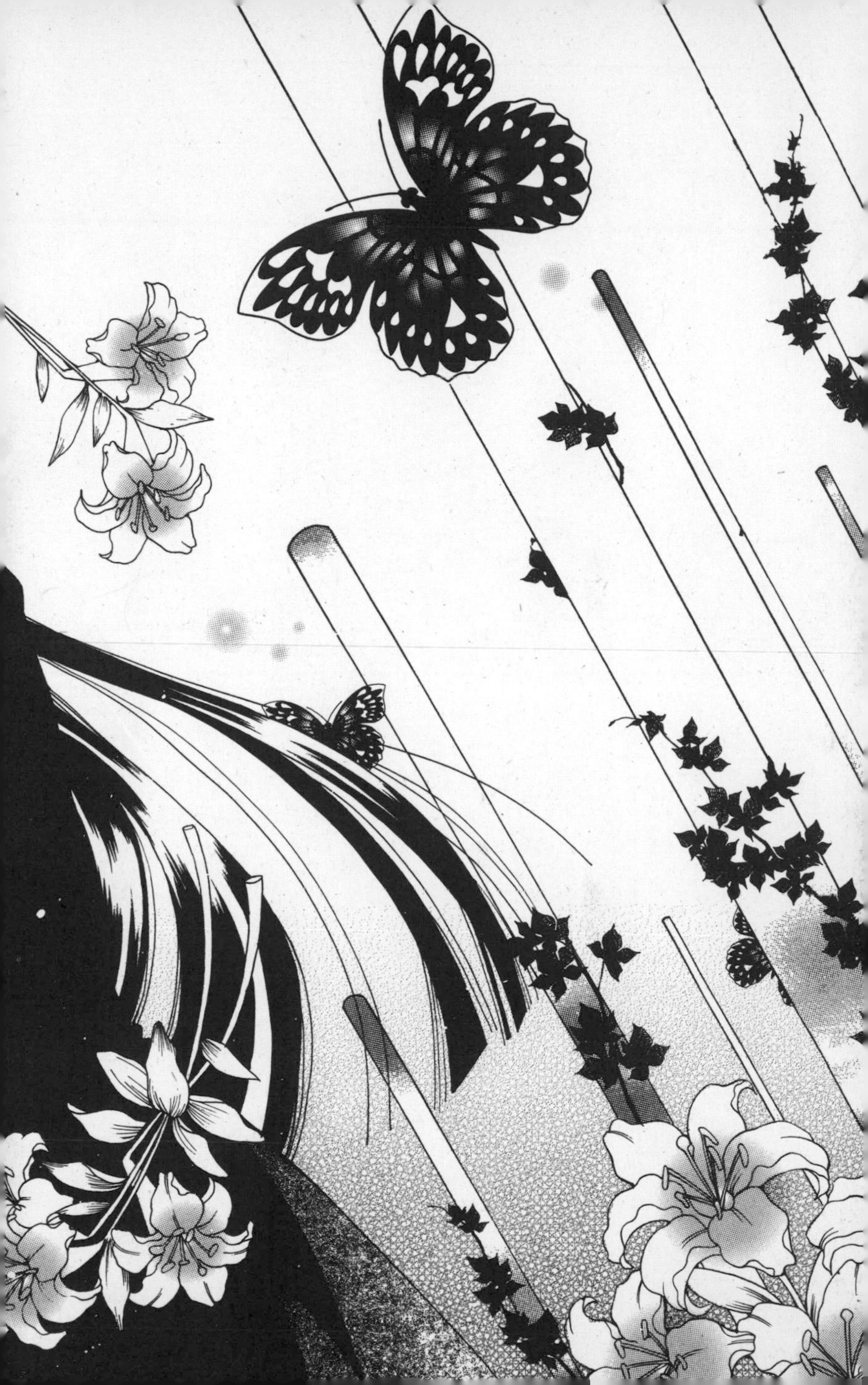

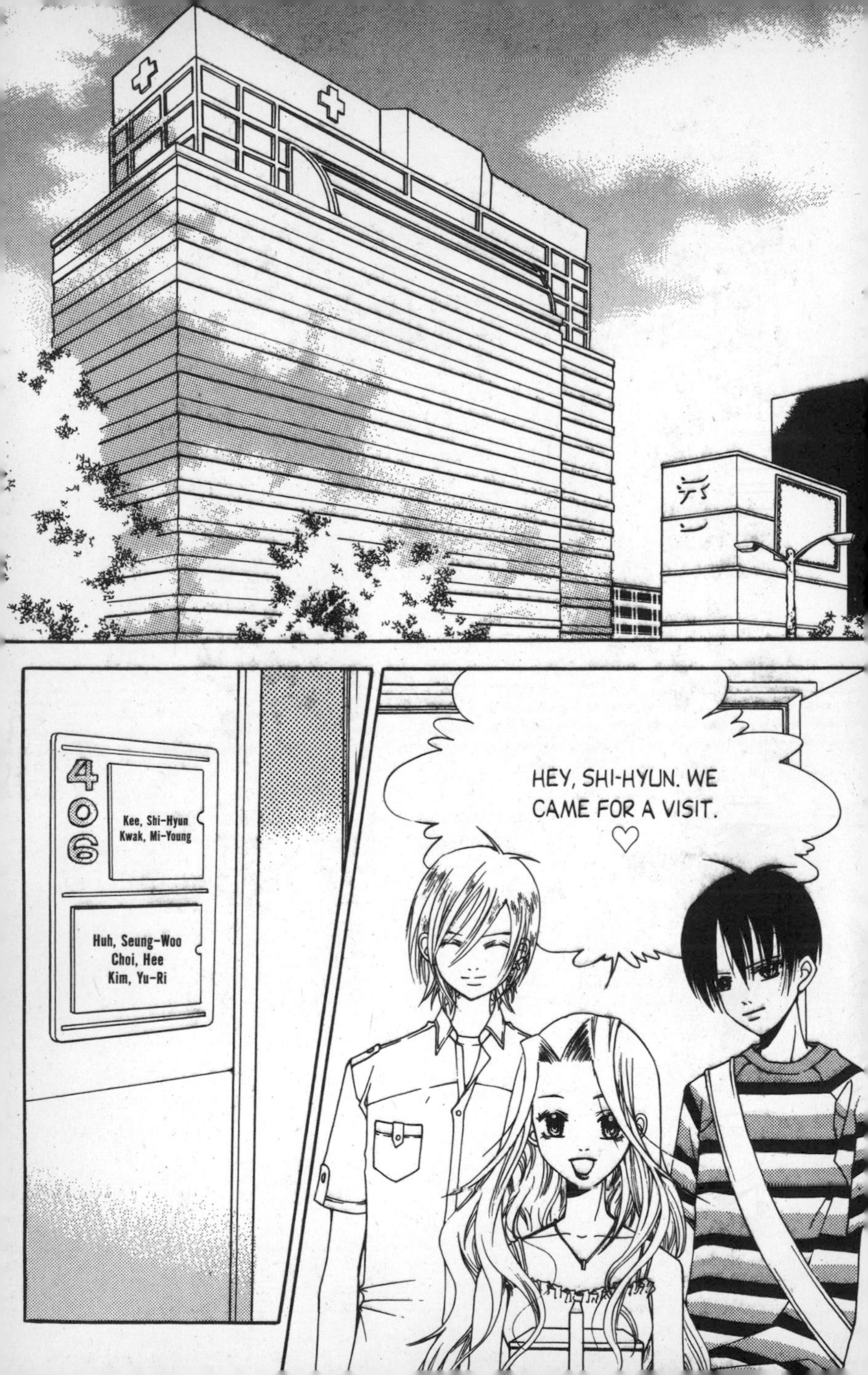
406
Kee, Shi-Hyun
Kwak, Mi-Young
Huh, Seung-Woo
Choi, Hee
Kim, Yu-Ri
HEY, SHI-HYUN. WE CAME FOR A VISIT. ♡

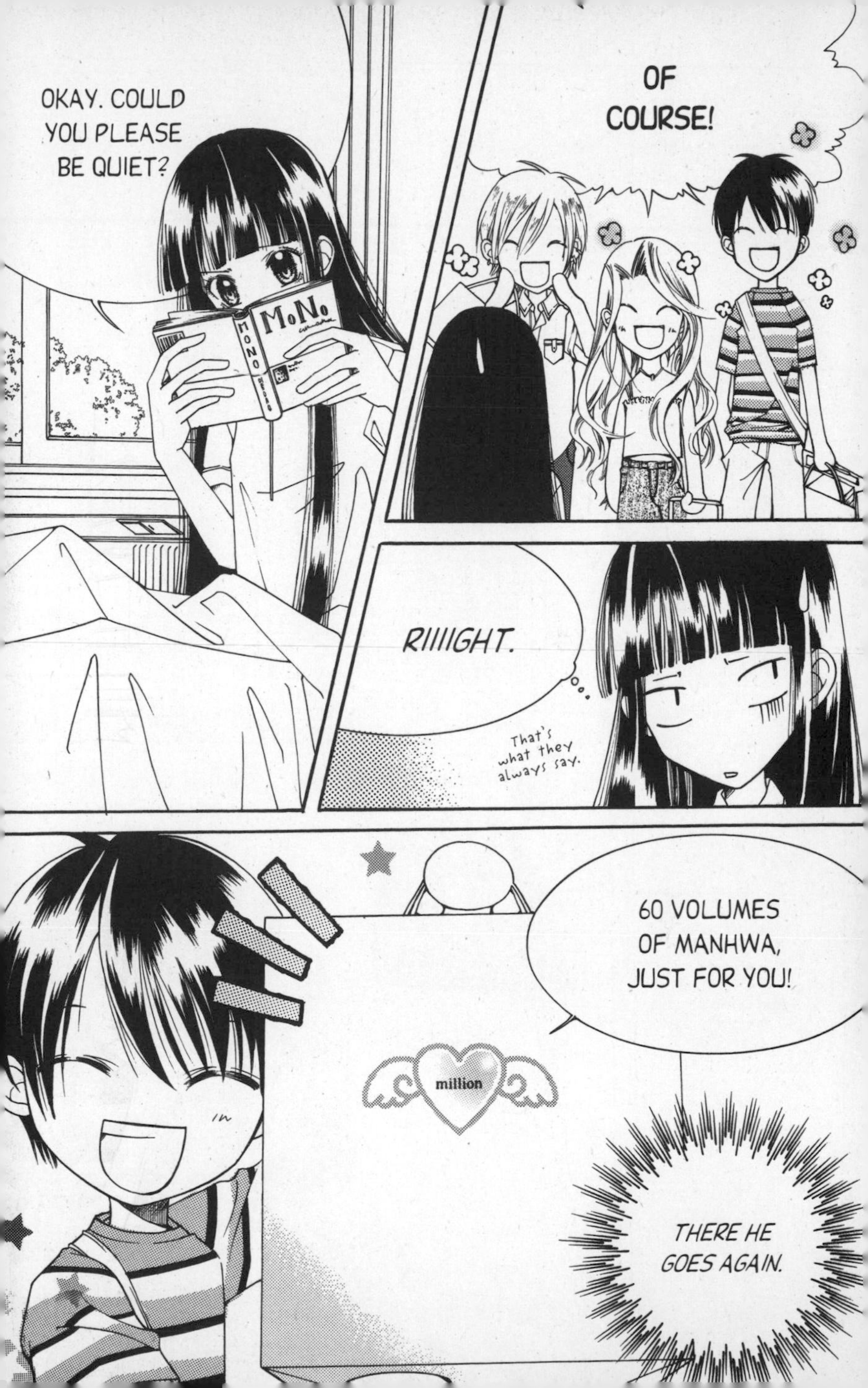
OKAY. COULD YOU PLEASE BE QUIET?
OF COURSE!
RIIIGHT.
That's what they always say.
60 VOLUMES OF MANHWA, JUST FOR YOU!
million
THERE HE GOES AGAIN.

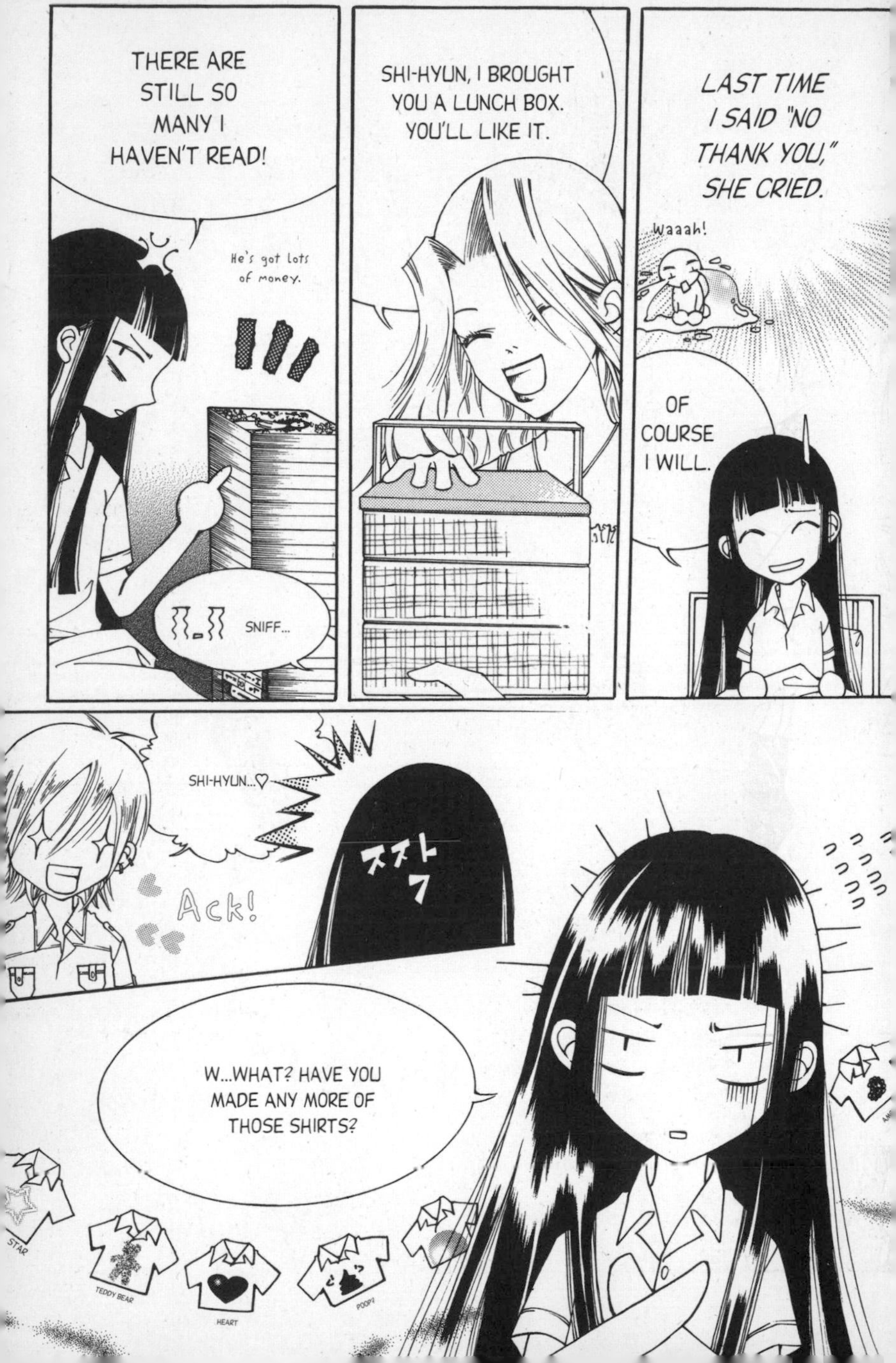
THERE ARE STILL SO MANY I HAVEN'T READ!
He's got lots of money.
ㅠ_ㅠ SNIFF...
SHI-HYUN, I BROUGHT YOU A LUNCH BOX. YOU'LL LIKE IT.
LAST TIME I SAID "NO THANK YOU," SHE CRIED.
Waaah!
OF COURSE I WILL.
SHI-HYUN...♡
Ack!
W...WHAT? HAVE YOU MADE ANY MORE OF THOSE SHIRTS?
STAR
TEDDY BEAR
HEART
POOP?

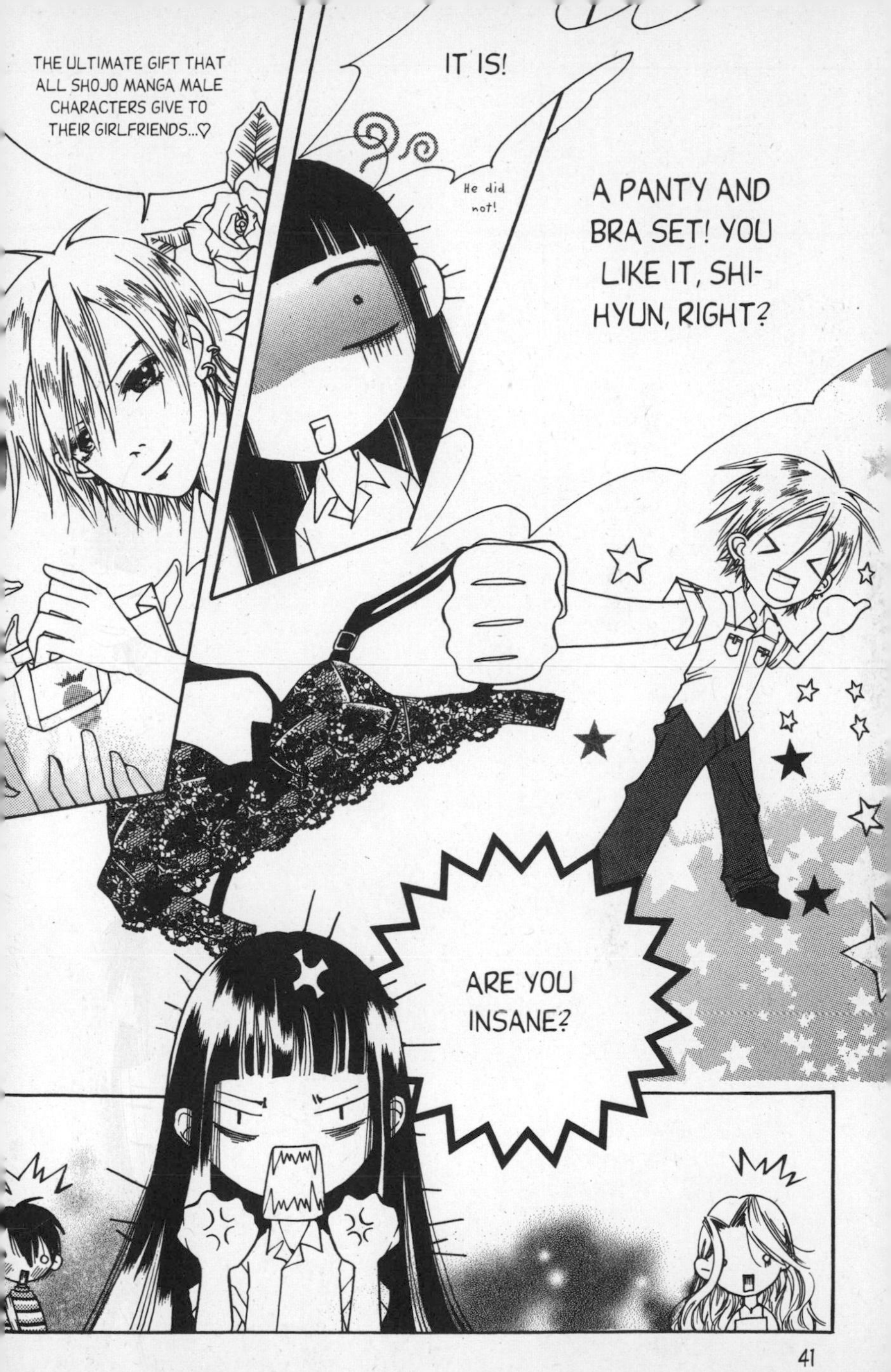
THE ULTIMATE GIFT THAT ALL SHOJO MANGA MALE CHARACTERS GIVE TO THEIR GIRLFRIENDS...♡
IT IS!
He did not!
A PANTY AND BRA SET! YOU LIKE IT, SHI-HYUN, RIGHT?
ARE YOU INSANE?

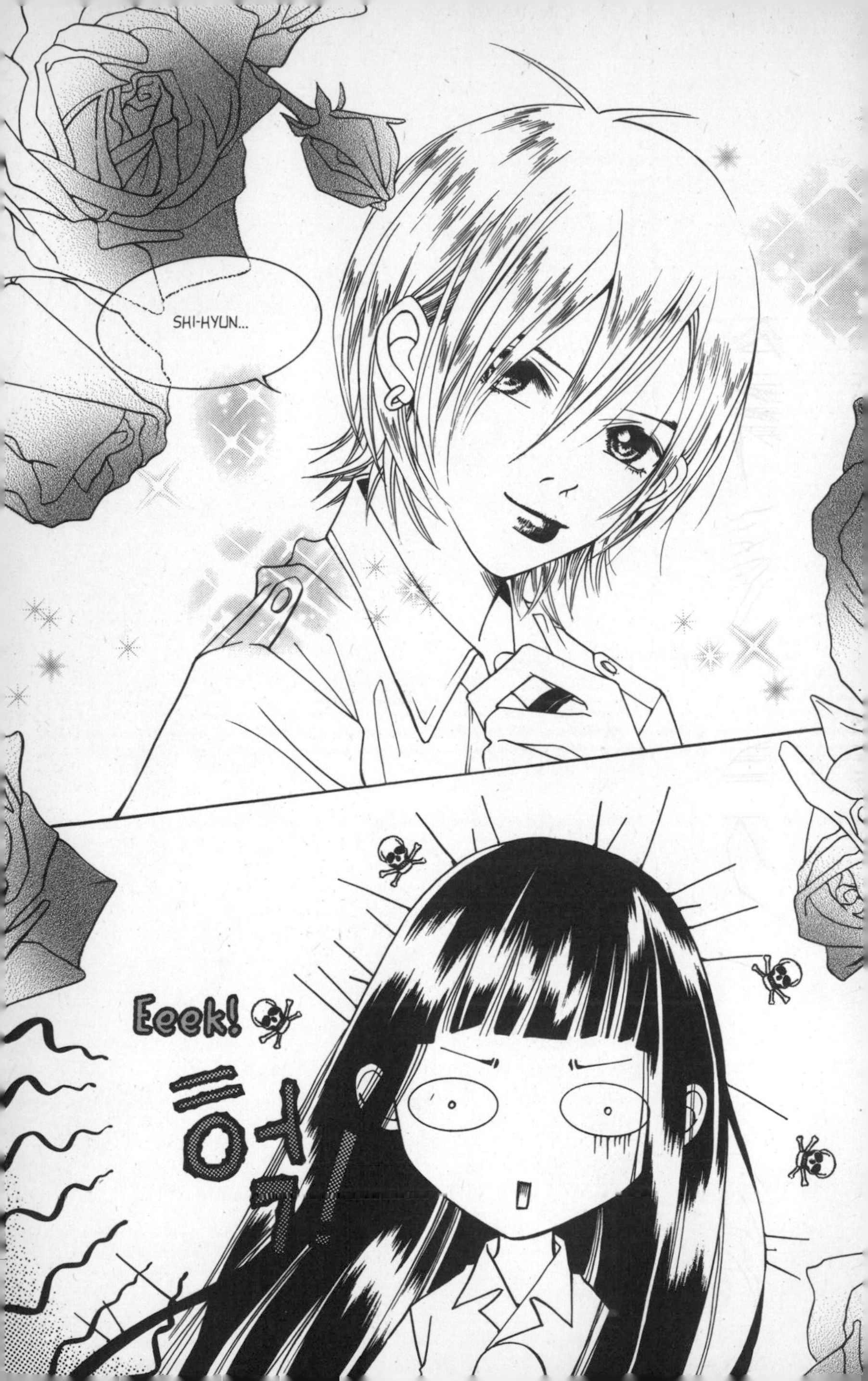
SHI-HYUN...
Eeek!
흐억!

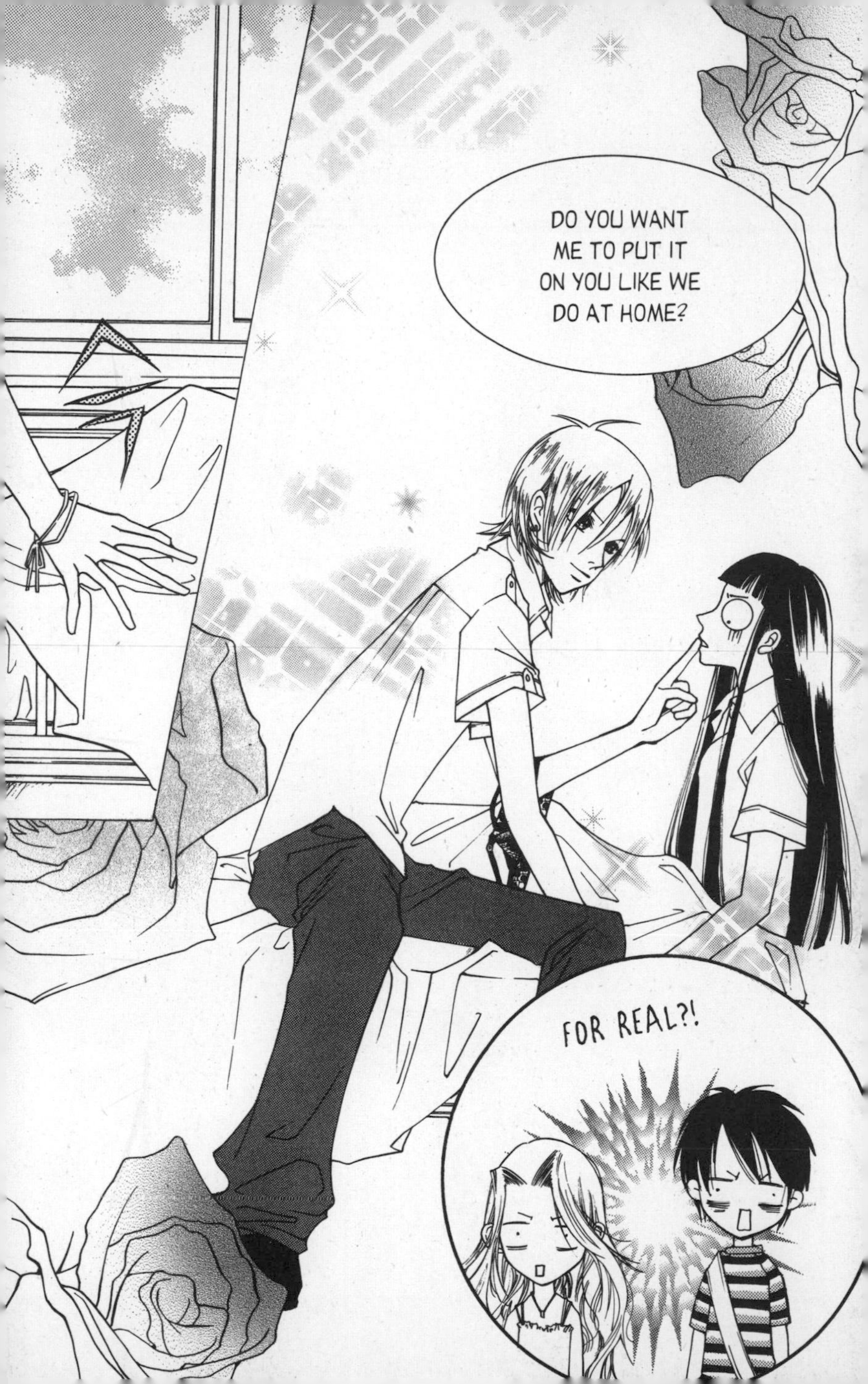
DO YOU WANT ME TO PUT IT ON YOU LIKE WE DO AT HOME?
FOR REAL?!

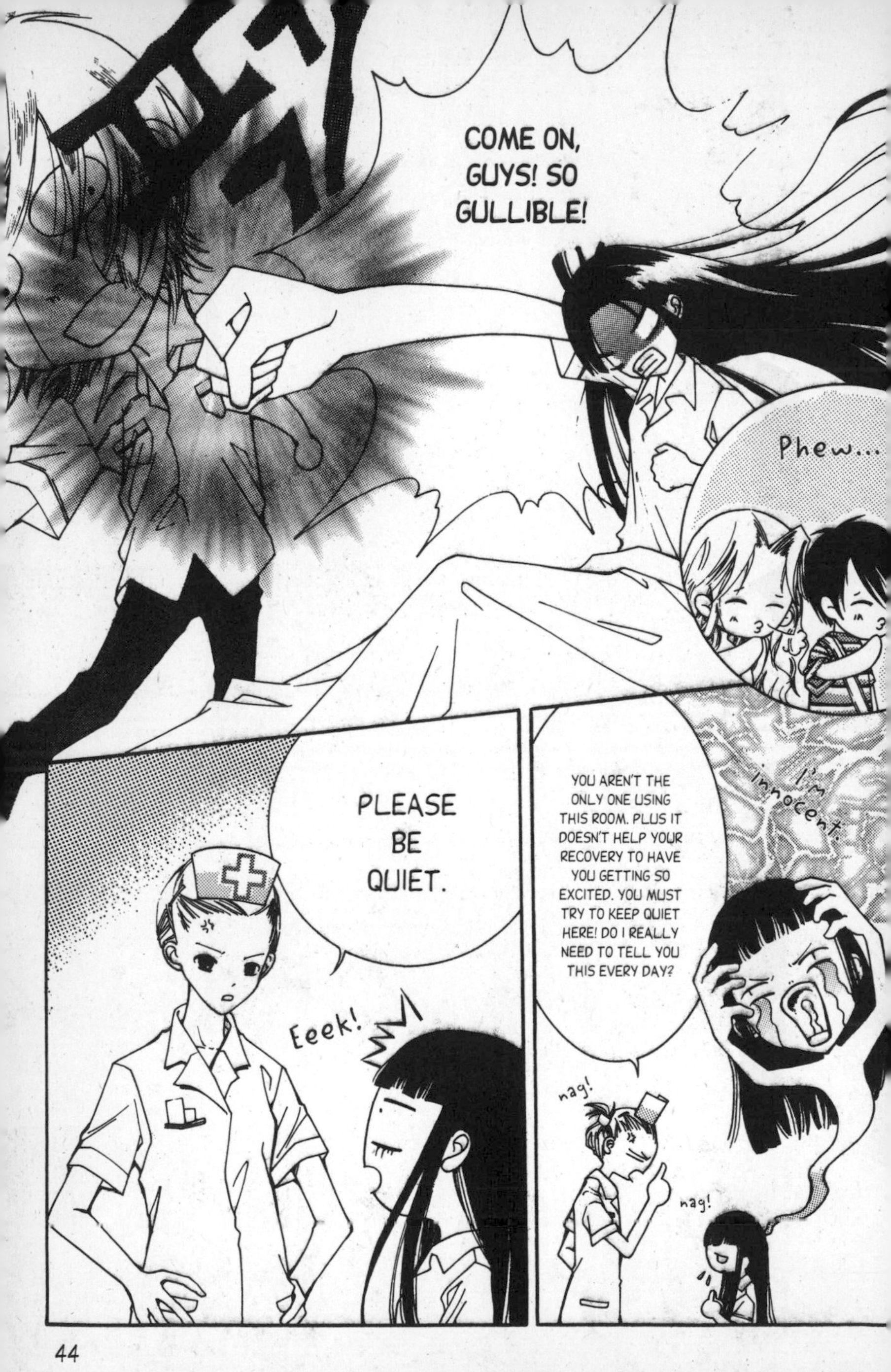
COME ON, GUYS! SO GULLIBLE!
Phew...
PLEASE BE QUIET.
Eeek!
YOU AREN'T THE ONLY ONE USING THIS ROOM. PLUS IT DOESN'T HELP YOUR RECOVERY TO HAVE YOU GETTING SO EXCITED. YOU MUST TRY TO KEEP QUIET HERE! DO I REALLY NEED TO TELL YOU THIS EVERY DAY?
I'm innocent.
nag!
nag!

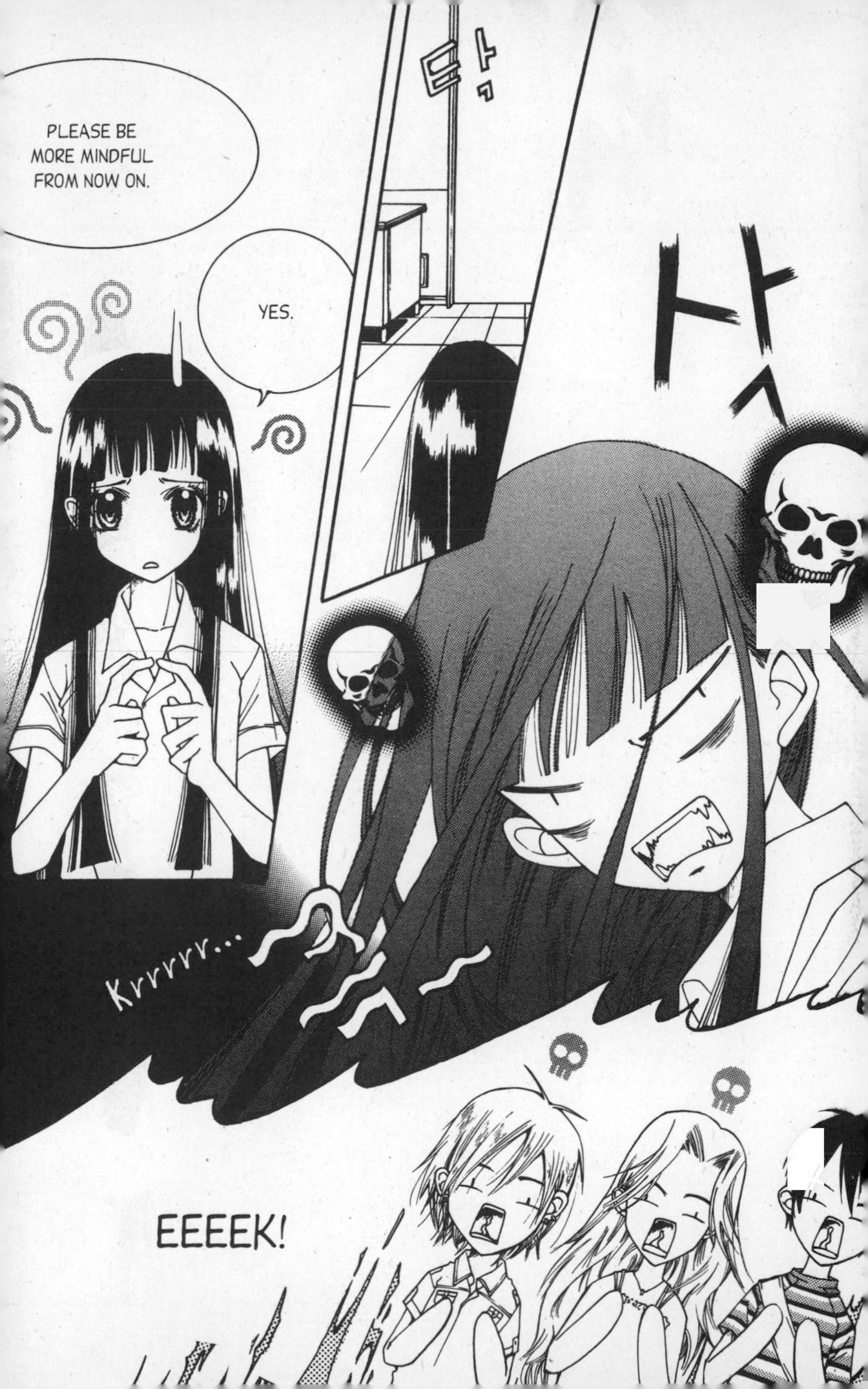
PLEASE BE MORE MINDFUL FROM NOW ON.
YES.
Krrrrr...
EEEEK!

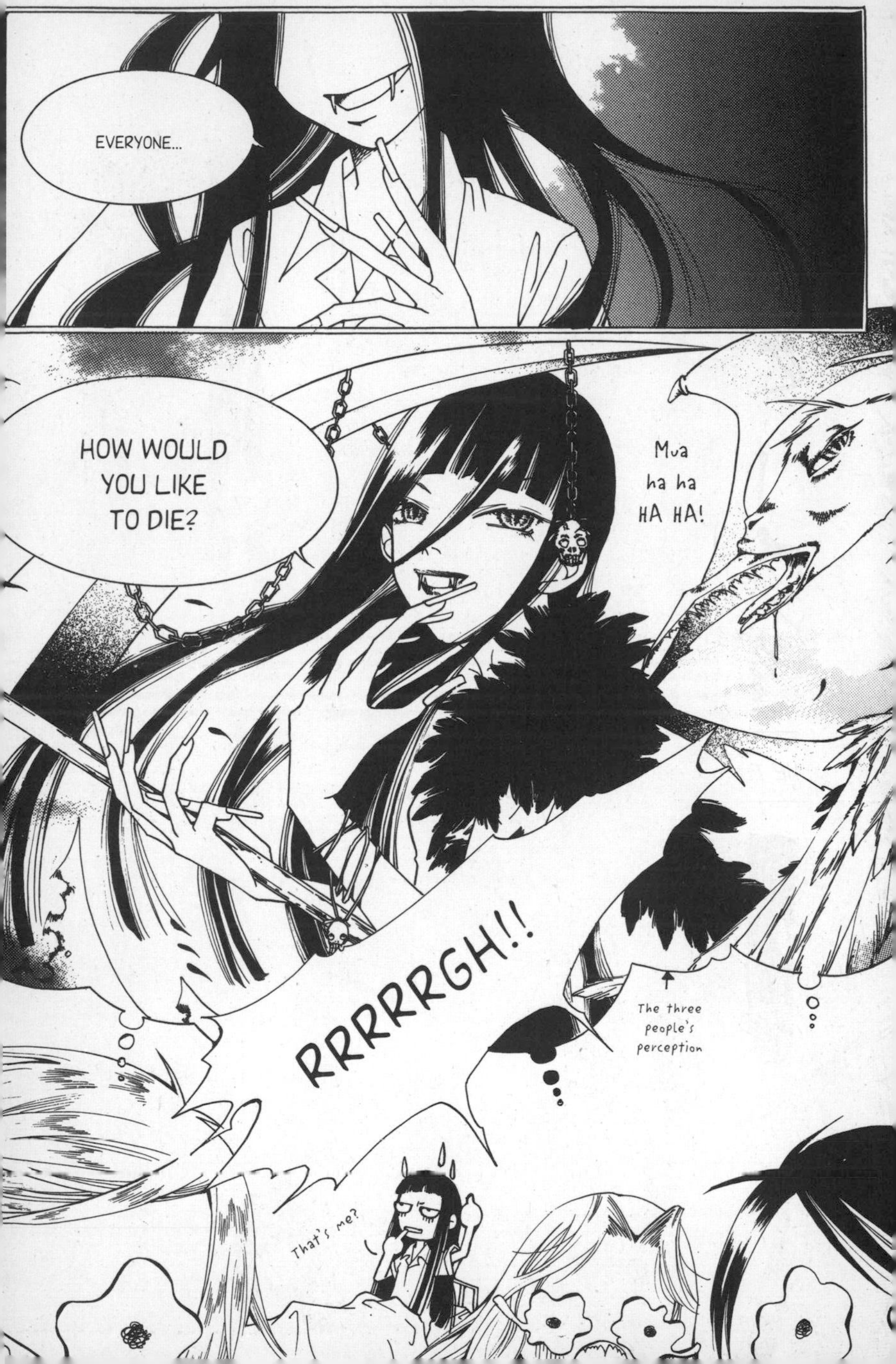
EVERYONE...
HOW WOULD YOU LIKE TO DIE?
Mua ha ha HA HA!
RRRRRGH!!
The three people's perception
That's me?

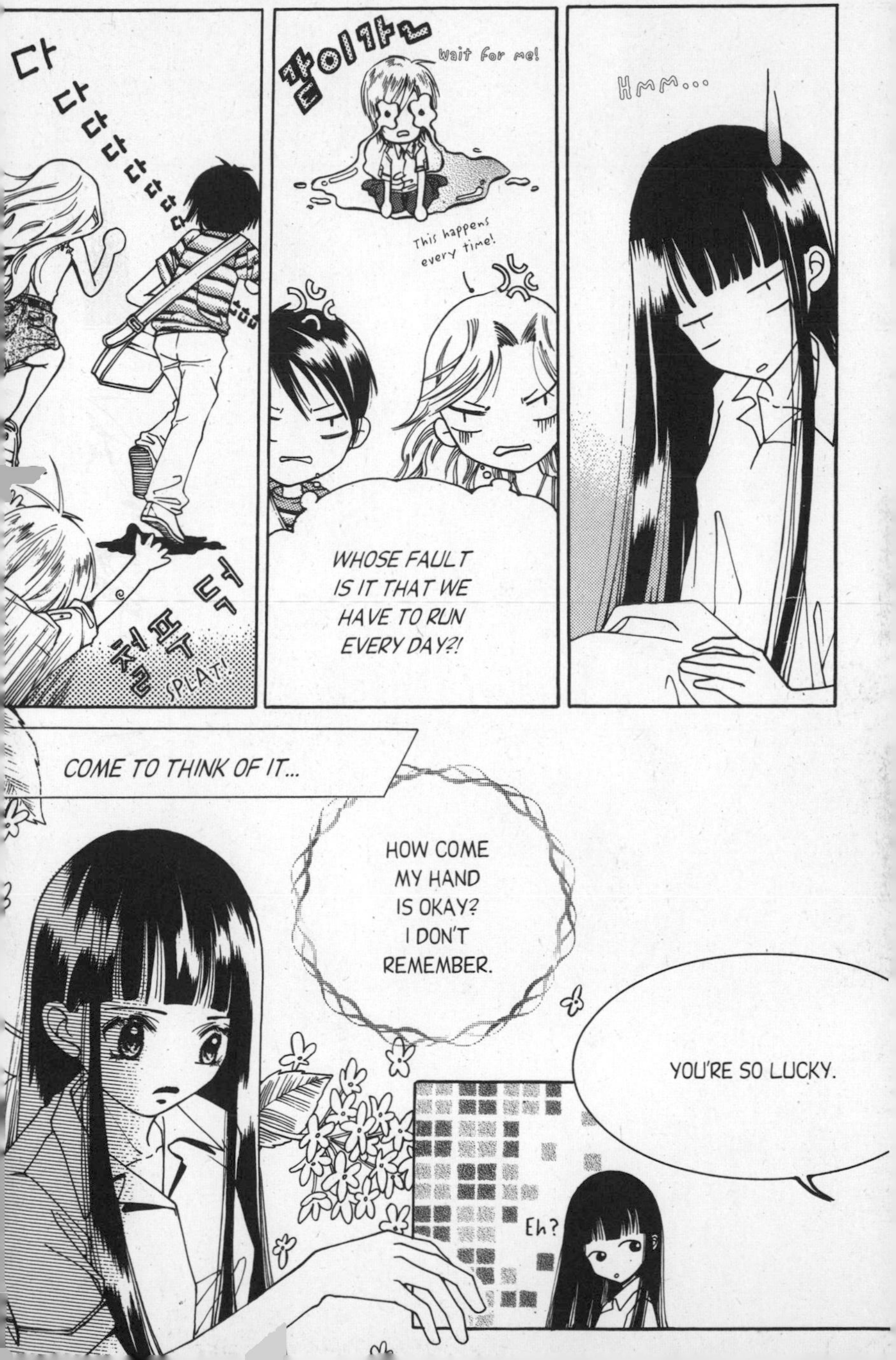
다다다다다다다다
철퍽
SPLAT!
같이가
wait for me!
This happens every time!
WHOSE FAULT IS IT THAT WE HAVE TO RUN EVERY DAY?!
Hmm...
COME TO THINK OF IT...
HOW COME MY HAND IS OKAY? I DON'T REMEMBER.
YOU'RE SO LUCKY.
Eh?

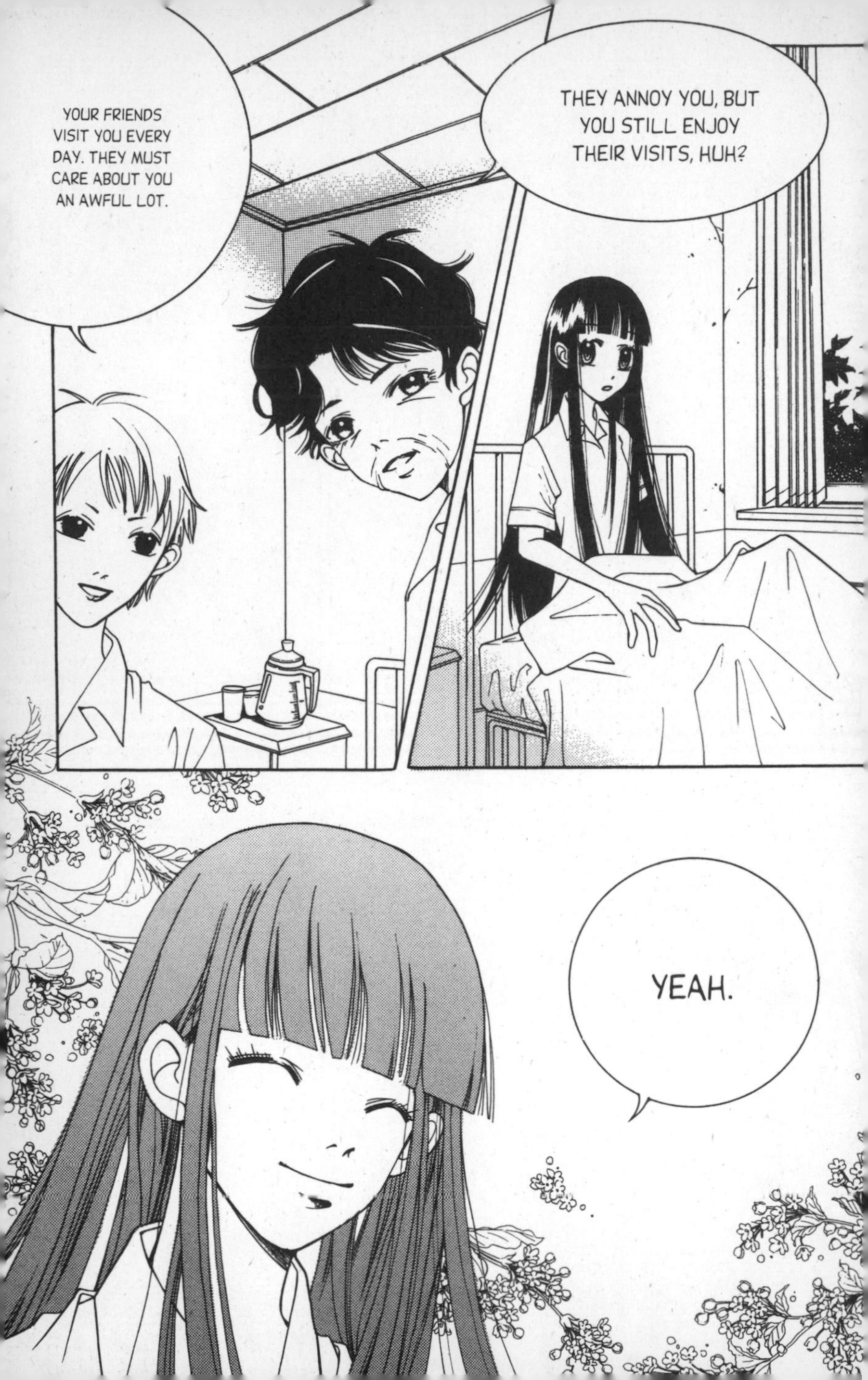
YOUR FRIENDS VISIT YOU EVERY DAY. THEY MUST CARE ABOUT YOU AN AWFUL LOT.
THEY ANNOY YOU, BUT YOU STILL ENJOY THEIR VISITS, HUH?
YEAH.

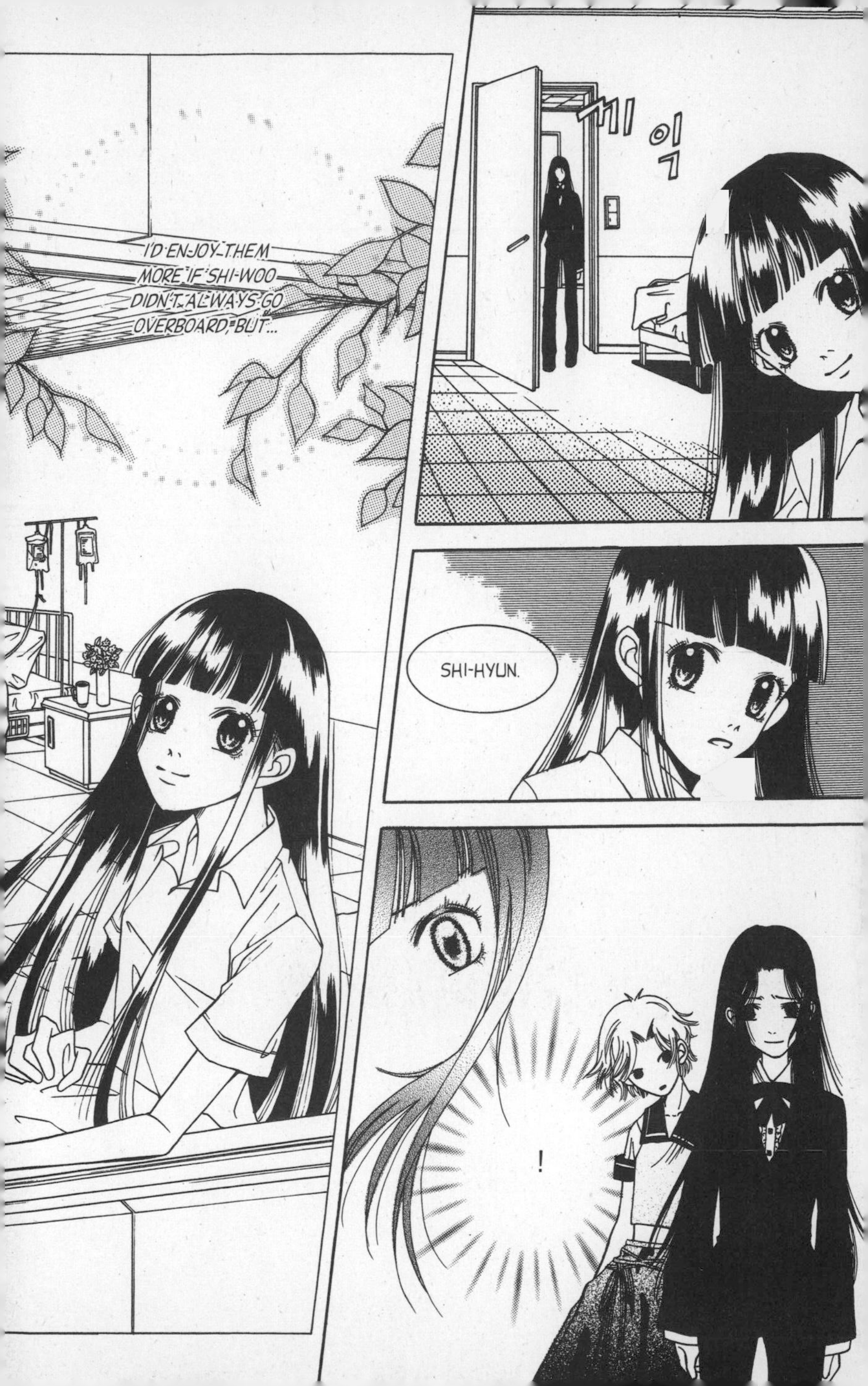
I'D ENJOY THEM MORE IF SHI-WOO DIDN'T ALWAYS GO OVERBOARD, BUT...
끼이익
SHI-HYUN.
!

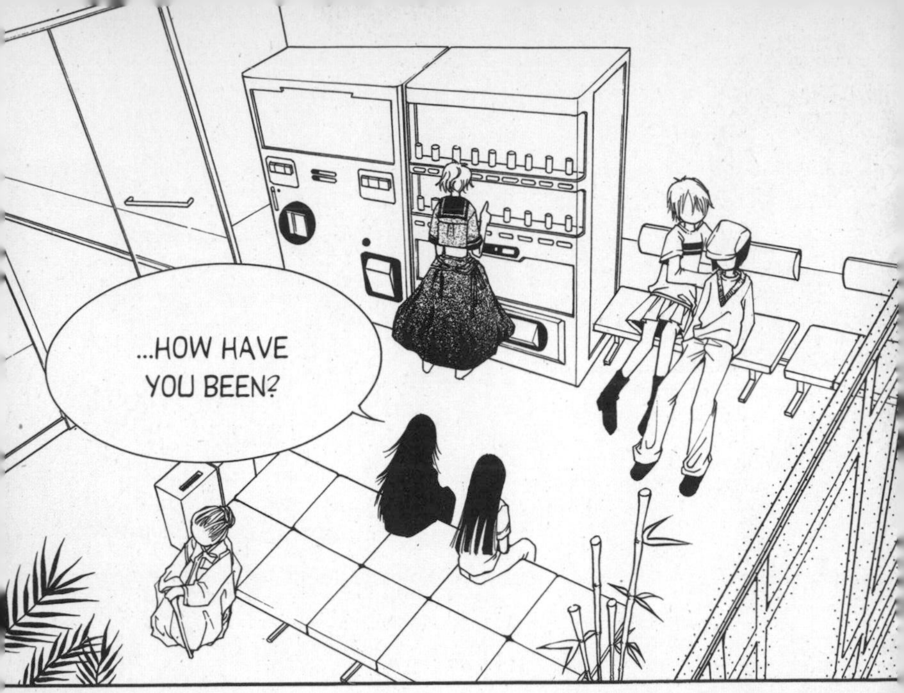
...HOW HAVE YOU BEEN?

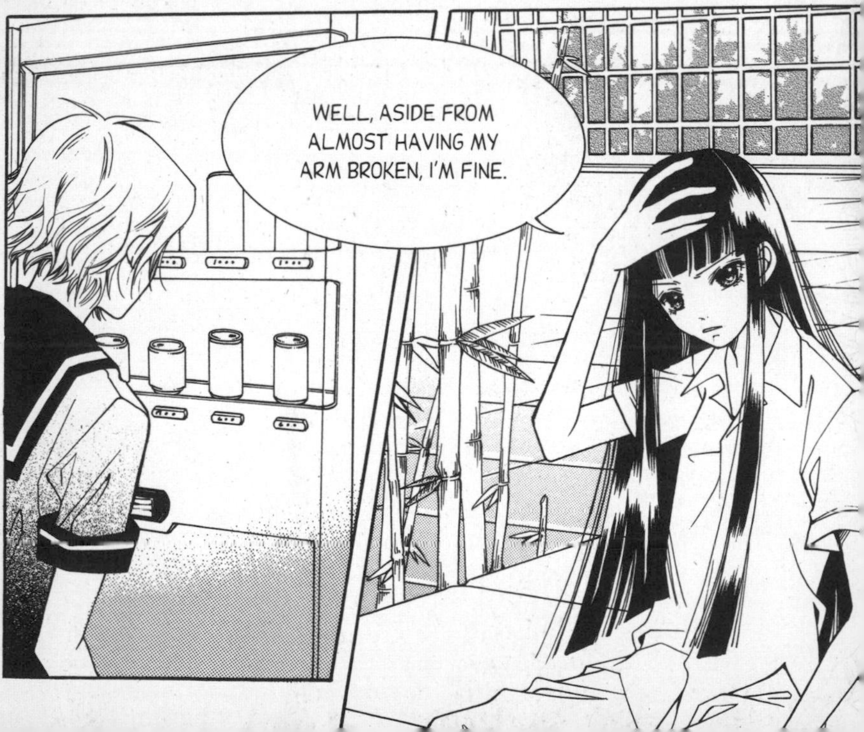
WELL, ASIDE FROM ALMOST HAVING MY ARM BROKEN, I'M FINE.

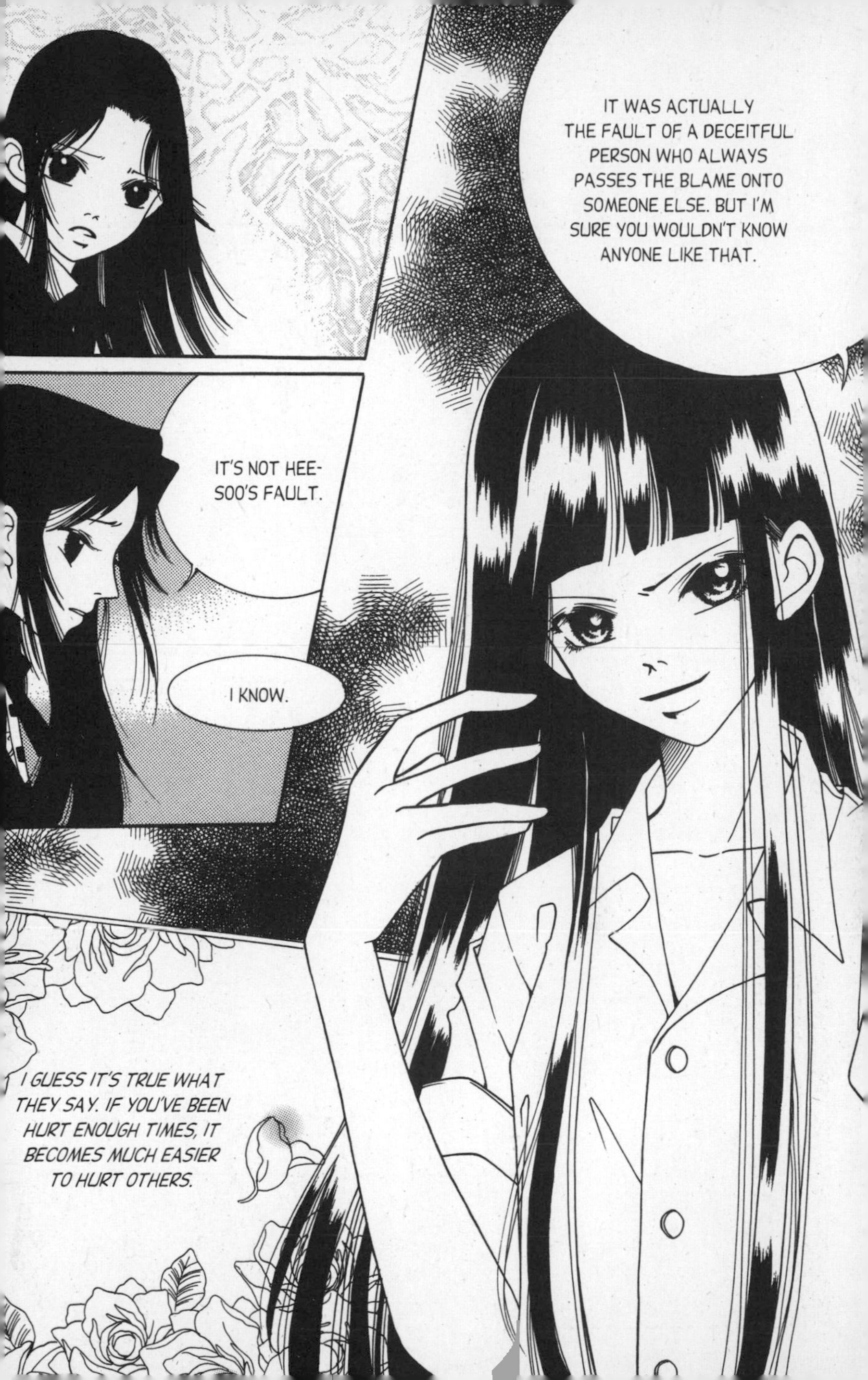
IT'S NOT HEE-SOO'S FAULT.
I KNOW.
IT WAS ACTUALLY THE FAULT OF A DECEITFUL PERSON WHO ALWAYS PASSES THE BLAME ONTO SOMEONE ELSE. BUT I'M SURE YOU WOULDN'T KNOW ANYONE LIKE THAT.
I GUESS IT'S TRUE WHAT THEY SAY. IF YOU'VE BEEN HURT ENOUGH TIMES, IT BECOMES MUCH EASIER TO HURT OTHERS.

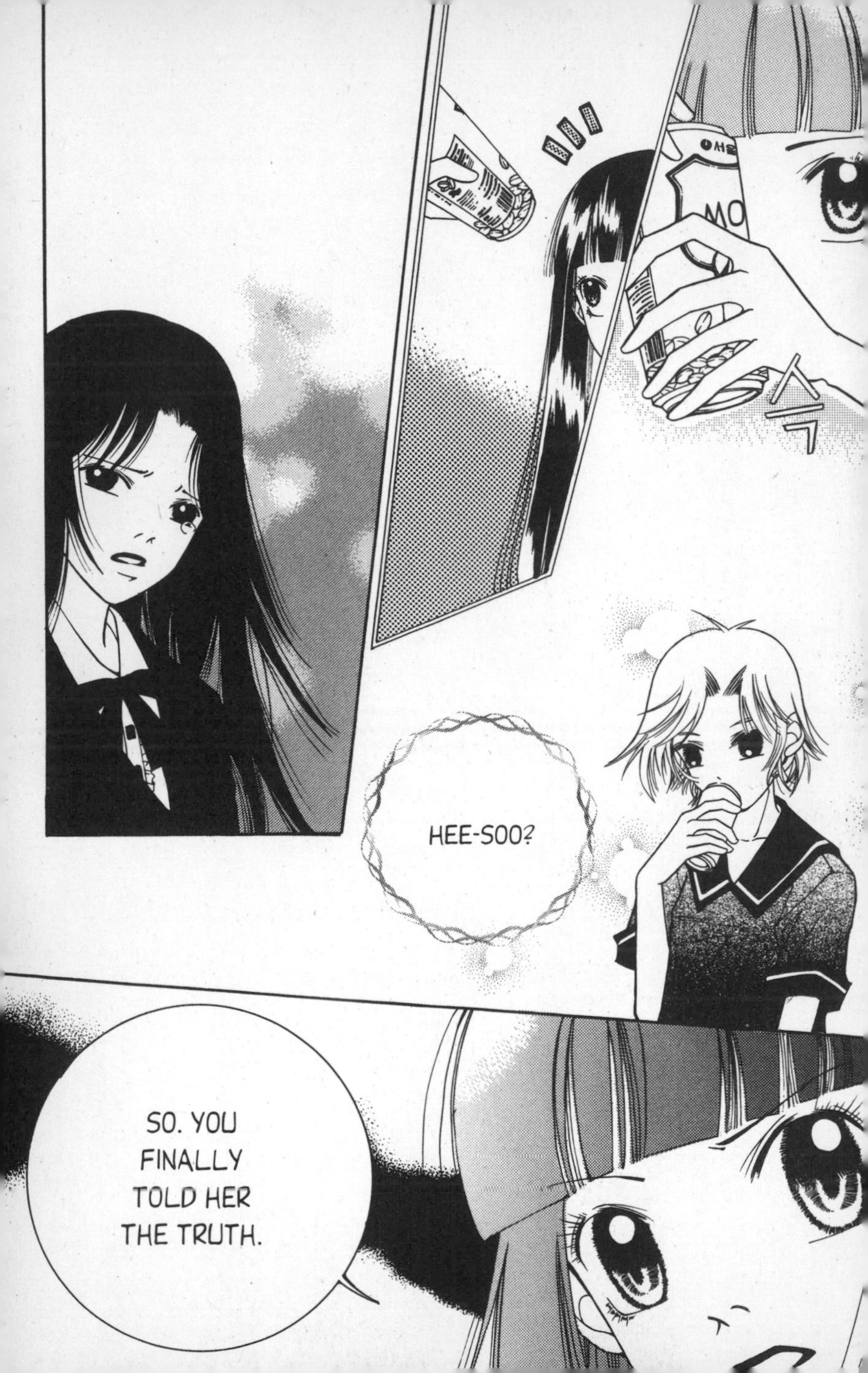
HEE-SOO?
SO. YOU FINALLY TOLD HER THE TRUTH.

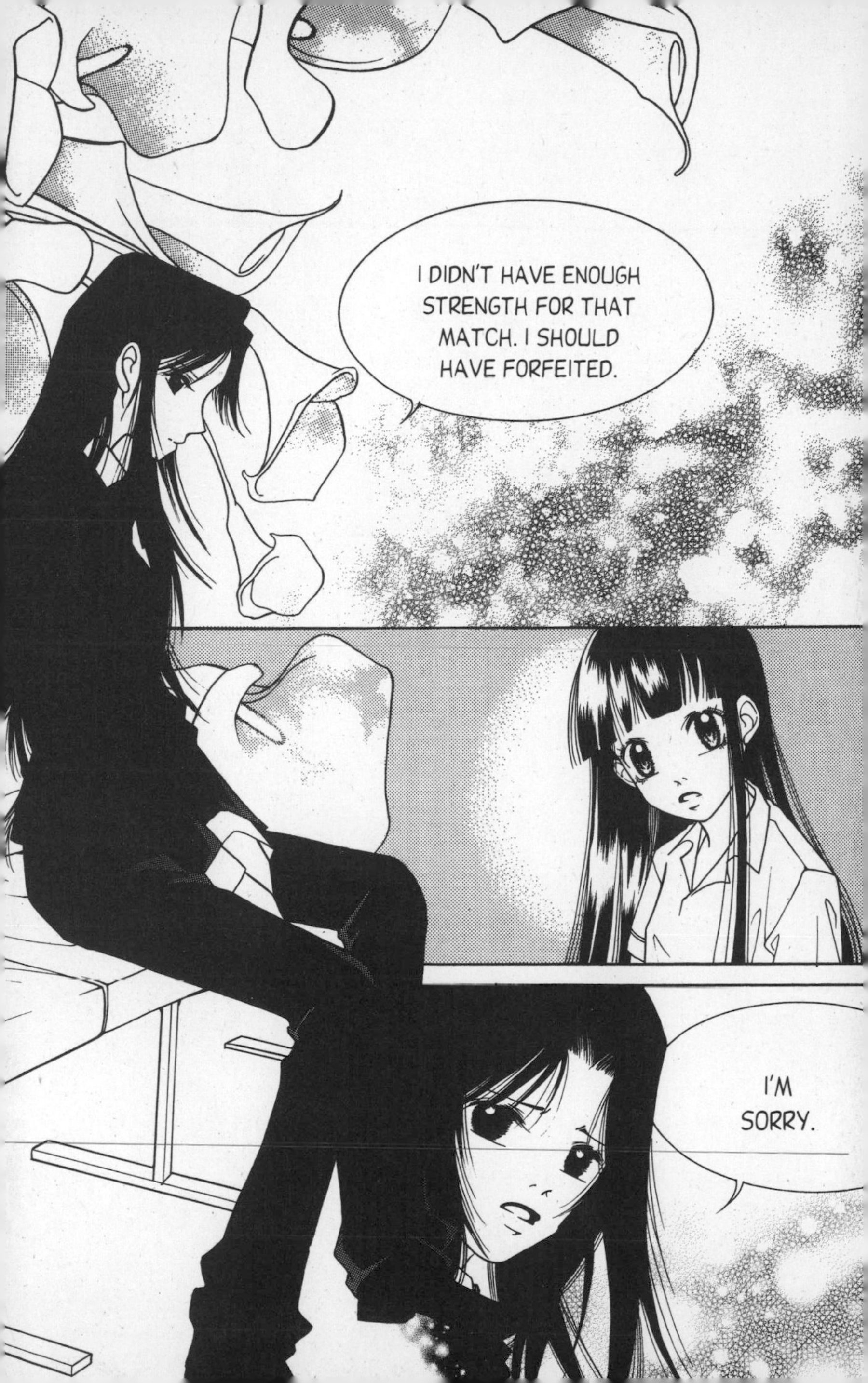
I DIDN'T HAVE ENOUGH STRENGTH FOR THAT MATCH. I SHOULD HAVE FORFEITED.
I'M SORRY.

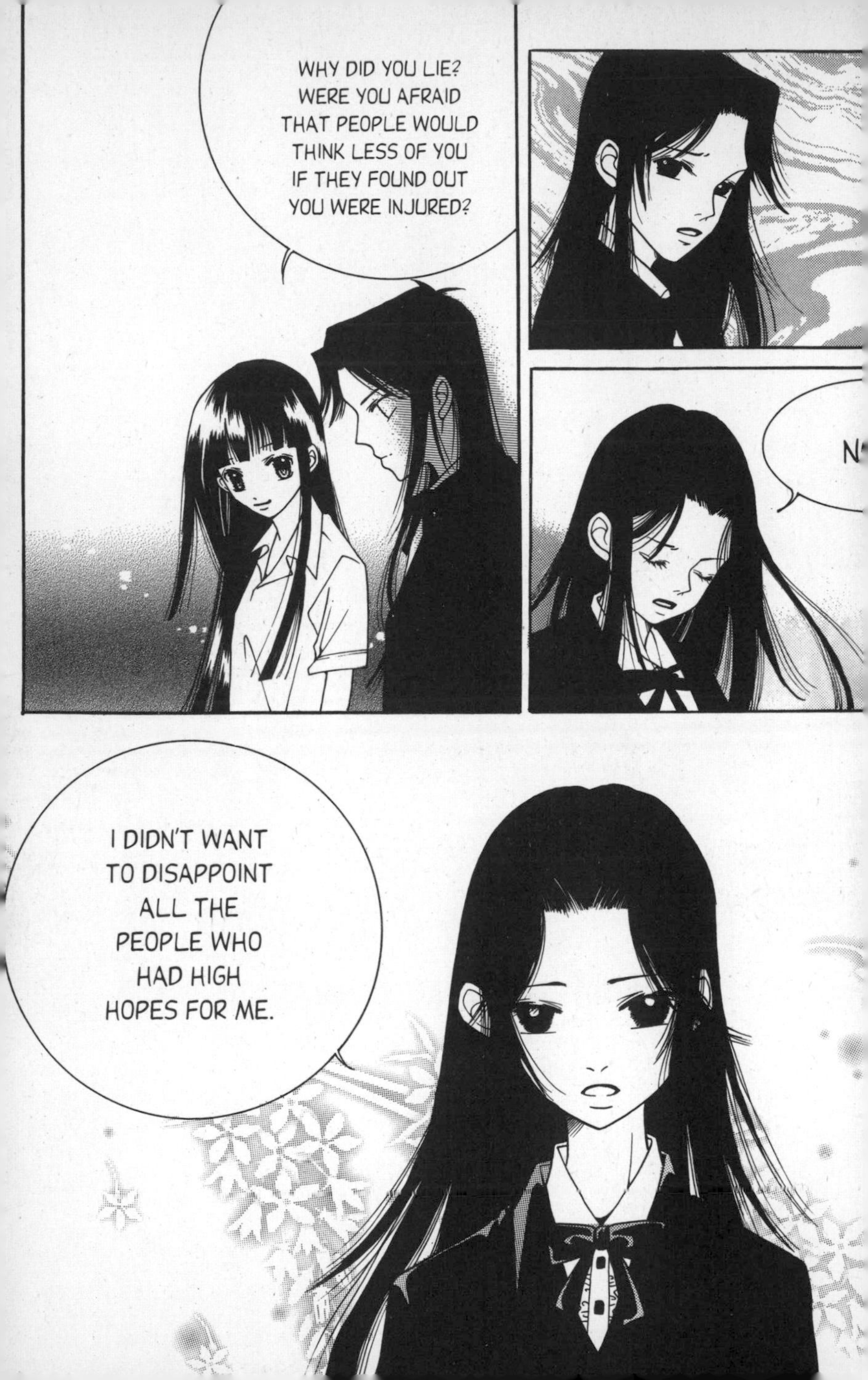
WHY DID YOU LIE? WERE YOU AFRAID THAT PEOPLE WOULD THINK LESS OF YOU IF THEY FOUND OUT YOU WERE INJURED?
I DIDN'T WANT TO DISAPPOINT ALL THE PEOPLE WHO HAD HIGH HOPES FOR ME.

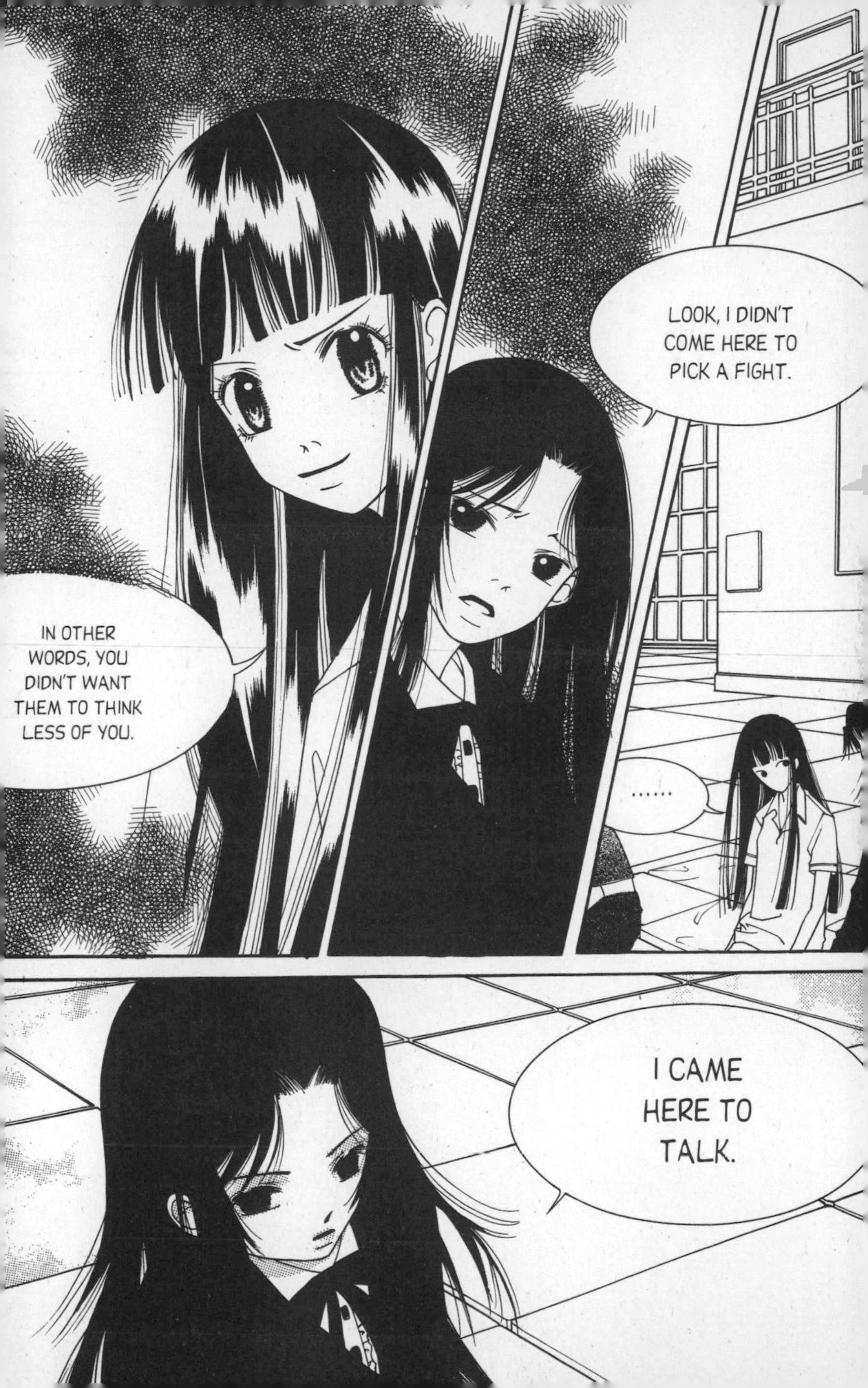
IN OTHER WORDS, YOU DIDN'T WANT THEM TO THINK LESS OF YOU.
LOOK, I DIDN'T COME HERE TO PICK A FIGHT.
......
I CAME HERE TO TALK.

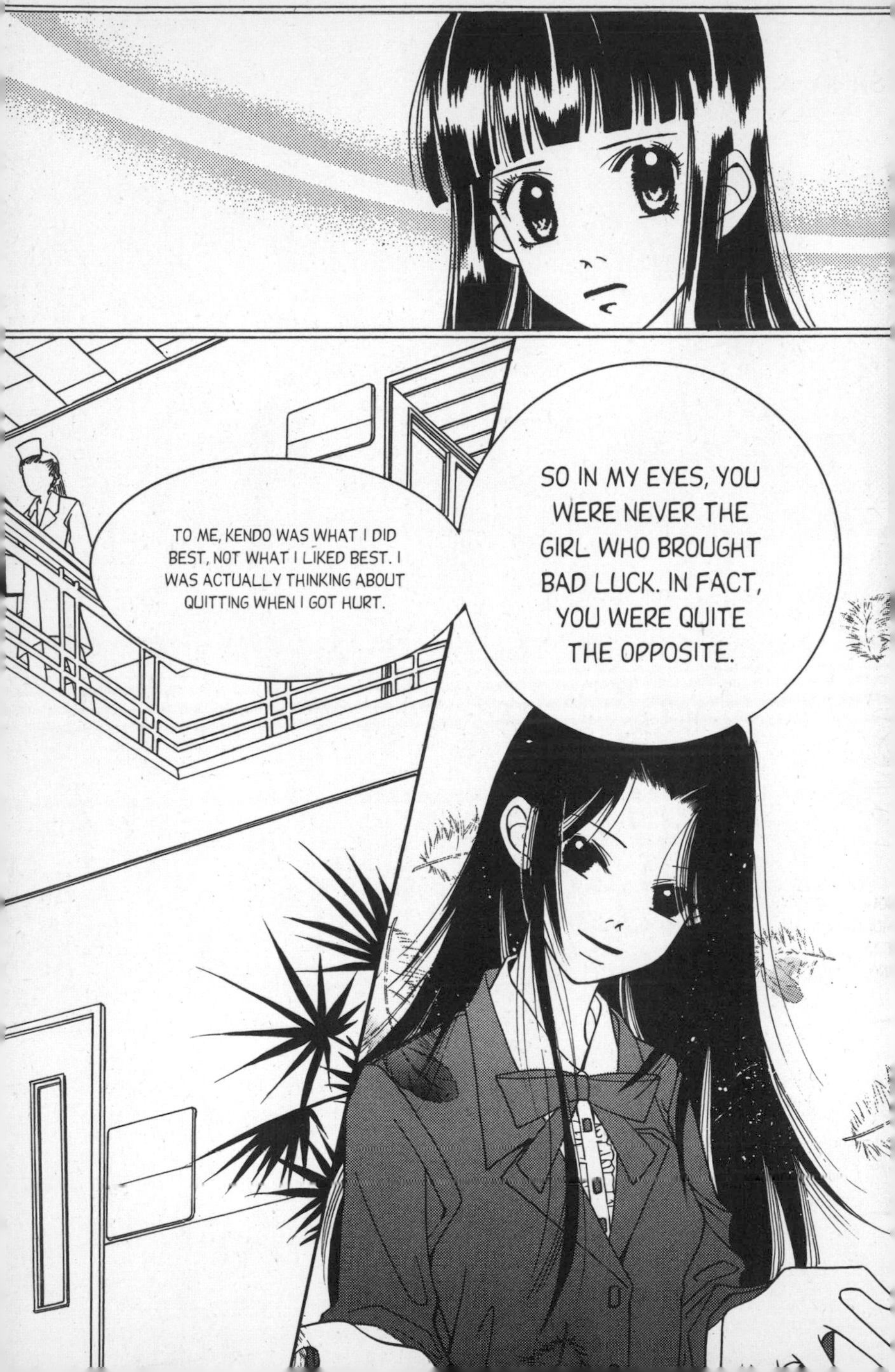
TO ME, KENDO WAS WHAT I DID BEST, NOT WHAT I LIKED BEST. I WAS ACTUALLY THINKING ABOUT QUITTING WHEN I GOT HURT.
SO IN MY EYES, YOU WERE NEVER THE GIRL WHO BROUGHT BAD LUCK. IN FACT, YOU WERE QUITE THE OPPOSITE.

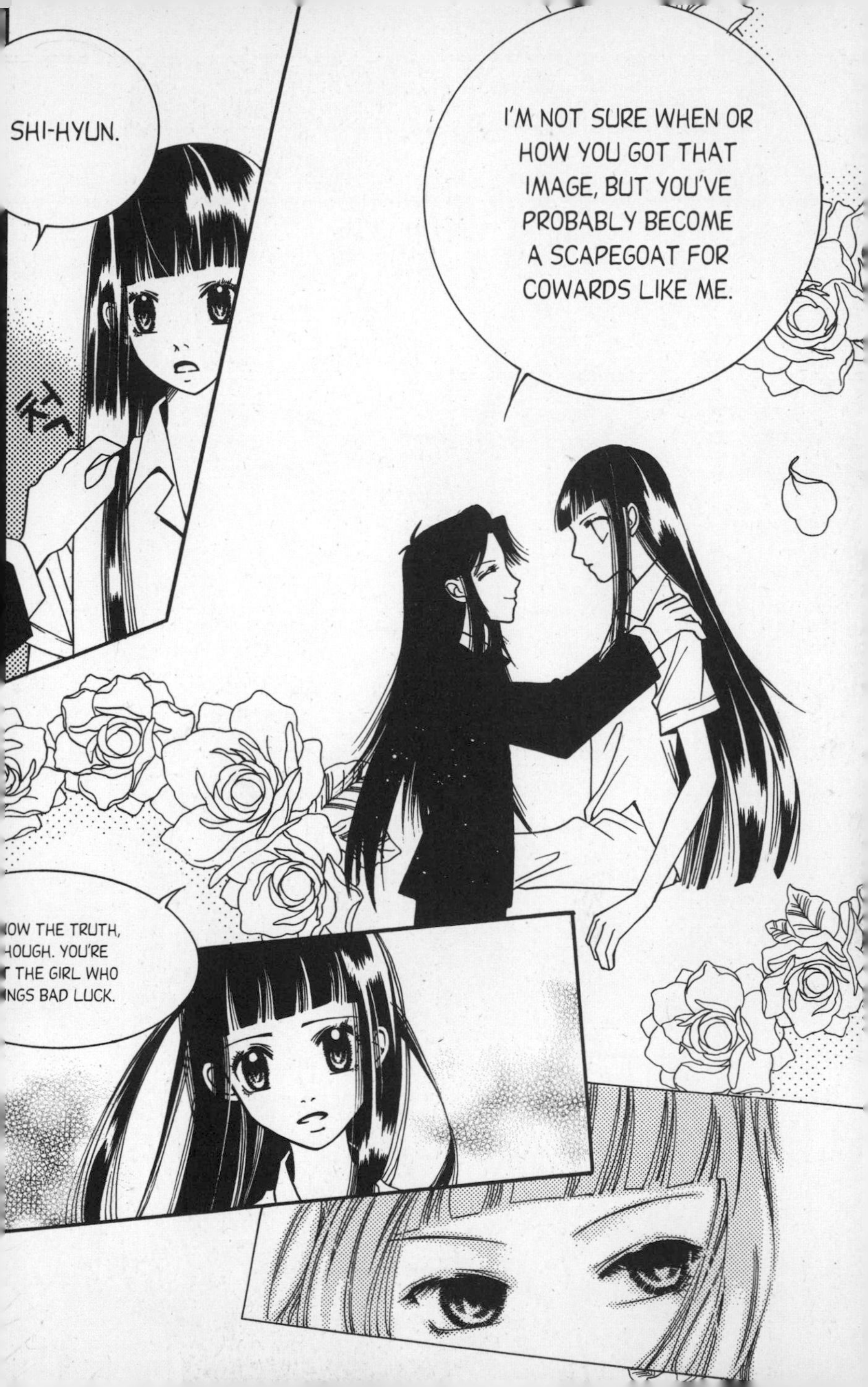
SHI-HYUN.
I'M NOT SURE WHEN OR HOW YOU GOT THAT IMAGE, BUT YOU'VE PROBABLY BECOME A SCAPEGOAT FOR COWARDS LIKE ME.
OW THE TRUTH, HOUGH. YOU'RE T THE GIRL WHO NGS BAD LUCK.

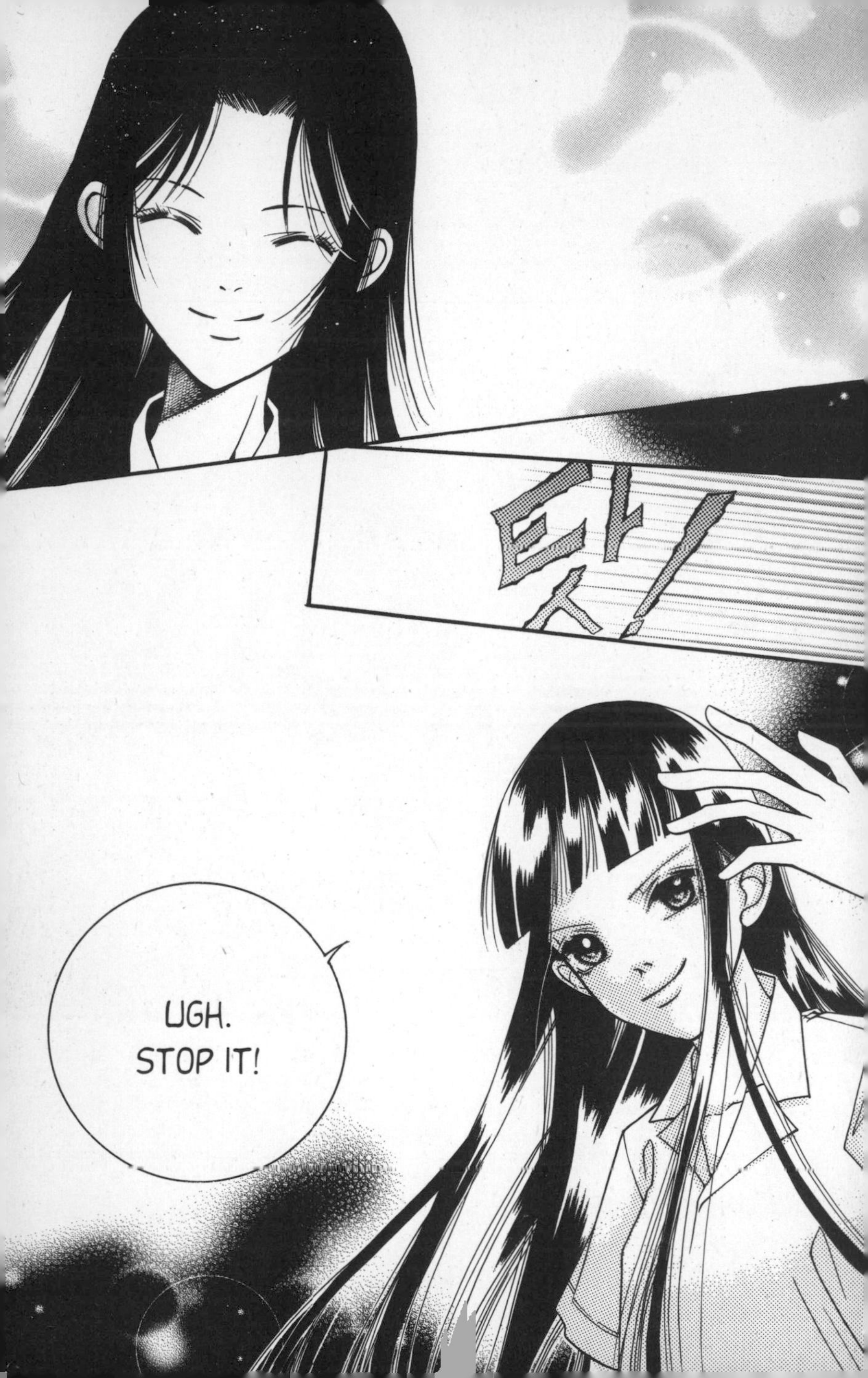
탓!
UGH. STOP IT!

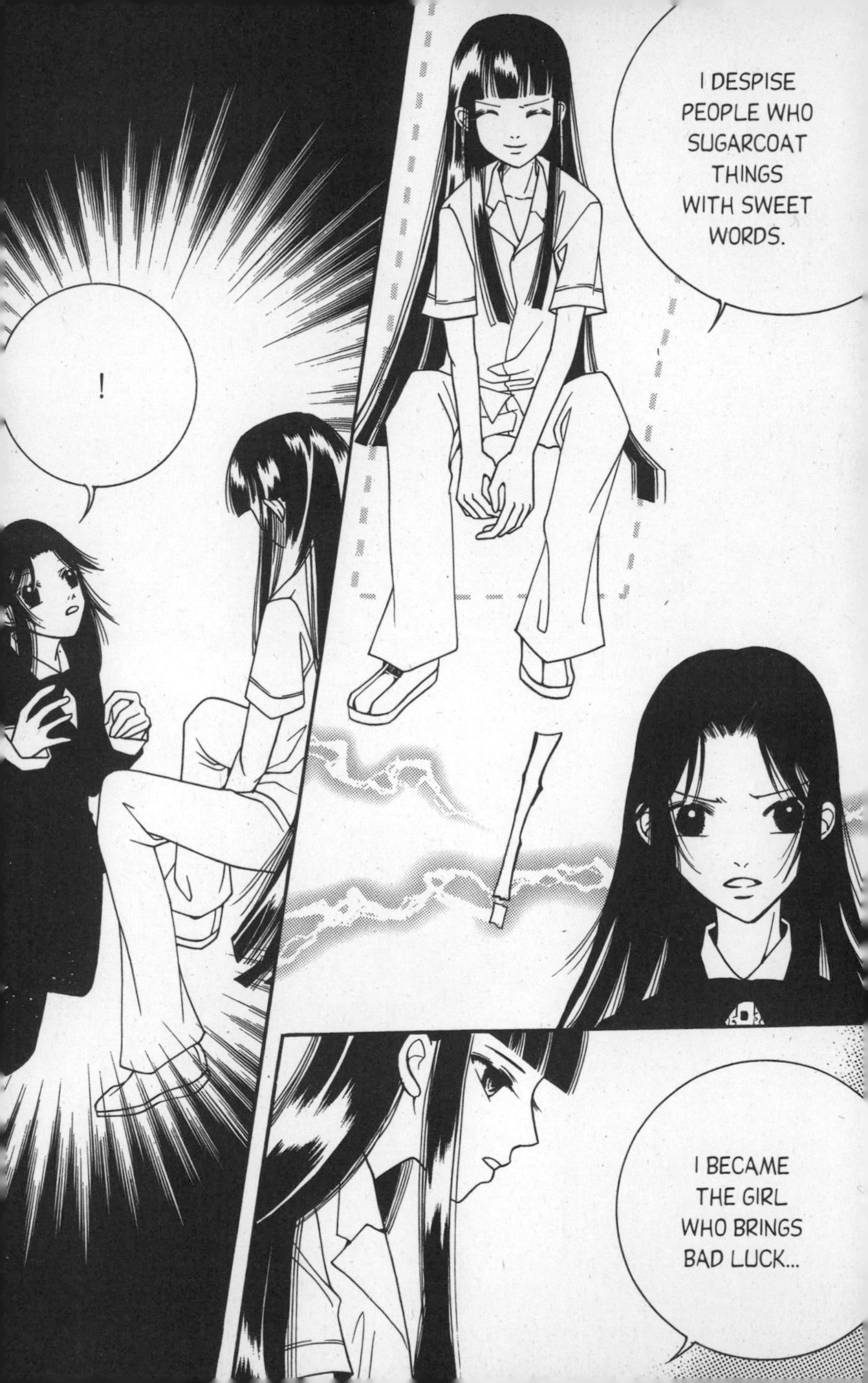
!
I DESPISE PEOPLE WHO SUGARCOAT THINGS WITH SWEET WORDS.
I BECAME THE GIRL WHO BRINGS BAD LUCK...

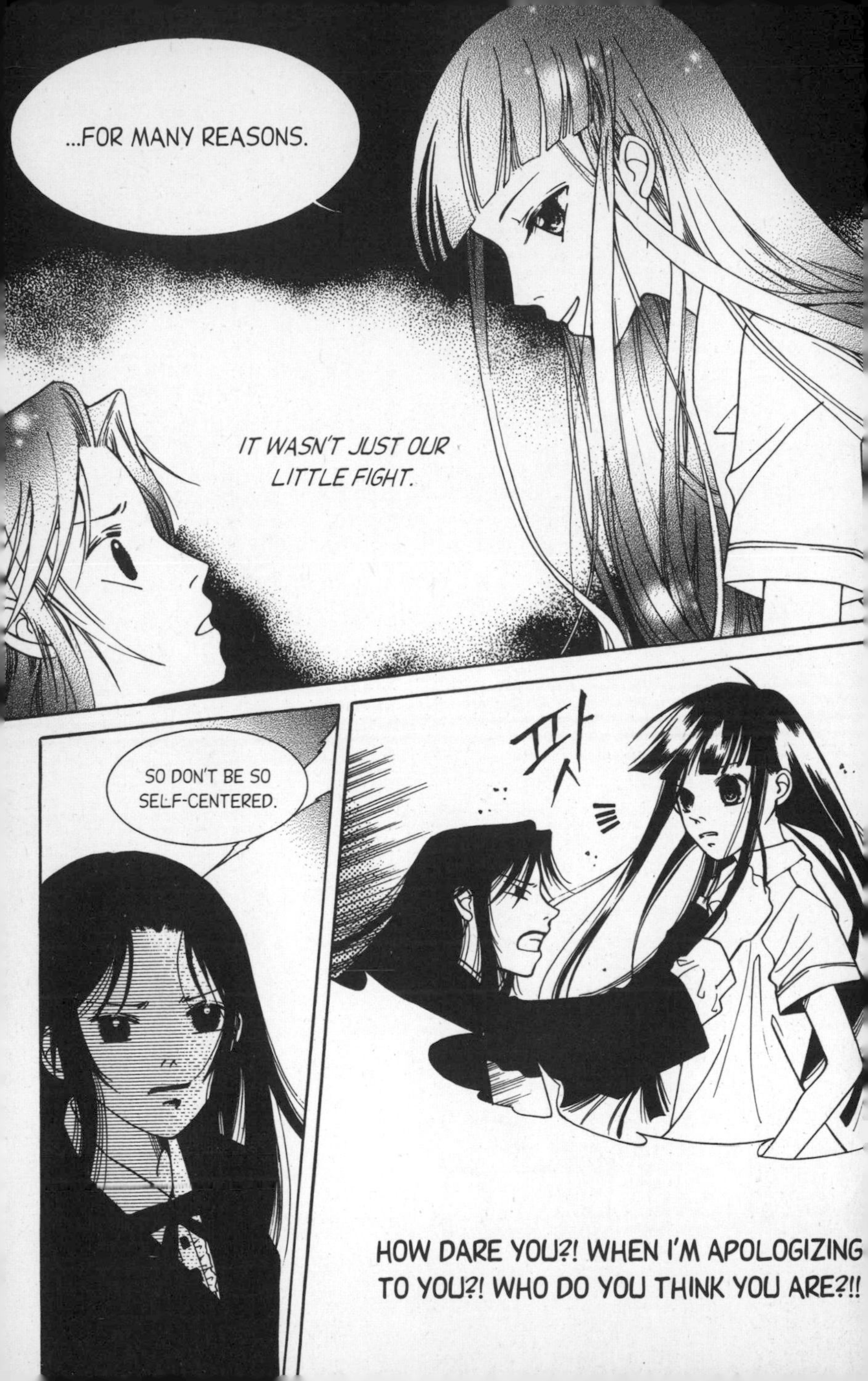
...FOR MANY REASONS.
IT WASN'T JUST OUR LITTLE FIGHT.
SO DON'T BE SO SELF-CENTERED.
팟
HOW DARE YOU?! WHEN I'M APOLOGIZING TO YOU?! WHO DO YOU THINK YOU ARE?!!

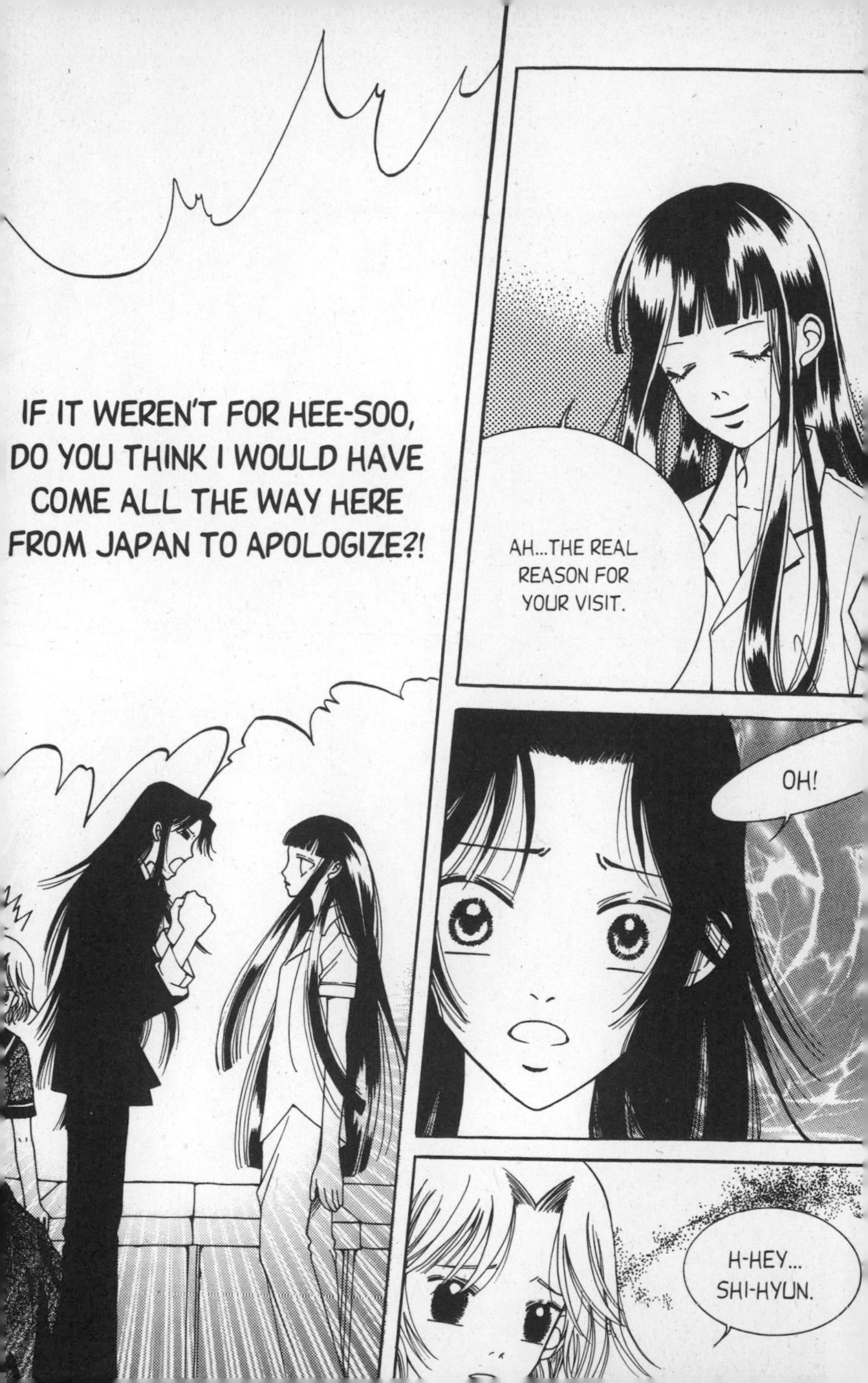
IF IT WEREN'T FOR HEE-SOO, DO YOU THINK I WOULD HAVE COME ALL THE WAY HERE FROM JAPAN TO APOLOGIZE?!
AH...THE REAL REASON FOR YOUR VISIT.
OH!
H-HEY... SHI-HYUN.

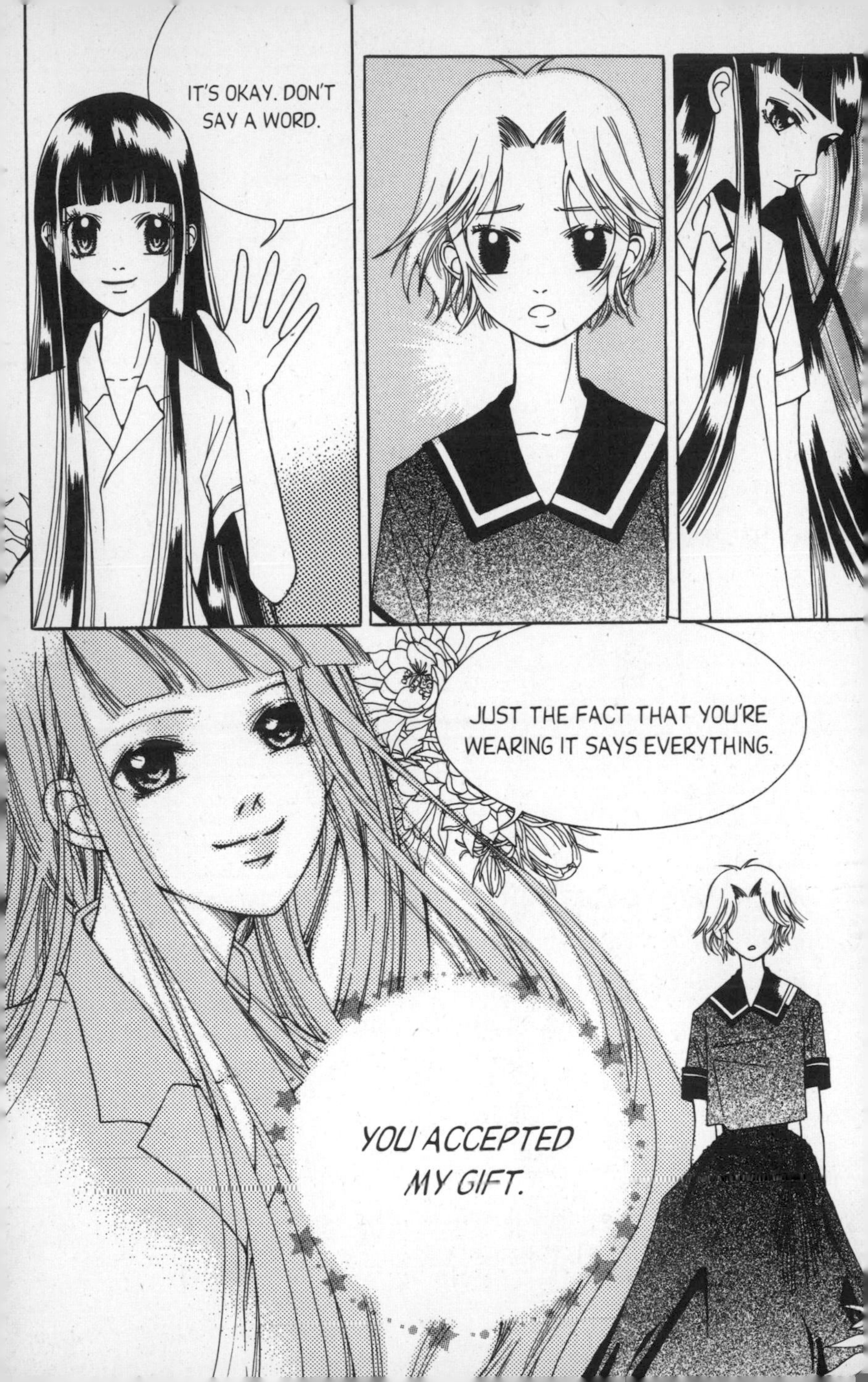
IT'S OKAY. DON'T SAY A WORD.
JUST THE FACT THAT YOU'RE WEARING IT SAYS EVERYTHING.
YOU ACCEPTED MY GIFT.

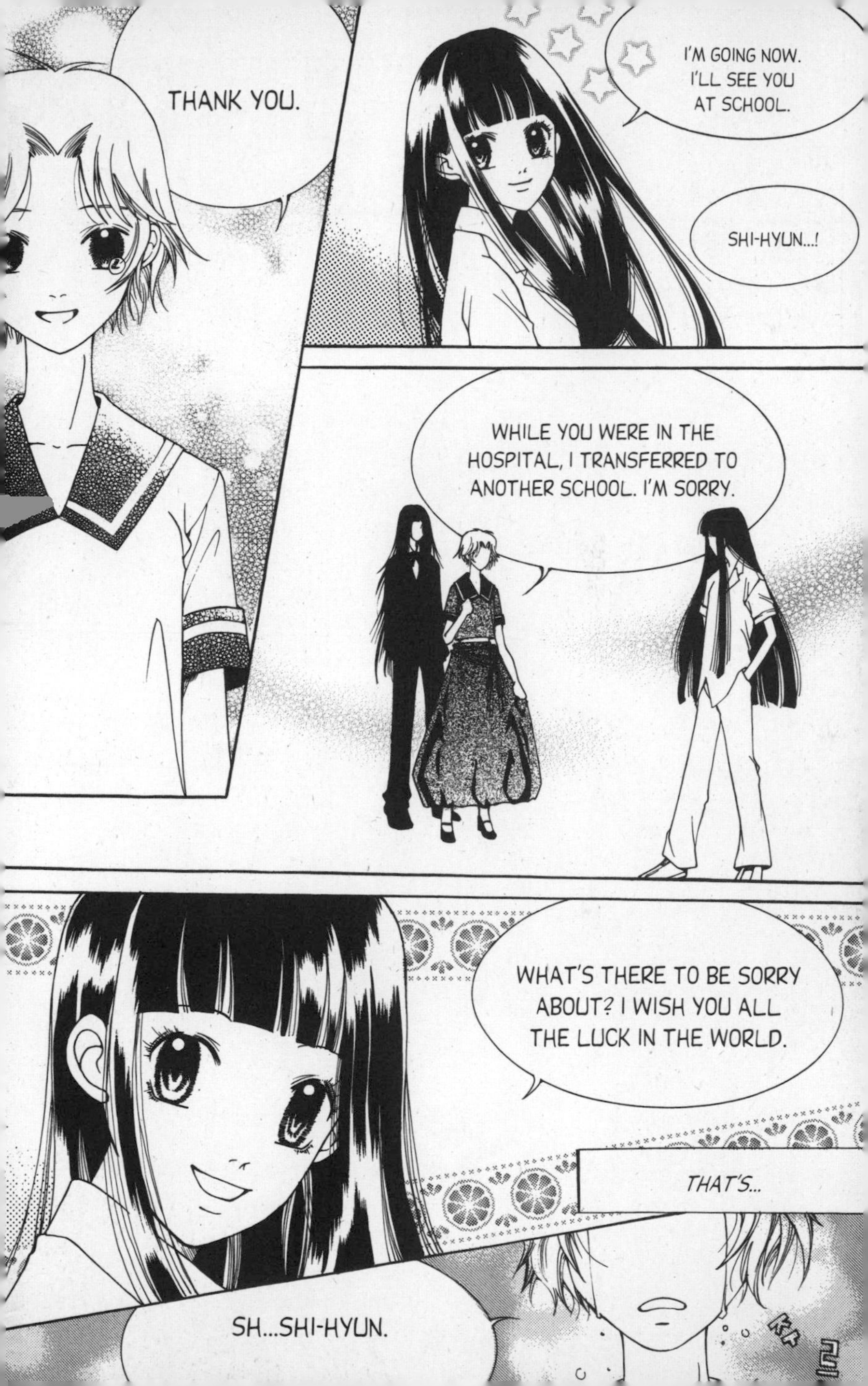
THANK YOU.
I'M GOING NOW. I'LL SEE YOU AT SCHOOL.
SHI-HYUN...!
WHILE YOU WERE IN THE HOSPITAL, I TRANSFERRED TO ANOTHER SCHOOL. I'M SORRY.
WHAT'S THERE TO BE SORRY ABOUT? I WISH YOU ALL THE LUCK IN THE WORLD.
THAT'S...
SH...SHI-HYUN.

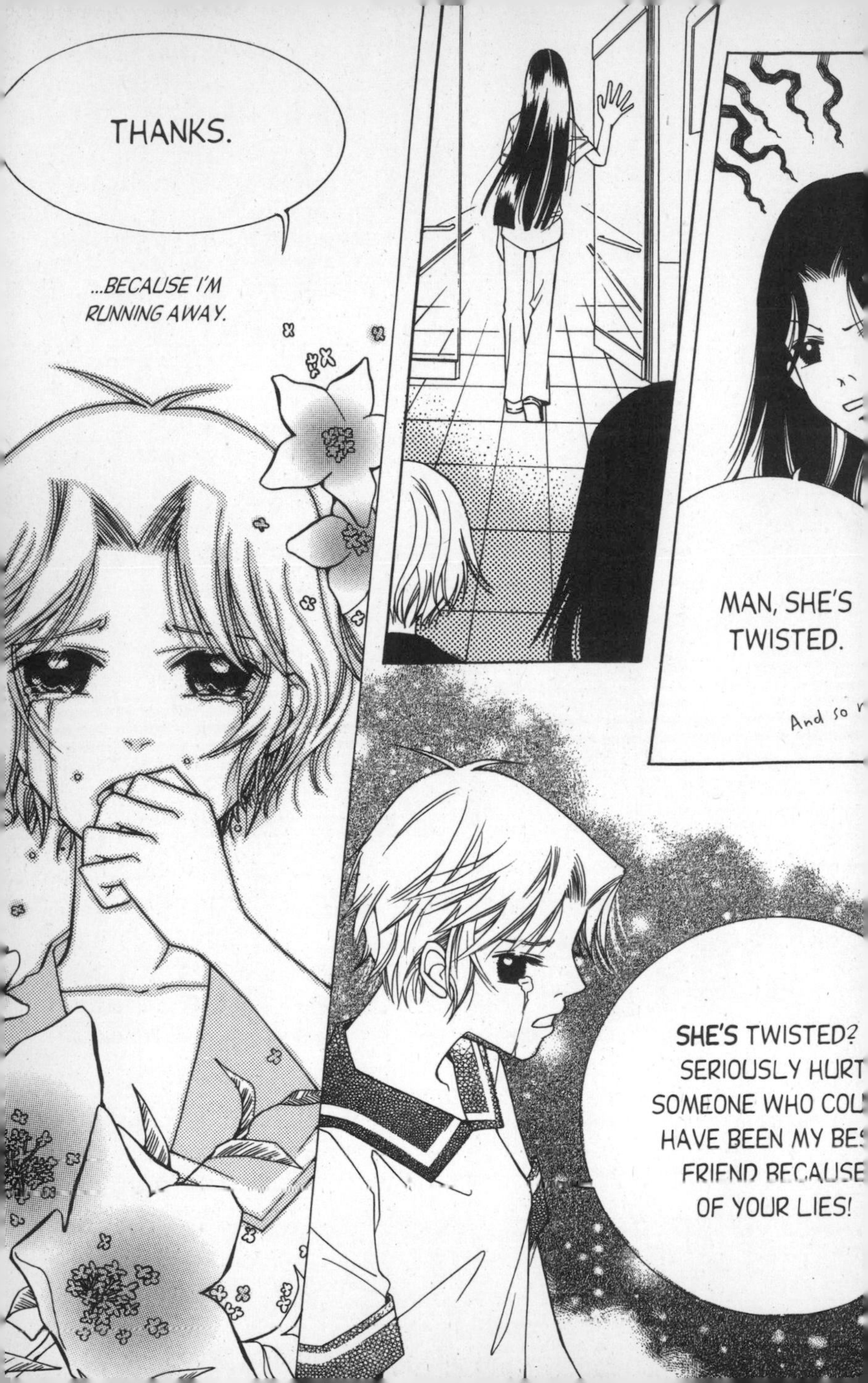

THANKS.
...BECAUSE I'M RUNNING AWAY.
MAN, SHE'S TWISTED.
SHE'S TWISTED? SERIOUSLY HURT SOMEONE WHO COU HAVE BEEN MY BES FRIEND BECAUSE OF YOUR LIES!

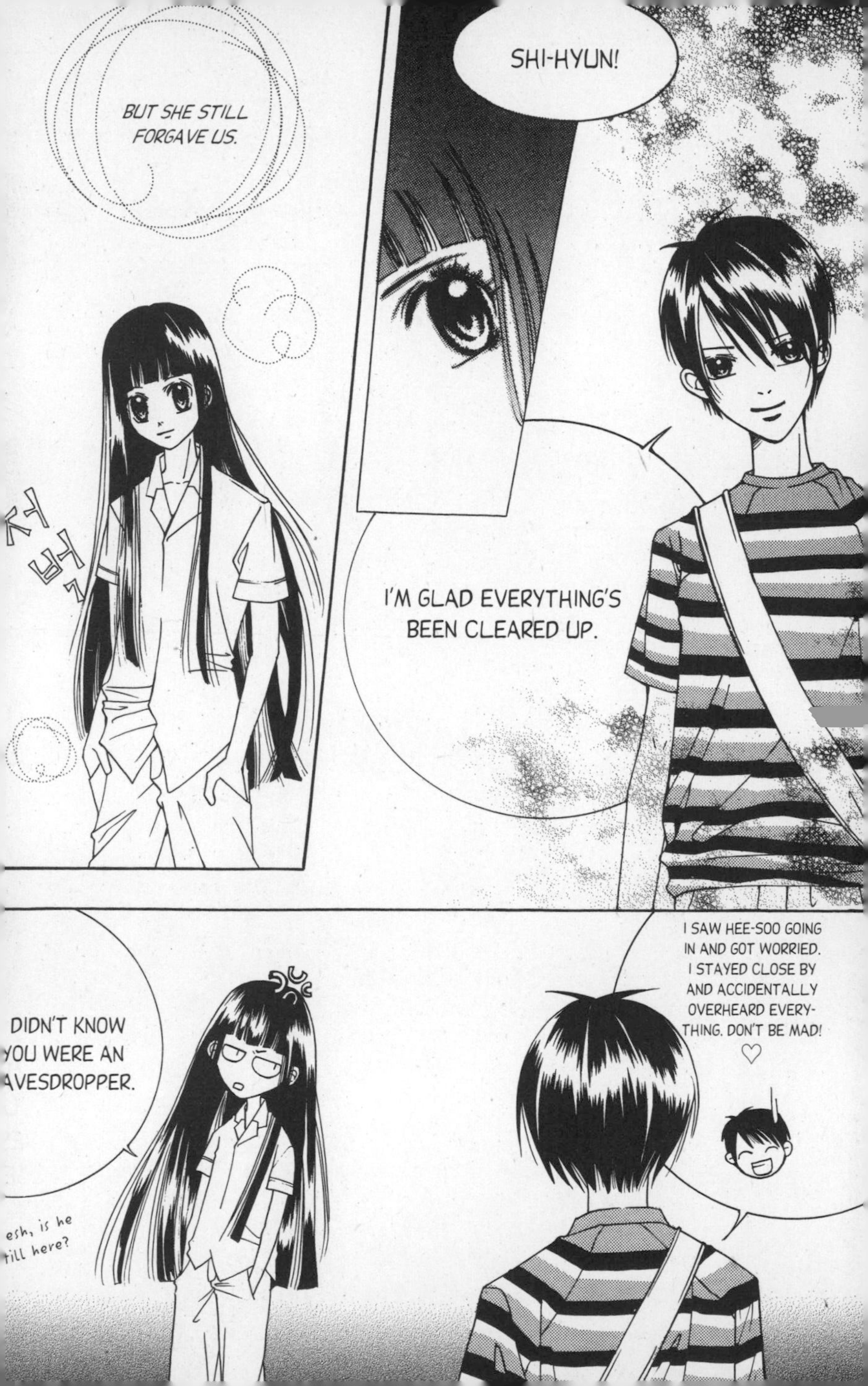
BUT SHE STILL FORGAVE US.
SHI-HYUN!
I'M GLAD EVERYTHING'S BEEN CLEARED UP.
DIDN'T KNOW YOU WERE AN AVESDROPPER.
esh, is he till here?
I SAW HEE-SOO GOING IN AND GOT WORRIED. I STAYED CLOSE BY AND ACCIDENTALLY OVERHEARD EVERY-THING. DON'T BE MAD! ♡

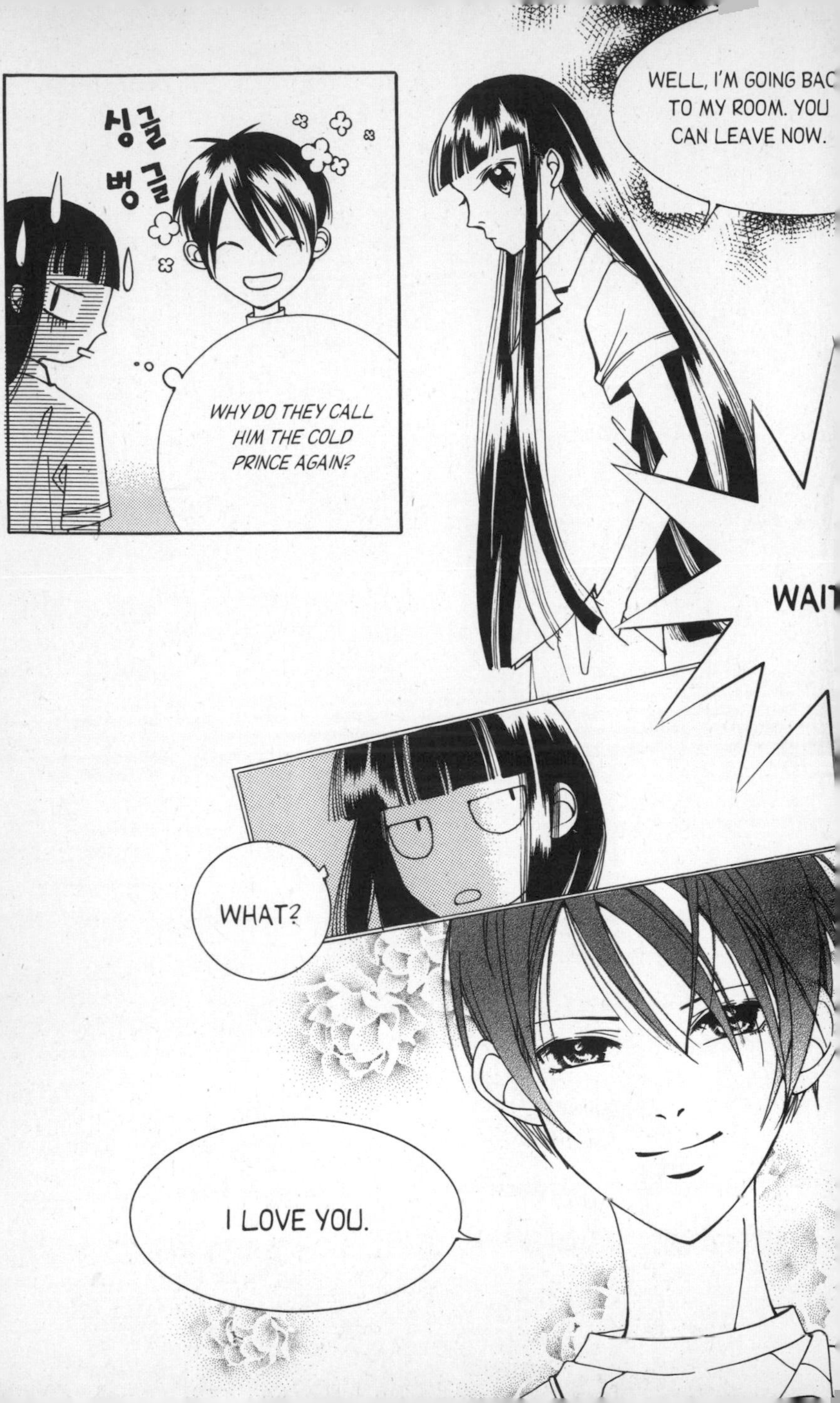
싱글벙글
WHY DO THEY CALL HIM THE COLD PRINCE AGAIN?
WELL, I'M GOING BAC TO MY ROOM. YOU CAN LEAVE NOW.
WAIT
WHAT?
I LOVE YOU.

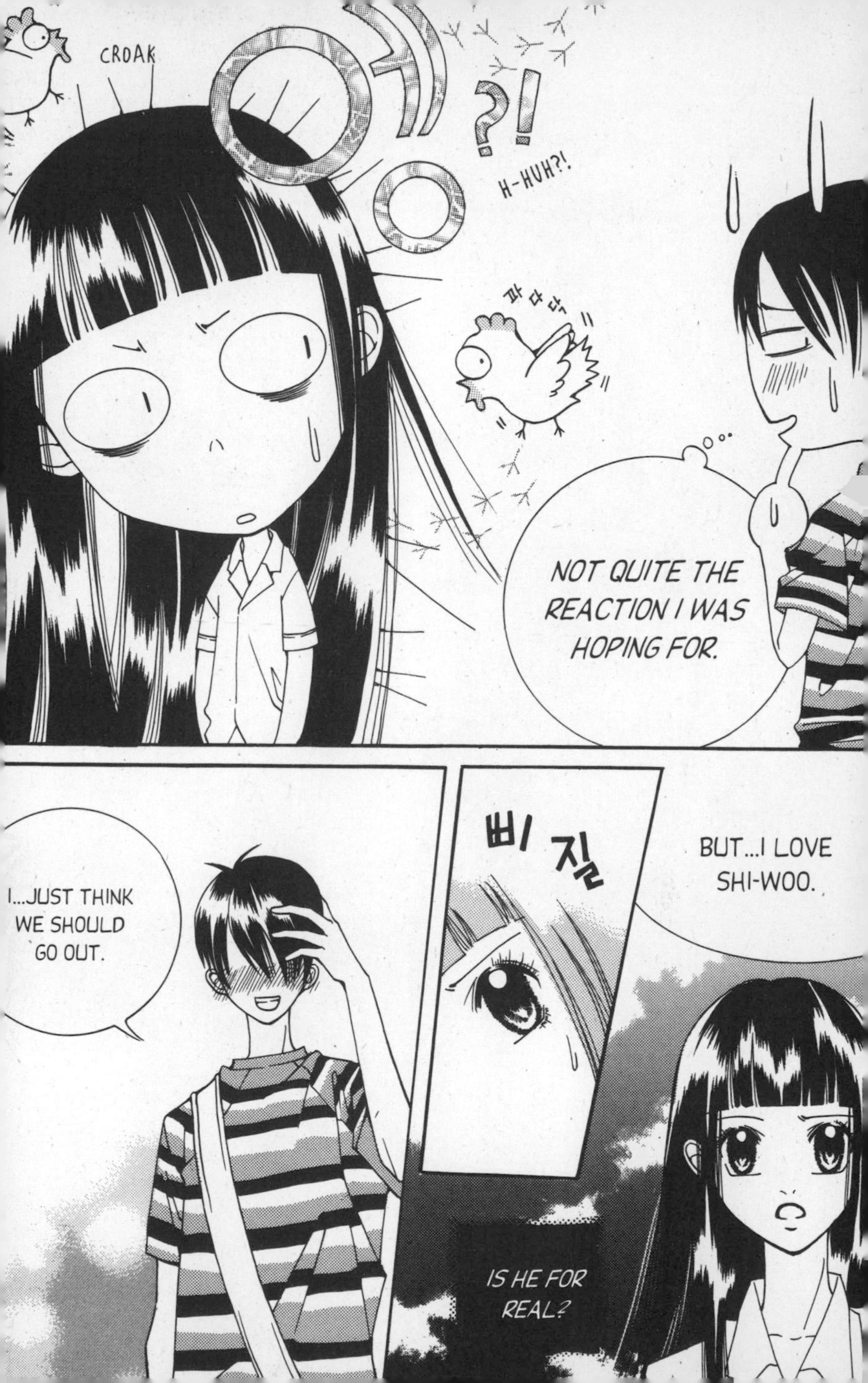
CROAK
?!
H-HUH?!
NOT QUITE THE REACTION I WAS HOPING FOR.
I...JUST THINK WE SHOULD GO OUT.
삐 질
BUT...I LOVE SHI-WOO.
IS HE FOR REAL?

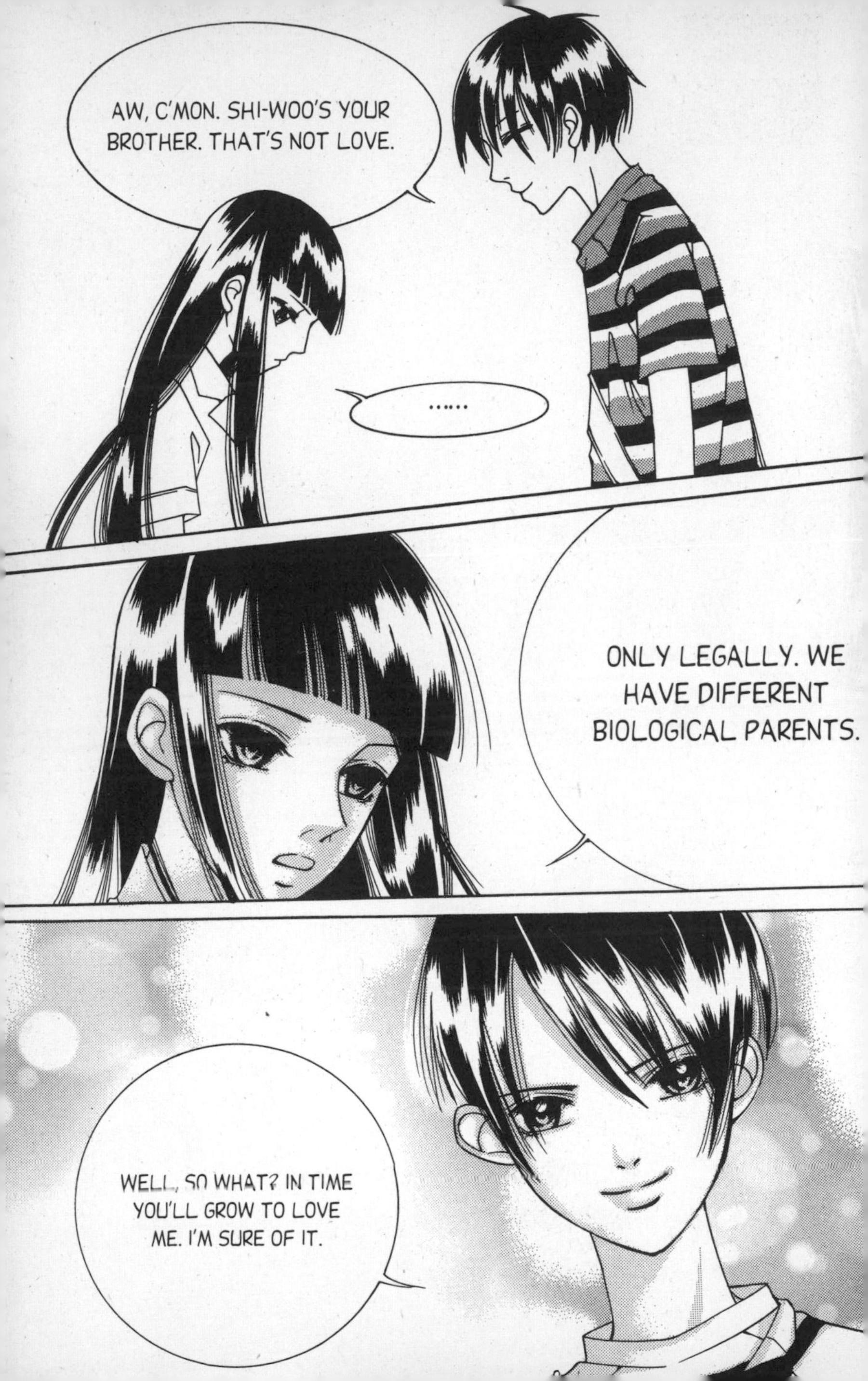
AW, C'MON. SHI-WOO'S YOUR BROTHER. THAT'S NOT LOVE.
......
ONLY LEGALLY. WE HAVE DIFFERENT BIOLOGICAL PARENTS.
WELL, SO WHAT? IN TIME YOU'LL GROW TO LOVE ME. I'M SURE OF IT.

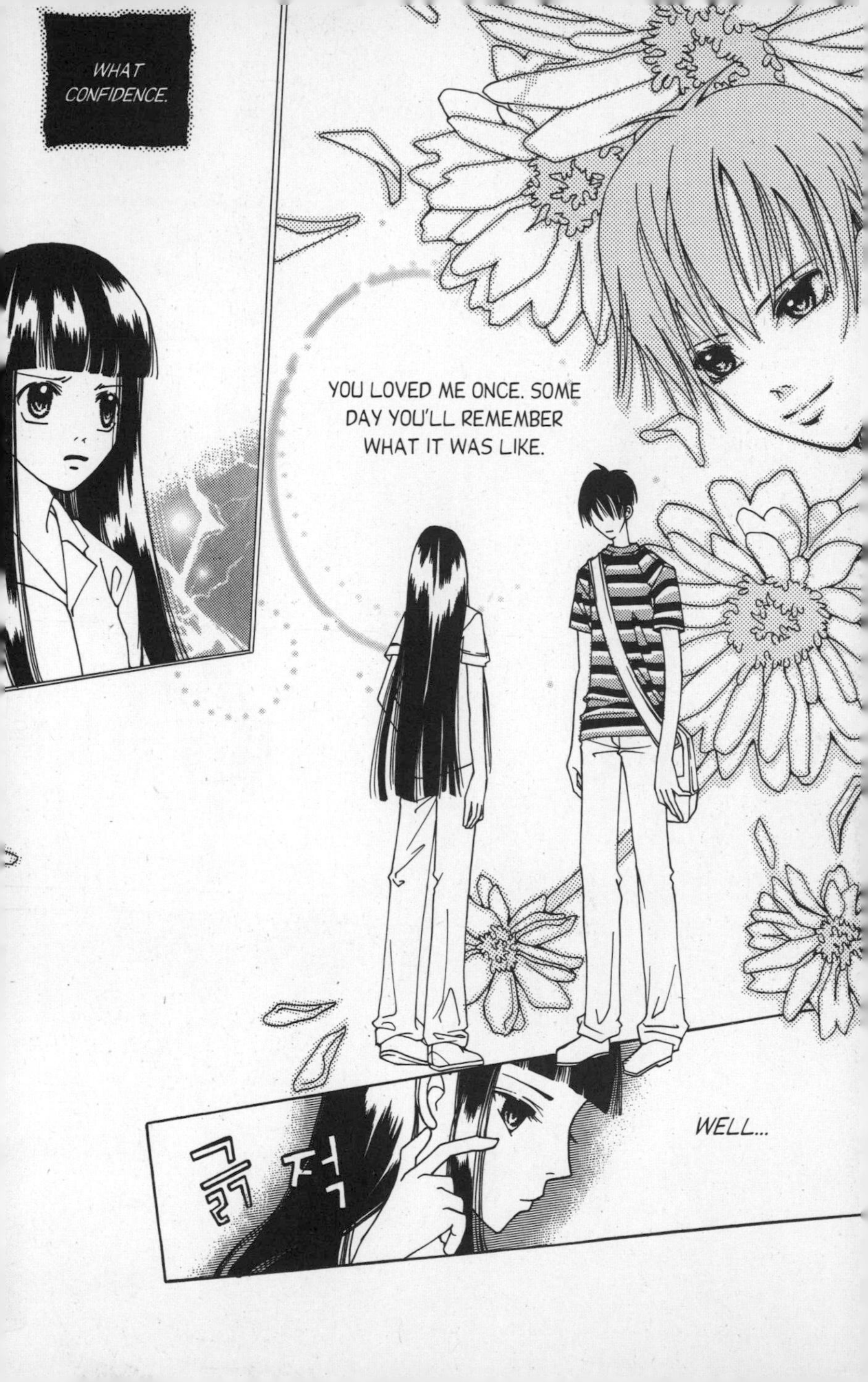
WHAT CONFIDENCE.
YOU LOVED ME ONCE. SOME DAY YOU'LL REMEMBER WHAT IT WAS LIKE.
긁적
WELL...

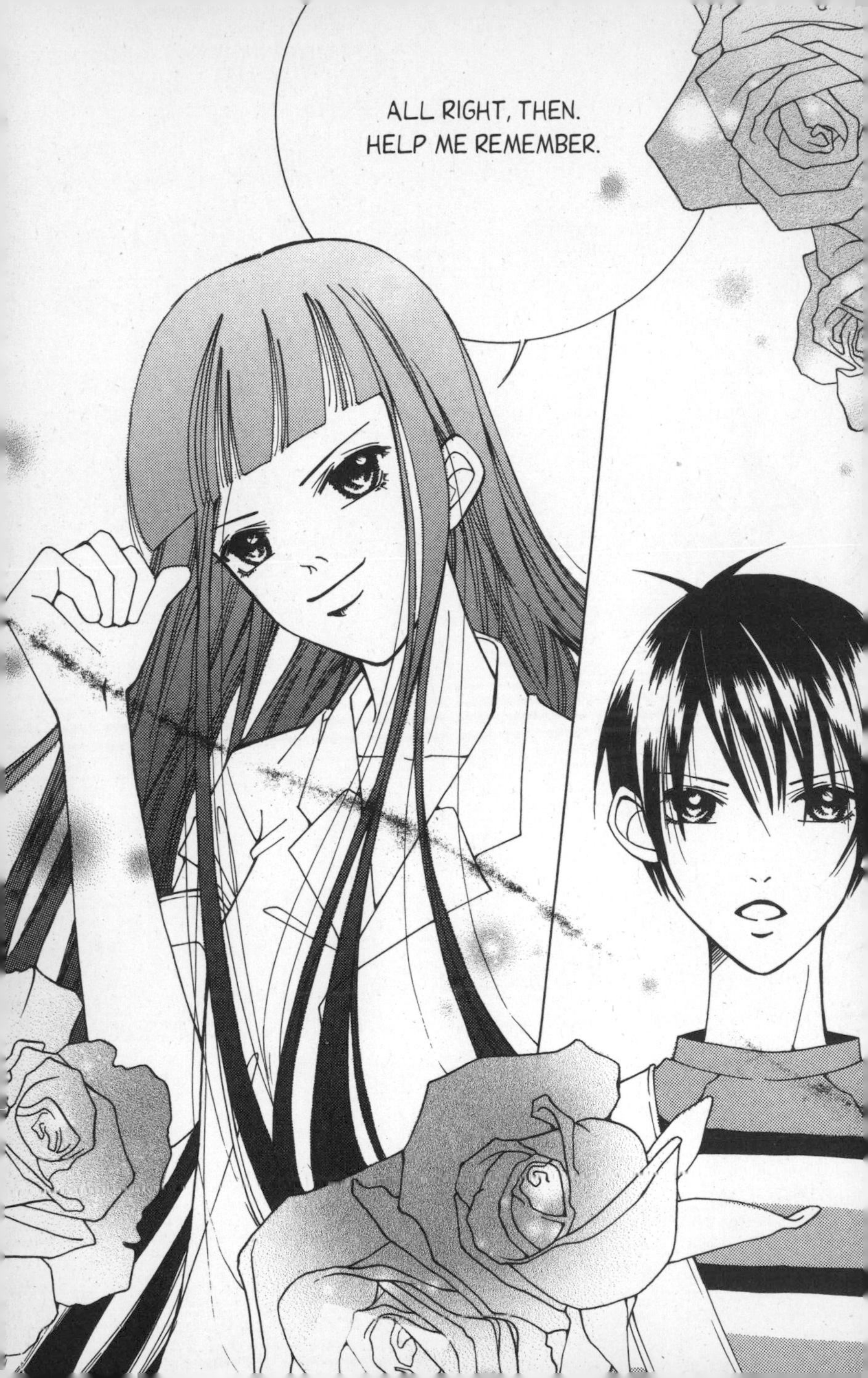
ALL RIGHT, THEN. HELP ME REMEMBER.

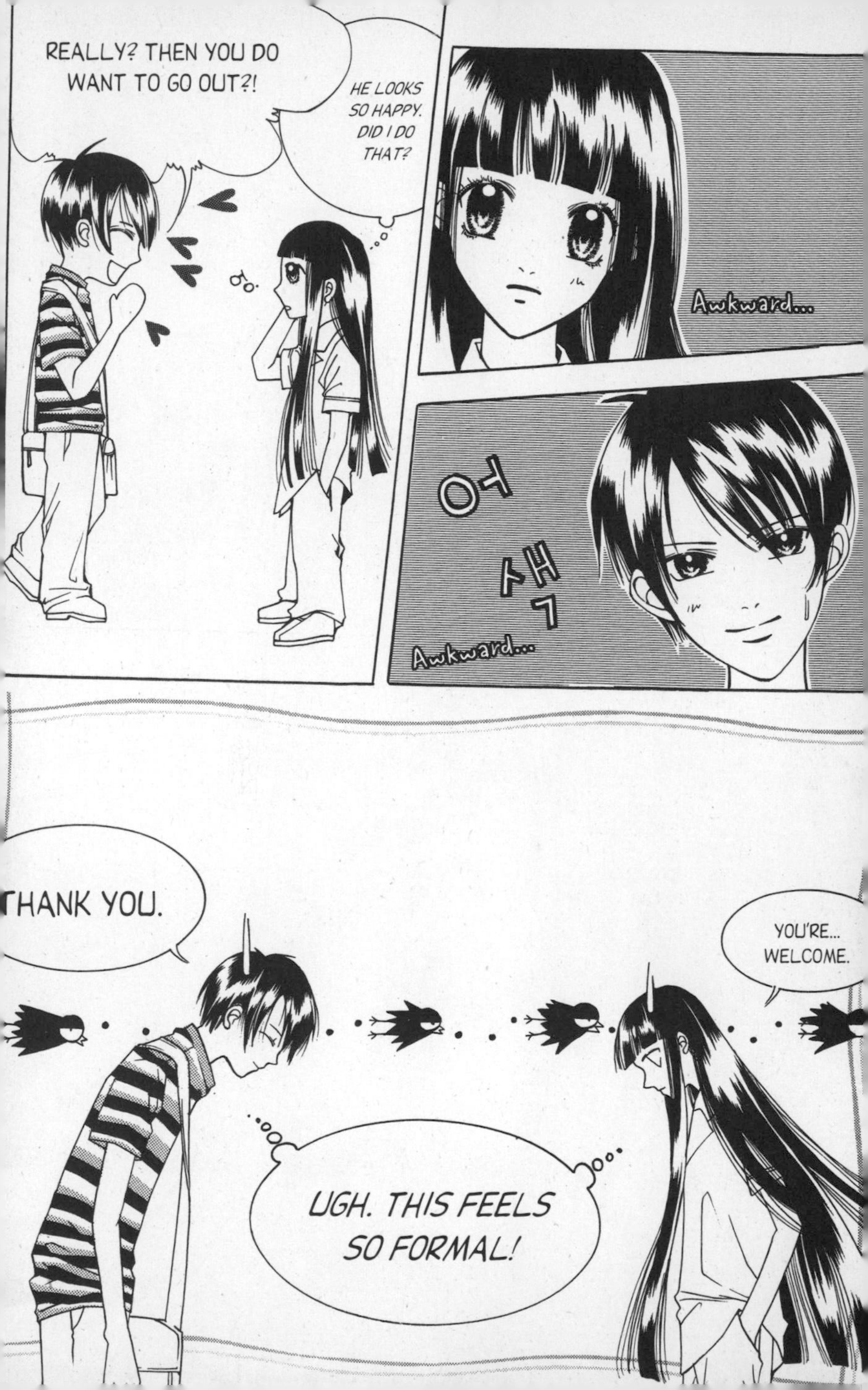
REALLY? THEN YOU DO WANT TO GO OUT?!
HE LOOKS SO HAPPY. DID I DO THAT?
Awkward...
Awkward...
THANK YOU.
YOU'RE... WELCOME.
UGH. THIS FEELS SO FORMAL!

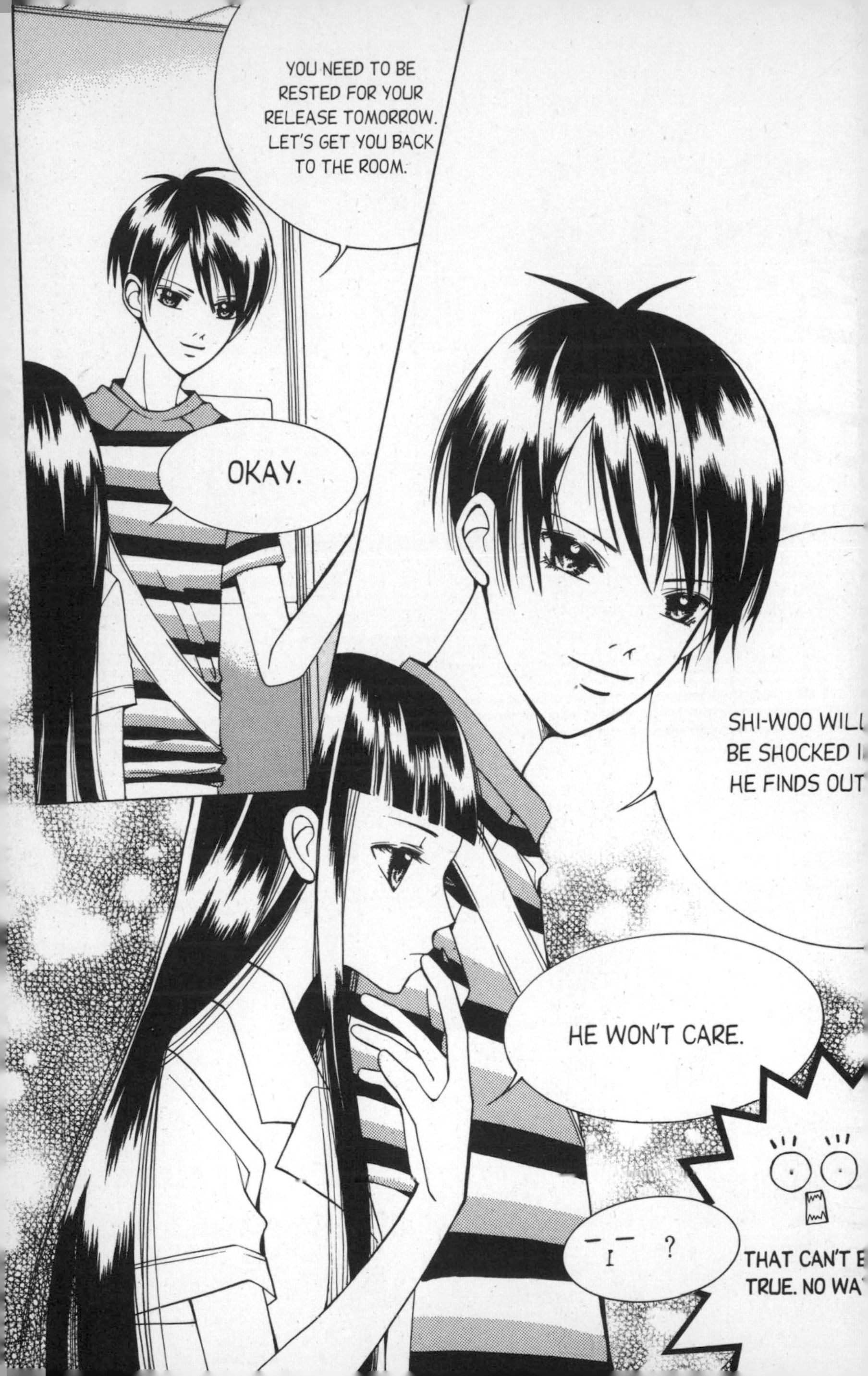
YOU NEED TO BE RESTED FOR YOUR RELEASE TOMORROW. LET'S GET YOU BACK TO THE ROOM.
OKAY.
SHI-WOO WIL BE SHOCKED I HE FINDS OUT
HE WON'T CARE.
THAT CAN'T TRUE. NO WA

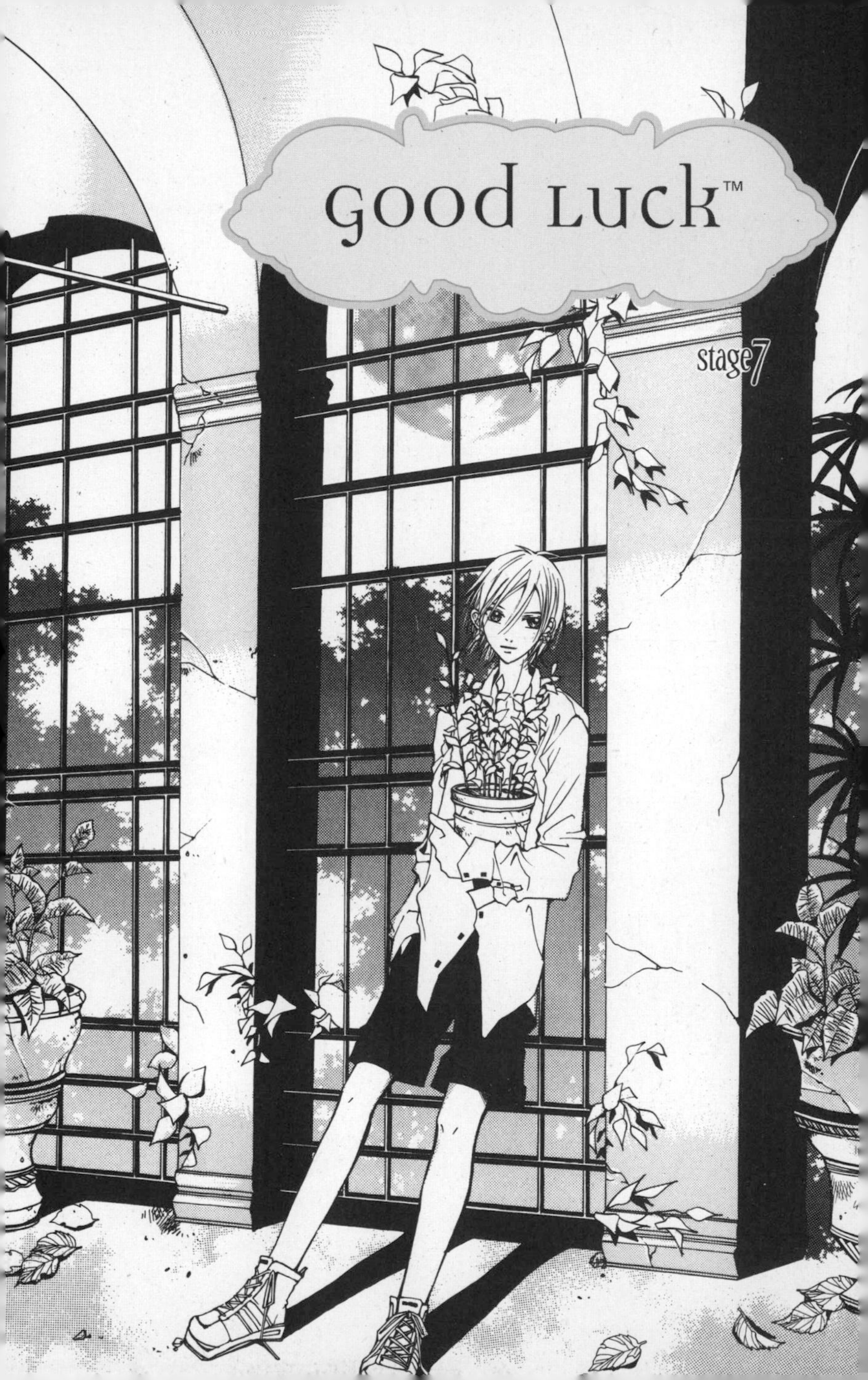
good luck™
stage7

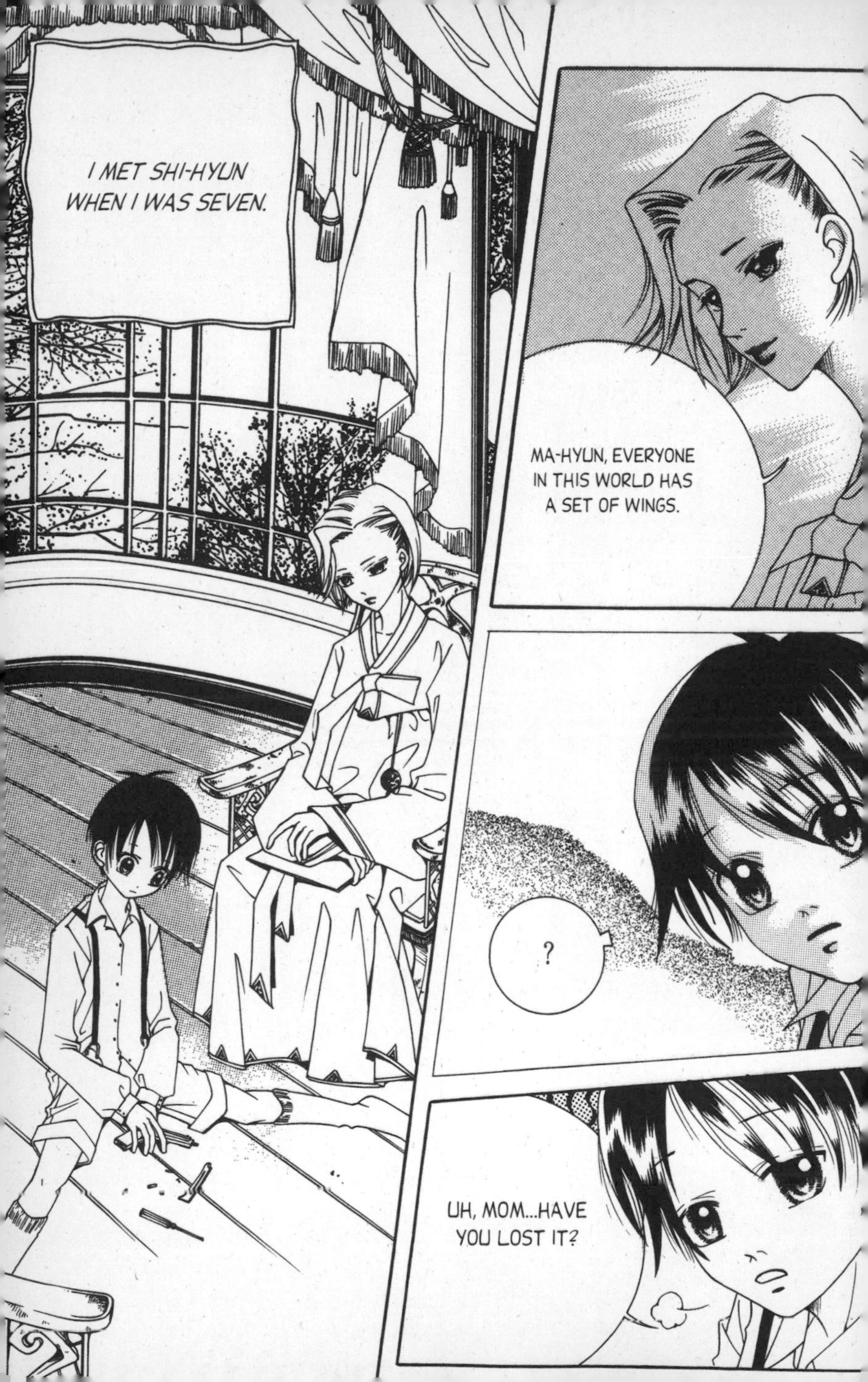
I MET SHI-HYUN WHEN I WAS SEVEN.
MA-HYUN, EVERYONE IN THIS WORLD HAS A SET OF WINGS.
?
UH, MOM...HAVE YOU LOST IT?

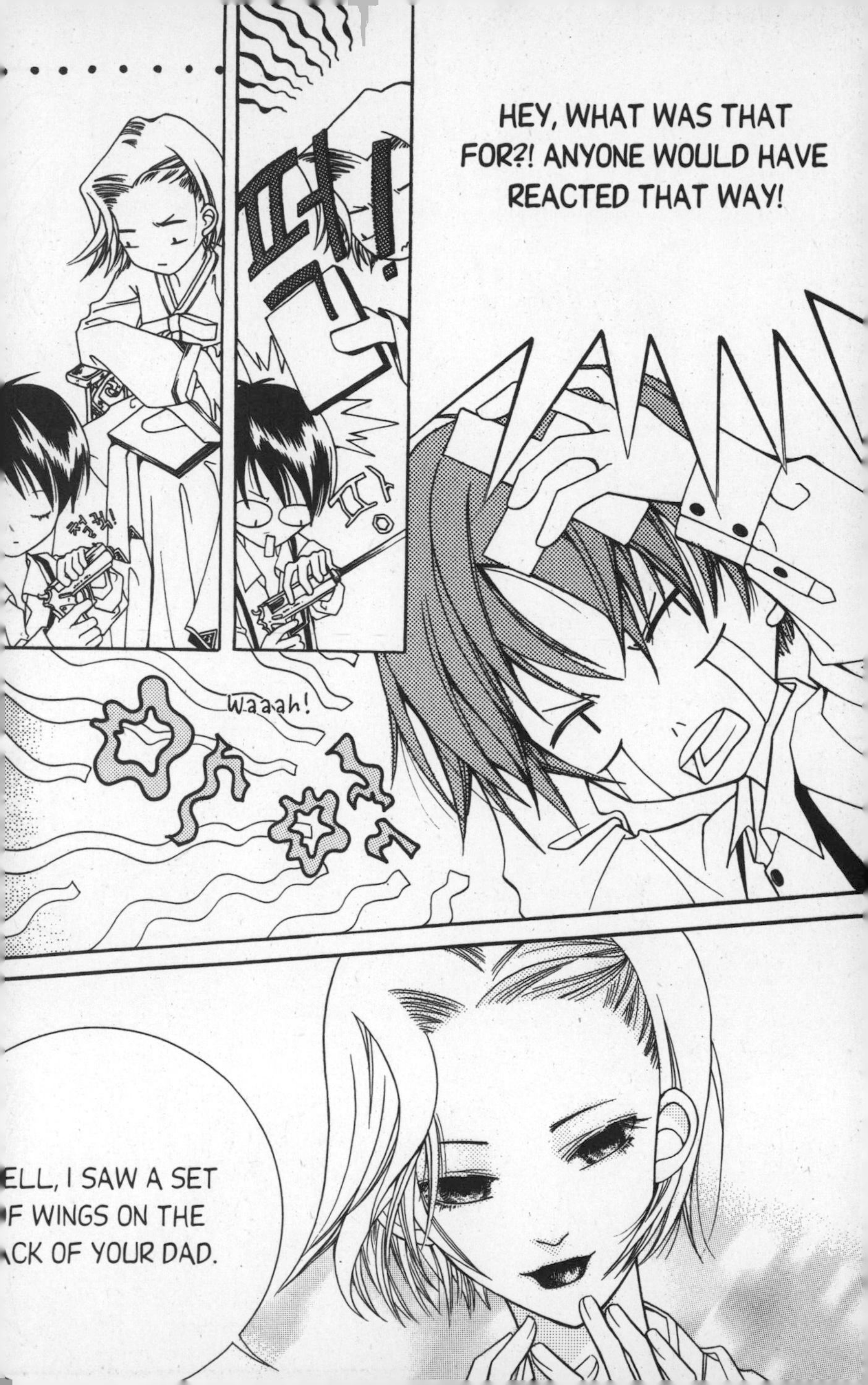

....
HEY, WHAT WAS THAT FOR?! ANYONE WOULD HAVE REACTED THAT WAY!
Waaah!
ELL, I SAW A SET
F WINGS ON THE
CK OF YOUR DAD.

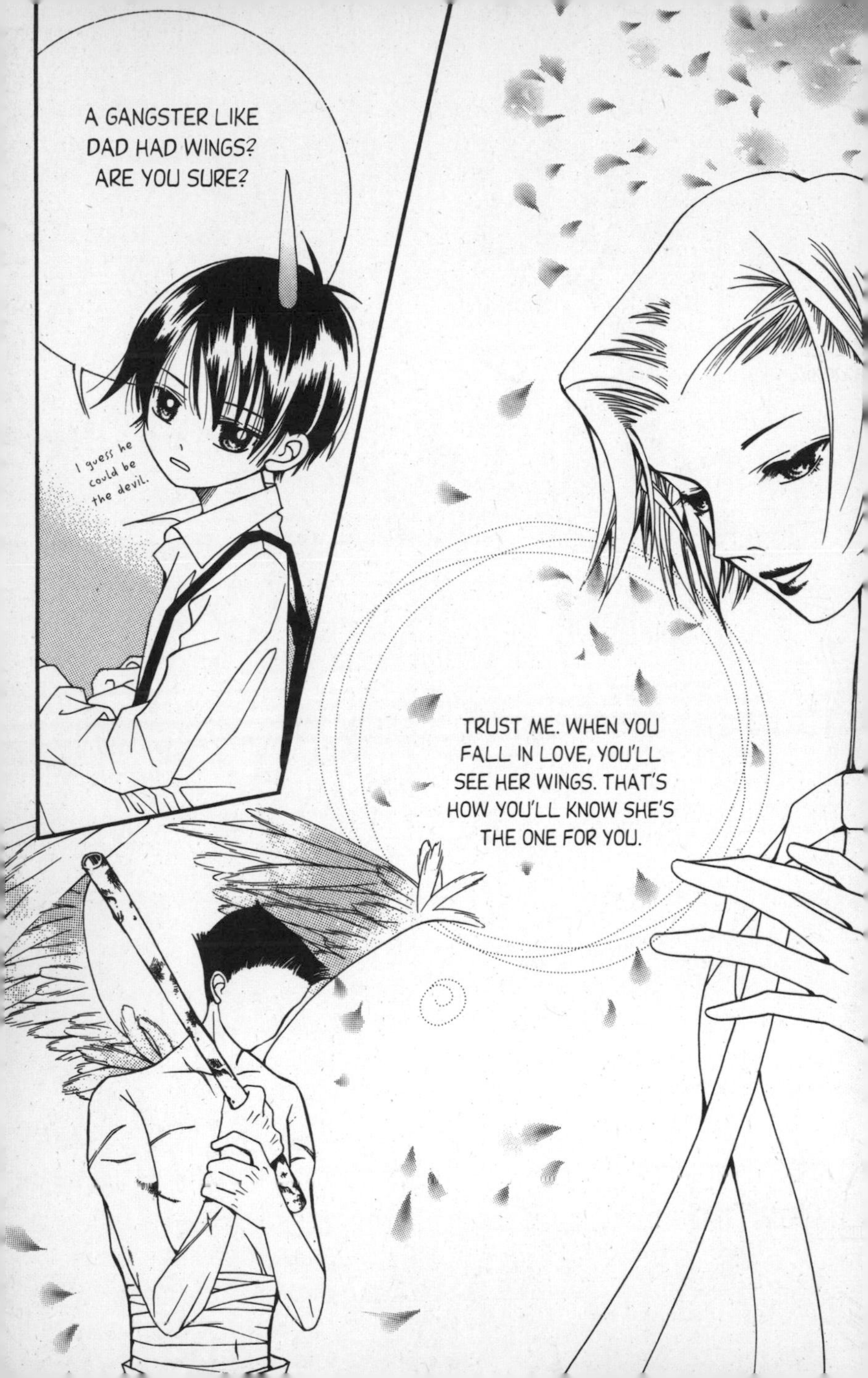
A GANGSTER LIKE DAD HAD WINGS? ARE YOU SURE?
I guess he could be the devil.
TRUST ME. WHEN YOU FALL IN LOVE, YOU'LL SEE HER WINGS. THAT'S HOW YOU'LL KNOW SHE'S THE ONE FOR YOU.

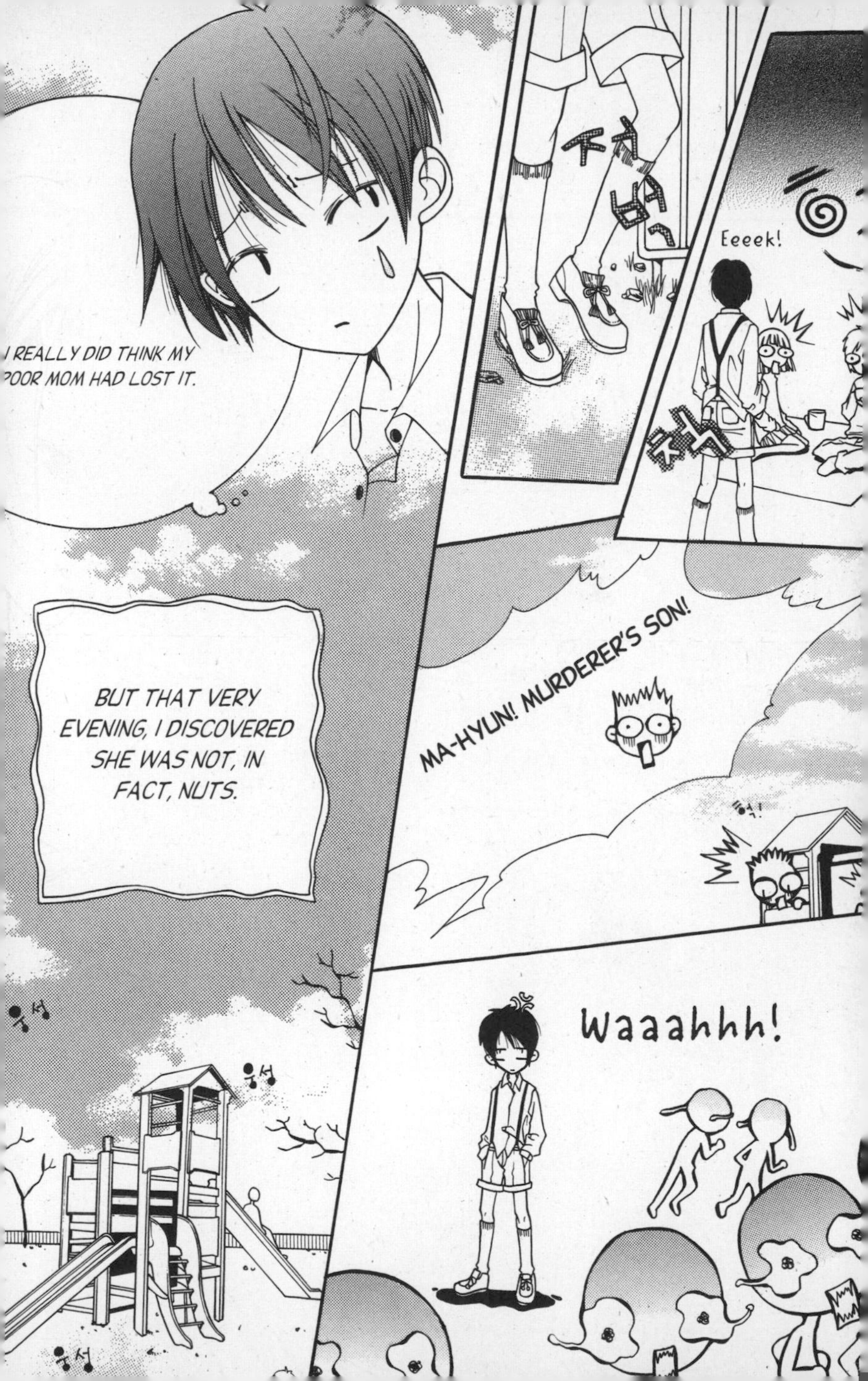

I REALLY DID THINK MY POOR MOM HAD LOST IT.
BUT THAT VERY EVENING, I DISCOVERED SHE WAS NOT, IN FACT, NUTS.
Eeeek!
MA-HYUN! MURDERER'S SON!
Waaahhh!

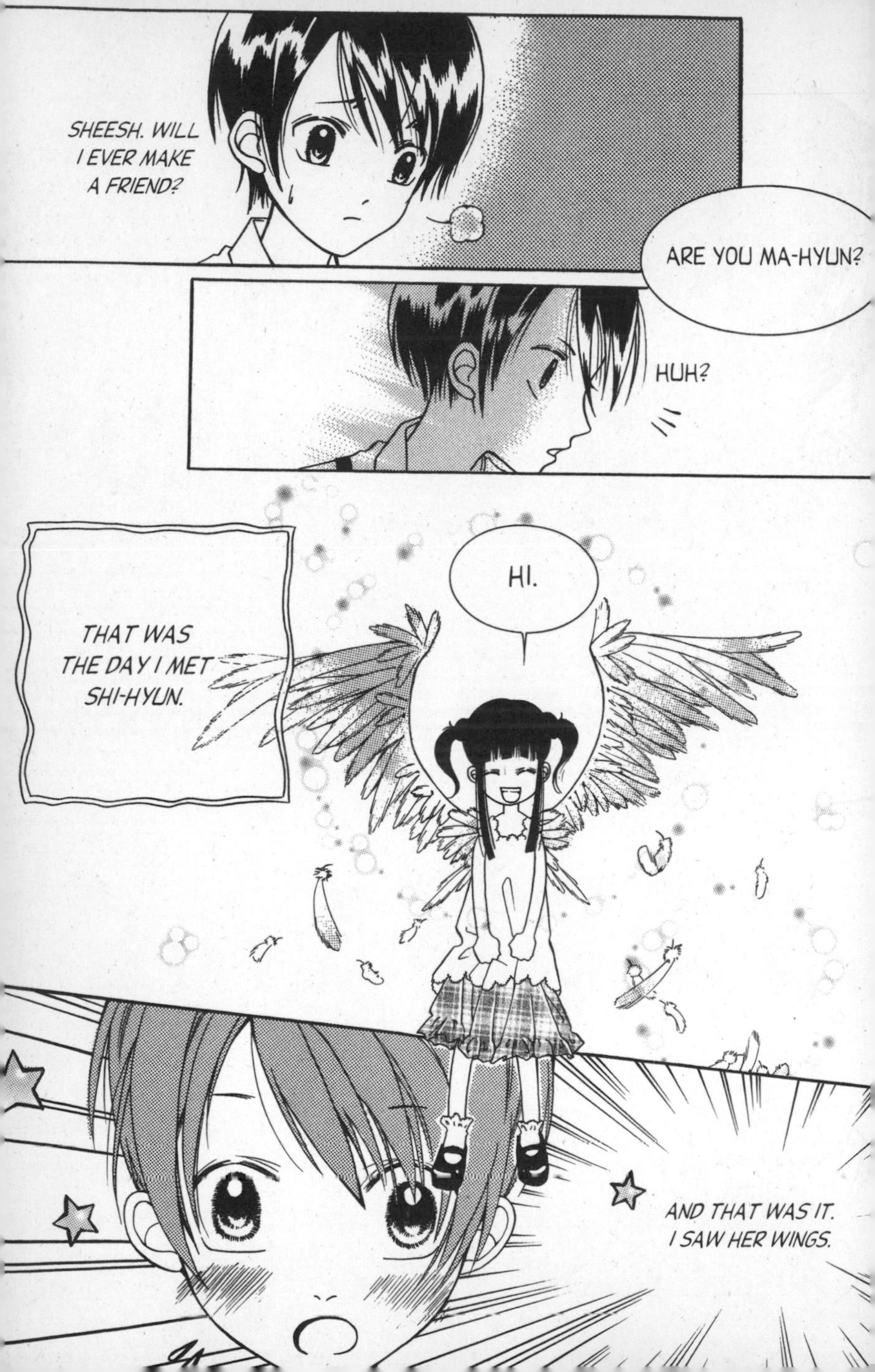
SHEESH. WILL I EVER MAKE A FRIEND?
ARE YOU MA-HYUN?
HUH?
THAT WAS THE DAY I MET SHI-HYUN.
HI.
AND THAT WAS IT. I SAW HER WINGS.

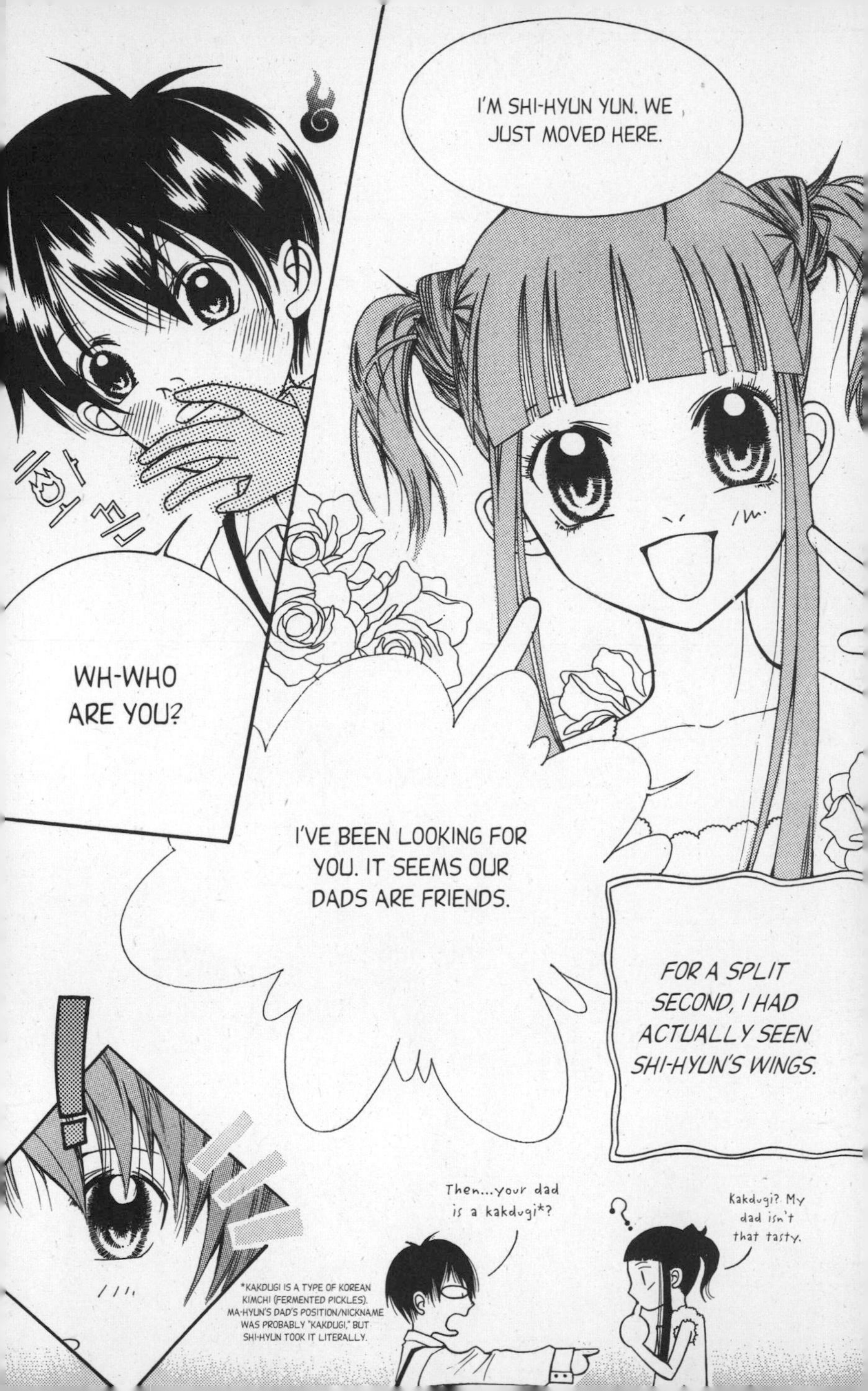
WH-WHO ARE YOU?
I'M SHI-HYUN YUN. WE JUST MOVED HERE.
I'VE BEEN LOOKING FOR YOU. IT SEEMS OUR DADS ARE FRIENDS.
FOR A SPLIT SECOND, I HAD ACTUALLY SEEN SHI-HYUN'S WINGS.
Then...your dad is a kakdugi*?
Kakdugi? My dad isn't that tasty.
*KAKDUGI IS A TYPE OF KOREAN KIMCHI (FERMENTED PICKLES). MA-HYUN'S DAD'S POSITION/NICKNAME WAS PROBABLY "KAKDUGI," BUT SHI-HYUN TOOK IT LITERALLY.

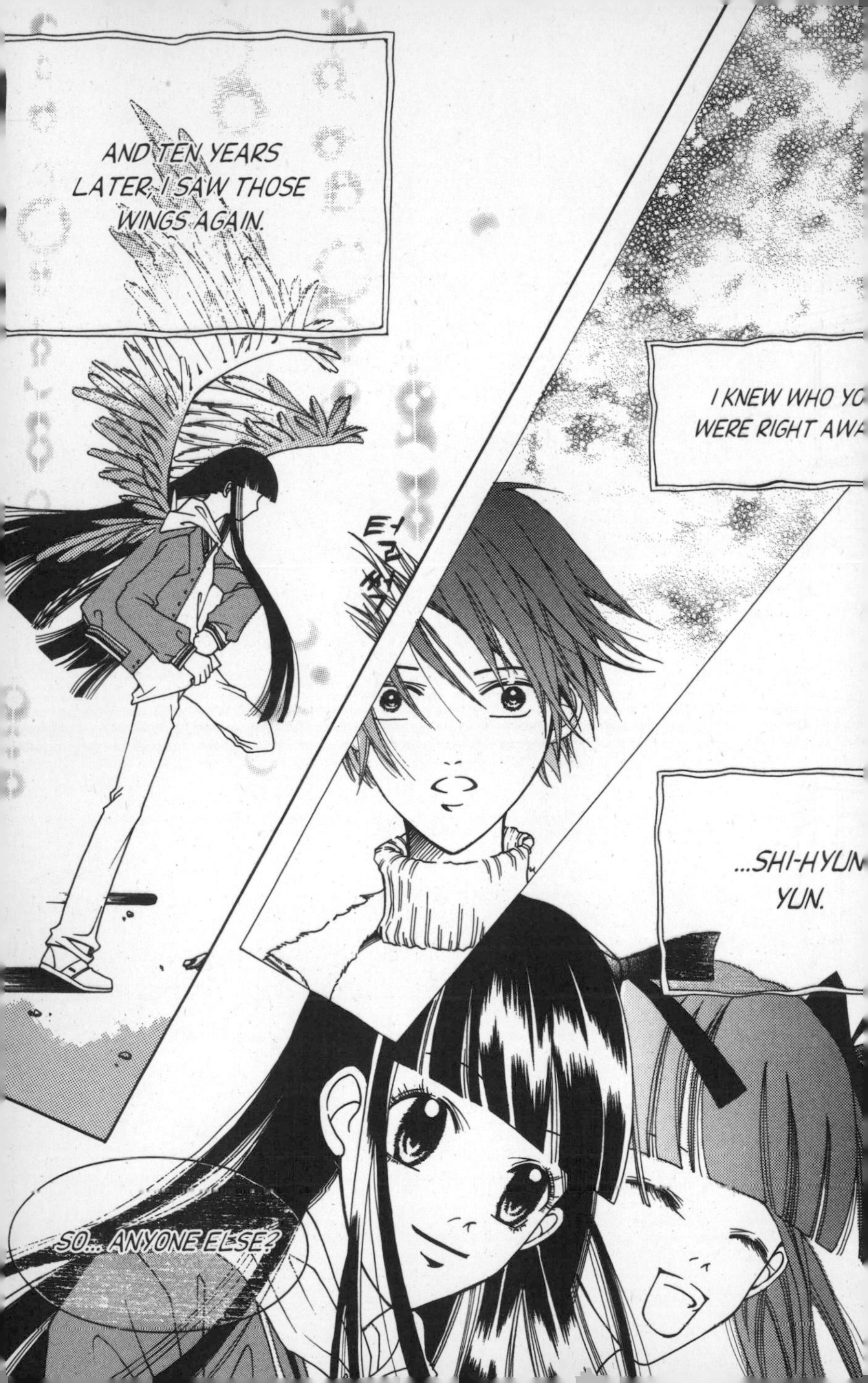
AND TEN YEARS LATER, I SAW THOSE WINGS AGAIN.
I KNEW WHO YO
WERE RIGHT AWA
...SHI-HYUN YUN.
SO... ANYONE ELSE?

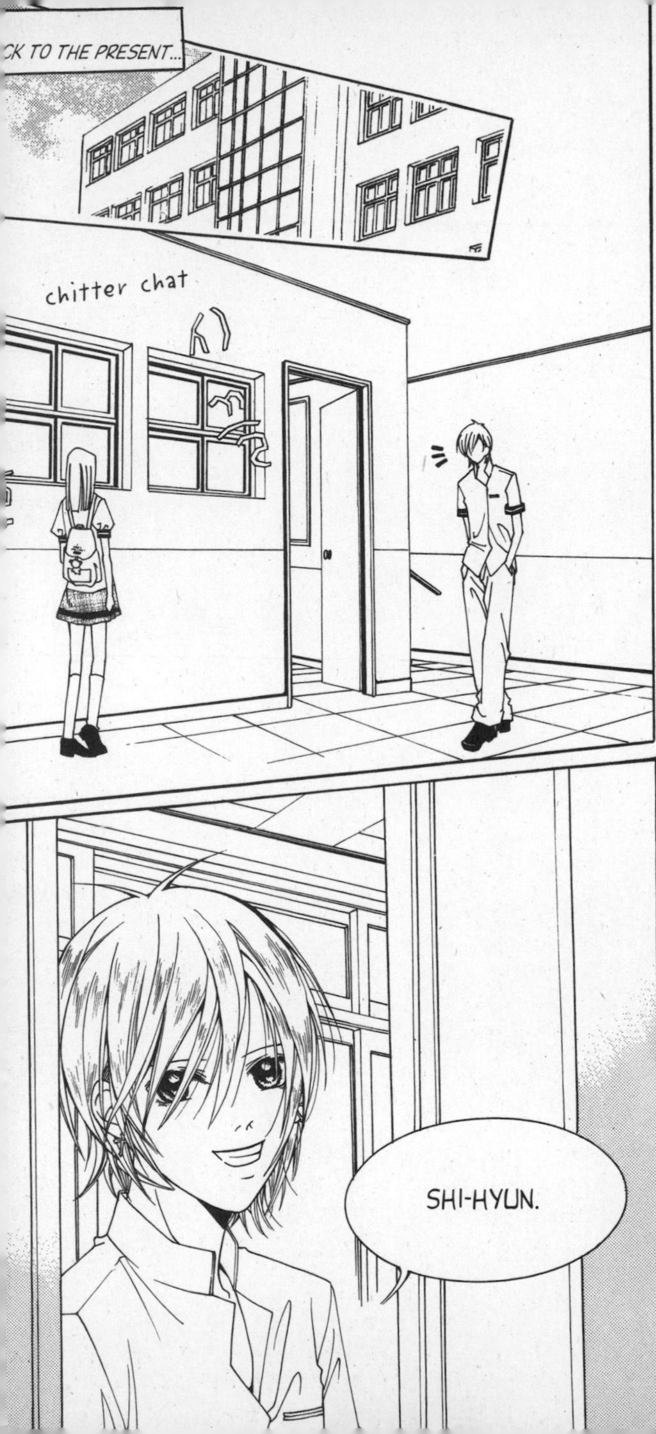
CK TO THE PRESENT...
chitter chat
SHI-HYUN.

Sidebar

Finally, a bit of Ma-Hyun and Shi-Hyun's past has been revealed! ^^* Can't fully guess what's happened, though, can you? Don't worry. More will be revealed, bit by bit. >v<~* Ma-Hyun looked very different when he was younger, but Shi-Hyun hasn't changed much at all, since she's got such a baby face. (She feels slightly different, though, right?) Anyway, please keep reading! ♥

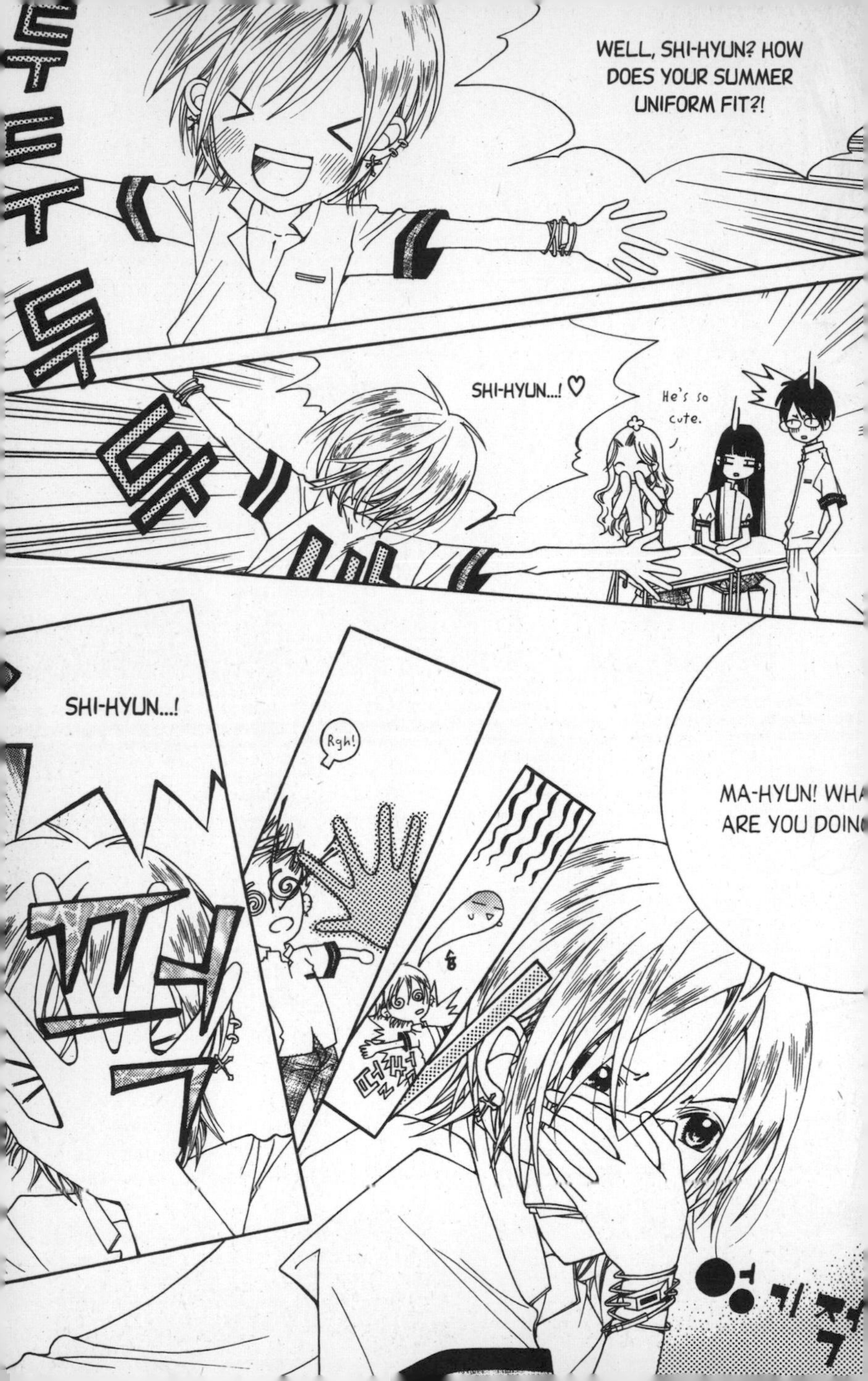
WELL, SHI-HYUN? HOW DOES YOUR SUMMER UNIFORM FIT?!
SHI-HYUN...! ♡
He's so cute.
SHI-HYUN...!
Rgh!
MA-HYUN! WHA ARE YOU DOIN

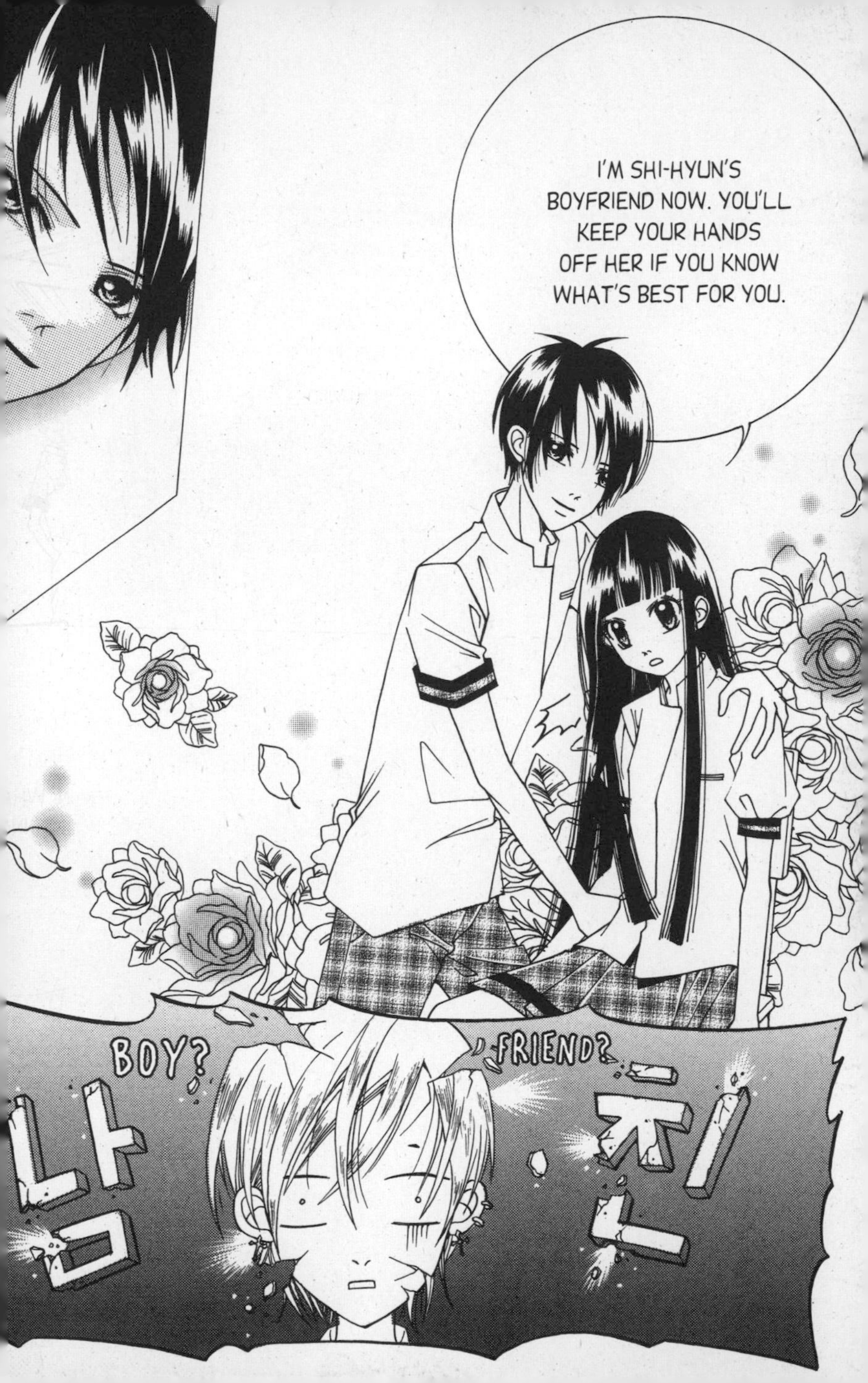
I'M SHI-HYUN'S BOYFRIEND NOW. YOU'LL KEEP YOUR HANDS OFF HER IF YOU KNOW WHAT'S BEST FOR YOU.
BOY?
FRIEND?

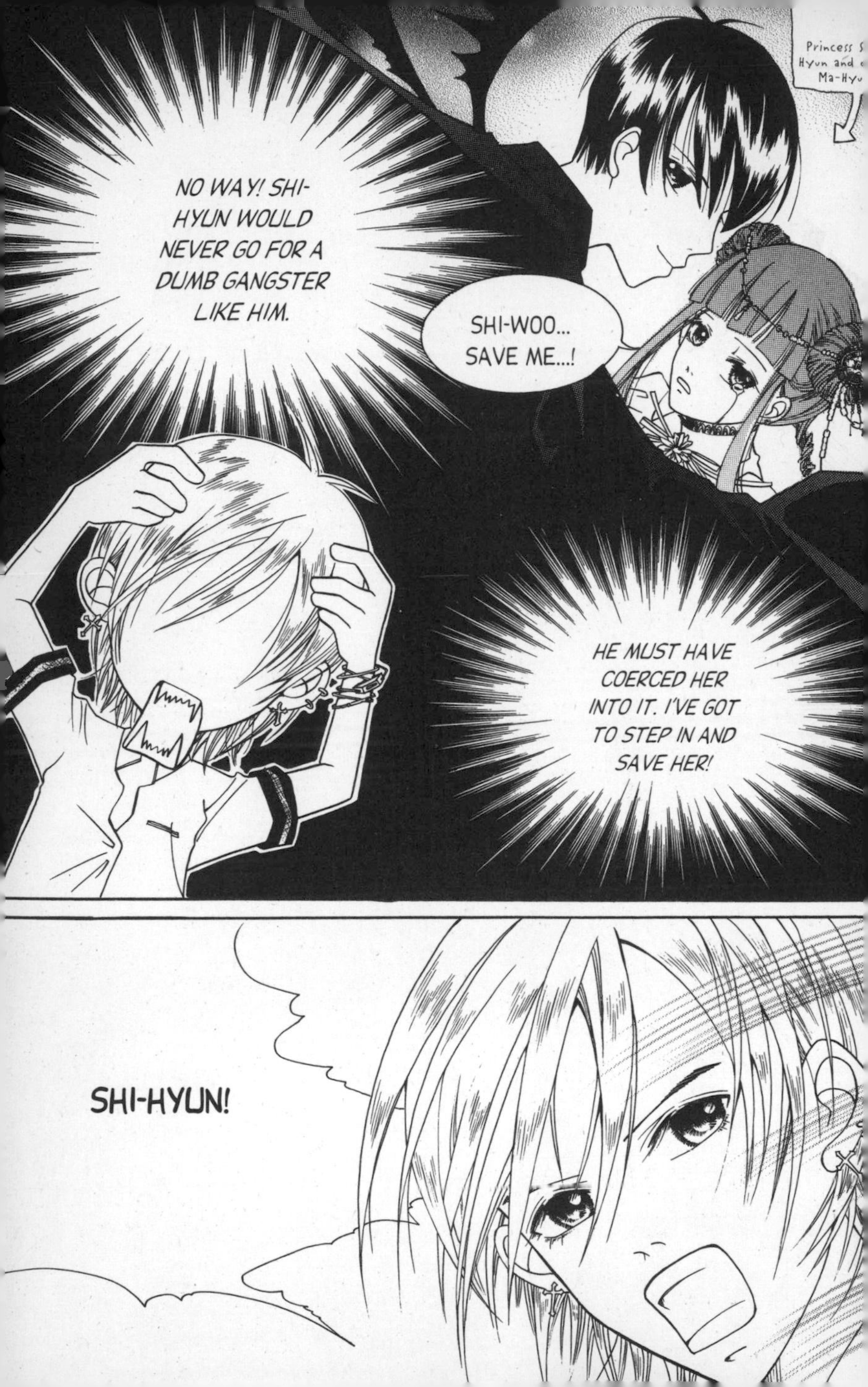
NO WAY! SHI-HYUN WOULD NEVER GO FOR A DUMB GANGSTER LIKE HIM.
Princess S
Hyun and
Ma-Hyu
SHI-WOO... SAVE ME...!
HE MUST HAVE COERCED HER INTO IT. I'VE GOT TO STEP IN AND SAVE HER!
SHI-HYUN!

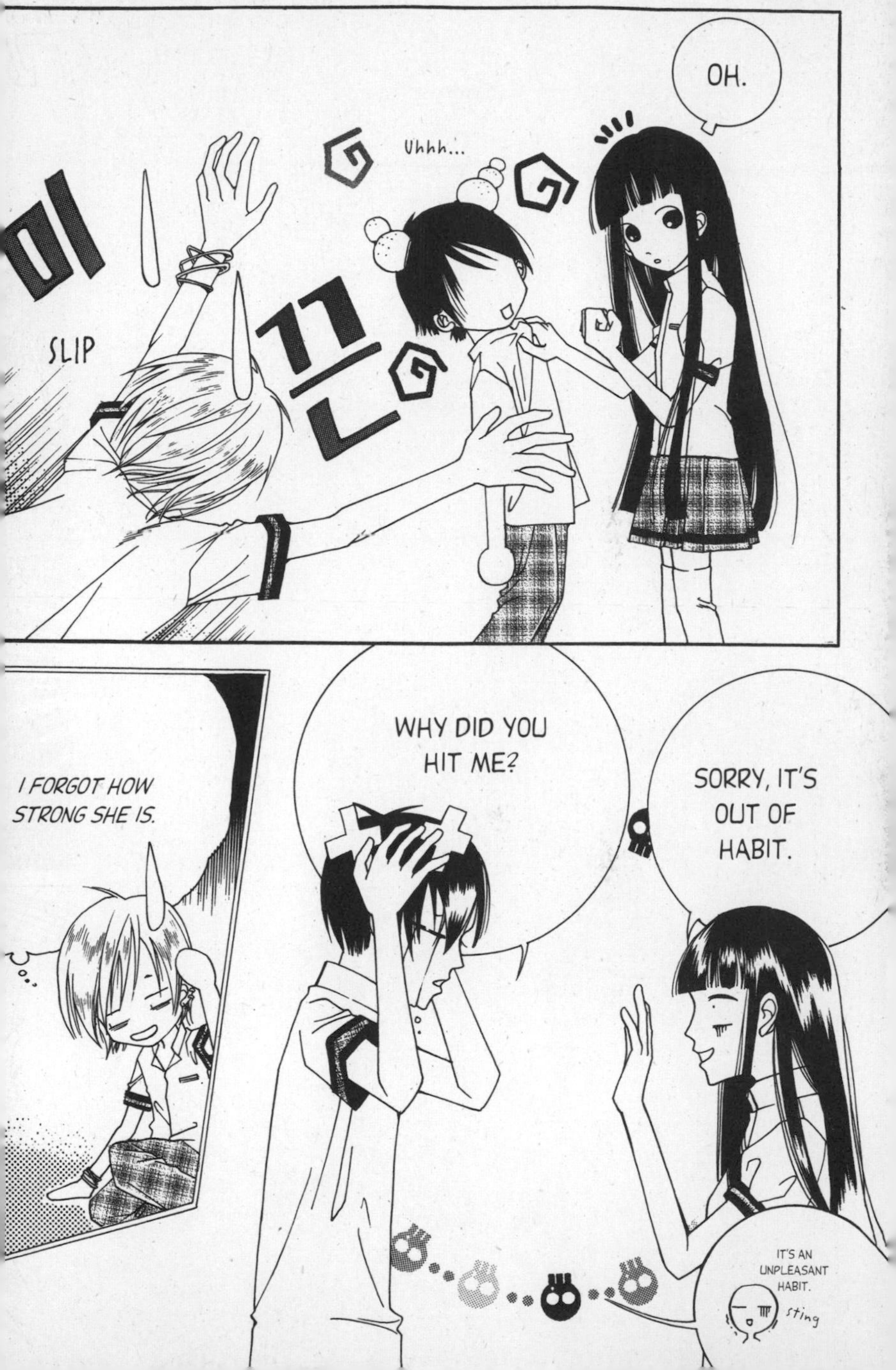
SLIP
Uhhh...
OH.
I FORGOT HOW STRONG SHE IS.
WHY DID YOU HIT ME?
SORRY, IT'S OUT OF HABIT.
IT'S AN UNPLEASANT HABIT.
sting

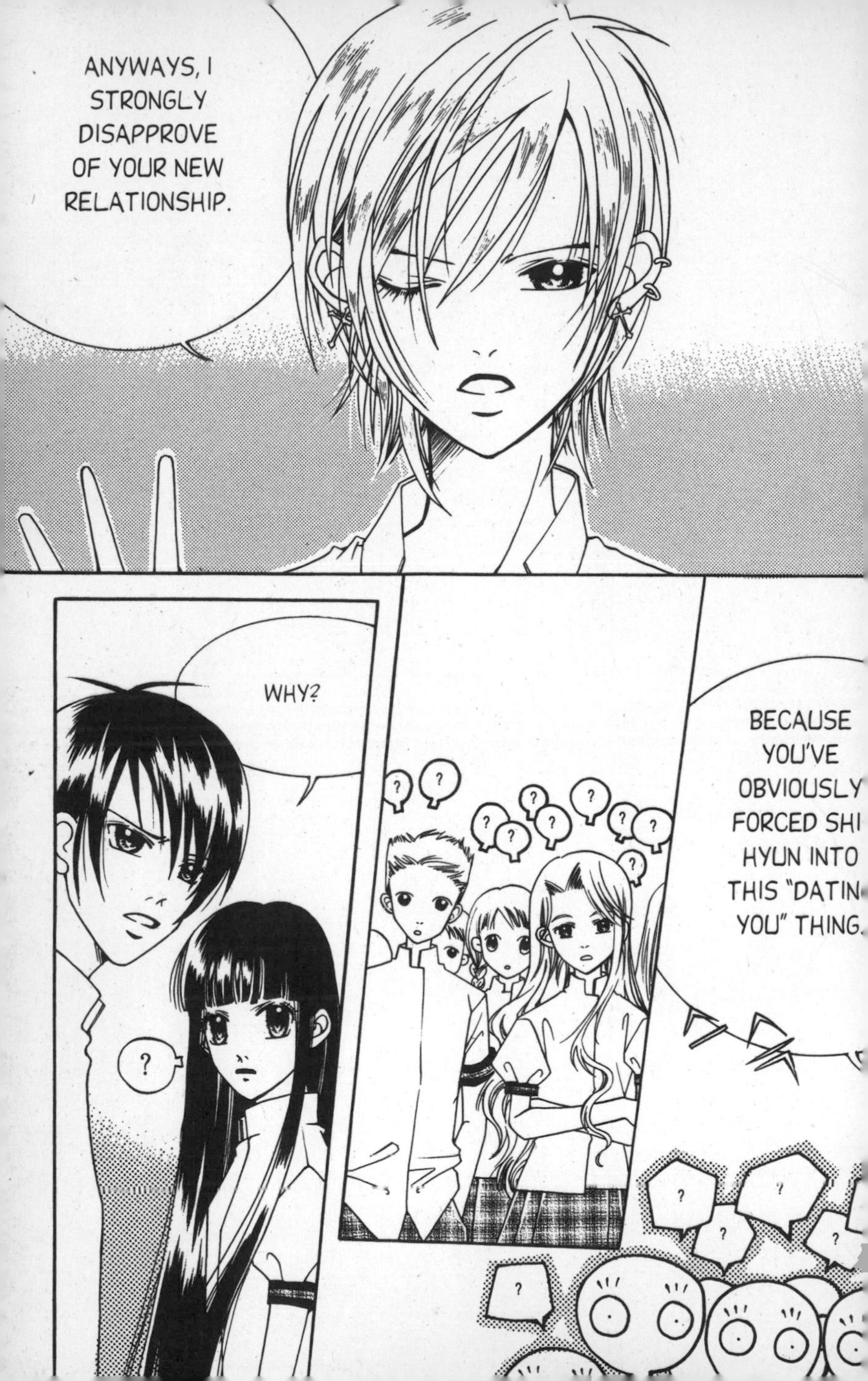
ANYWAYS, I STRONGLY DISAPPROVE OF YOUR NEW RELATIONSHIP.
WHY?
?
? ? ? ? ? ? ? ? ? ? ?
BECAUSE YOU'VE OBVIOUSLY FORCED SHI HYUN INTO THIS "DATIN YOU" THING.
? ? ? ? ?

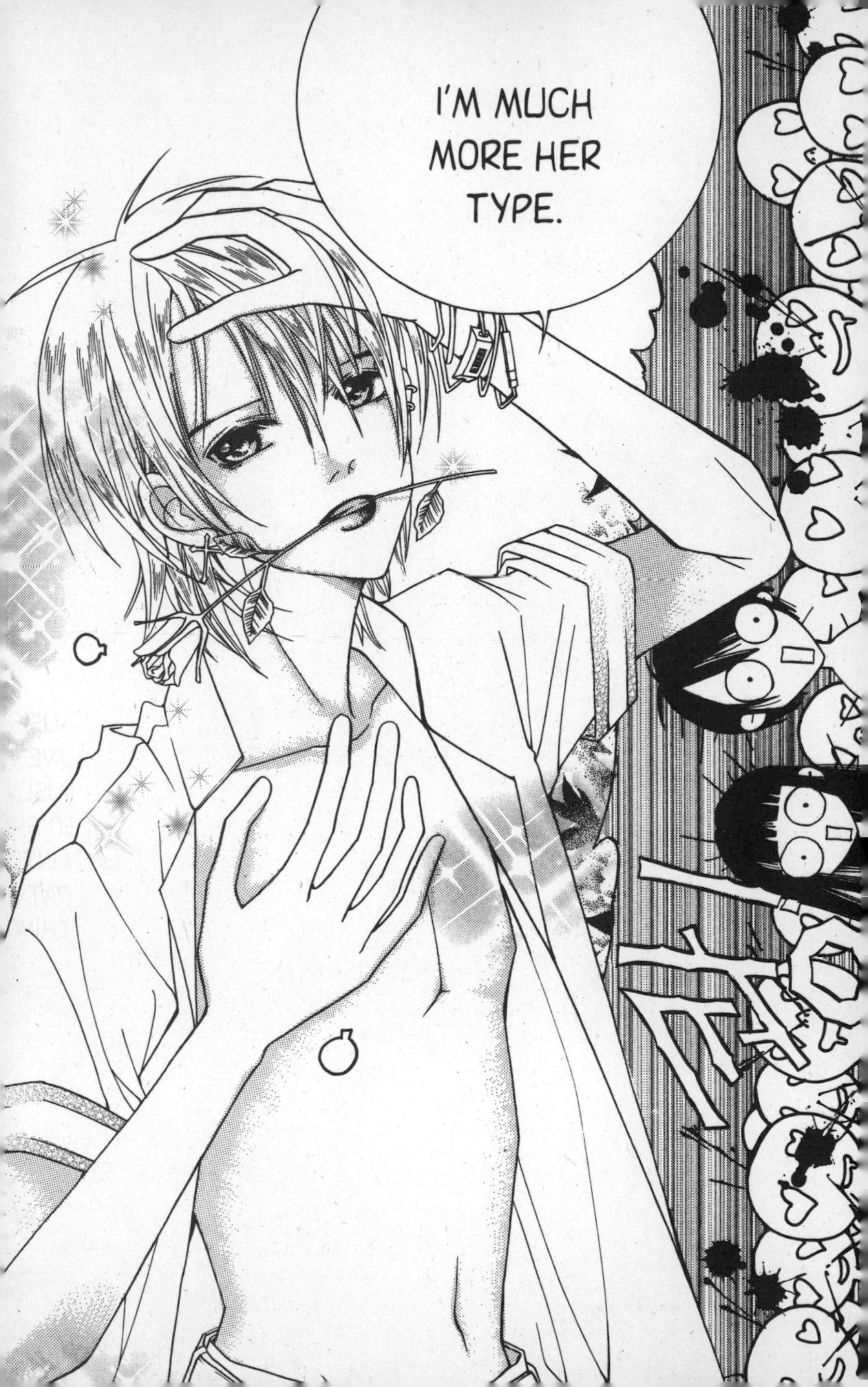
I'M MUCH MORE HER TYPE.

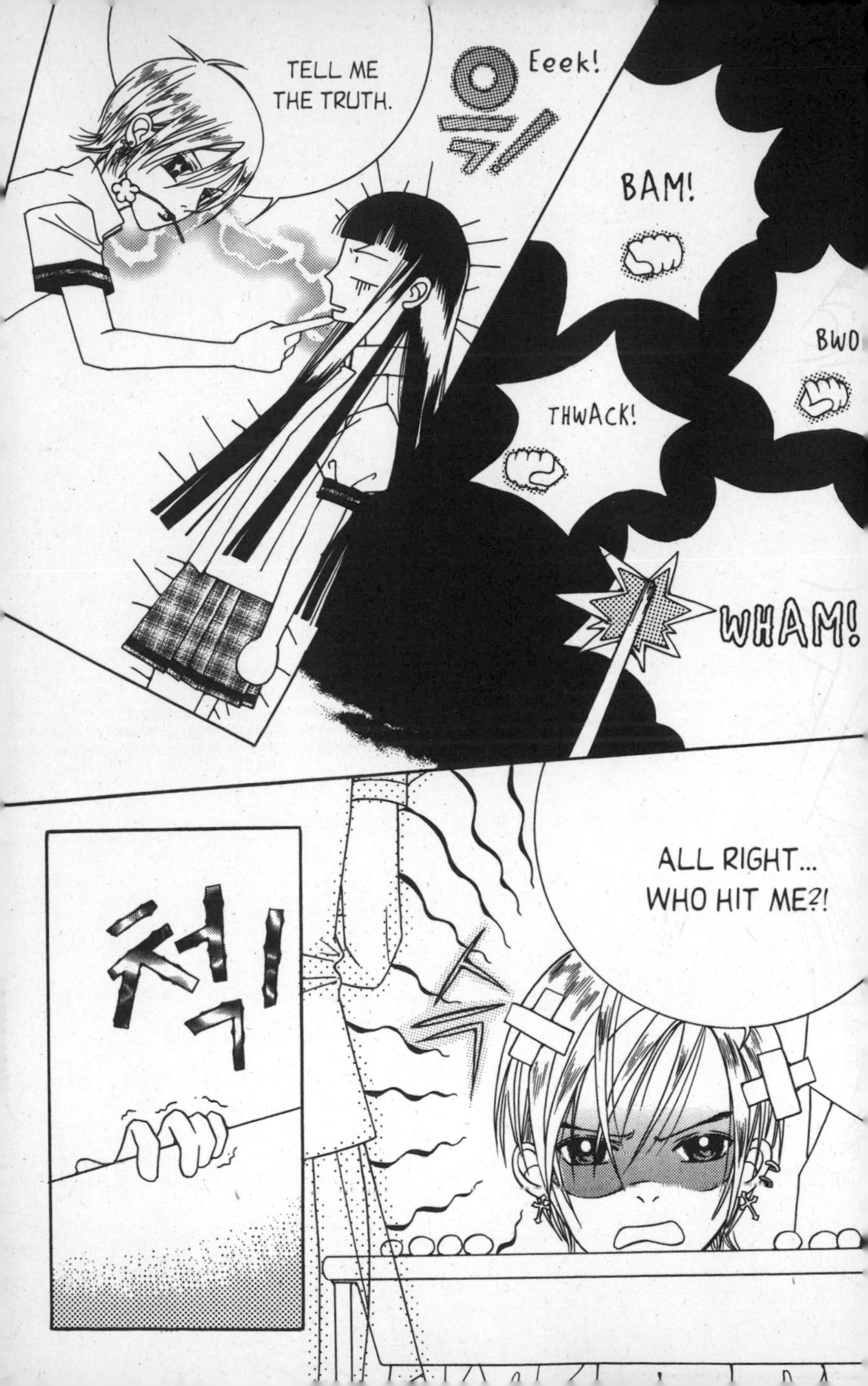
TELL ME THE TRUTH.
Eeek!
BAM!
BWO
THWACK!
WHAM!
ALL RIGHT... WHO HIT ME?!

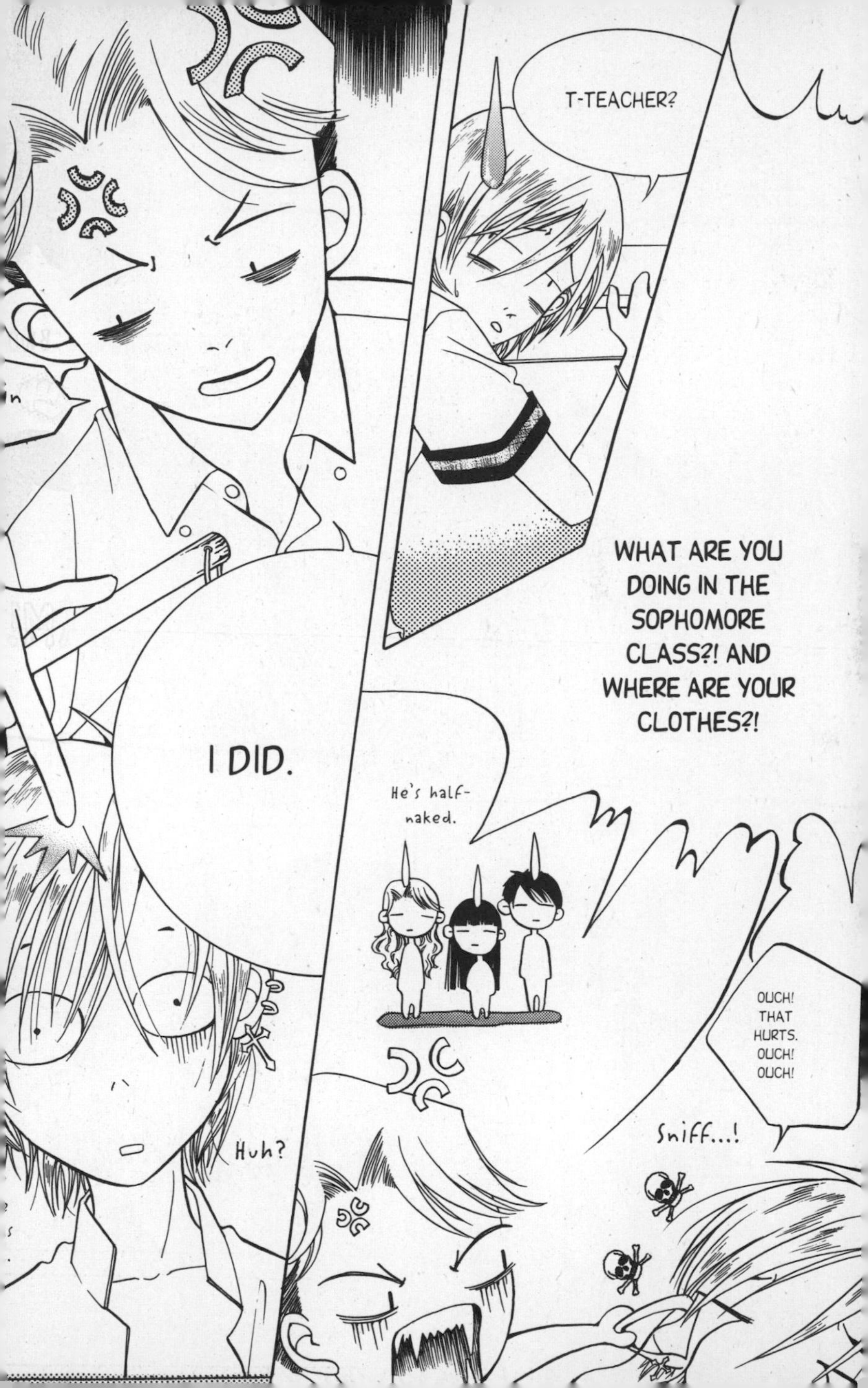
I DID.
Huh?
T-TEACHER?
WHAT ARE YOU DOING IN THE SOPHOMORE CLASS?! AND WHERE ARE YOUR CLOTHES?!
He's half-naked.
OUCH! THAT HURTS. OUCH! OUCH!
Sniff...!

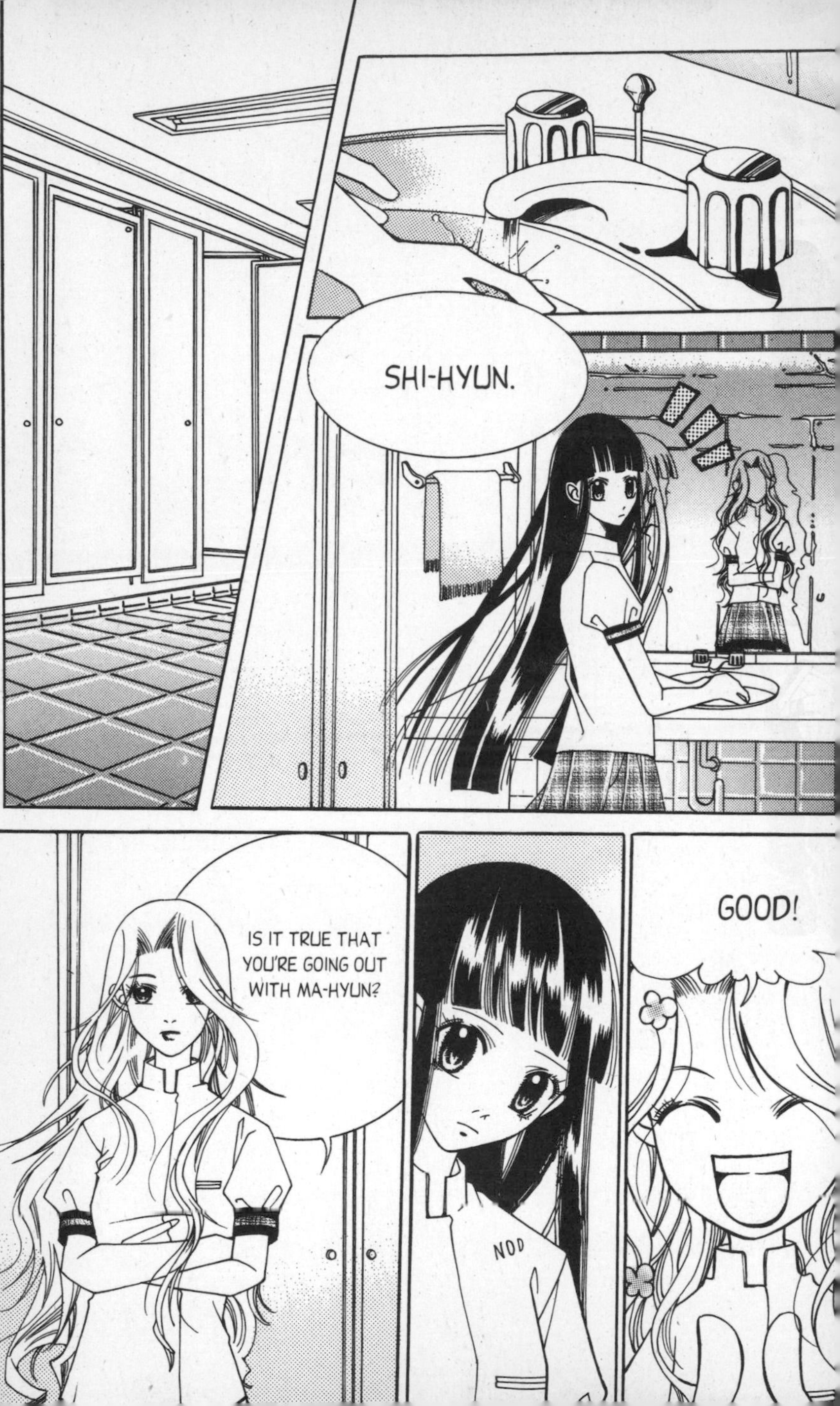
SHI-HYUN.
IS IT TRUE THAT YOU'RE GOING OUT WITH MA-HYUN?
NOD
GOOD!

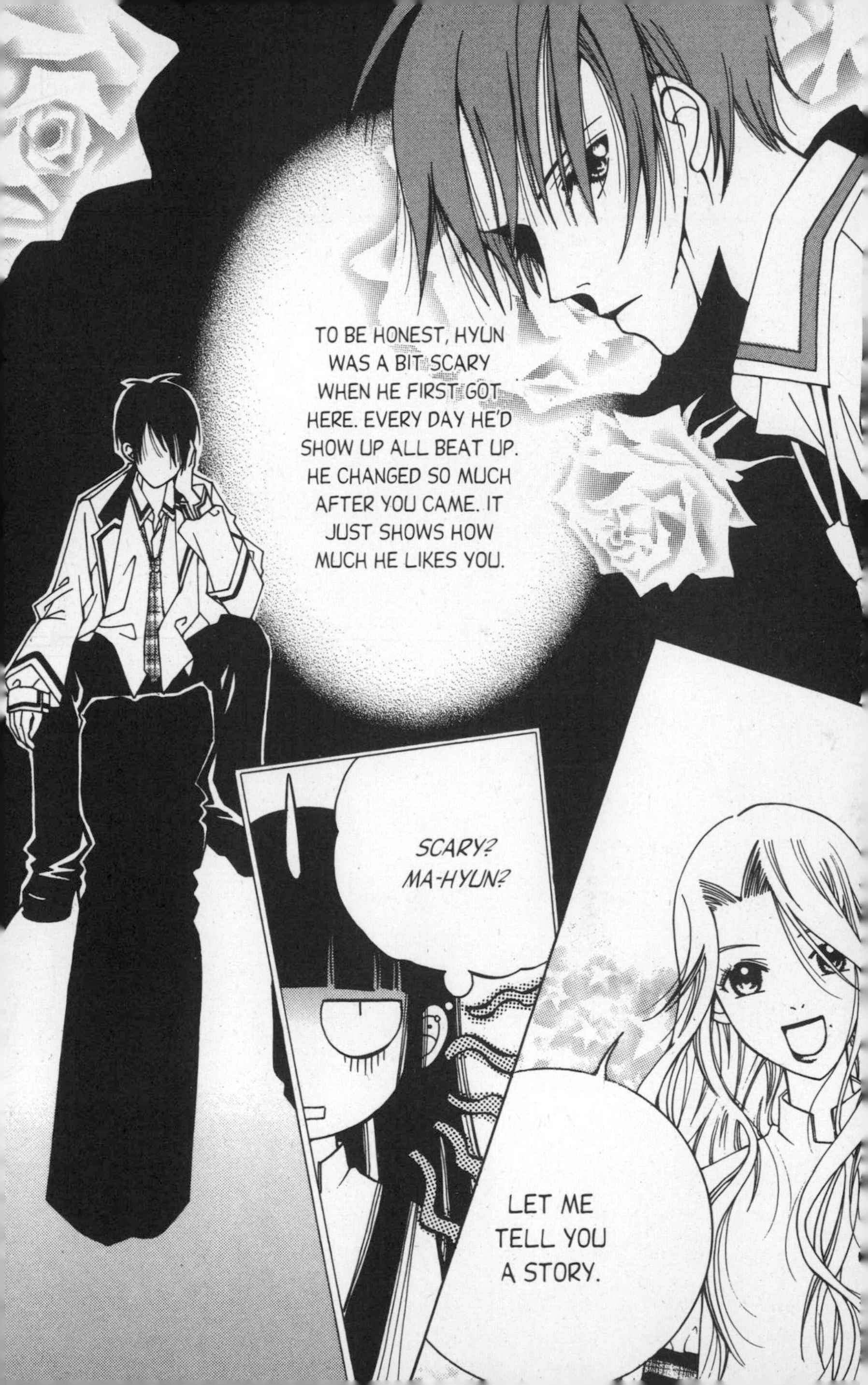
TO BE HONEST, HYUN WAS A BIT SCARY WHEN HE FIRST GOT HERE. EVERY DAY HE'D SHOW UP ALL BEAT UP. HE CHANGED SO MUCH AFTER YOU CAME. IT JUST SHOWS HOW MUCH HE LIKES YOU.
SCARY? MA-HYUN?
LET ME TELL YOU A STORY.

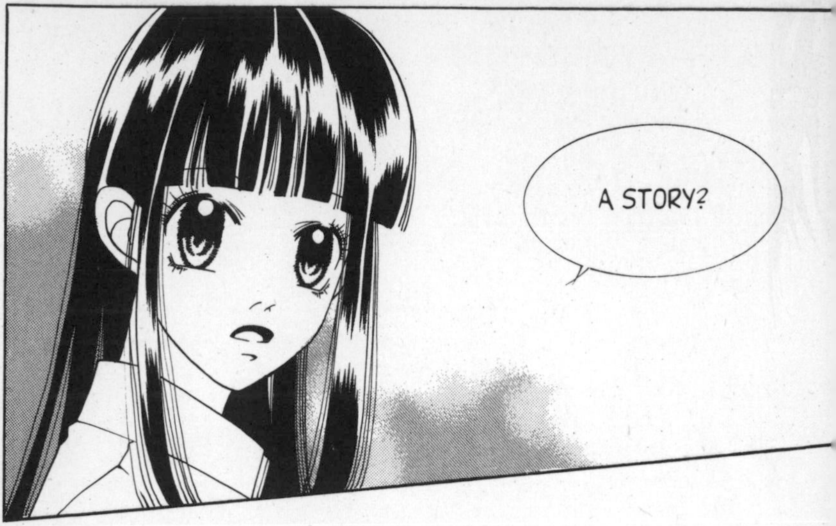
A STORY?
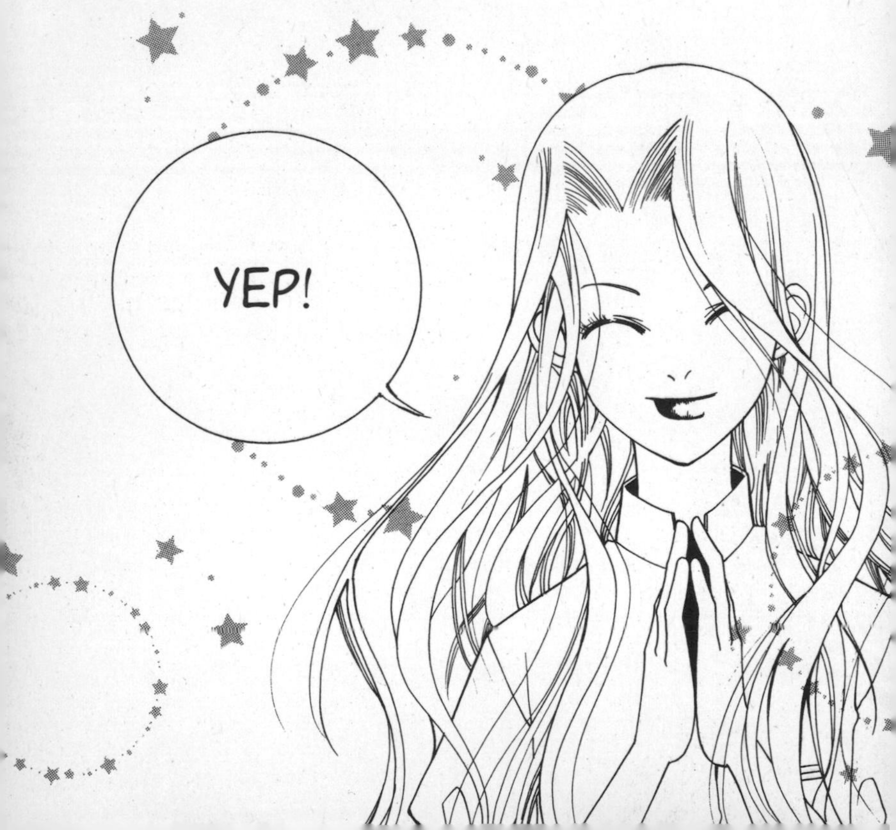
YEP!

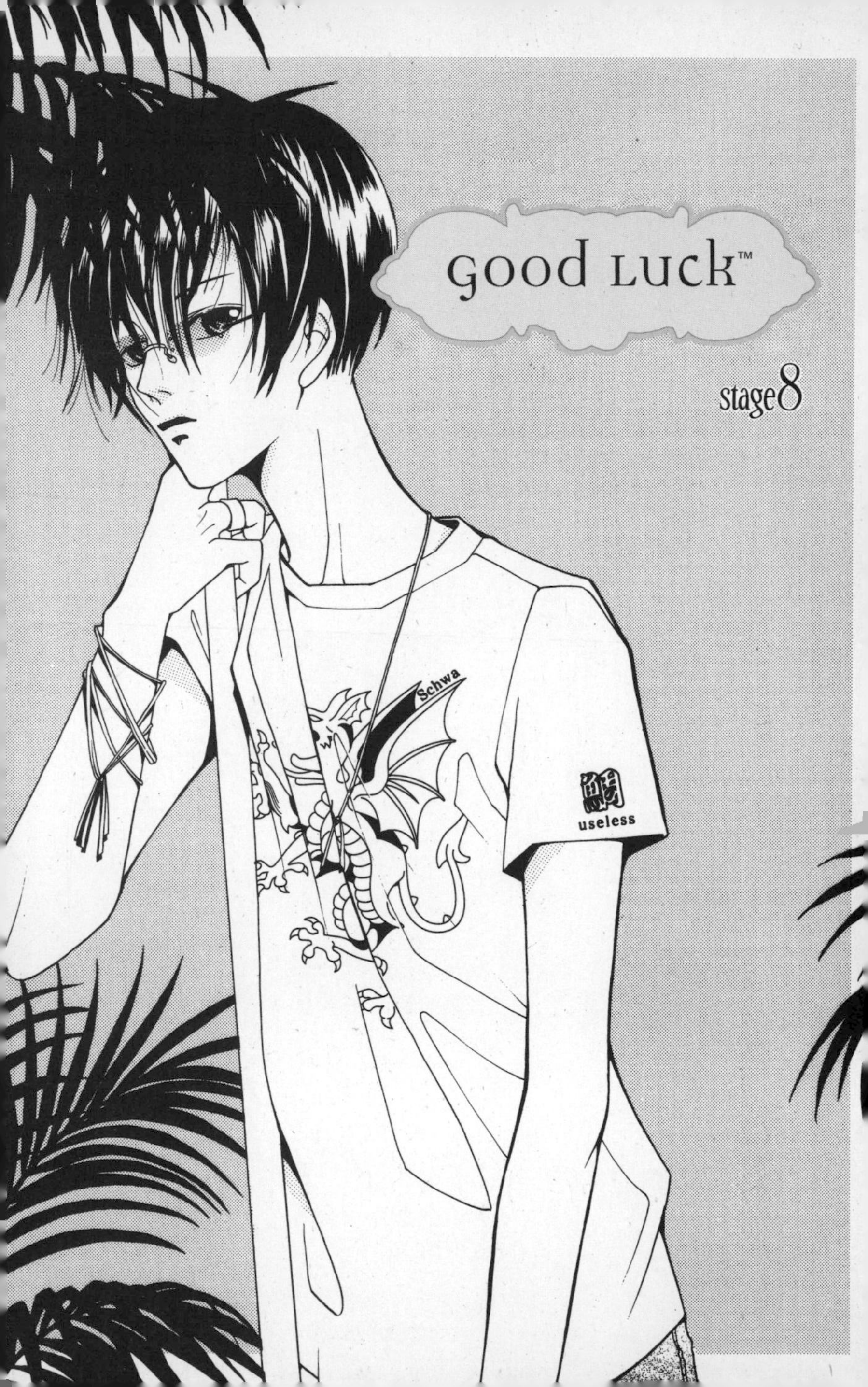
good luck™
stage8
Schwa
useless

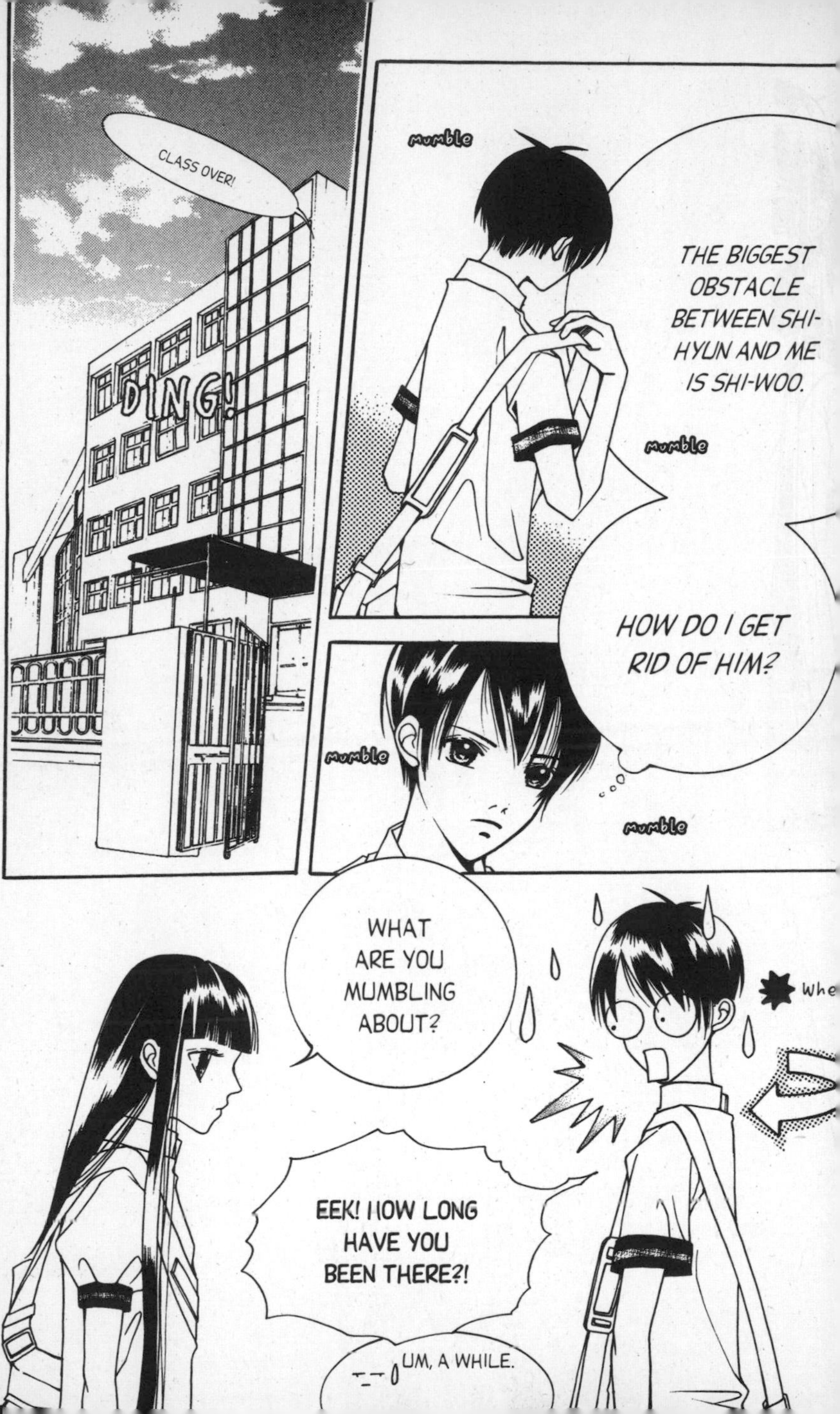
CLASS OVER!
DING!
mumble
THE BIGGEST OBSTACLE BETWEEN SHI-HYUN AND ME IS SHI-WOO.
mumble
HOW DO I GET RID OF HIM?
mumble
mumble
WHAT ARE YOU MUMBLING ABOUT?
EEK! HOW LONG HAVE YOU BEEN THERE?!
UM, A WHILE.

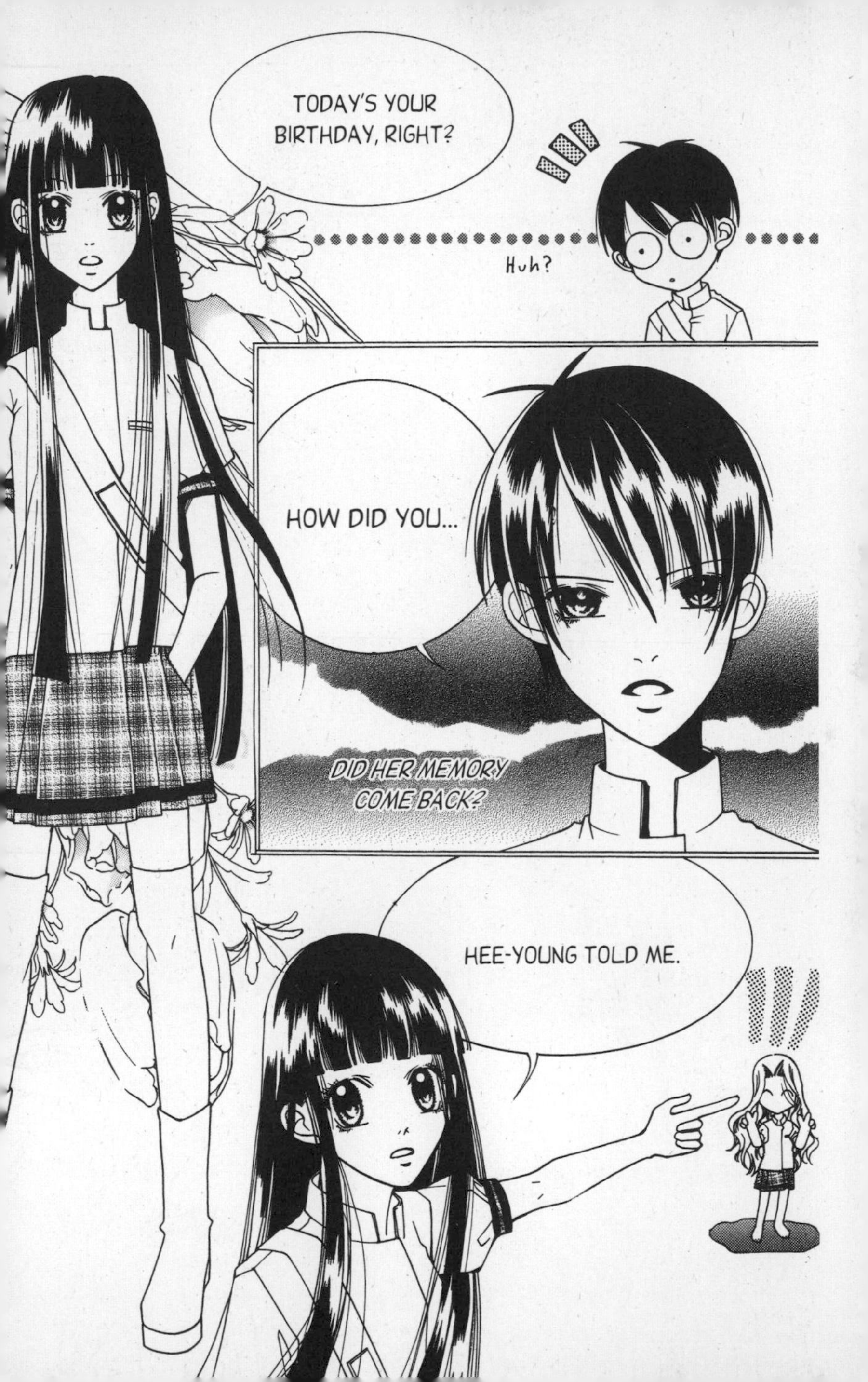
TODAY'S YOUR BIRTHDAY, RIGHT?
Huh?
HOW DID YOU...
DID HER MEMORY COME BACK?
HEE-YOUNG TOLD ME.

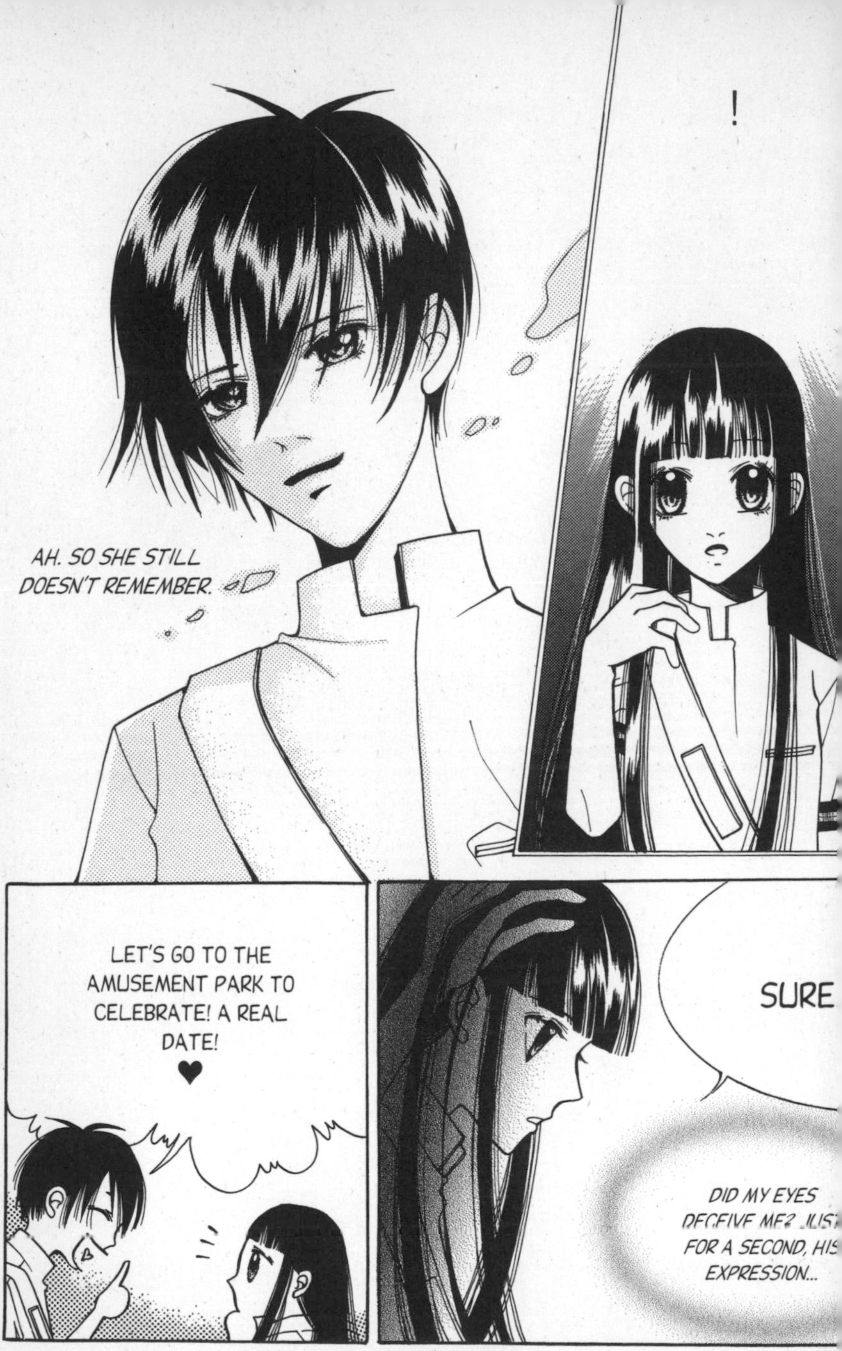
!
AH. SO SHE STILL DOESN'T REMEMBER.
LET'S GO TO THE AMUSEMENT PARK TO CELEBRATE! A REAL DATE! ♥
SURE
DID MY EYES DECEIVE ME? JUS
FOR A SECOND, HIS EXPRESSION...

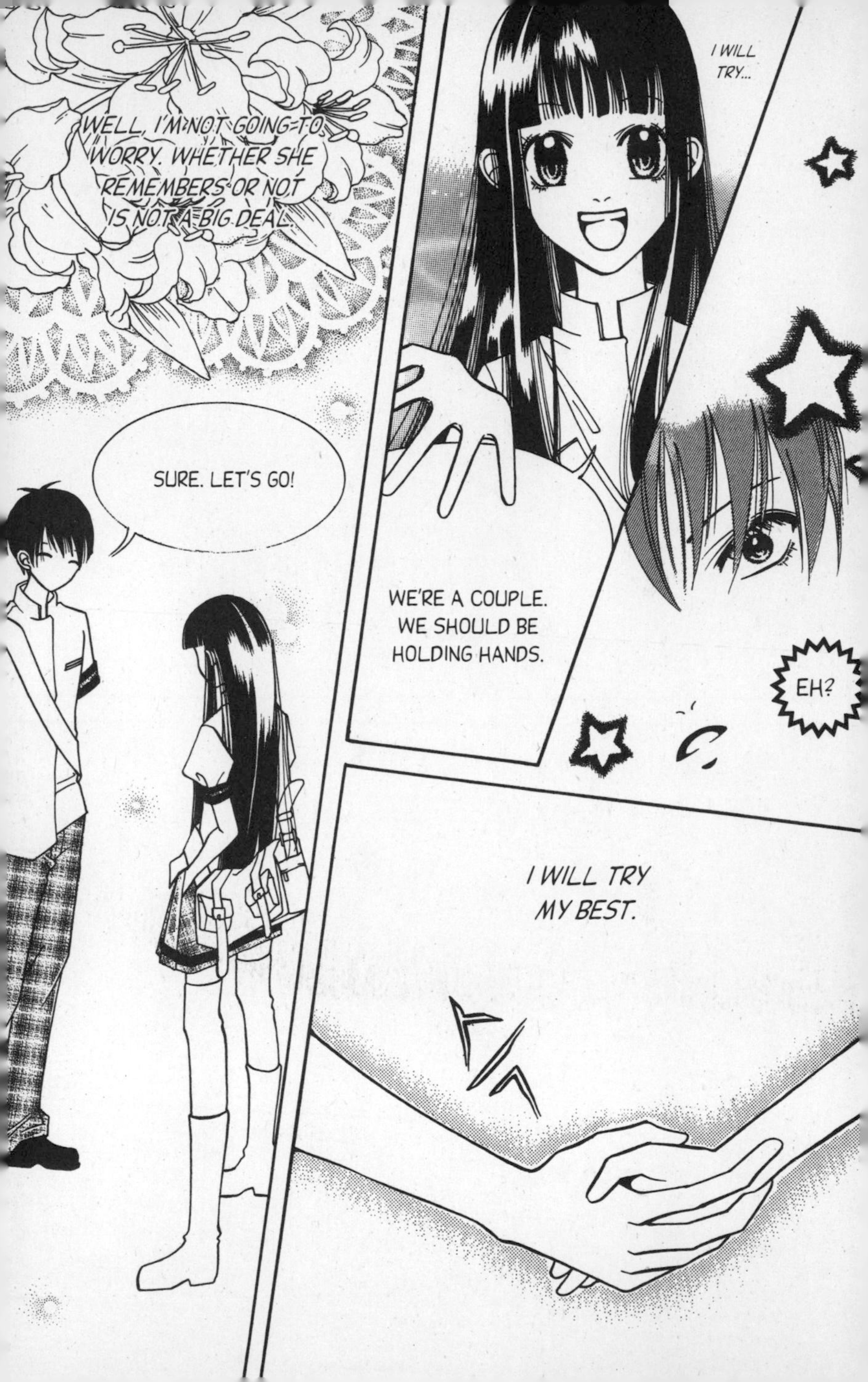
WELL, I'M NOT GOING TO WORRY. WHETHER SHE REMEMBERS OR NOT IS NOT A BIG DEAL.
SURE. LET'S GO!
I WILL TRY...
WE'RE A COUPLE. WE SHOULD BE HOLDING HANDS.
EH?
I WILL TRY MY BEST.

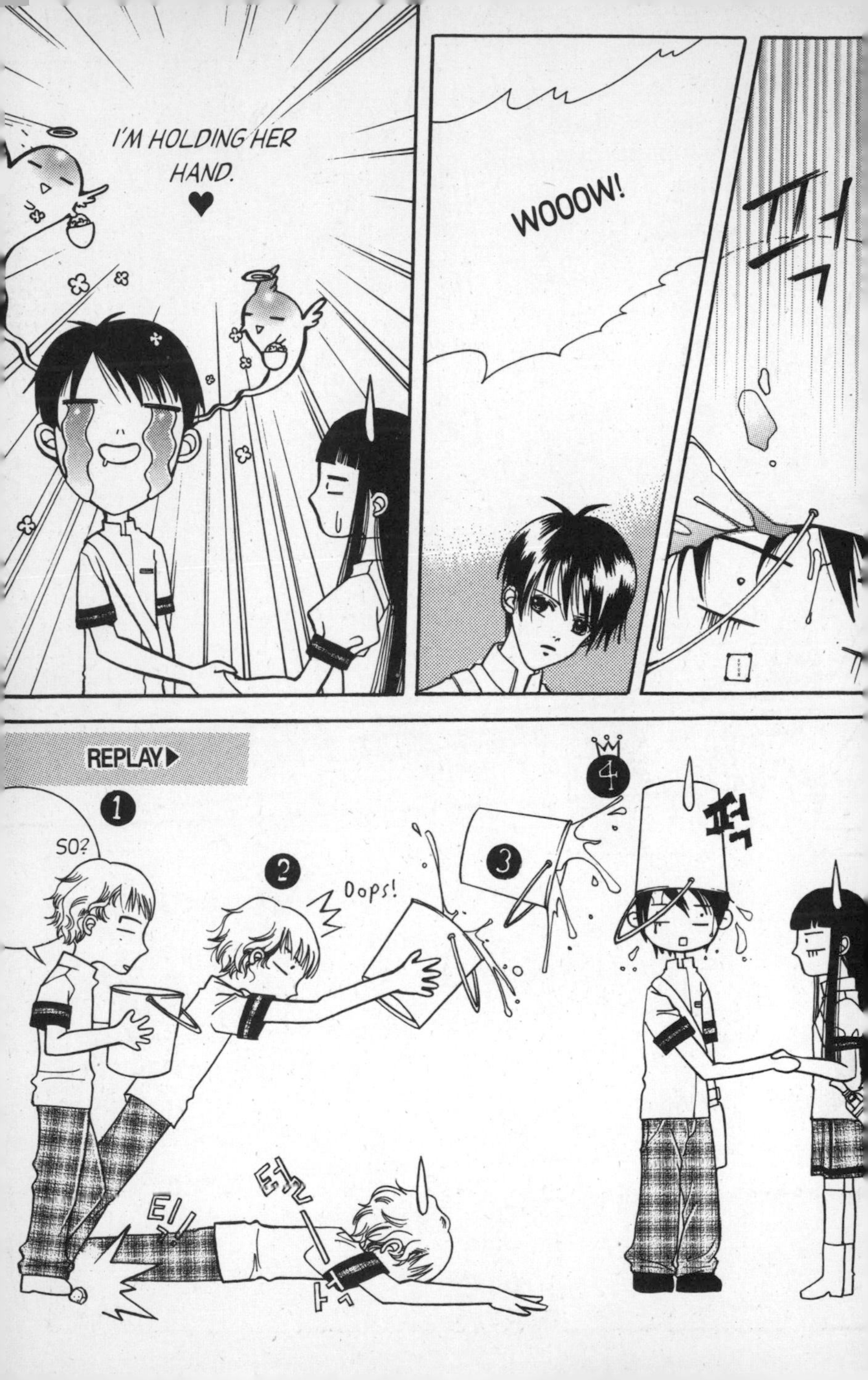
I'M HOLDING HER HAND. ♥
WOOOW!
퍽
REPLAY▶
1
SO?
2
Oops!
3
4
퍽

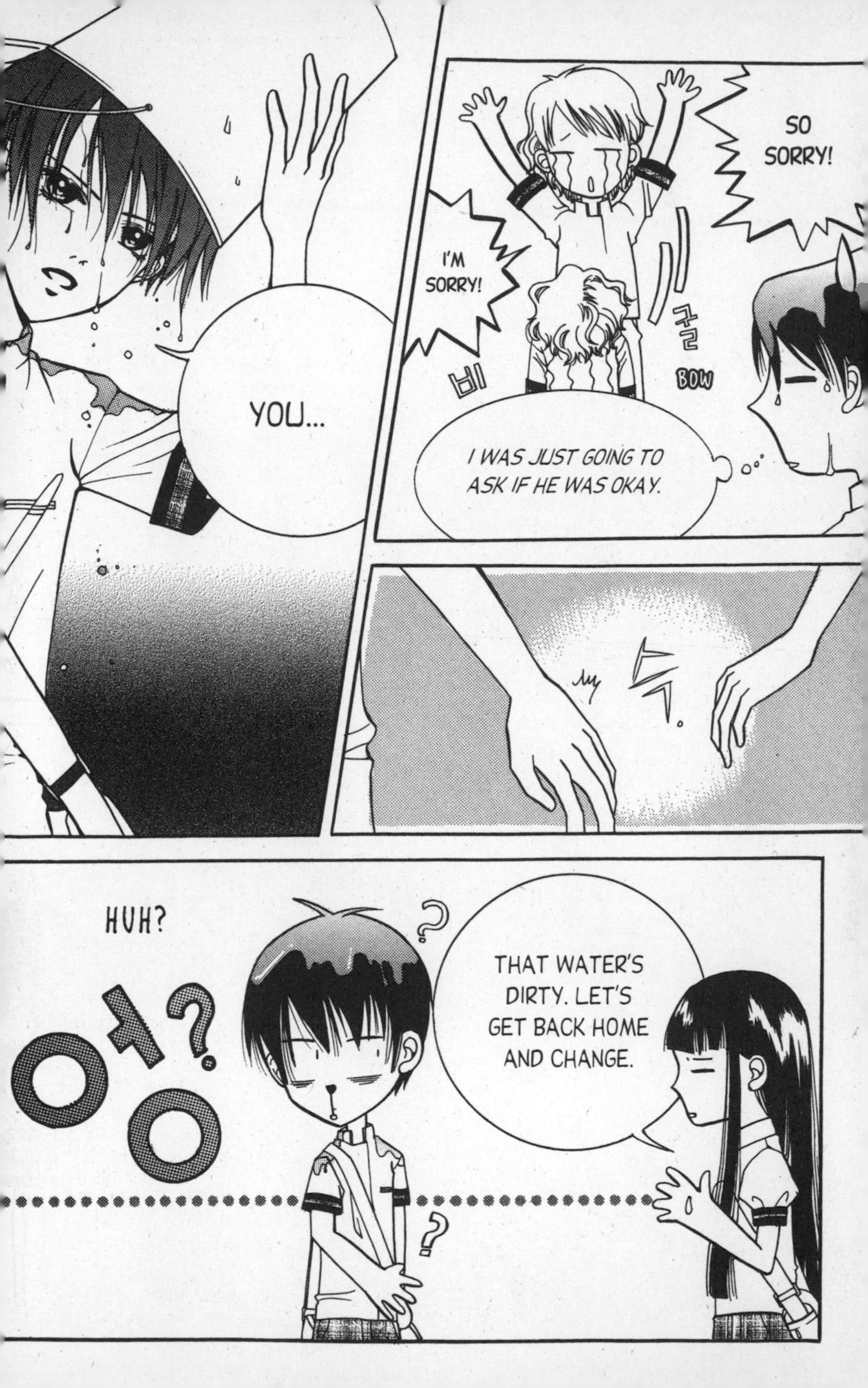
YOU...
I'M SORRY!
SO SORRY!
BOW
I WAS JUST GOING TO ASK IF HE WAS OKAY.
HUH?
THAT WATER'S DIRTY. LET'S GET BACK HOME AND CHANGE.

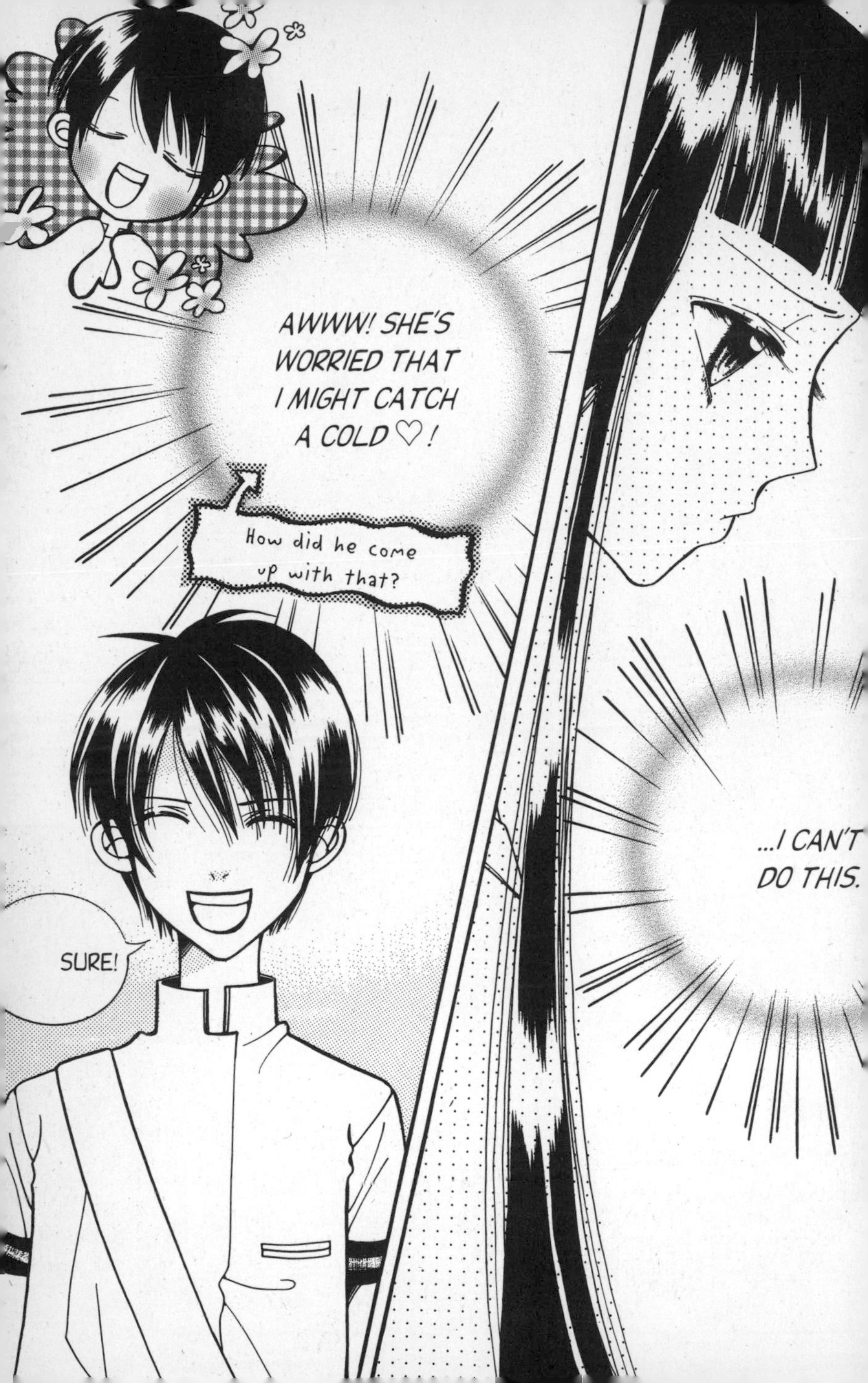
AWWW! SHE'S WORRIED THAT I MIGHT CATCH A COLD♡!
How did he come up with that?
SURE!
...I CAN'T DO THIS.

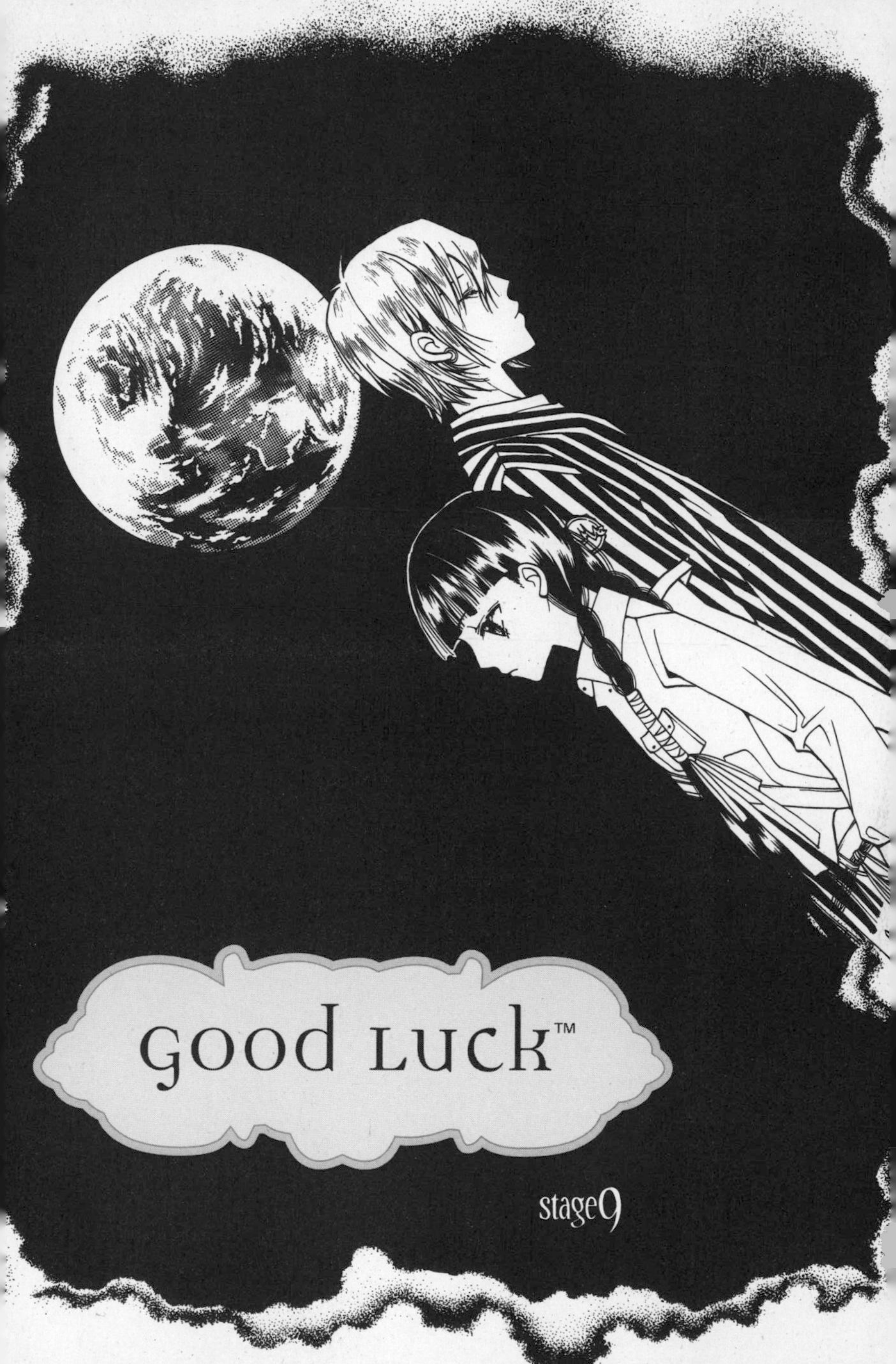
good luck™
stage9

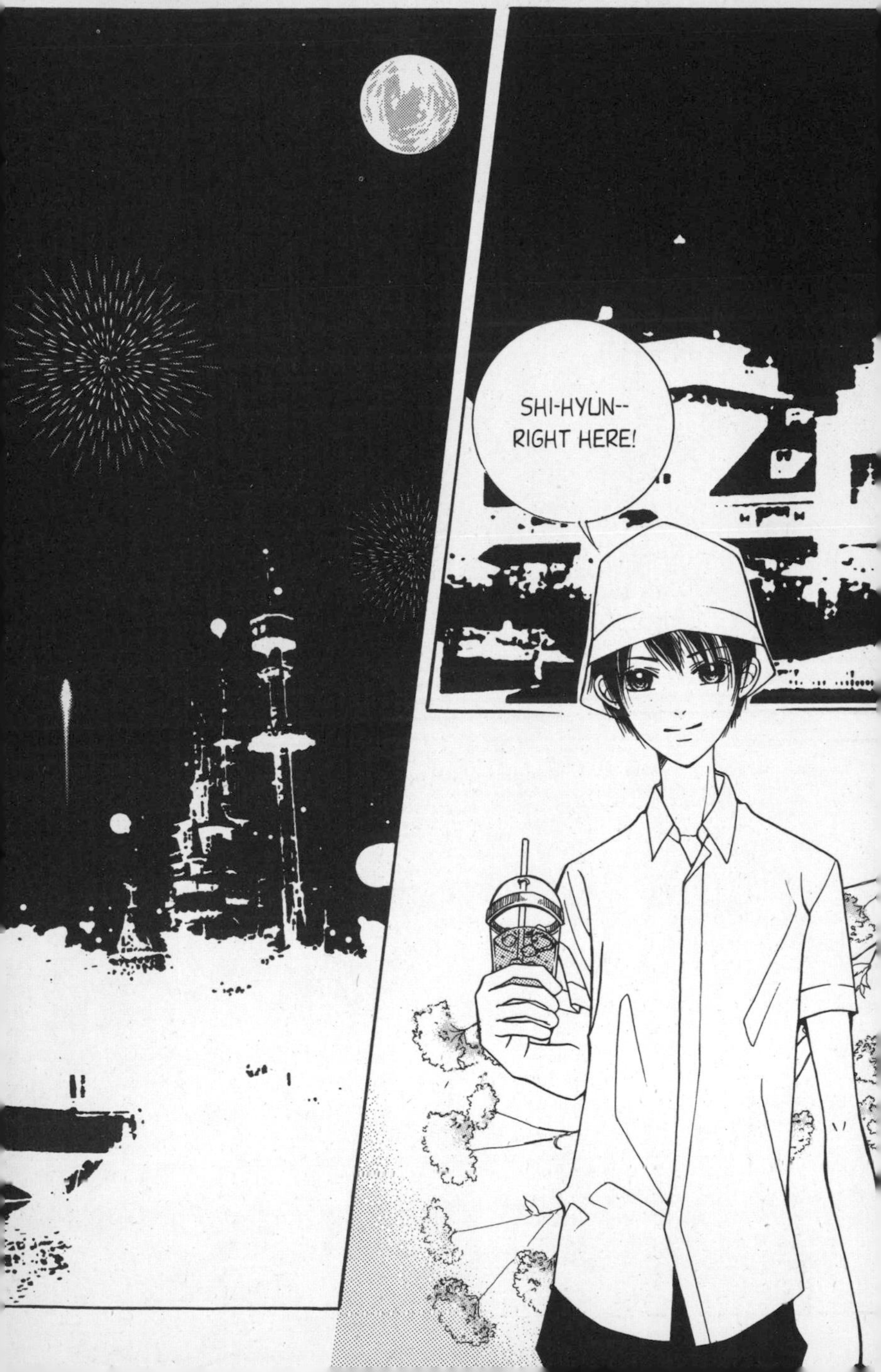
SHI-HYUN--
RIGHT HERE!

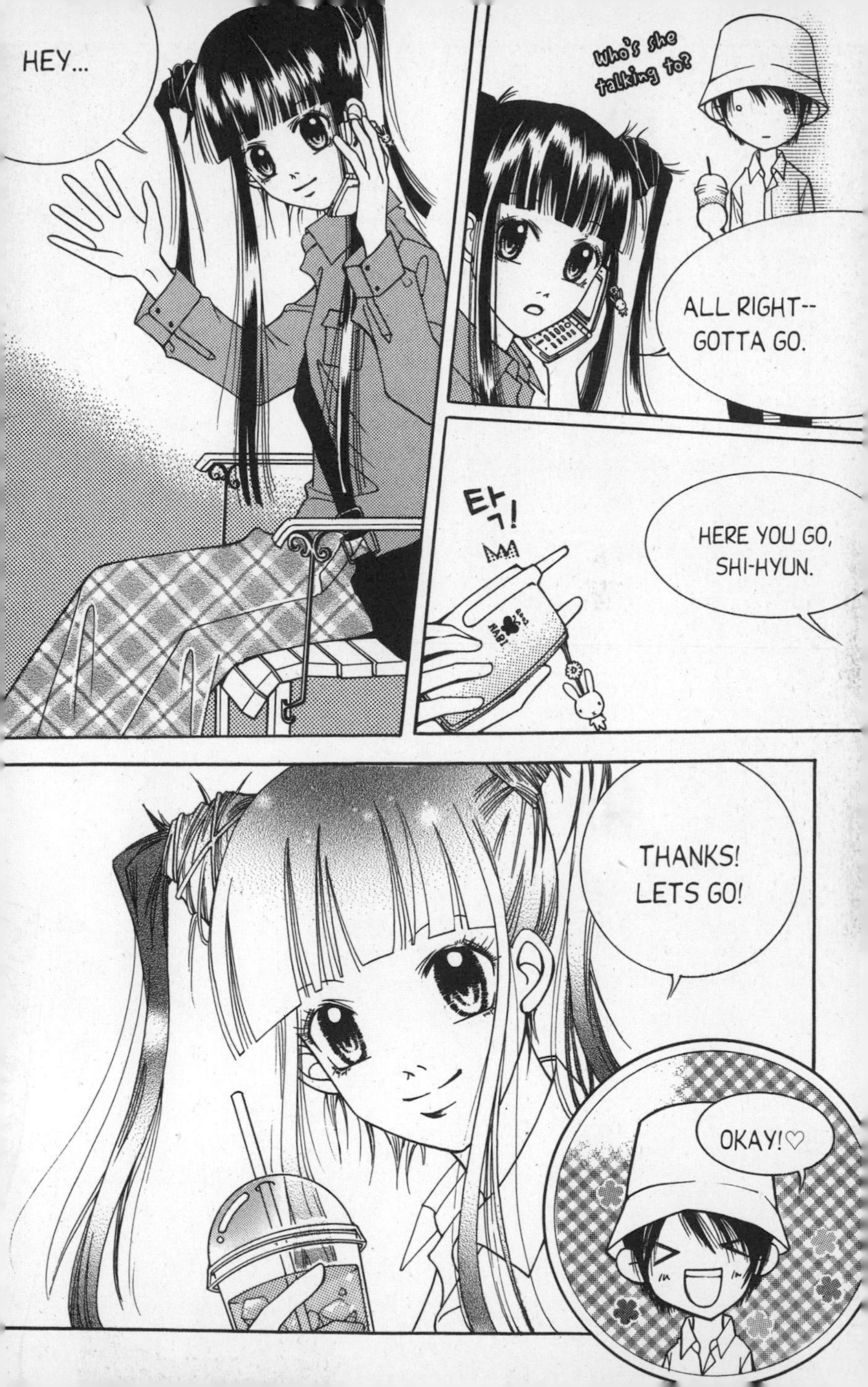
HEY...
Who's she talking to?
ALL RIGHT-- GOTTA GO.
탁!
HERE YOU GO, SHI-HYUN.
NABI
THANKS! LETS GO!
OKAY!♡

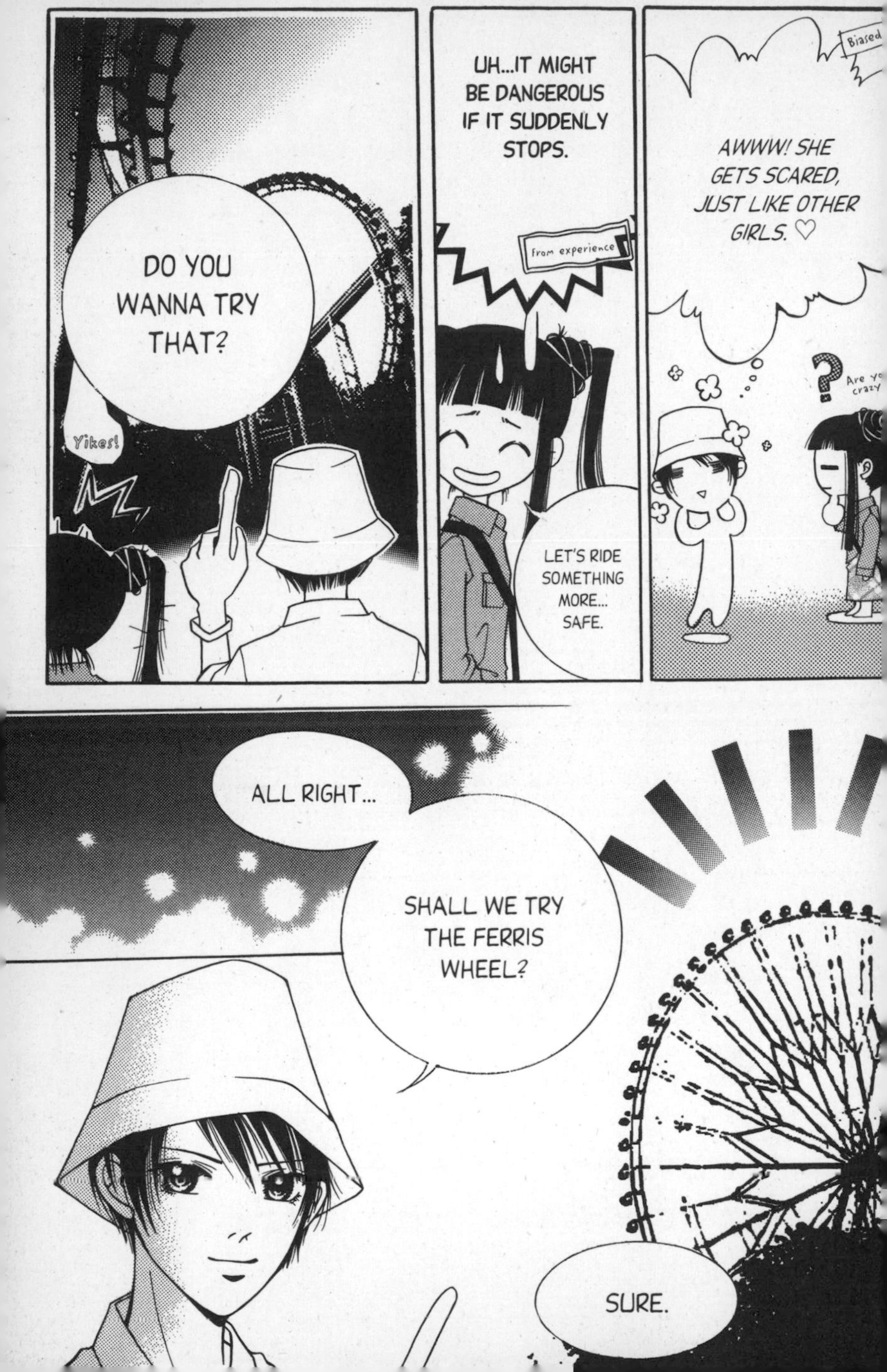
DO YOU WANNA TRY THAT?
Yikes!
UH...IT MIGHT BE DANGEROUS IF IT SUDDENLY STOPS.
from experience
LET'S RIDE SOMETHING MORE... SAFE.
Biased
AWWW! SHE GETS SCARED, JUST LIKE OTHER GIRLS. ♡
ALL RIGHT...
SHALL WE TRY THE FERRIS WHEEL?
SURE.

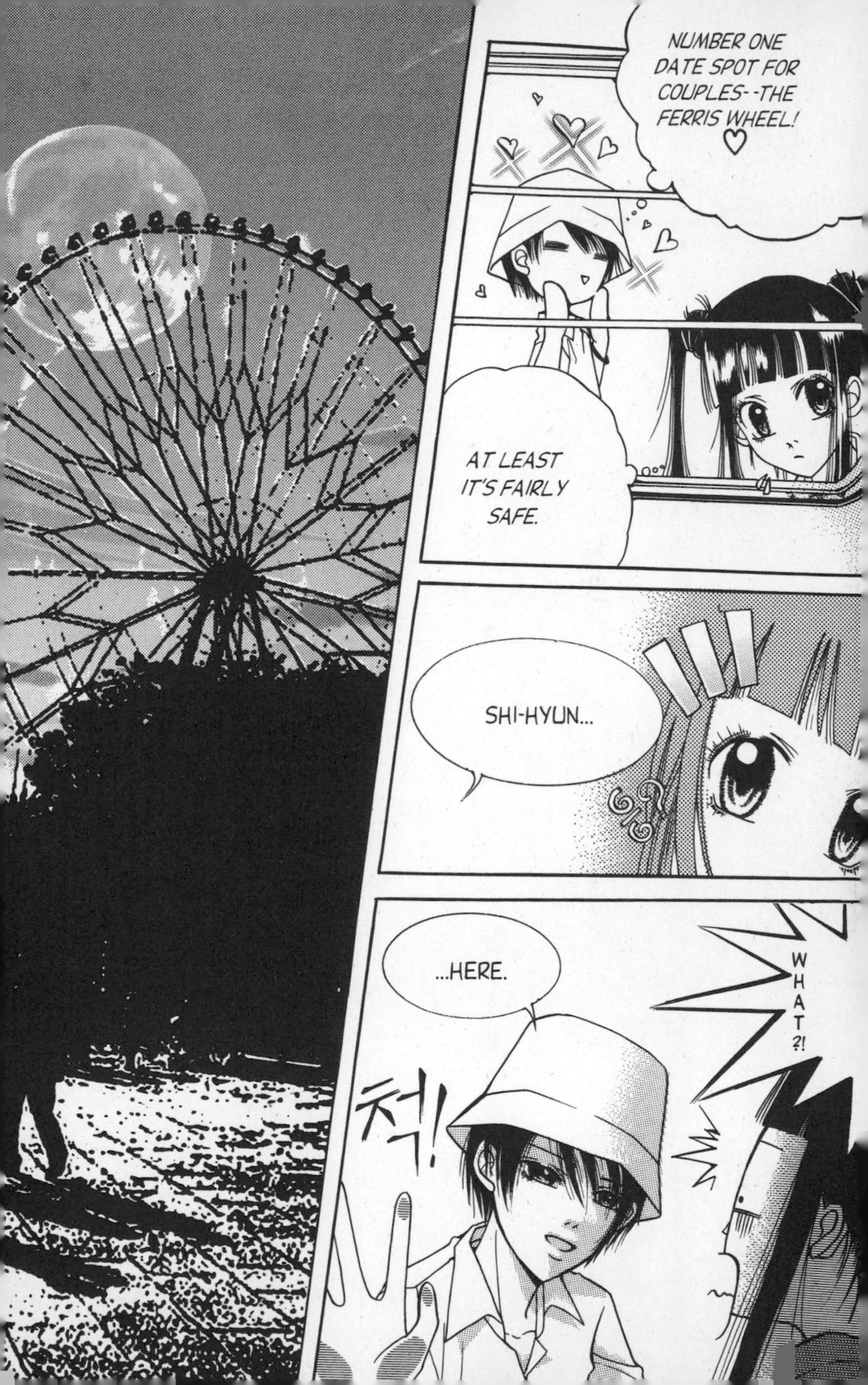
NUMBER ONE DATE SPOT FOR COUPLES--THE FERRIS WHEEL! ♡
AT LEAST IT'S FAIRLY SAFE.
SHI-HYUN...
...HERE.
WHAT?!
척!

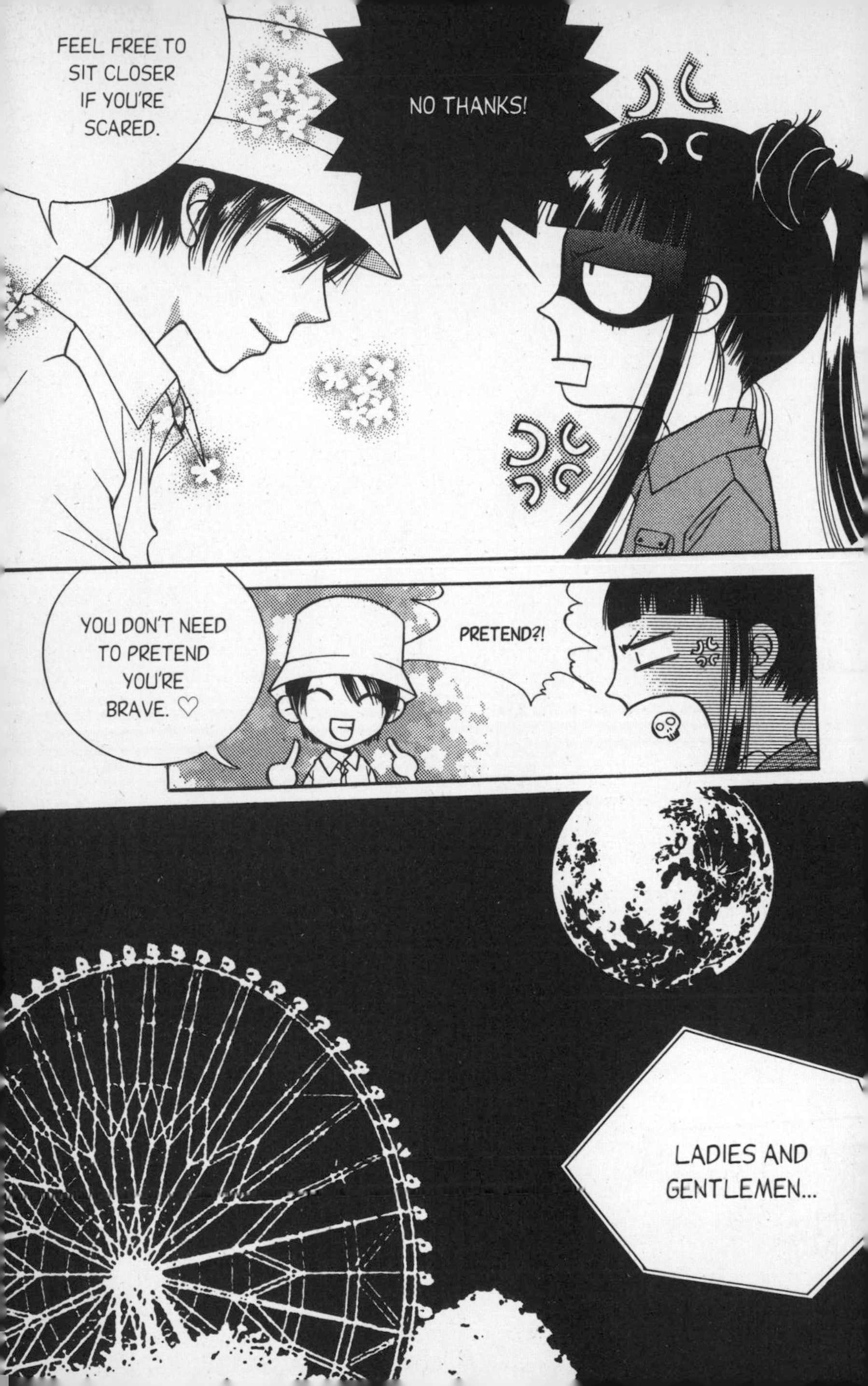

FEEL FREE TO SIT CLOSER IF YOU'RE SCARED.
NO THANKS!
YOU DON'T NEED TO PRETEND YOU'RE BRAVE. ♡
PRETEND?!
LADIES AND GENTLEMEN...

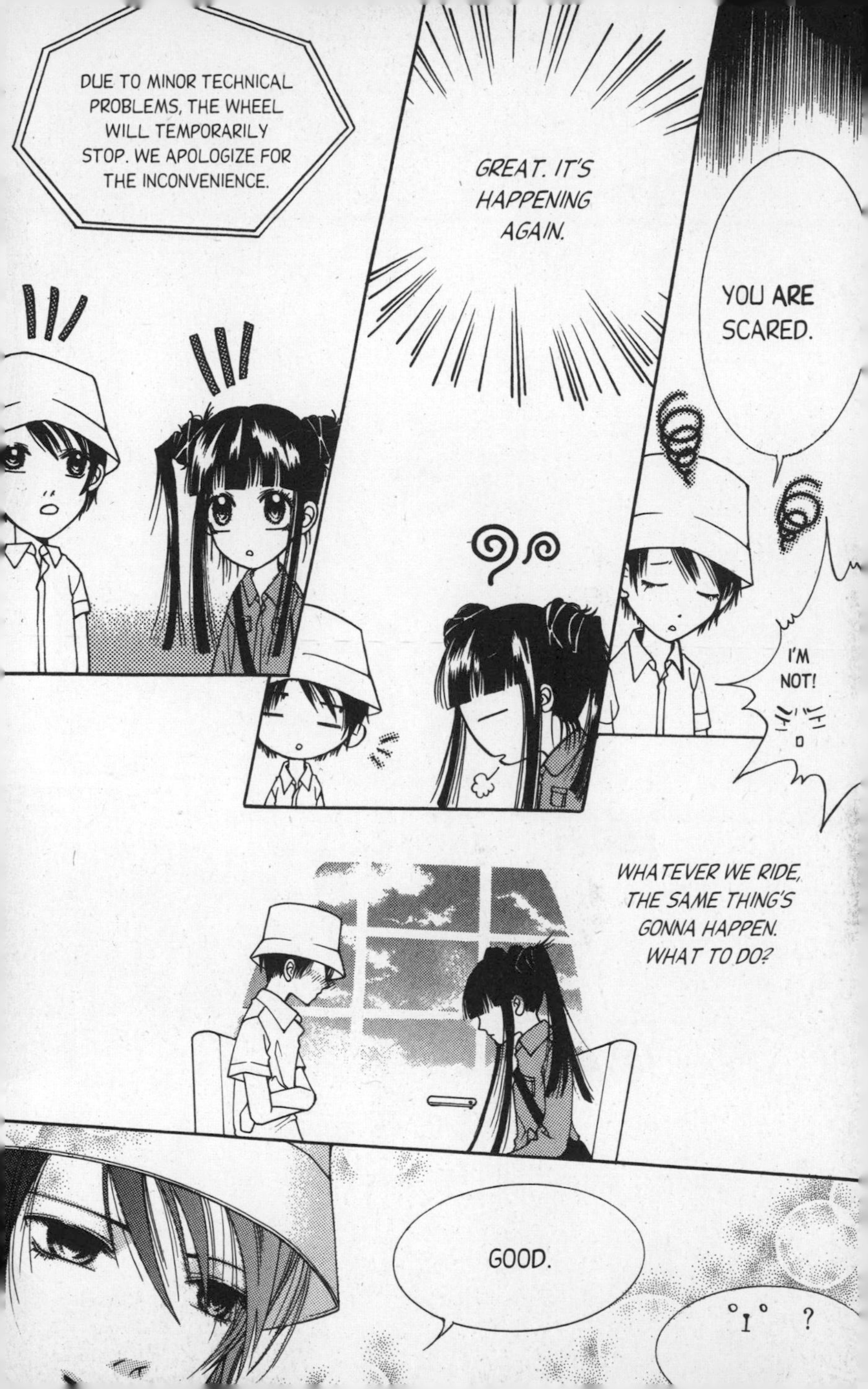
DUE TO MINOR TECHNICAL PROBLEMS, THE WHEEL WILL TEMPORARILY STOP. WE APOLOGIZE FOR THE INCONVENIENCE.
GREAT. IT'S HAPPENING AGAIN.
YOU ARE SCARED.
I'M NOT!
WHATEVER WE RIDE, THE SAME THING'S GONNA HAPPEN. WHAT TO DO?
GOOD.
?

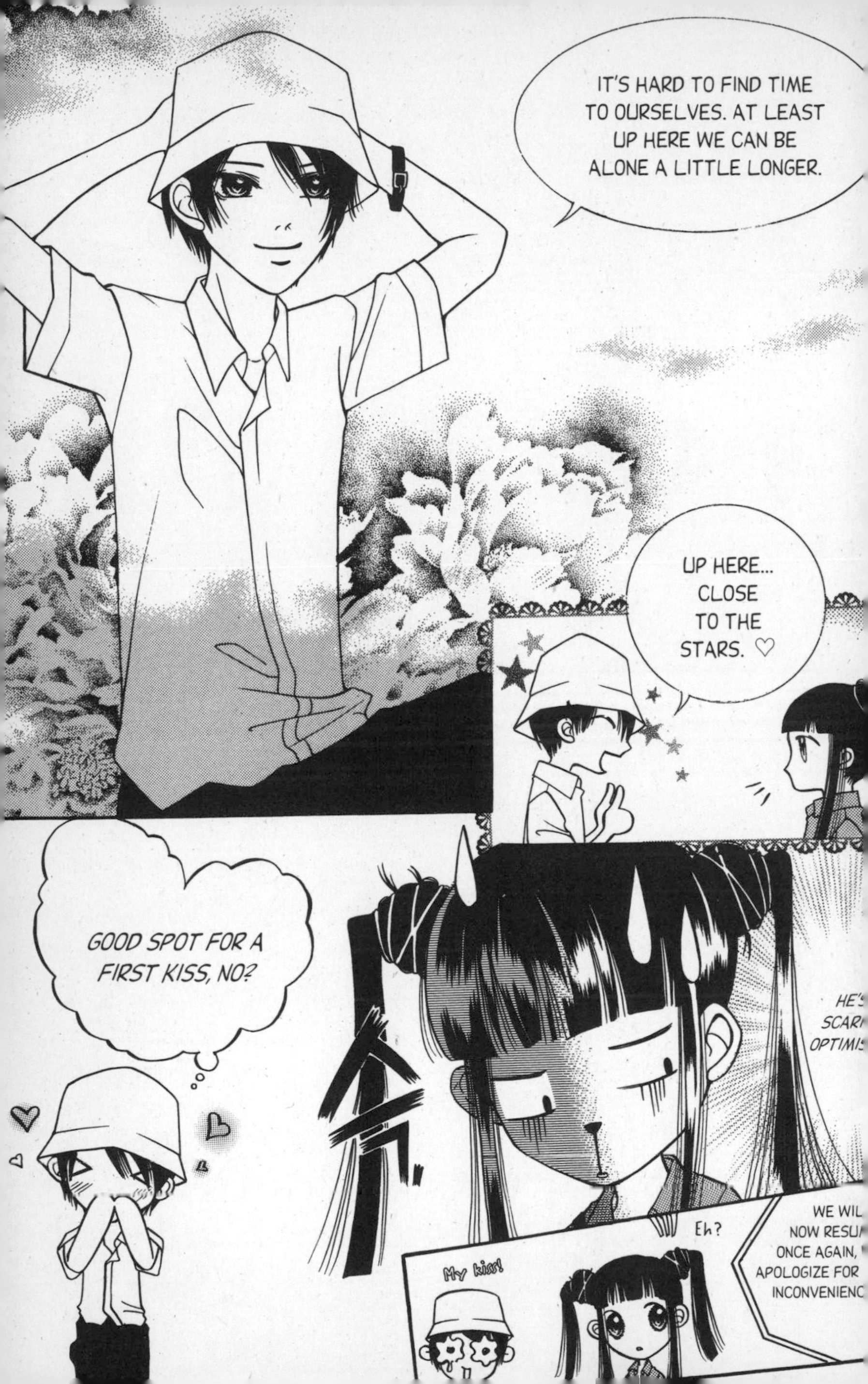
IT'S HARD TO FIND TIME TO OURSELVES. AT LEAST UP HERE WE CAN BE ALONE A LITTLE LONGER.
UP HERE... CLOSE TO THE STARS. ♡
GOOD SPOT FOR A FIRST KISS, NO?
HE'S SCAR OPTIMIS
Eh?
My kiss!
WE WIL NOW RESU ONCE AGAIN, APOLOGIZE FOR INCONVENIENC

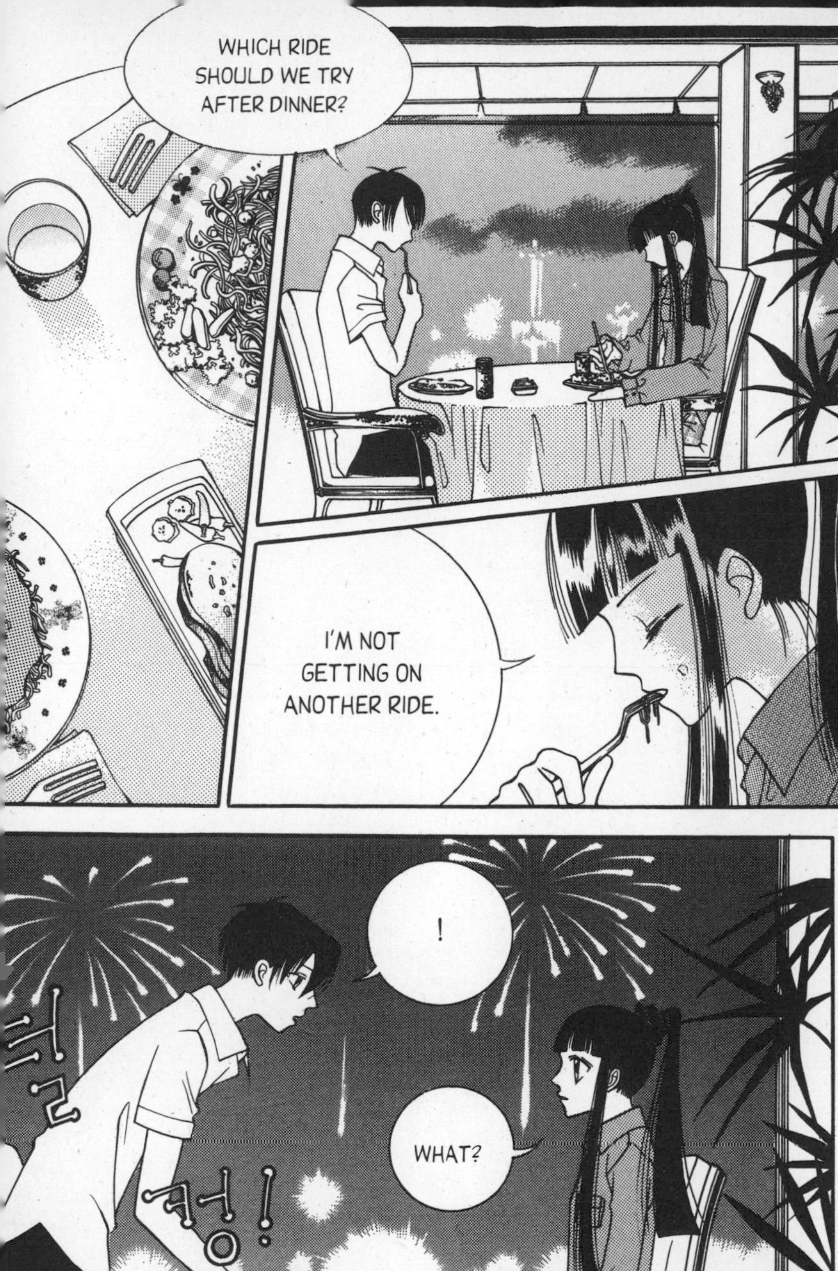
WHICH RIDE SHOULD WE TRY AFTER DINNER?
I'M NOT GETTING ON ANOTHER RIDE.
!
WHAT?

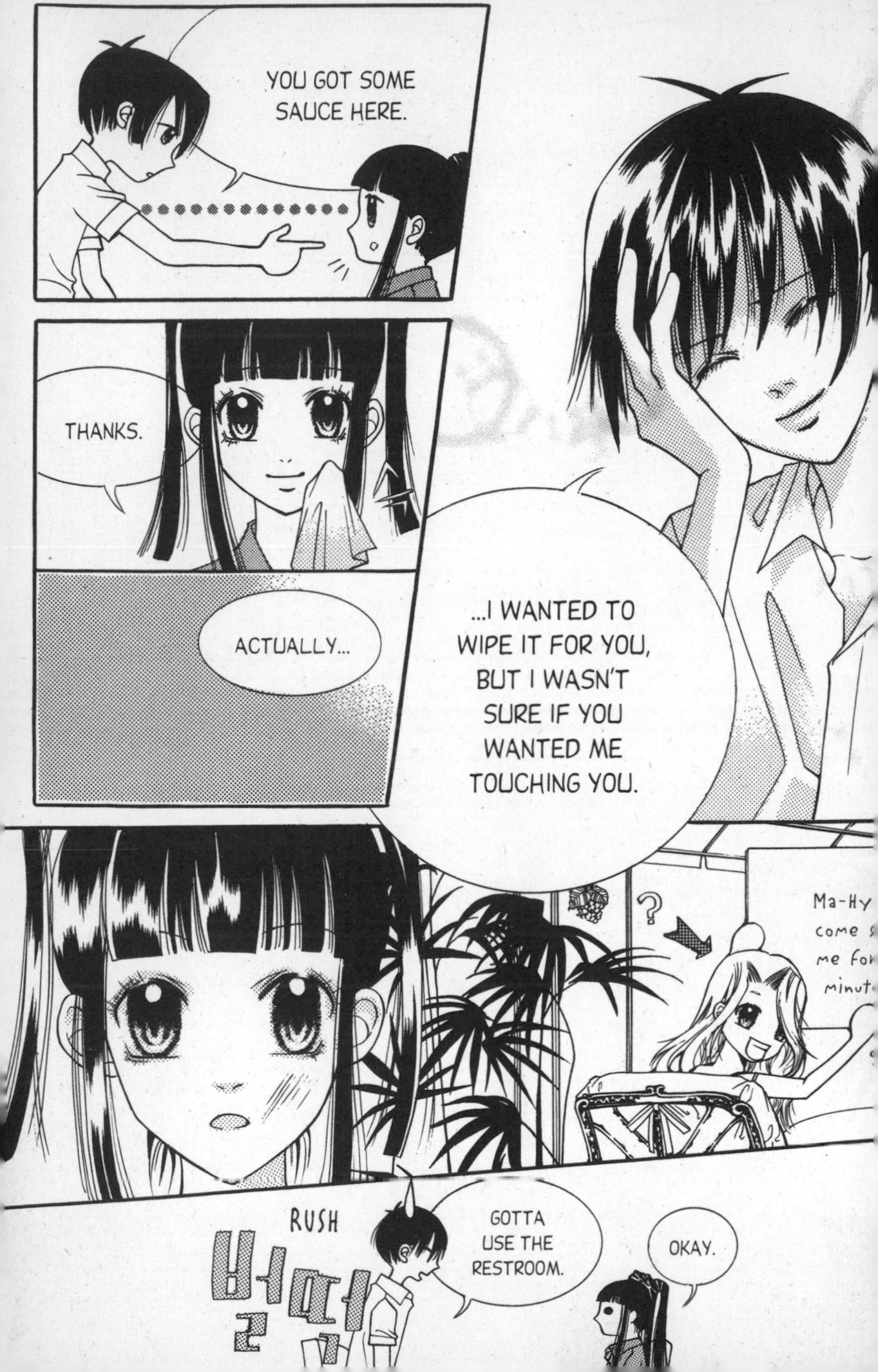

YOU GOT SOME SAUCE HERE.
THANKS.
ACTUALLY...
...I WANTED TO WIPE IT FOR YOU, BUT I WASN'T SURE IF YOU WANTED ME TOUCHING YOU.
RUSH
GOTTA USE THE RESTROOM.
OKAY.

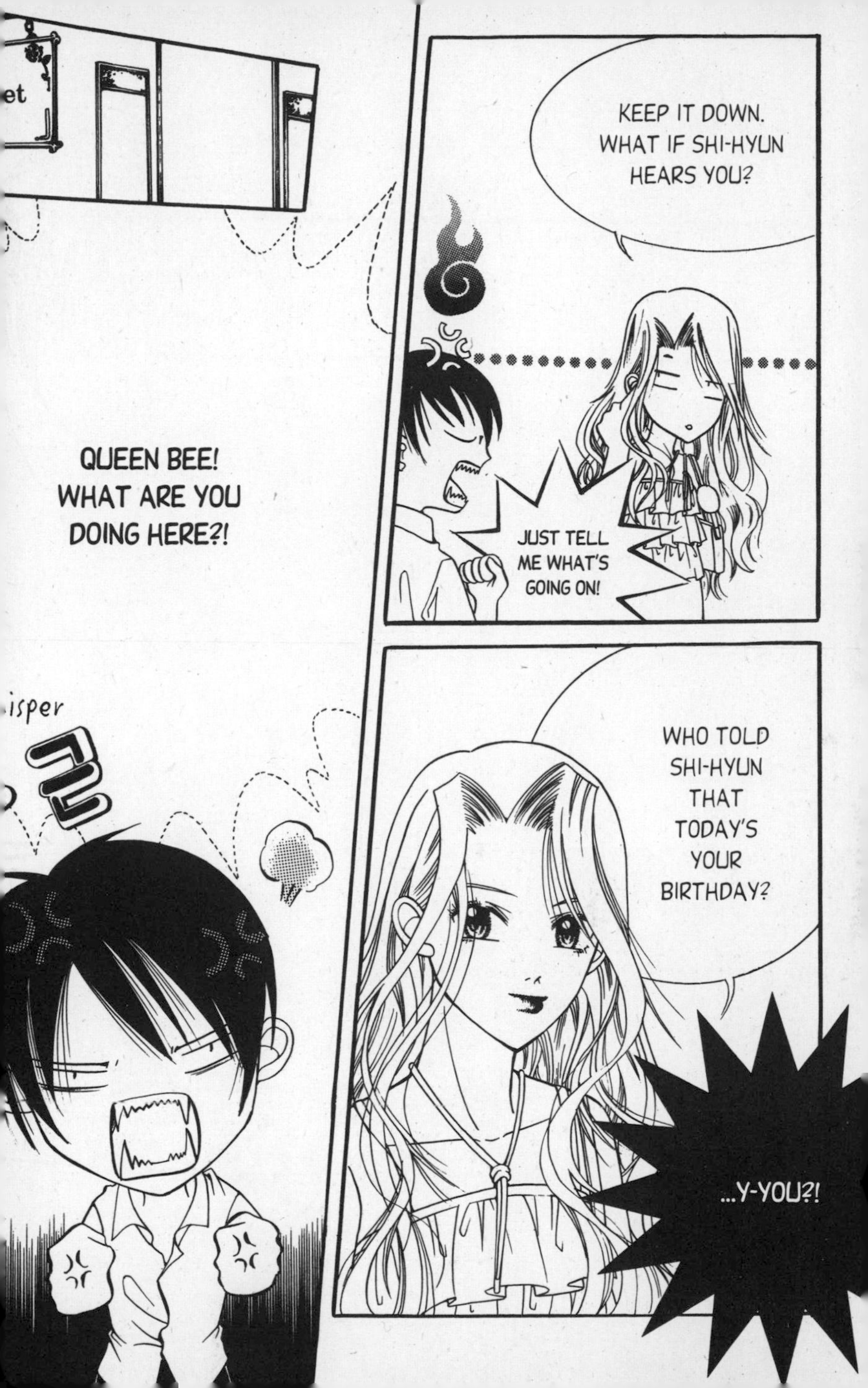
QUEEN BEE! WHAT ARE YOU DOING HERE?!
KEEP IT DOWN. WHAT IF SHI-HYUN HEARS YOU?
JUST TELL ME WHAT'S GOING ON!
WHO TOLD SHI-HYUN THAT TODAY'S YOUR BIRTHDAY?
...Y-YOU?!

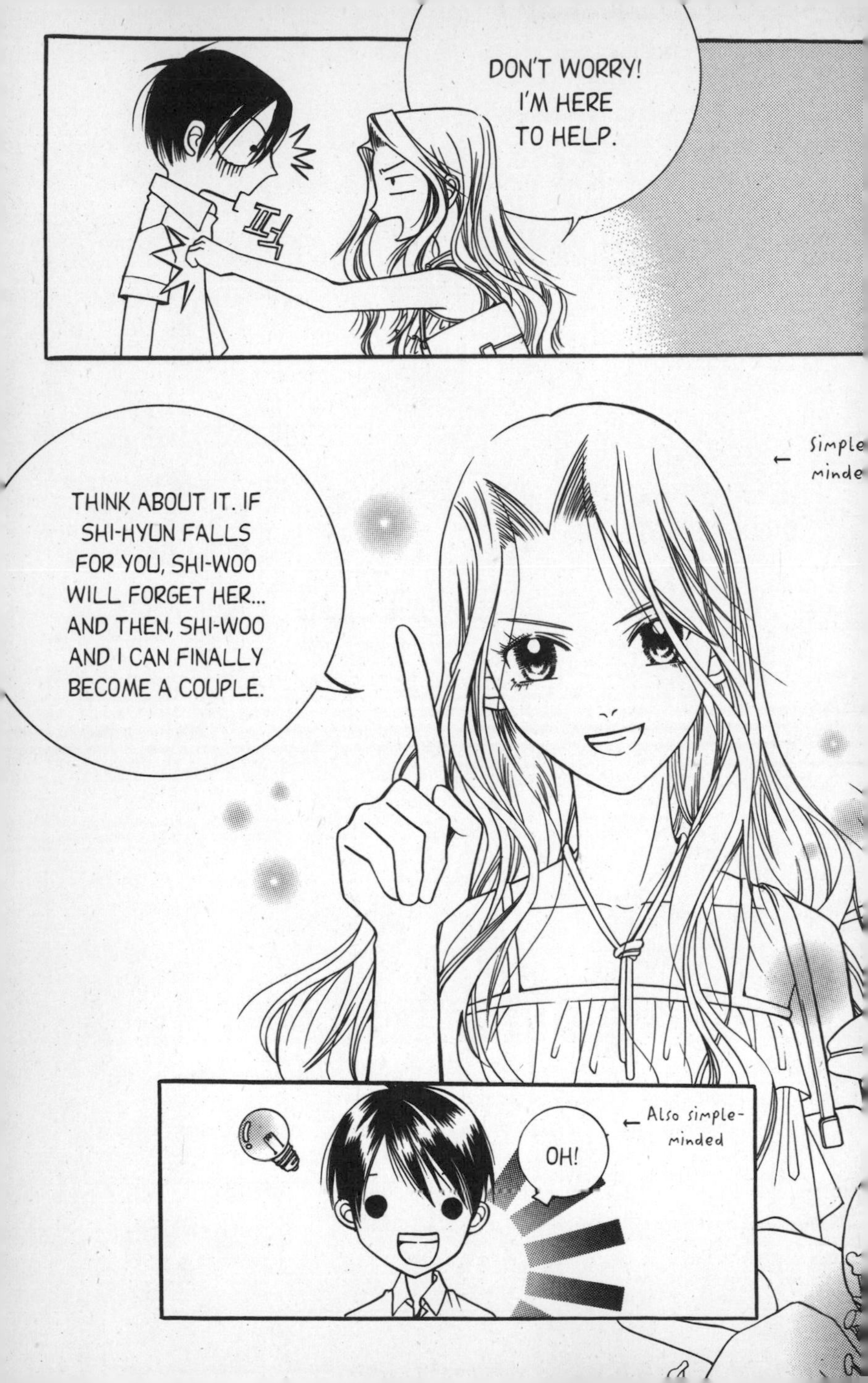
DON'T WORRY! I'M HERE TO HELP.
THINK ABOUT IT. IF SHI-HYUN FALLS FOR YOU, SHI-WOO WILL FORGET HER... AND THEN, SHI-WOO AND I CAN FINALLY BECOME A COUPLE.
← Simple minde
OH!
← Also simple-minded

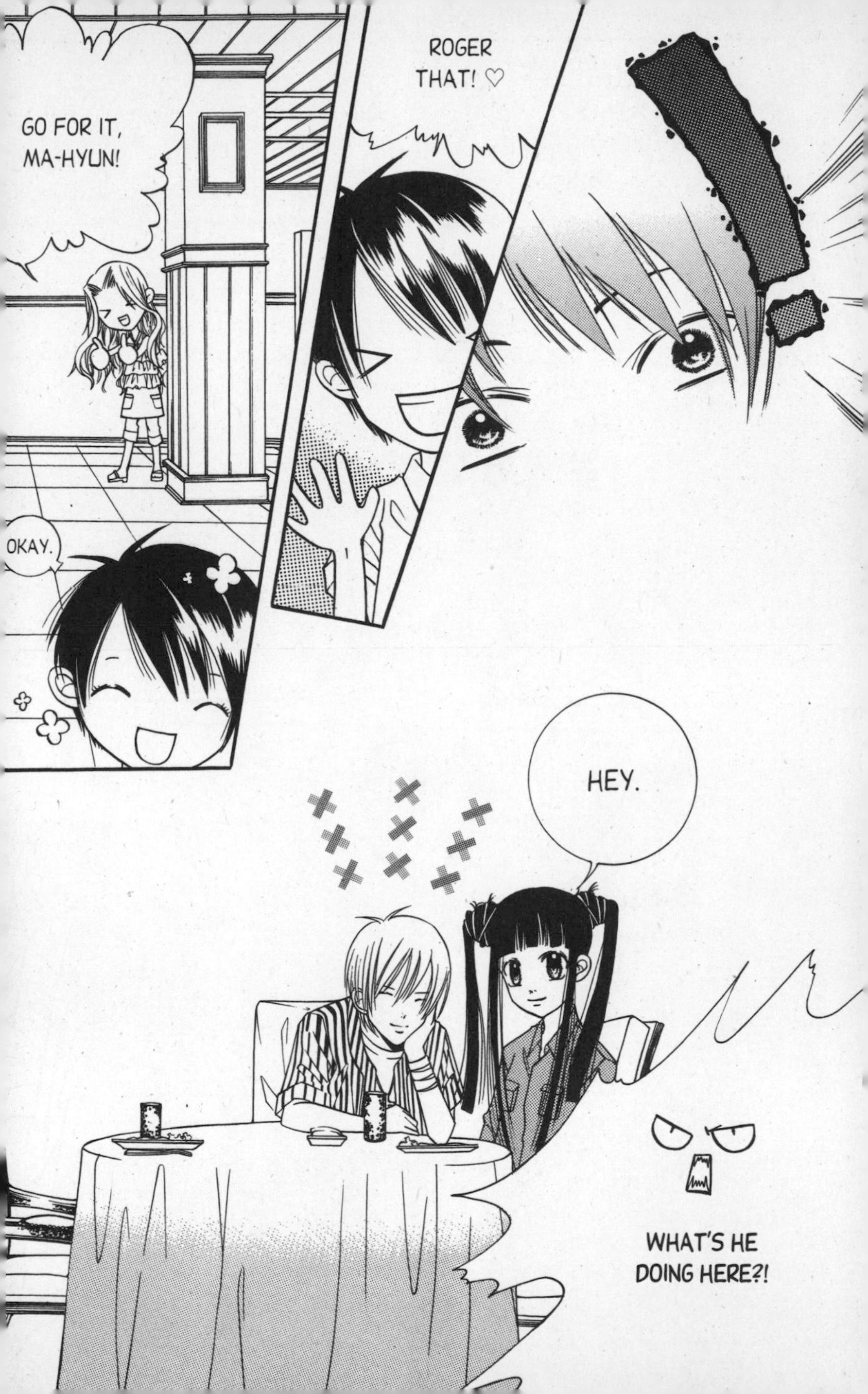
GO FOR IT, MA-HYUN!
OKAY.
ROGER THAT! ♡
HEY.
WHAT'S HE DOING HERE?!

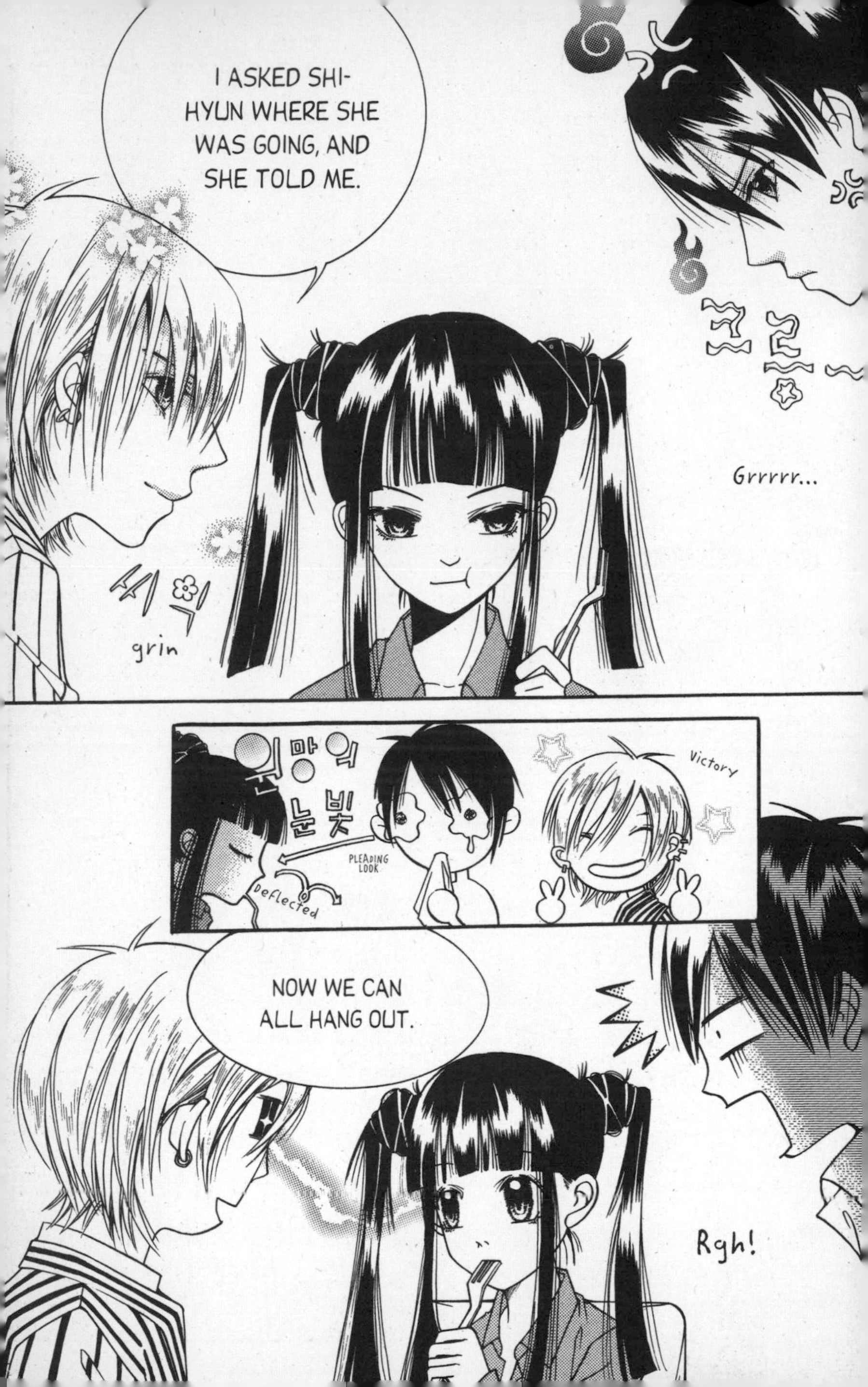
I ASKED SHI-HYUN WHERE SHE WAS GOING, AND SHE TOLD ME.
씨익
grin
Grrrrr...
원망의 눈빛
PLEADING LOOK
Deflected
Victory
NOW WE CAN ALL HANG OUT.
Rgh!

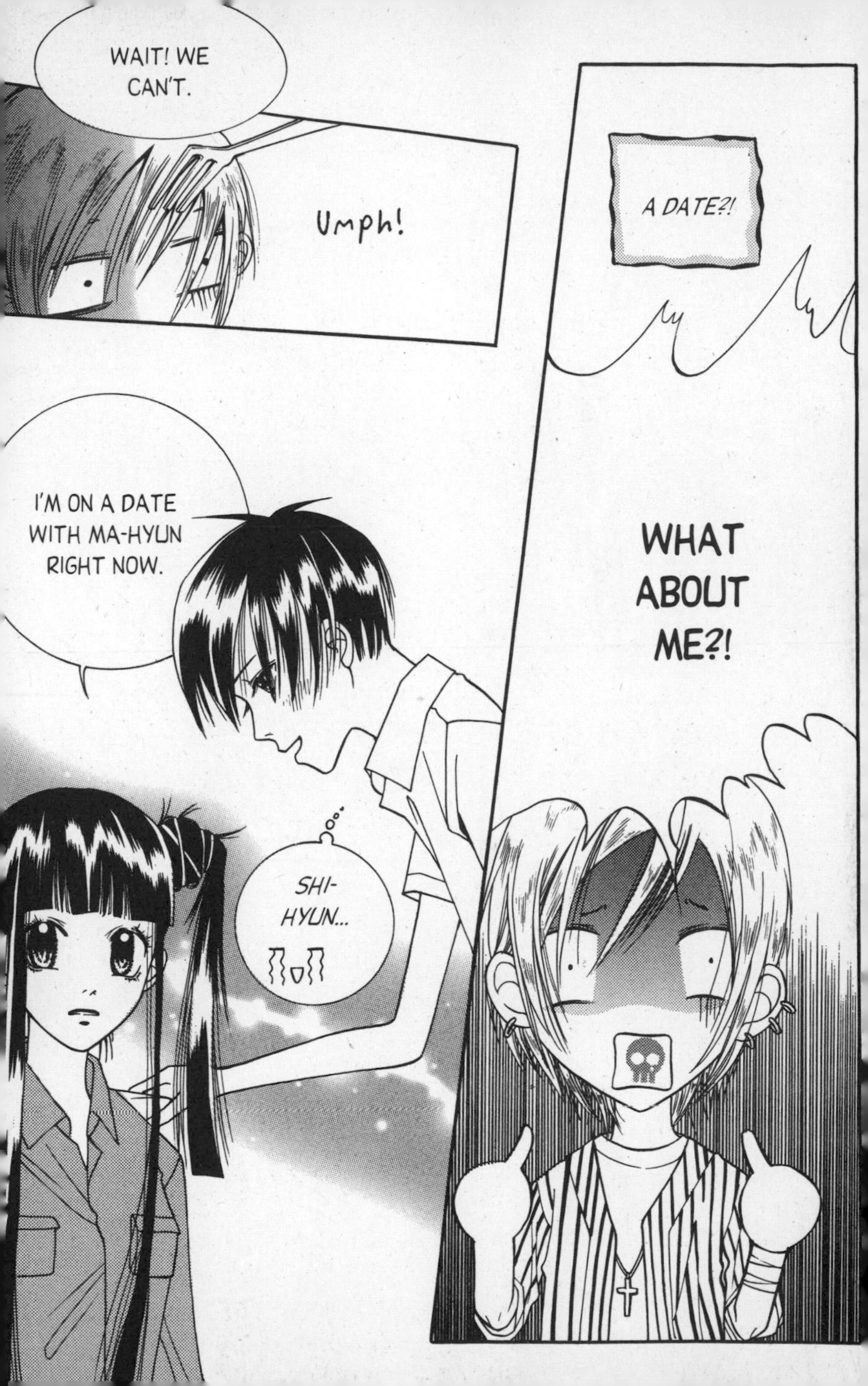
WAIT! WE CAN'T.
Umph!
A DATE?!
I'M ON A DATE WITH MA-HYUN RIGHT NOW.
SHI-HYUN...
WHAT ABOUT ME?!

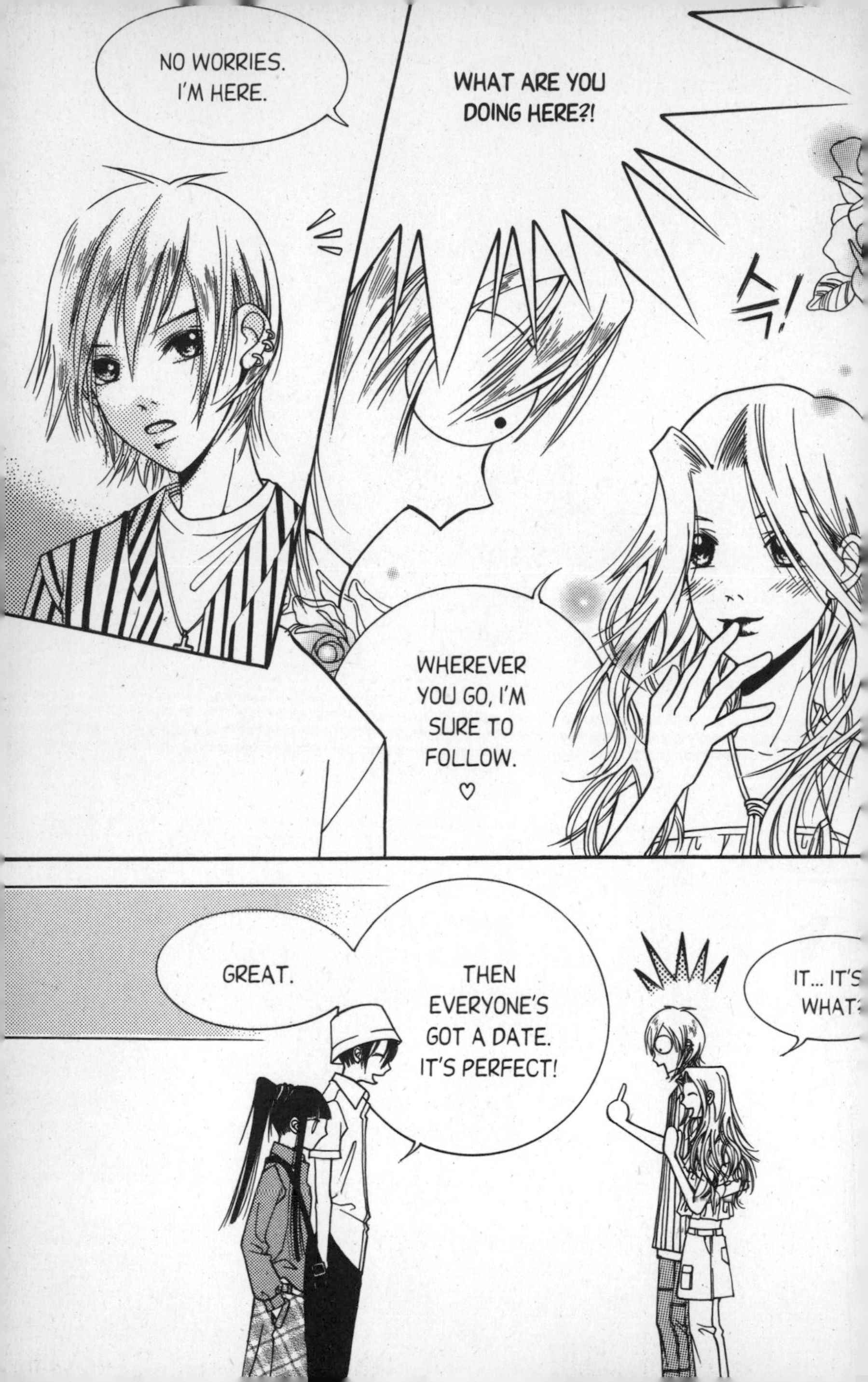
NO WORRIES. I'M HERE.
WHAT ARE YOU DOING HERE?!
슥!
WHEREVER YOU GO, I'M SURE TO FOLLOW. ♡
GREAT.
THEN EVERYONE'S GOT A DATE. IT'S PERFECT!
IT... IT'S WHAT?

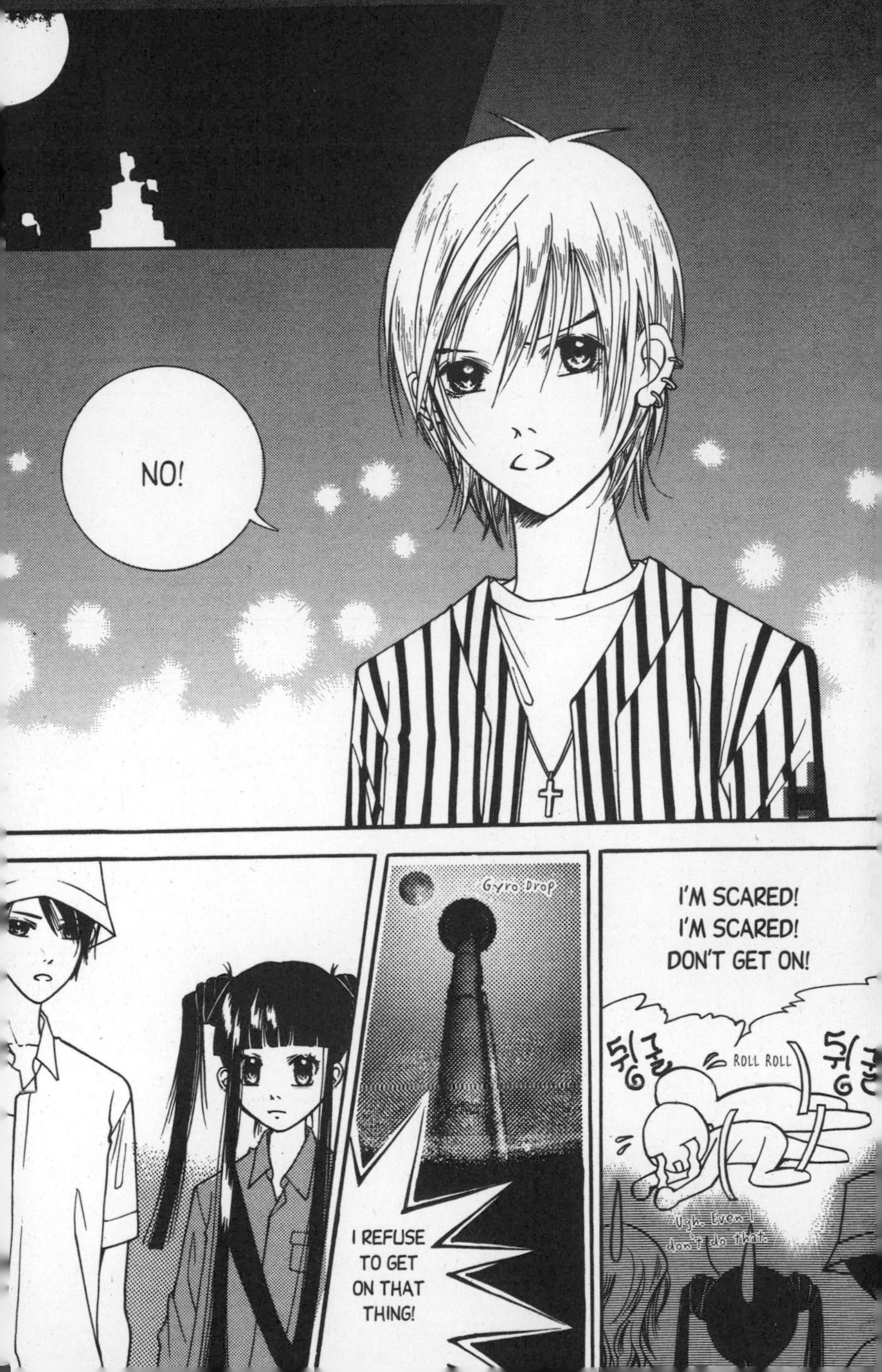
NO!
Gyro Drop
I REFUSE TO GET ON THAT THING!
I'M SCARED! I'M SCARED! DON'T GET ON!
뒹굴
ROLL ROLL
뒹굴
Ugh. Even I don't do that.

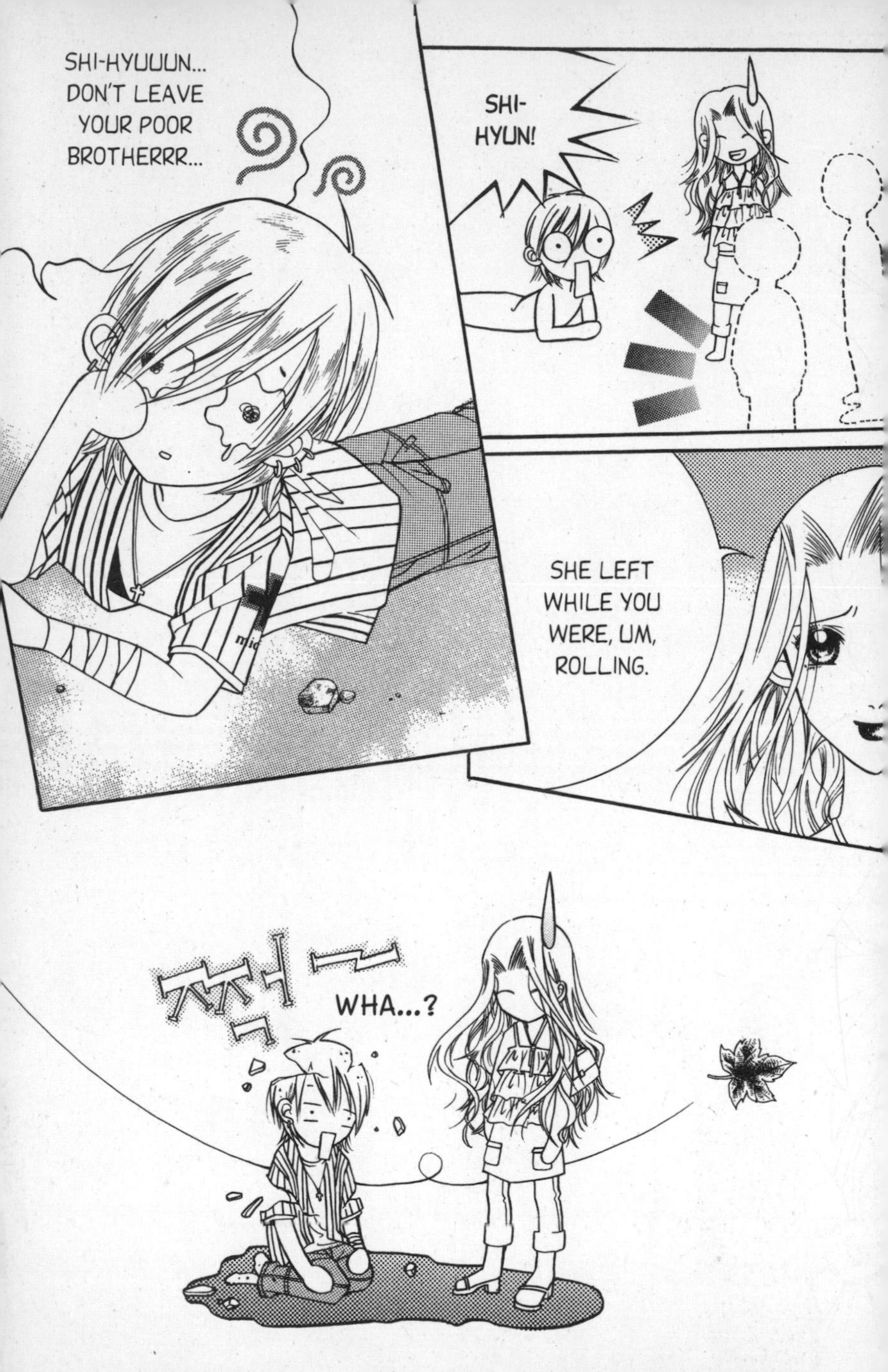
SHI-HYUUUN... DON'T LEAVE YOUR POOR BROTHERRR...
SHI-HYUN!
SHE LEFT WHILE YOU WERE, UM, ROLLING.
WHA...?

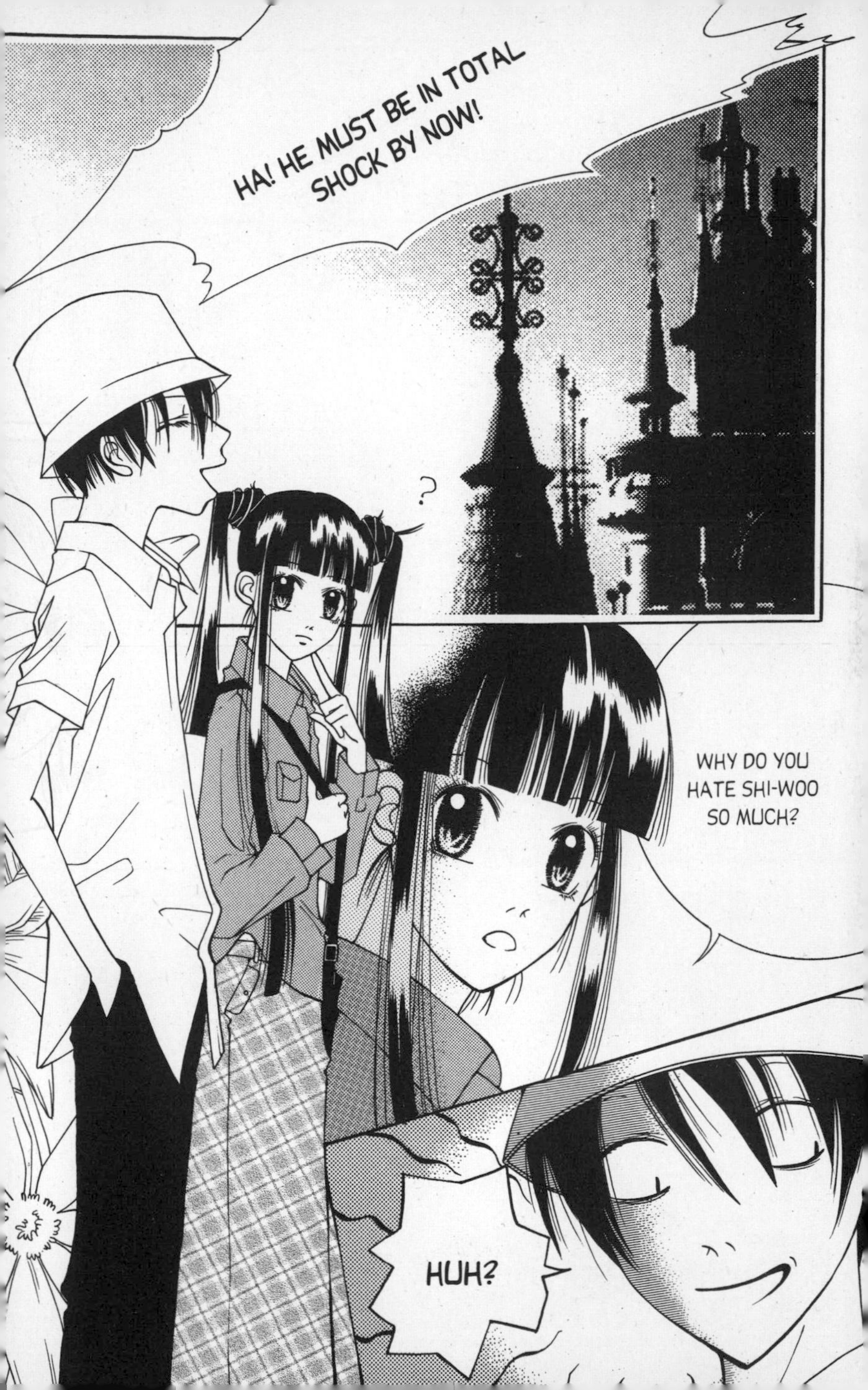
HA! HE MUST BE IN TOTAL SHOCK BY NOW!
?
WHY DO YOU HATE SHI-WOO SO MUCH?
HUH?

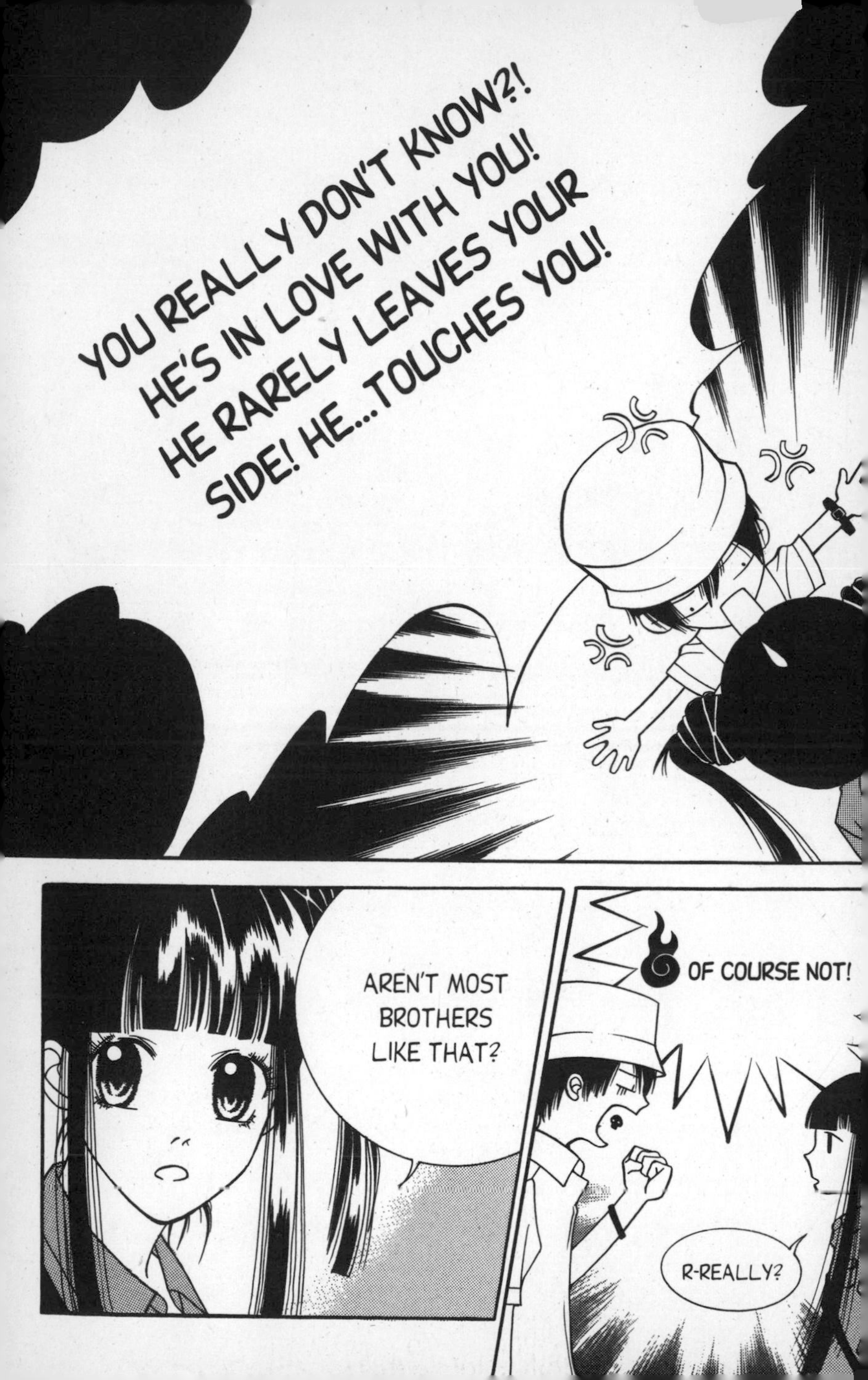
YOU REALLY DON'T KNOW?! HE'S IN LOVE WITH YOU! HE RARELY LEAVES YOUR SIDE! HE...TOUCHES YOU!
AREN'T MOST BROTHERS LIKE THAT?
OF COURSE NOT!
R-REALLY?

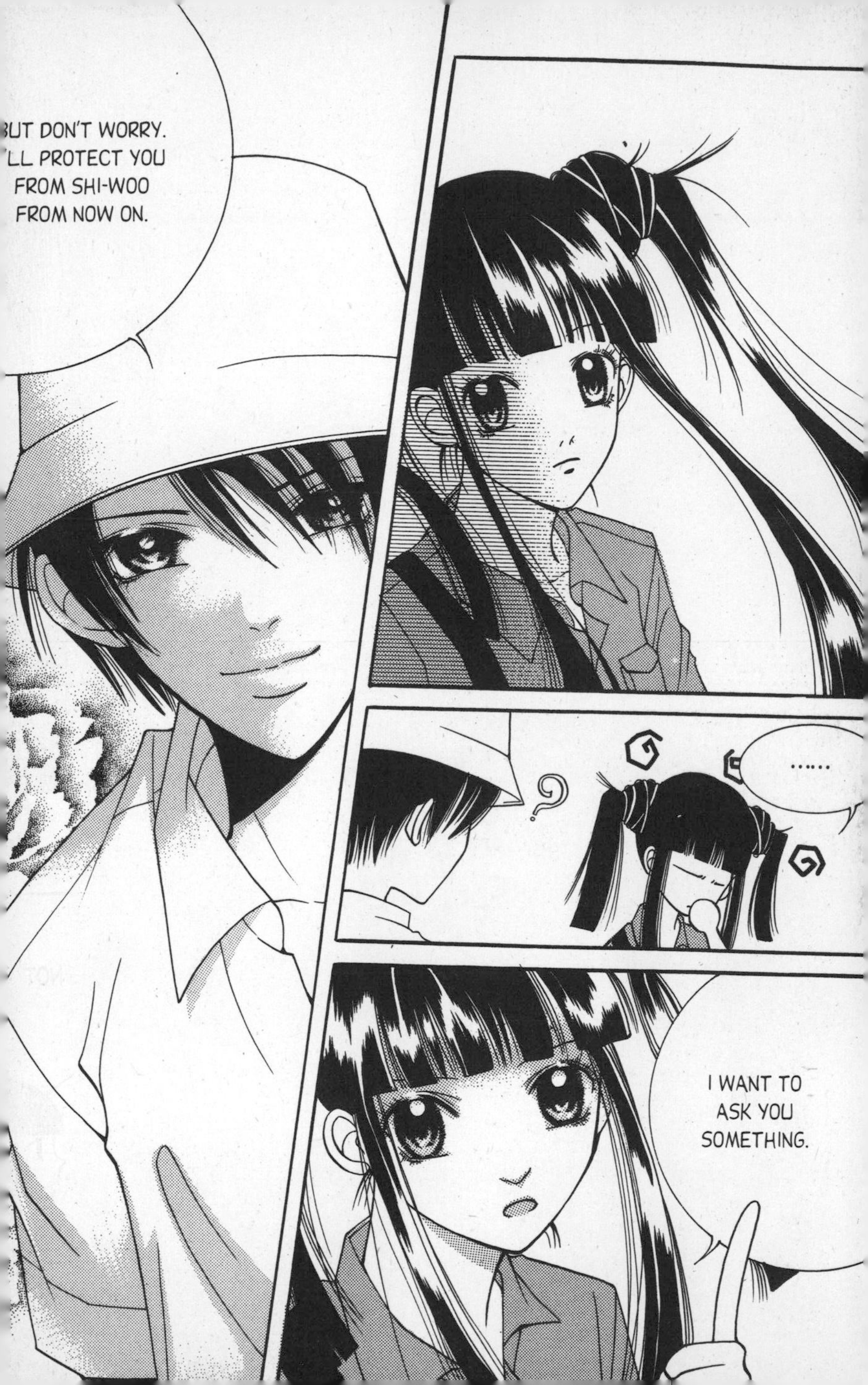
UT DON'T WORRY. 'LL PROTECT YOU FROM SHI-WOO FROM NOW ON.
......
I WANT TO ASK YOU SOMETHING.

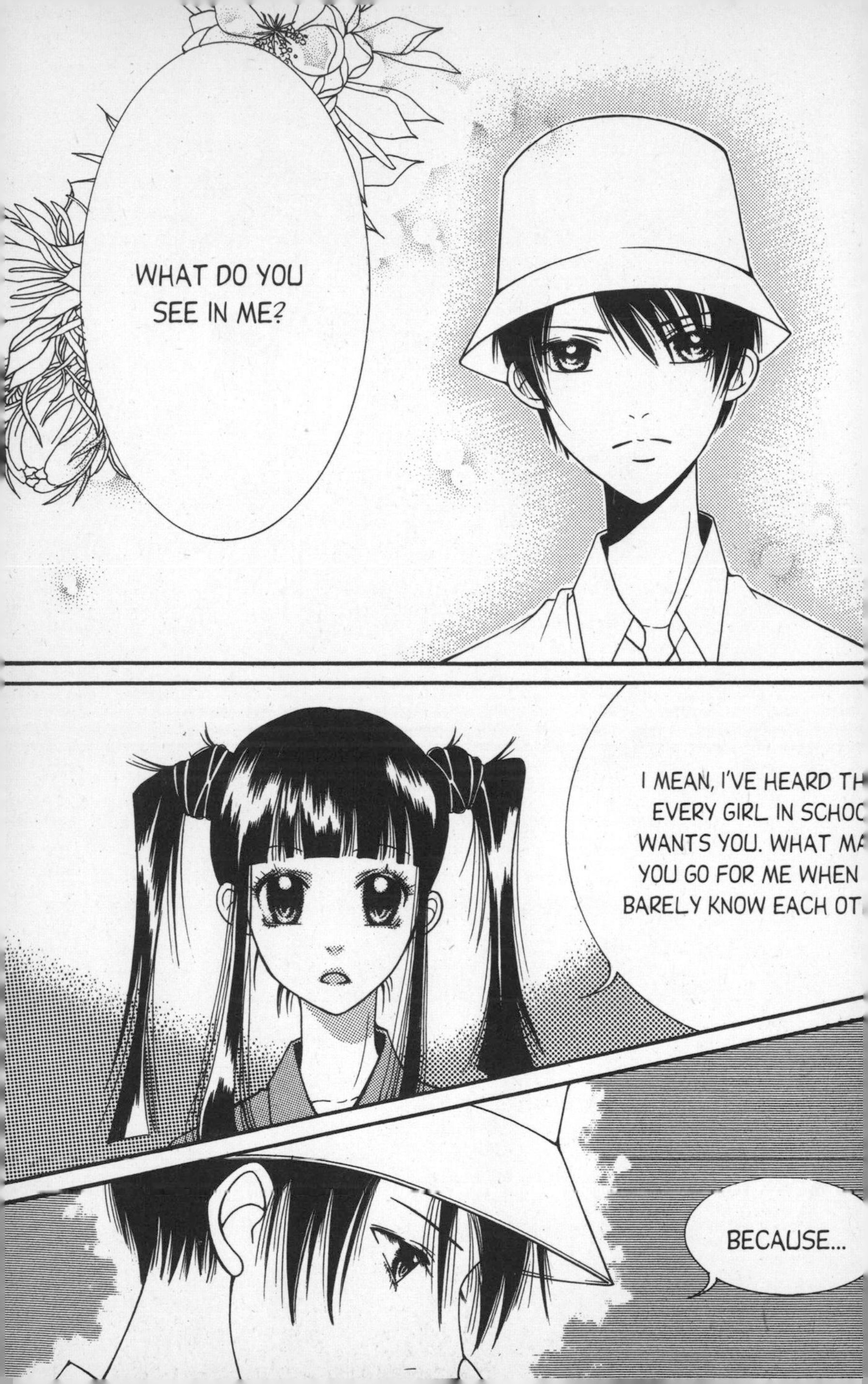
WHAT DO YOU SEE IN ME?
I MEAN, I'VE HEARD TH EVERY GIRL IN SCHOC WANTS YOU. WHAT MA YOU GO FOR ME WHEN BARELY KNOW EACH OT
BECAUSE...

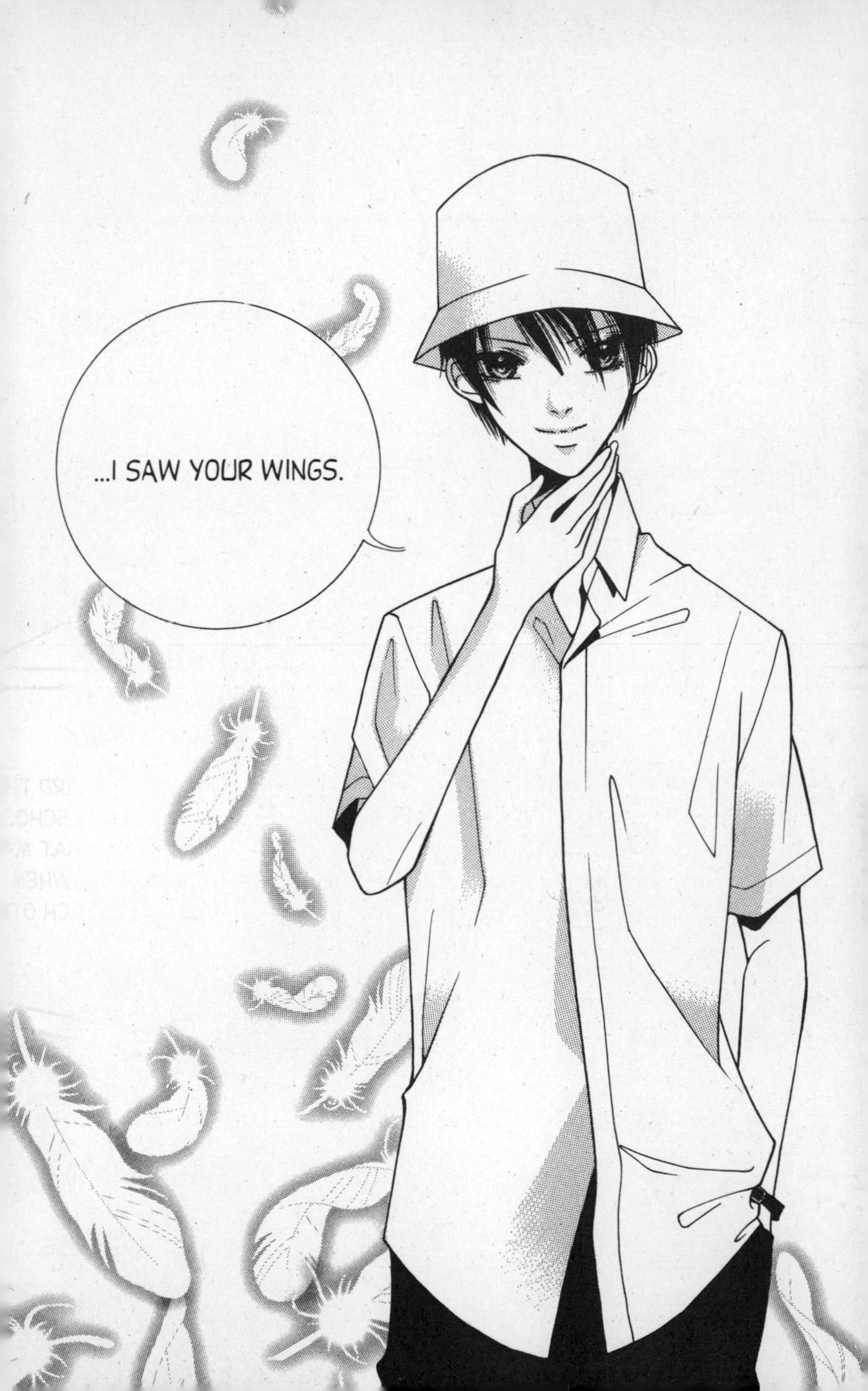
...I SAW YOUR WINGS.

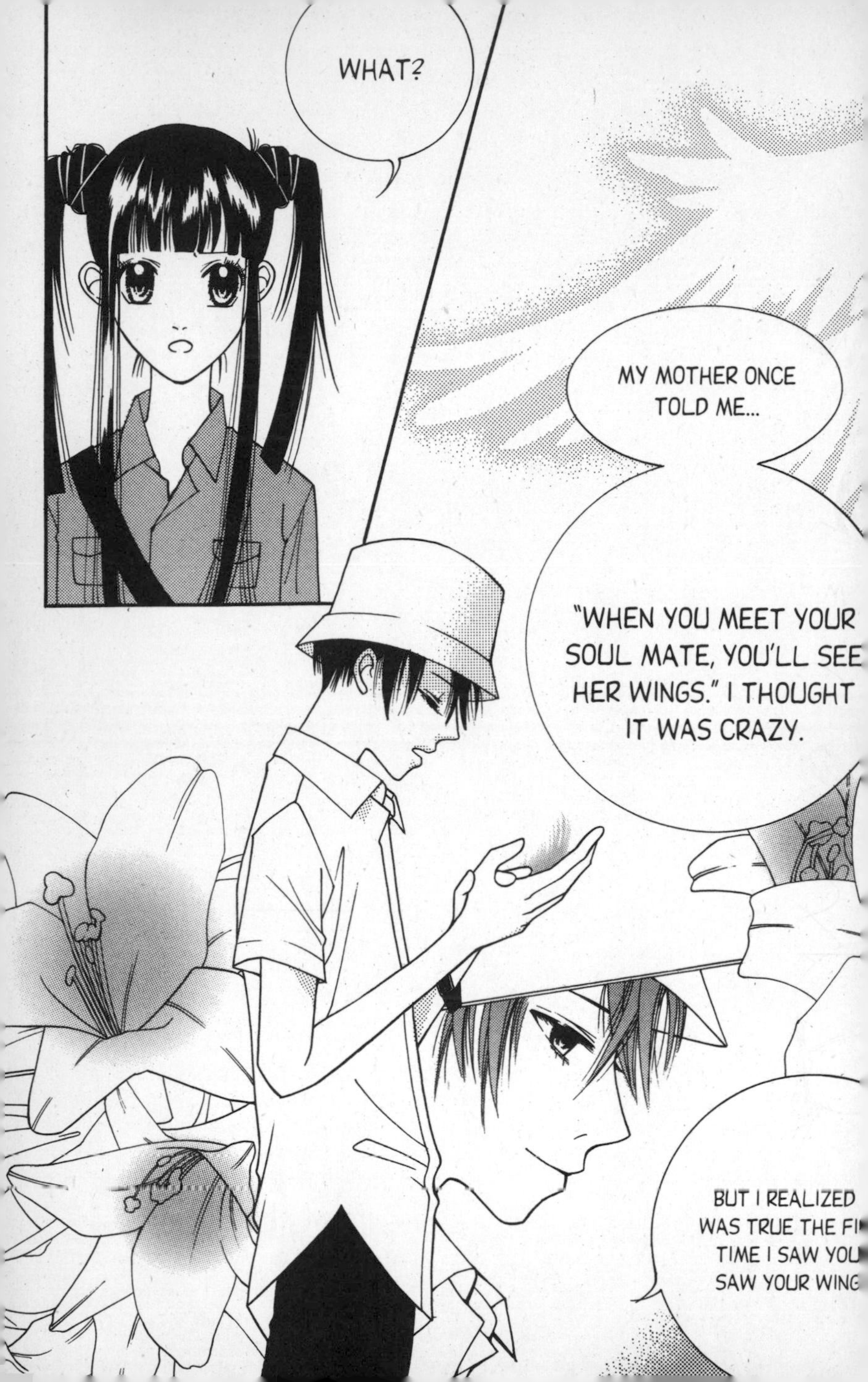
WHAT?
MY MOTHER ONCE TOLD ME...
"WHEN YOU MEET YOUR SOUL MATE, YOU'LL SEE HER WINGS." I THOUGHT IT WAS CRAZY.
BUT I REALIZED
WAS TRUE THE FI
TIME I SAW YOU
SAW YOUR WING

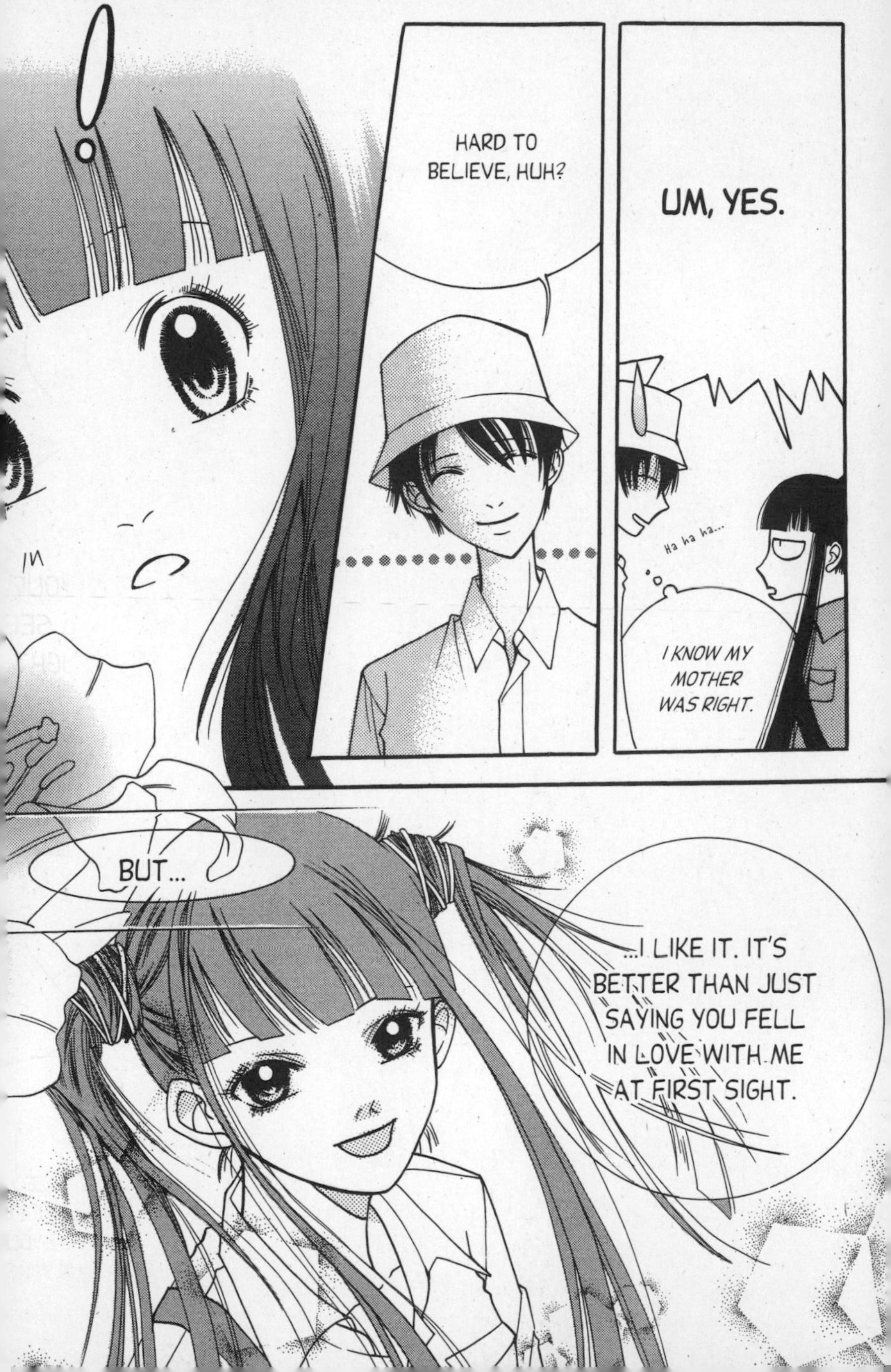
!
HARD TO BELIEVE, HUH?
UM, YES.
Ha ha ha...
I KNOW MY MOTHER WAS RIGHT.
BUT...
...I LIKE IT. IT'S BETTER THAN JUST SAYING YOU FELL IN LOVE WITH ME AT FIRST SIGHT.

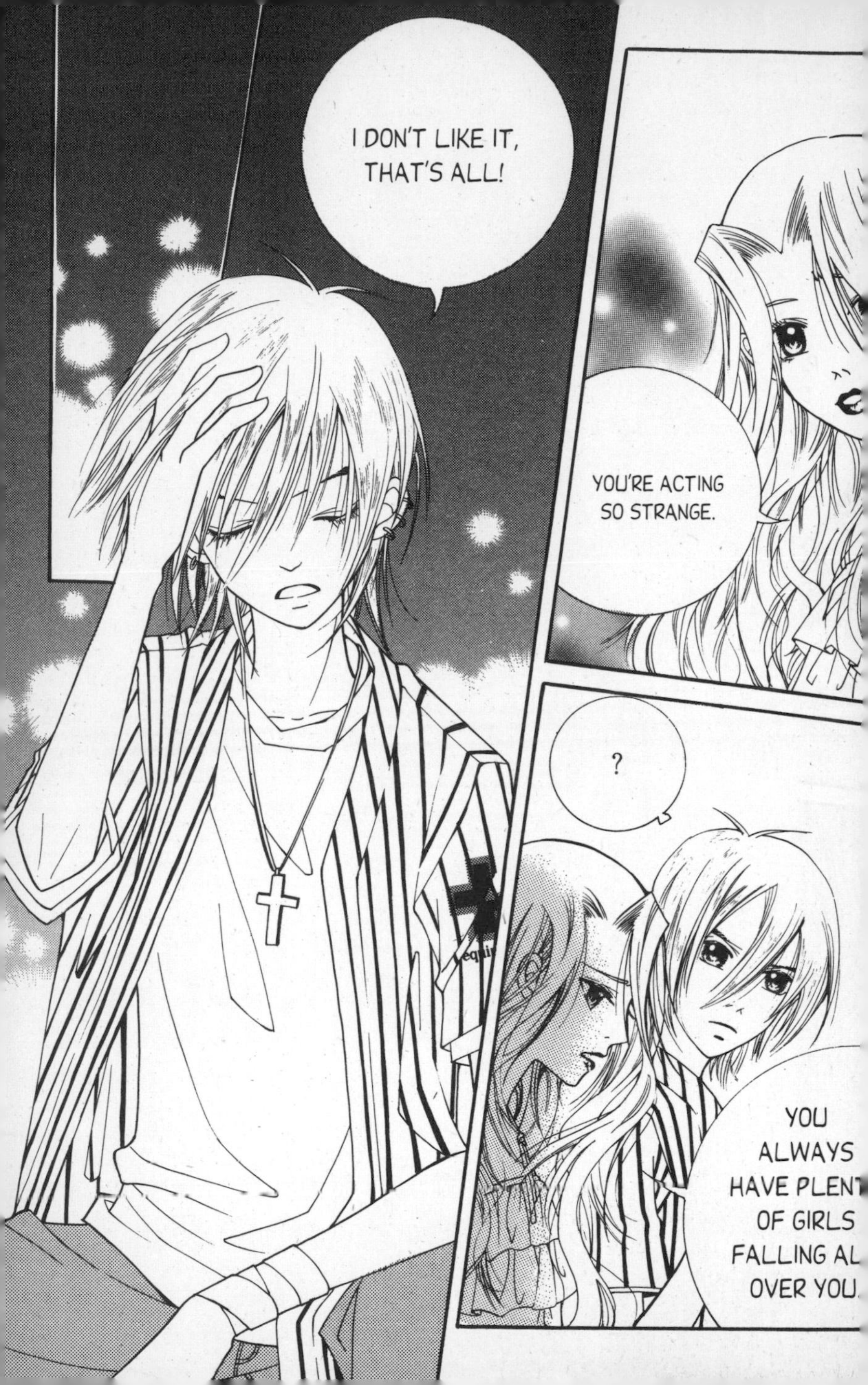
I DON'T LIKE IT, THAT'S ALL!
YOU'RE ACTING SO STRANGE.
?
YOU ALWAYS HAVE PLENT OF GIRLS FALLING AL OVER YOU.

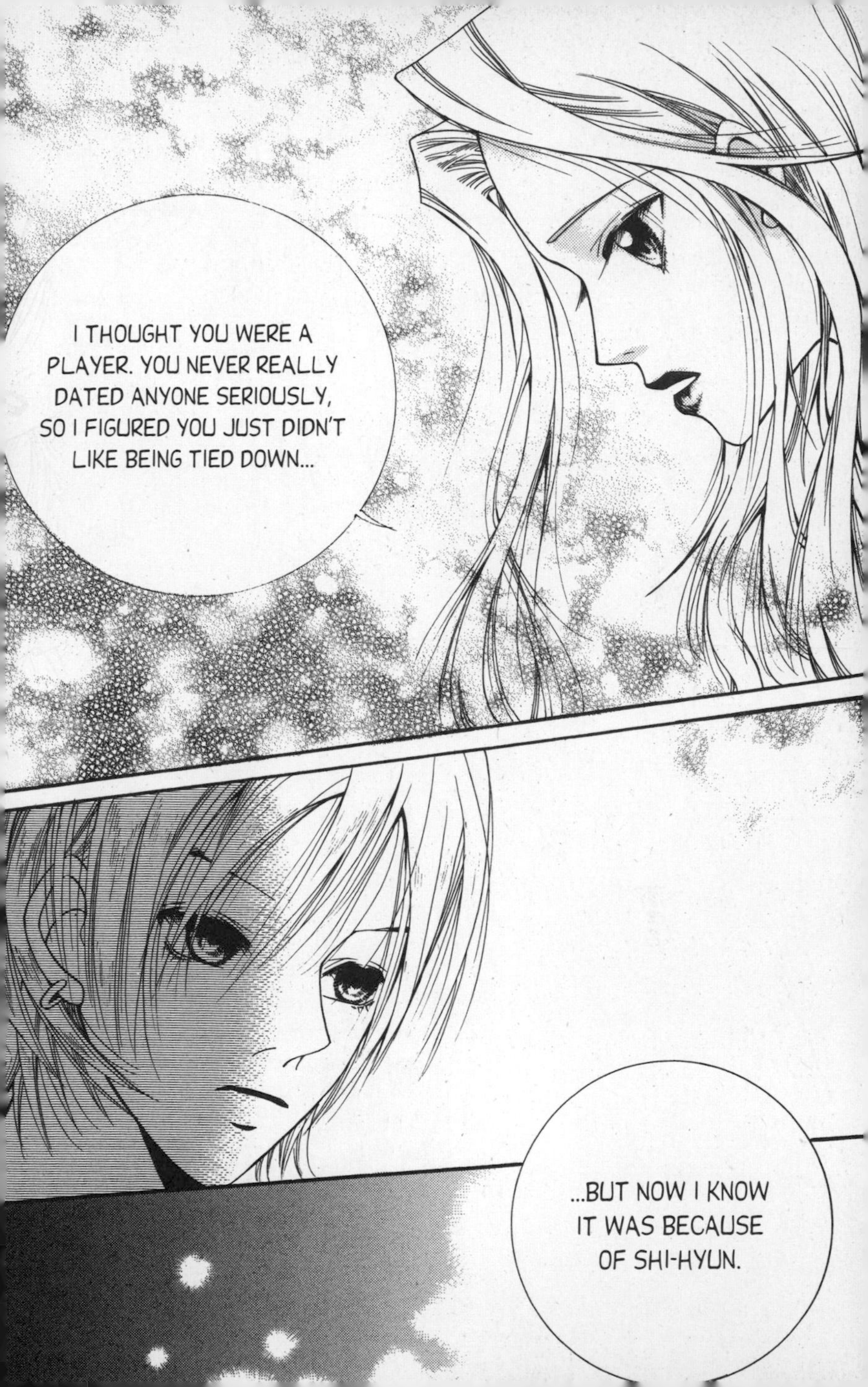
I THOUGHT YOU WERE A PLAYER. YOU NEVER REALLY DATED ANYONE SERIOUSLY, SO I FIGURED YOU JUST DIDN'T LIKE BEING TIED DOWN...
...BUT NOW I KNOW IT WAS BECAUSE OF SHI-HYUN.

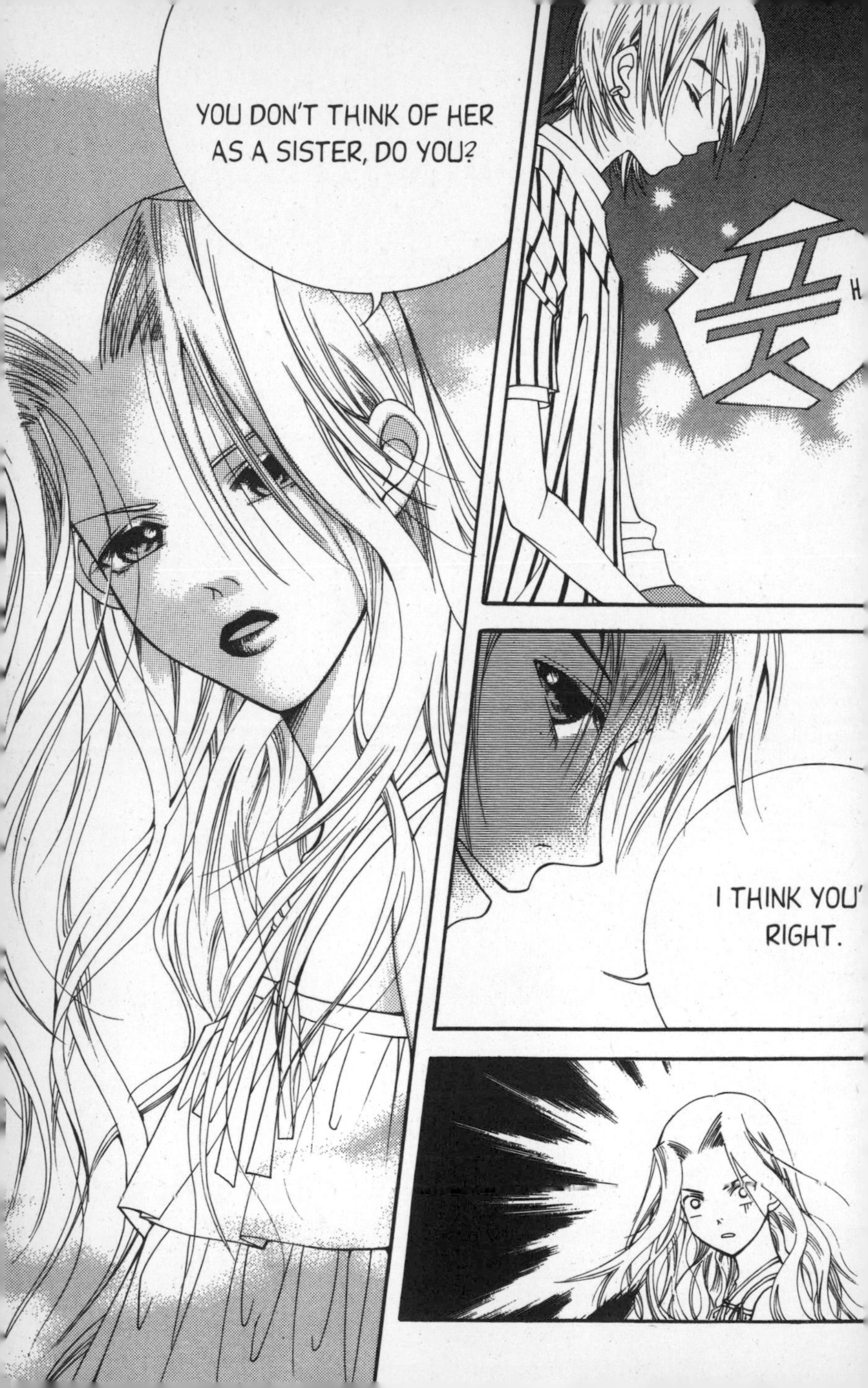
YOU DON'T THINK OF HER AS A SISTER, DO YOU?
H
I THINK YOU' RIGHT.

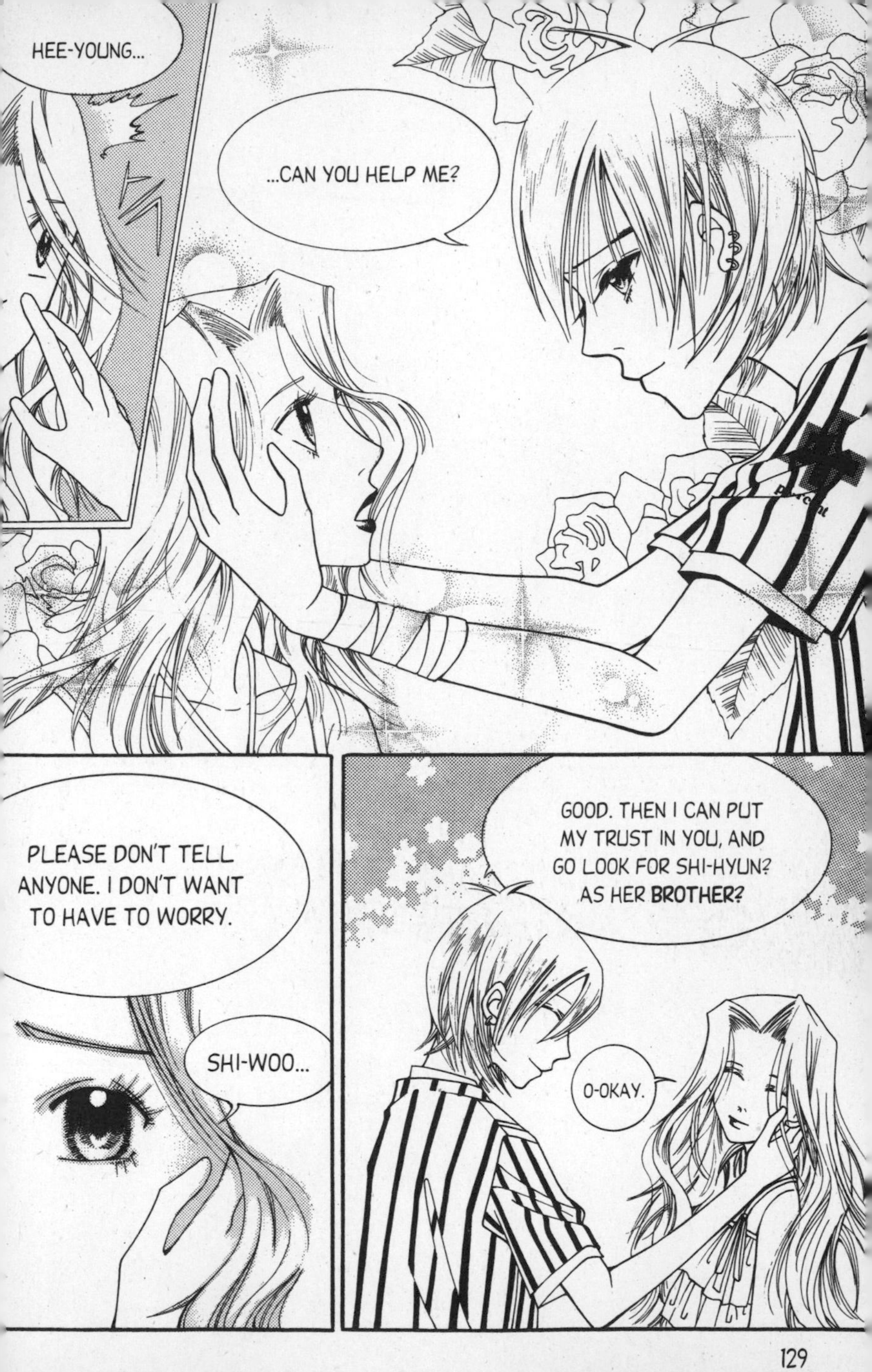
HEE-YOUNG...
...CAN YOU HELP ME?
PLEASE DON'T TELL ANYONE. I DON'T WANT TO HAVE TO WORRY.
SHI-WOO...
GOOD. THEN I CAN PUT MY TRUST IN YOU, AND GO LOOK FOR SHI-HYUN? AS HER **BROTHER**?
O-OKAY.

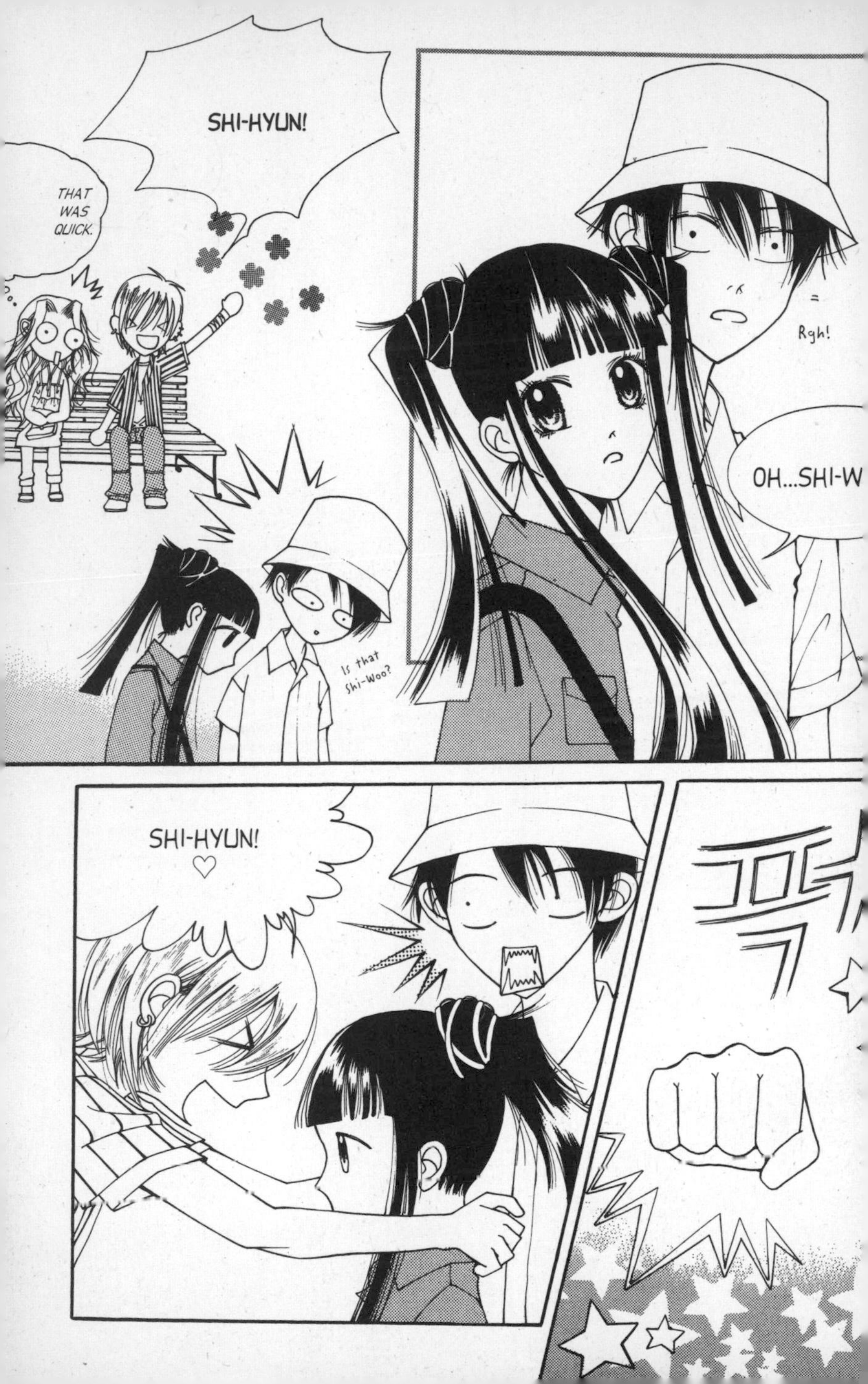
SHI-HYUN!
THAT WAS QUICK.
Is that Shi-Woo?
Rgh!
OH...SHI-W
SHI-HYUN! ♡

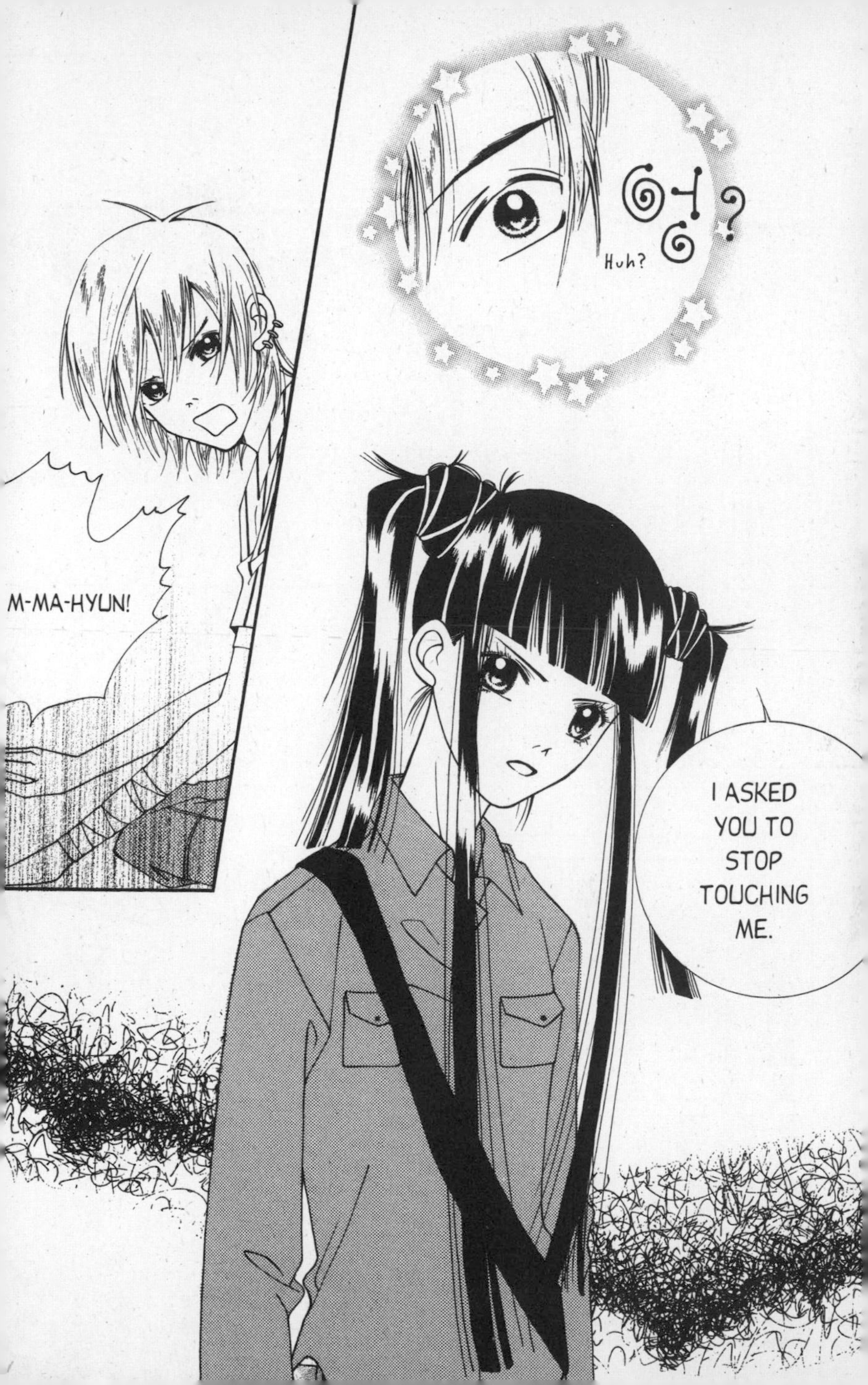
M-MA-HYUN!
엉?
Huh?
I ASKED YOU TO STOP TOUCHING ME.

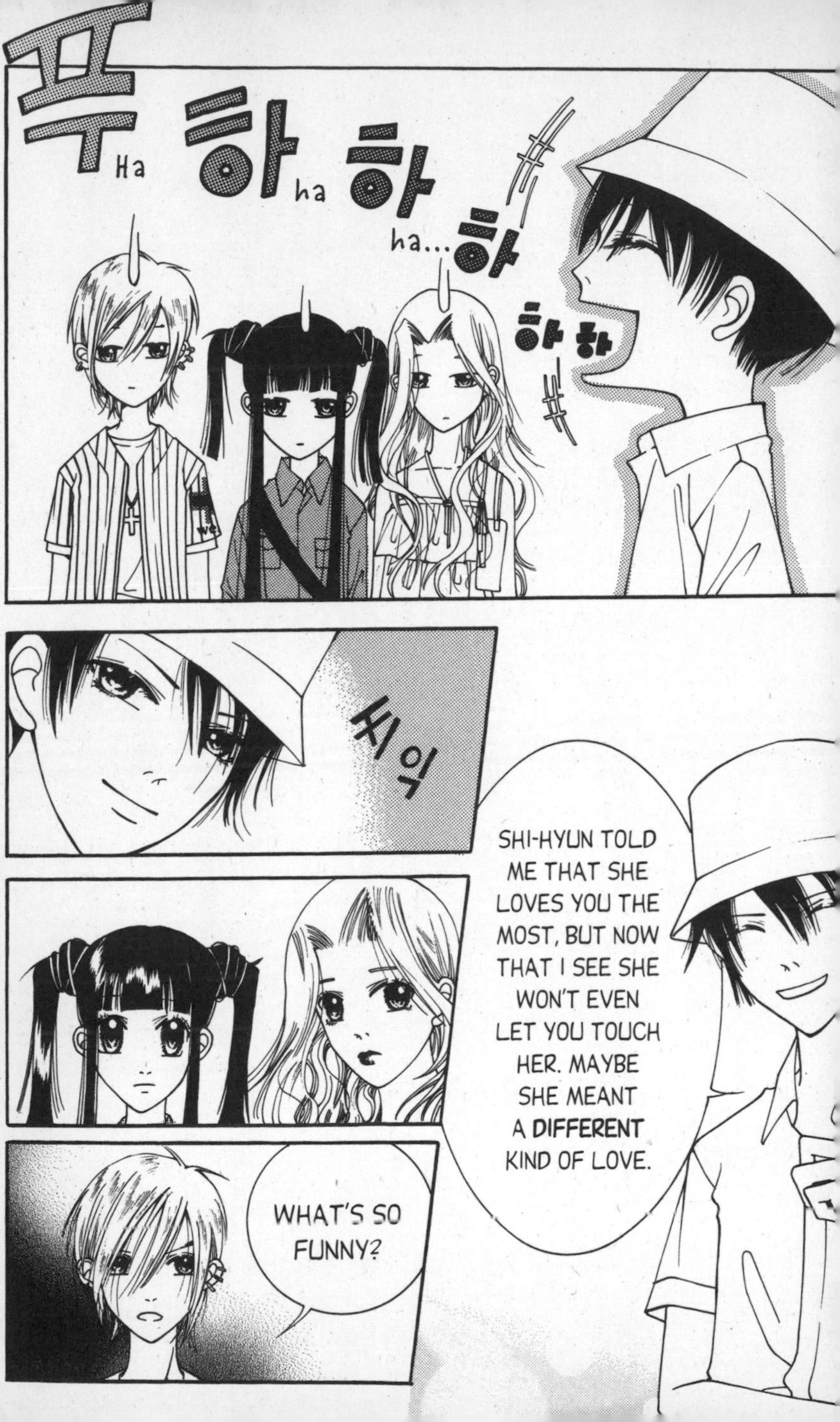
푸
Ha
하
ha
하
ha...
하
하 하
WHAT'S SO FUNNY?
SHI-HYUN TOLD ME THAT SHE LOVES YOU THE MOST, BUT NOW THAT I SEE SHE WON'T EVEN LET YOU TOUCH HER. MAYBE SHE MEANT A **DIFFERENT** KIND OF LOVE.

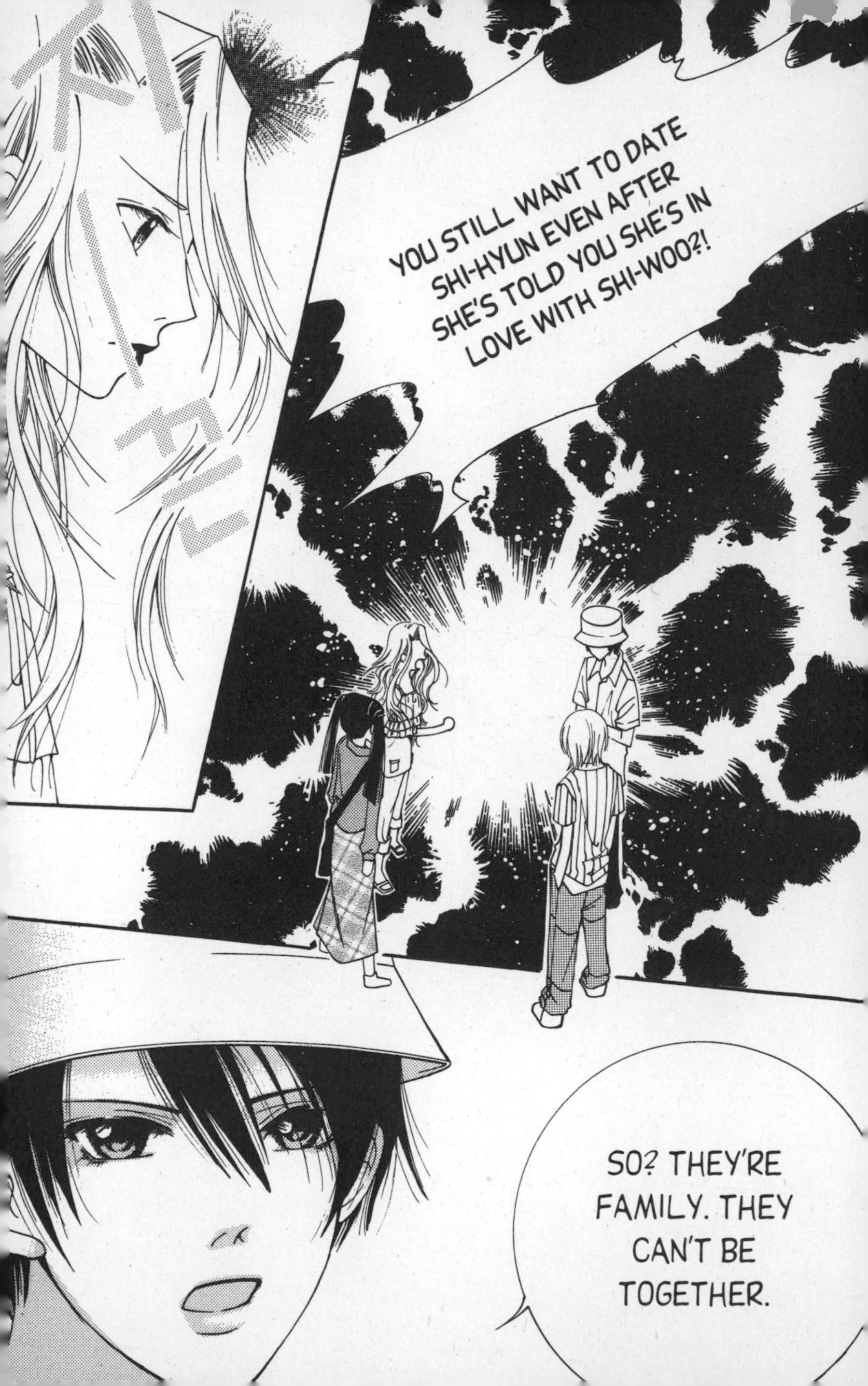
YOU STILL WANT TO DATE SHI-HYUN EVEN AFTER SHE'S TOLD YOU SHE'S IN LOVE WITH SHI-WOO?!
SO? THEY'RE FAMILY. THEY CAN'T BE TOGETHER.

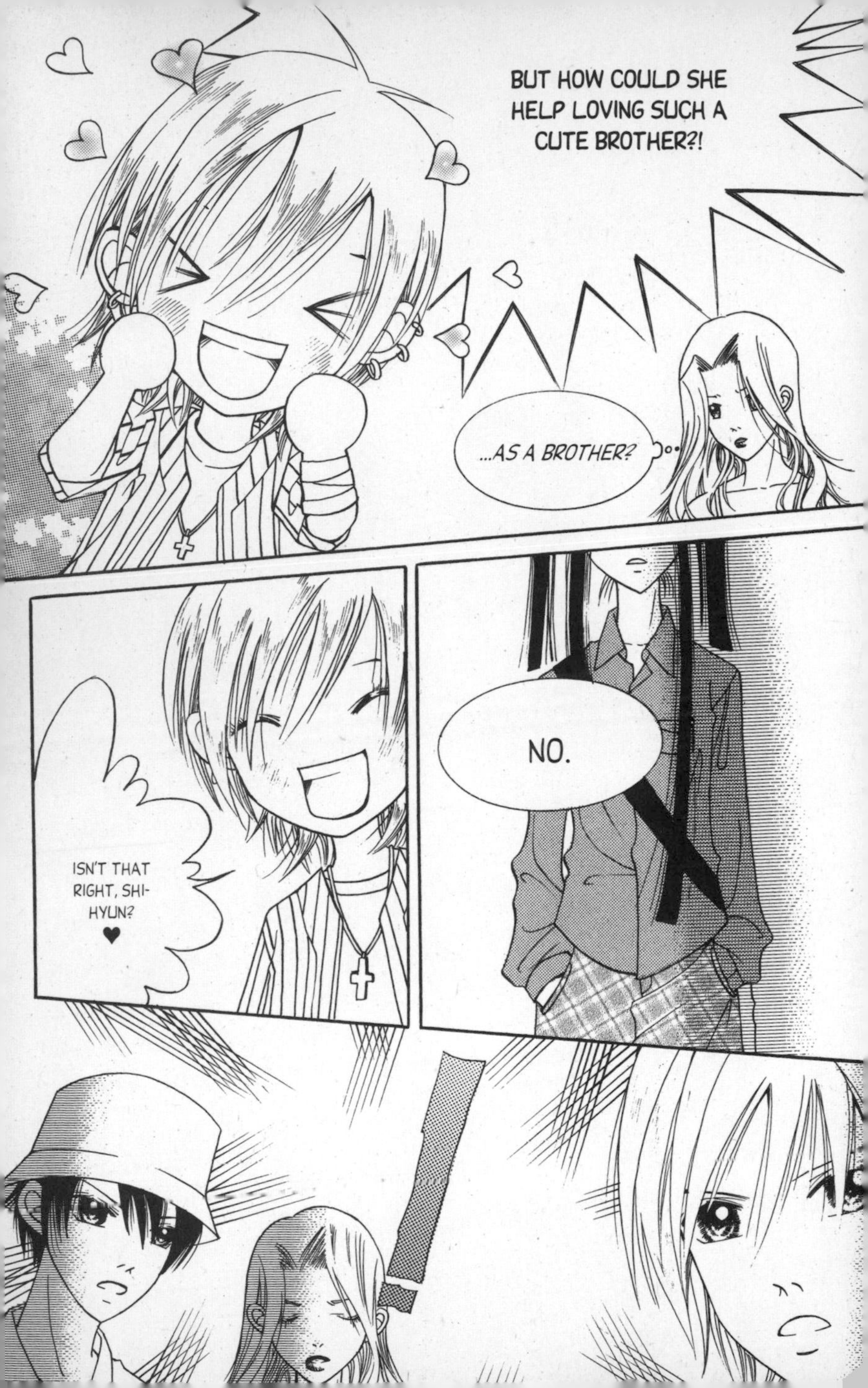
BUT HOW COULD SHE HELP LOVING SUCH A CUTE BROTHER?!
...AS A BROTHER?
ISN'T THAT RIGHT, SHI-HYUN? ♥
NO.

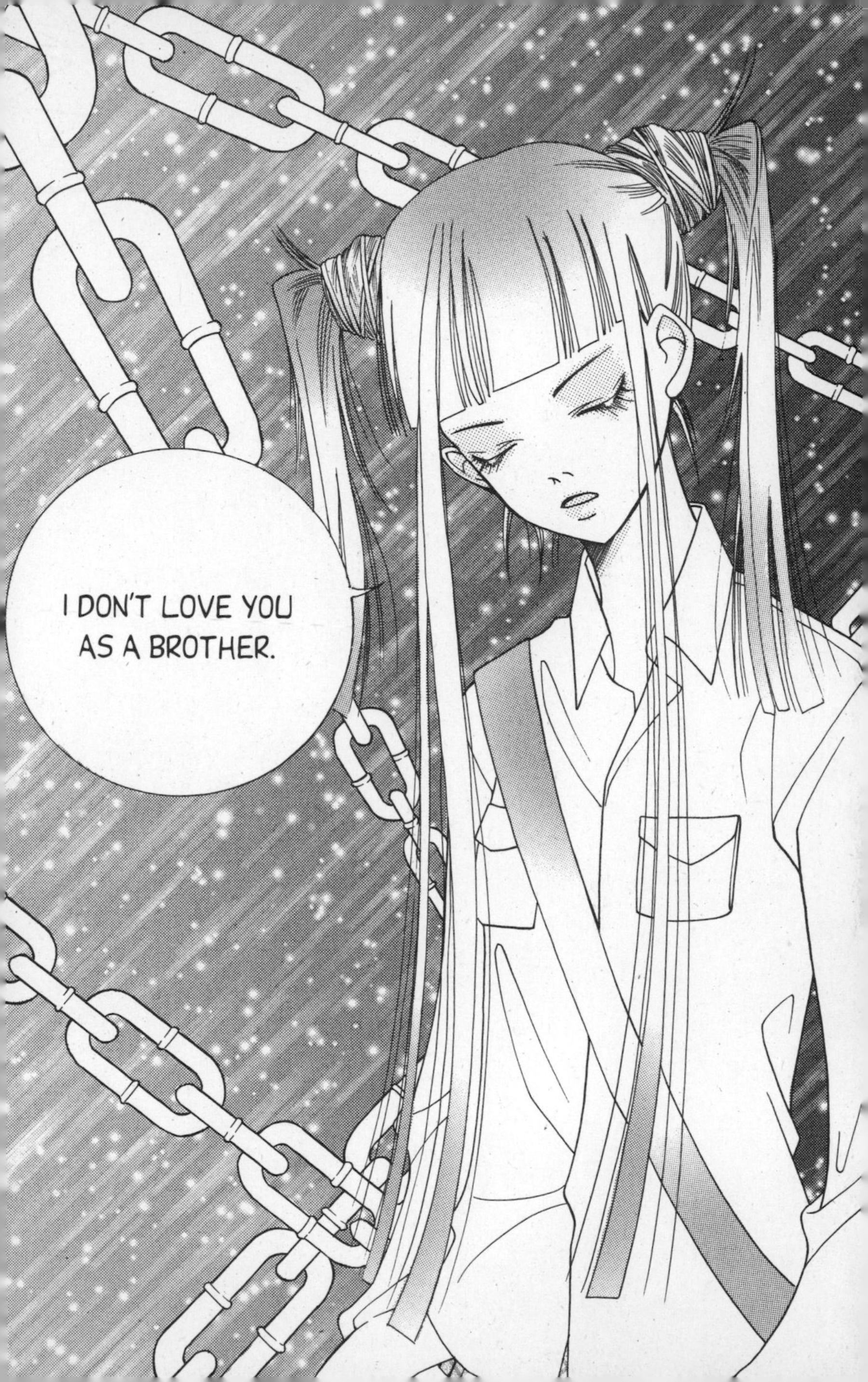
I DON'T LOVE YOU AS A BROTHER.

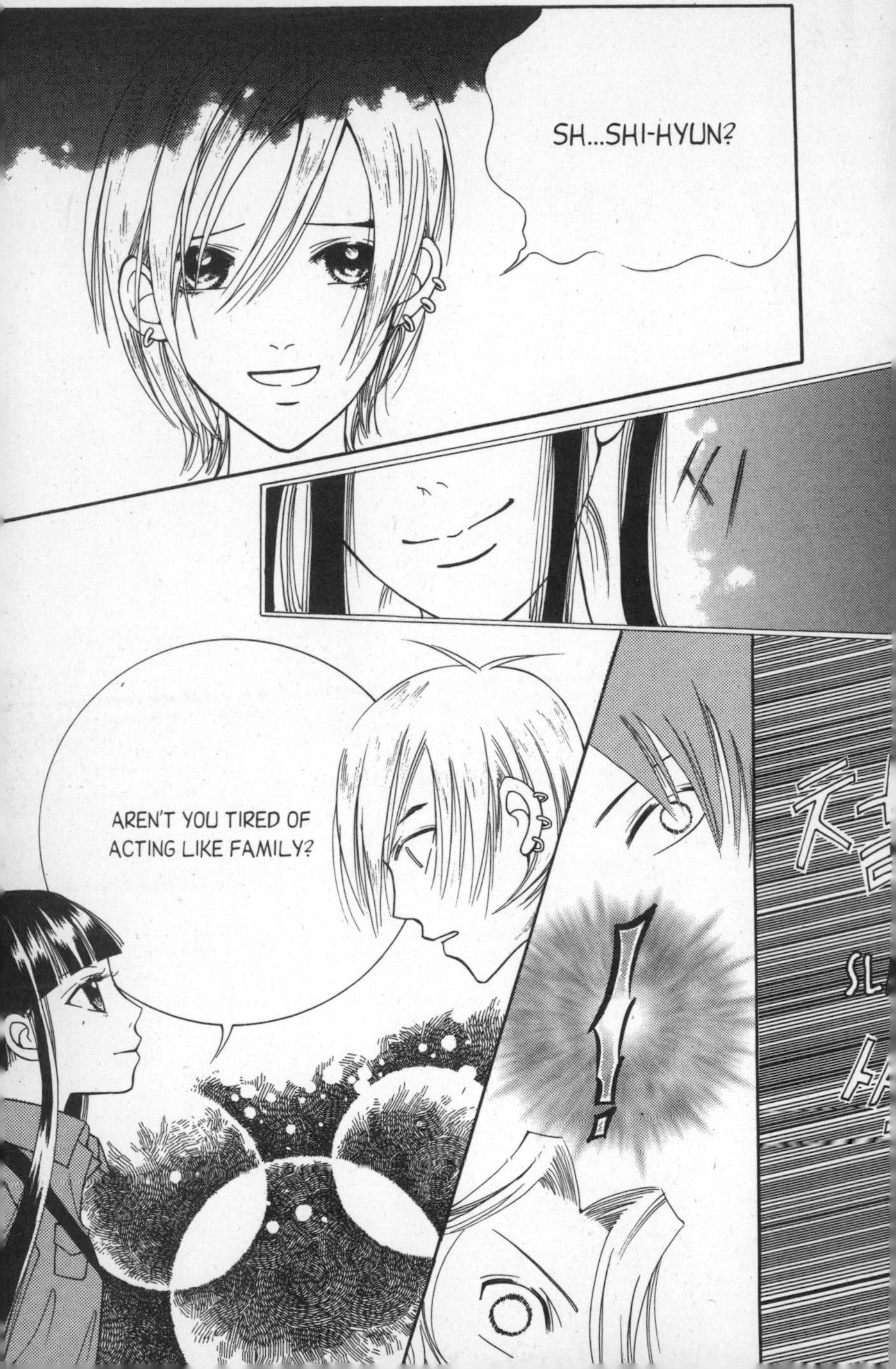
SH...SHI-HYUN?
AREN'T YOU TIRED OF ACTING LIKE FAMILY?

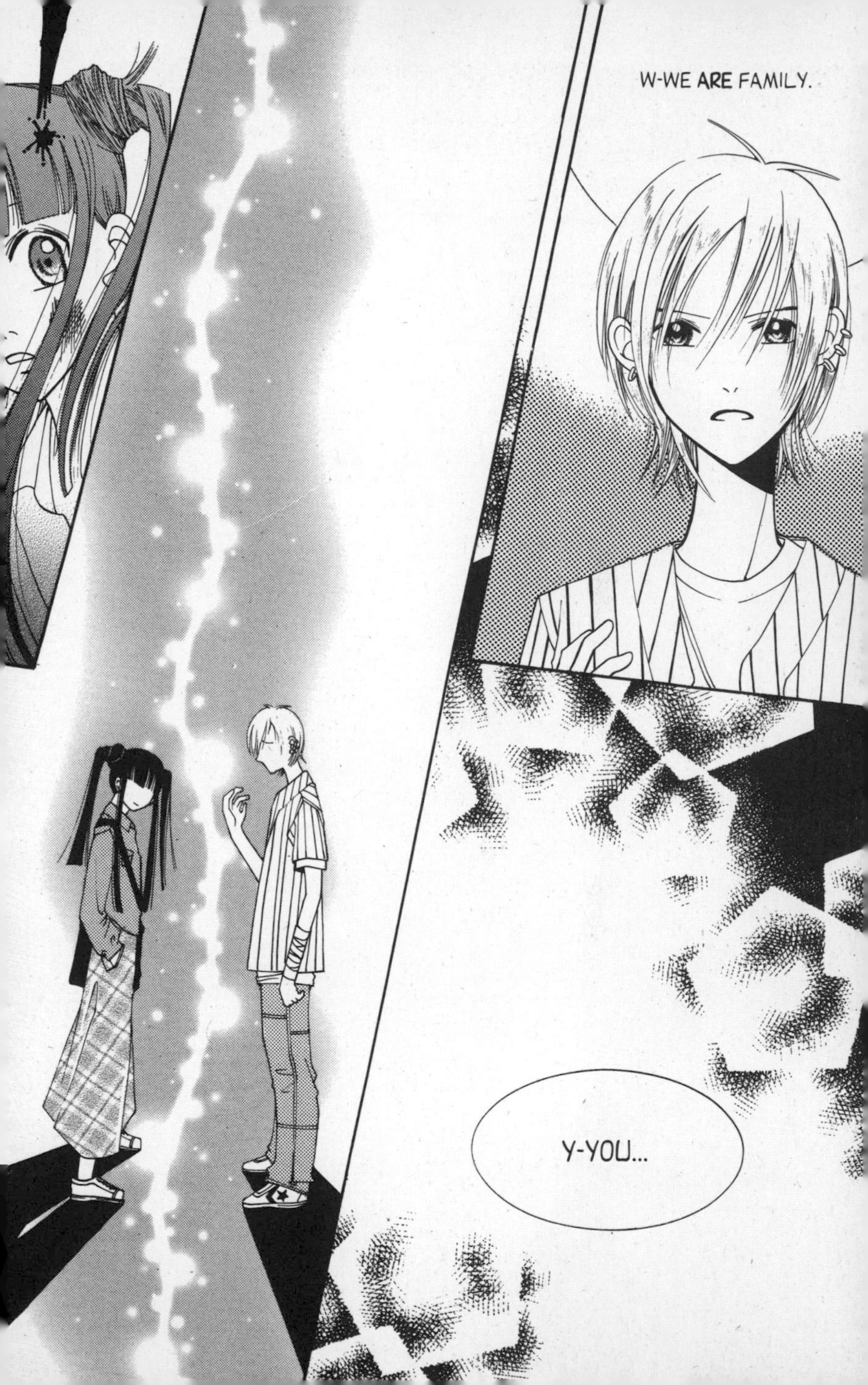
W-WE ARE FAMILY.
Y-YOU...

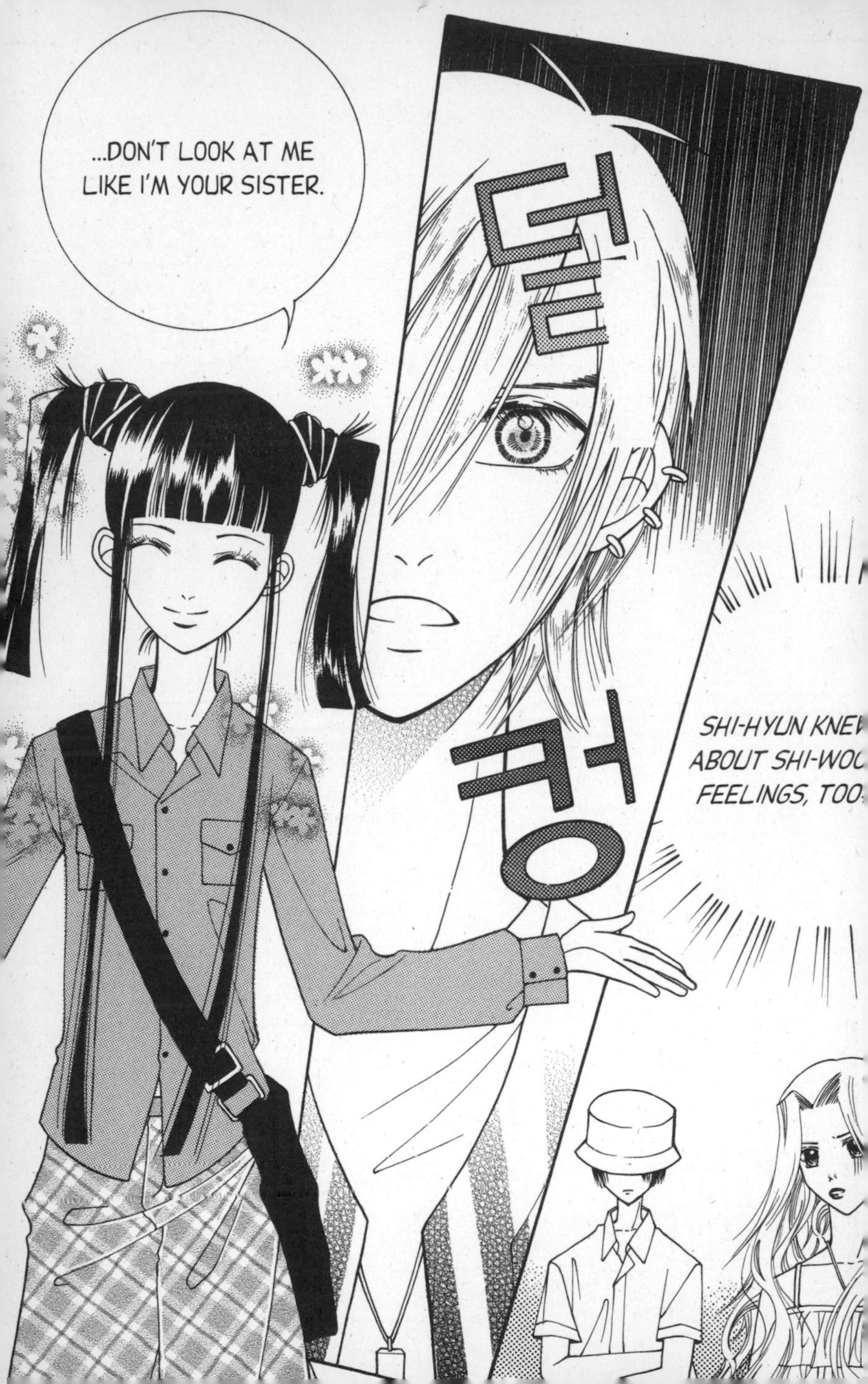
...DON'T LOOK AT ME LIKE I'M YOUR SISTER.
덜컹
SHI-HYUN KNEW ABOUT SHI-WOO FEELINGS, TOO

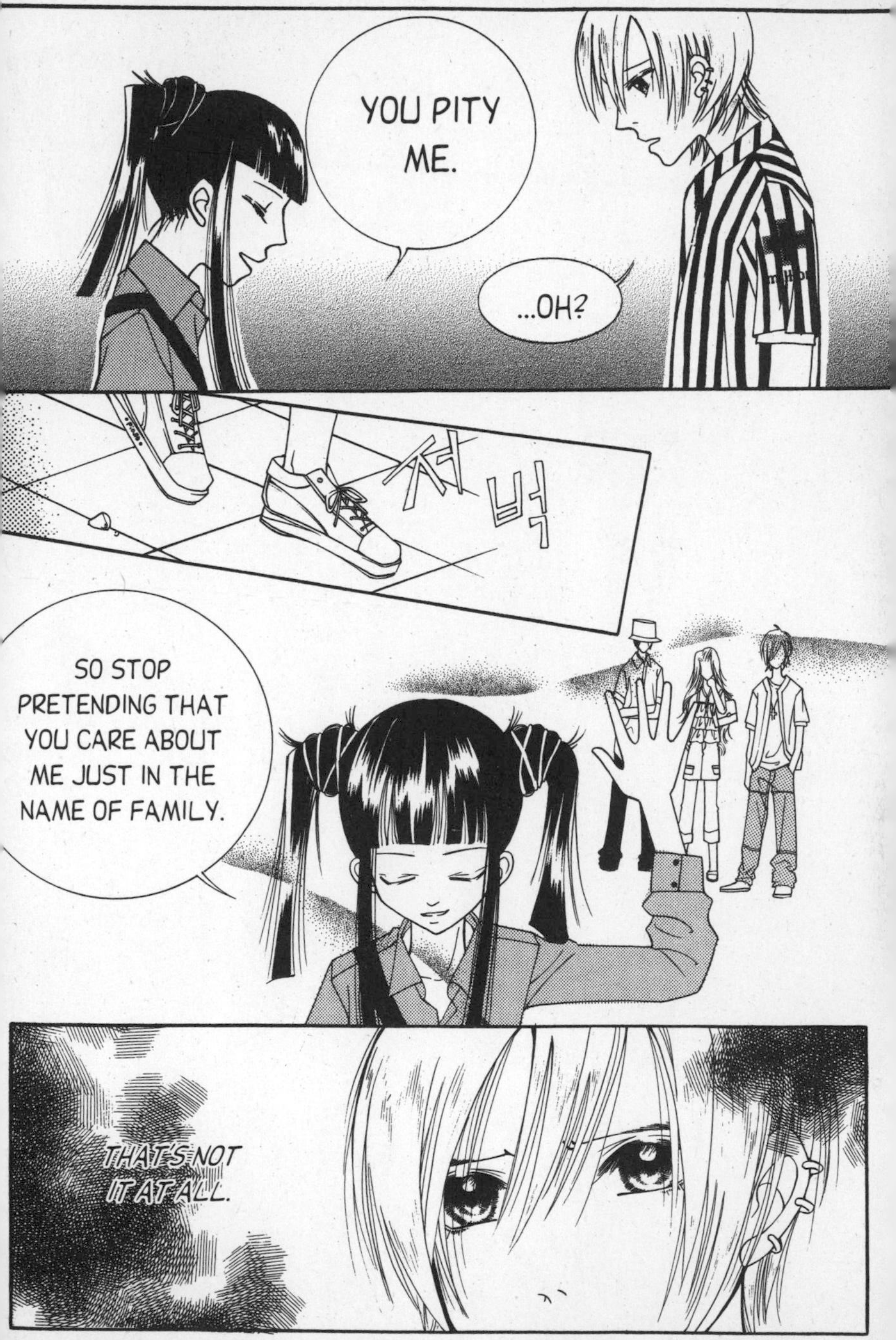
YOU PITY ME.
...OH?
서벅
SO STOP PRETENDING THAT YOU CARE ABOUT ME JUST IN THE NAME OF FAMILY.
THAT'S NOT IT AT ALL.

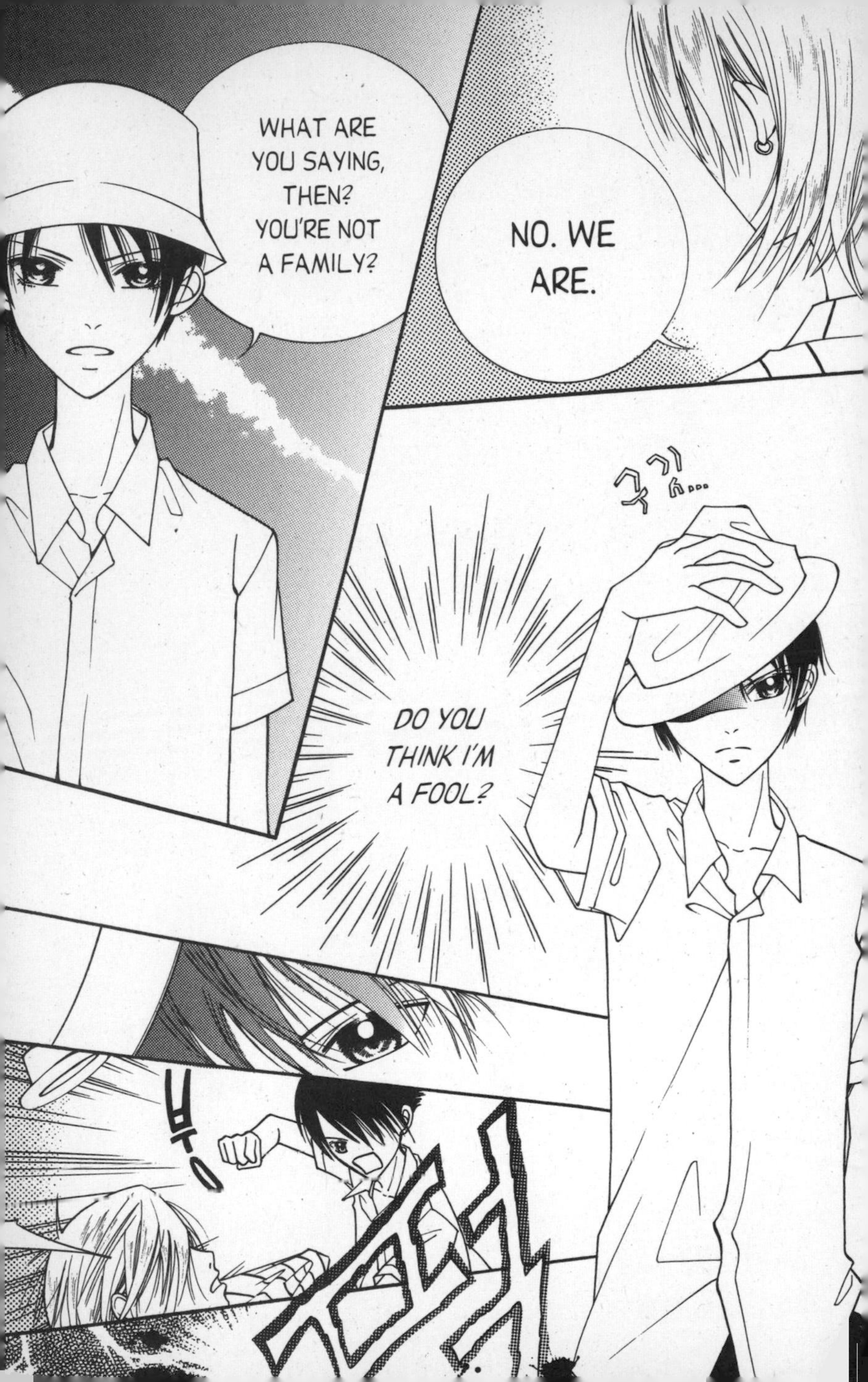
WHAT ARE YOU SAYING, THEN? YOU'RE NOT A FAMILY?
NO. WE ARE.
DO YOU THINK I'M A FOOL?

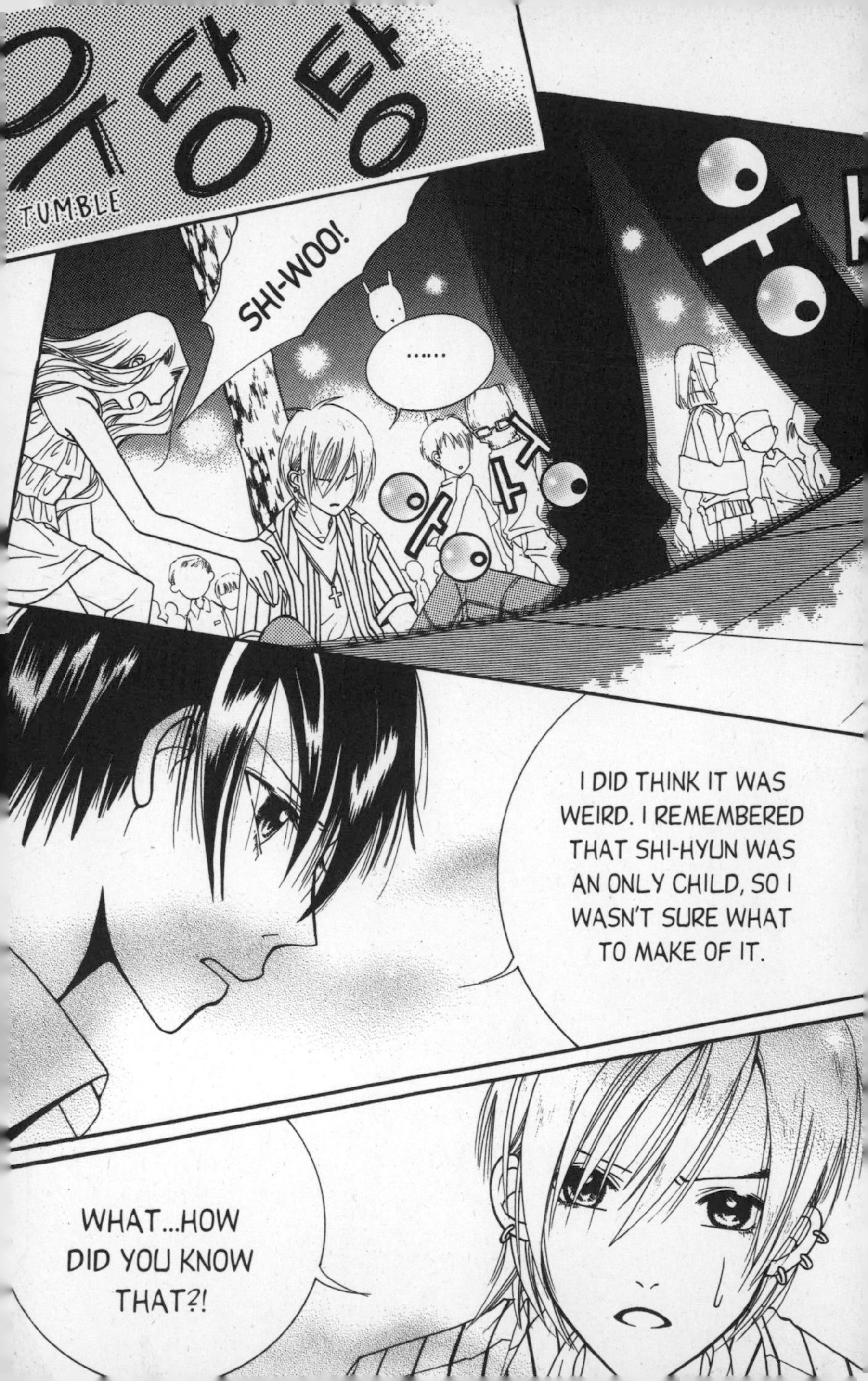
TUMBLE
SHI-WOO!
......
I DID THINK IT WAS WEIRD. I REMEMBERED THAT SHI-HYUN WAS AN ONLY CHILD, SO I WASN'T SURE WHAT TO MAKE OF IT.
WHAT...HOW DID YOU KNOW THAT?!

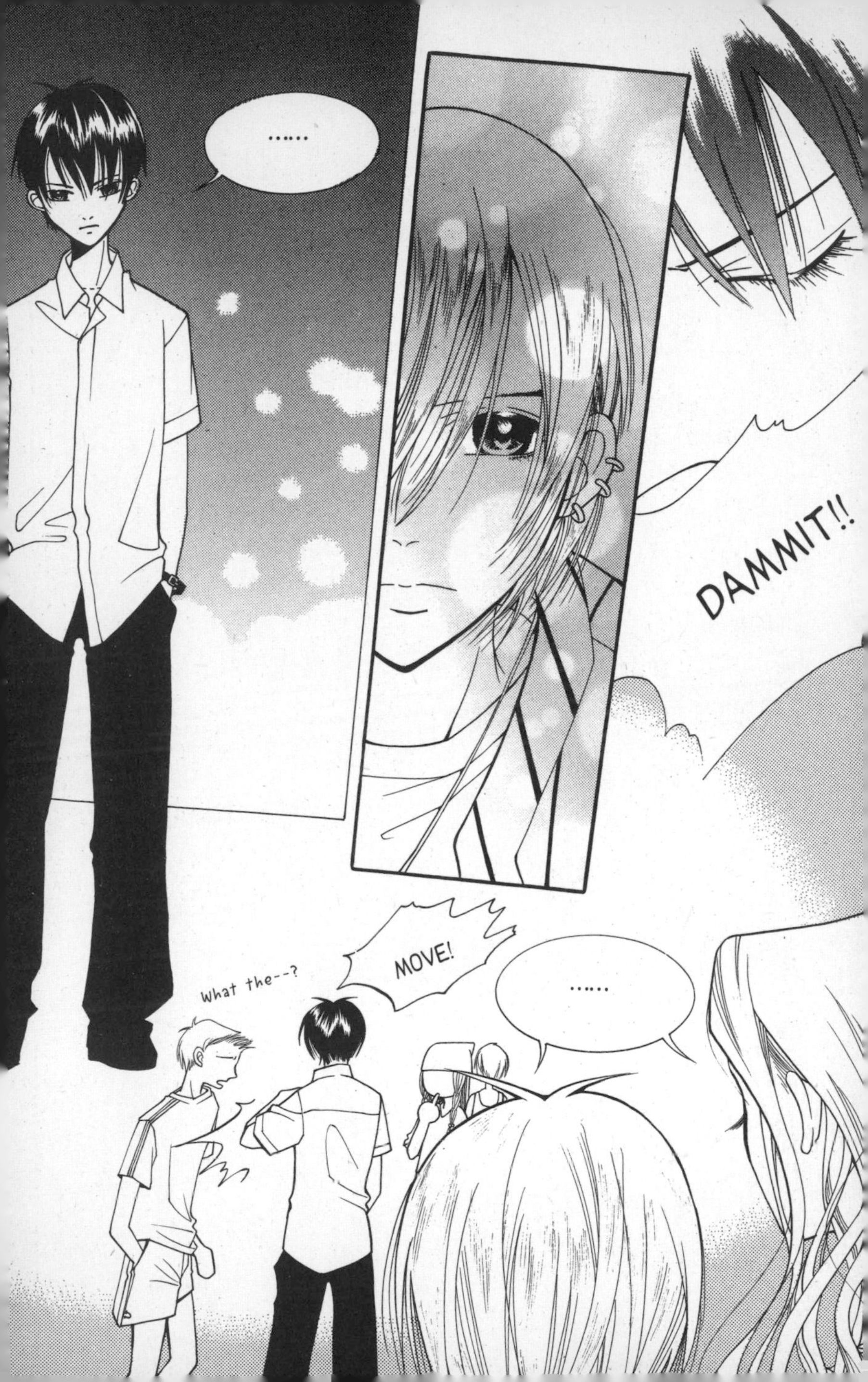
......
DAMMIT!!
What the--?
MOVE!
......

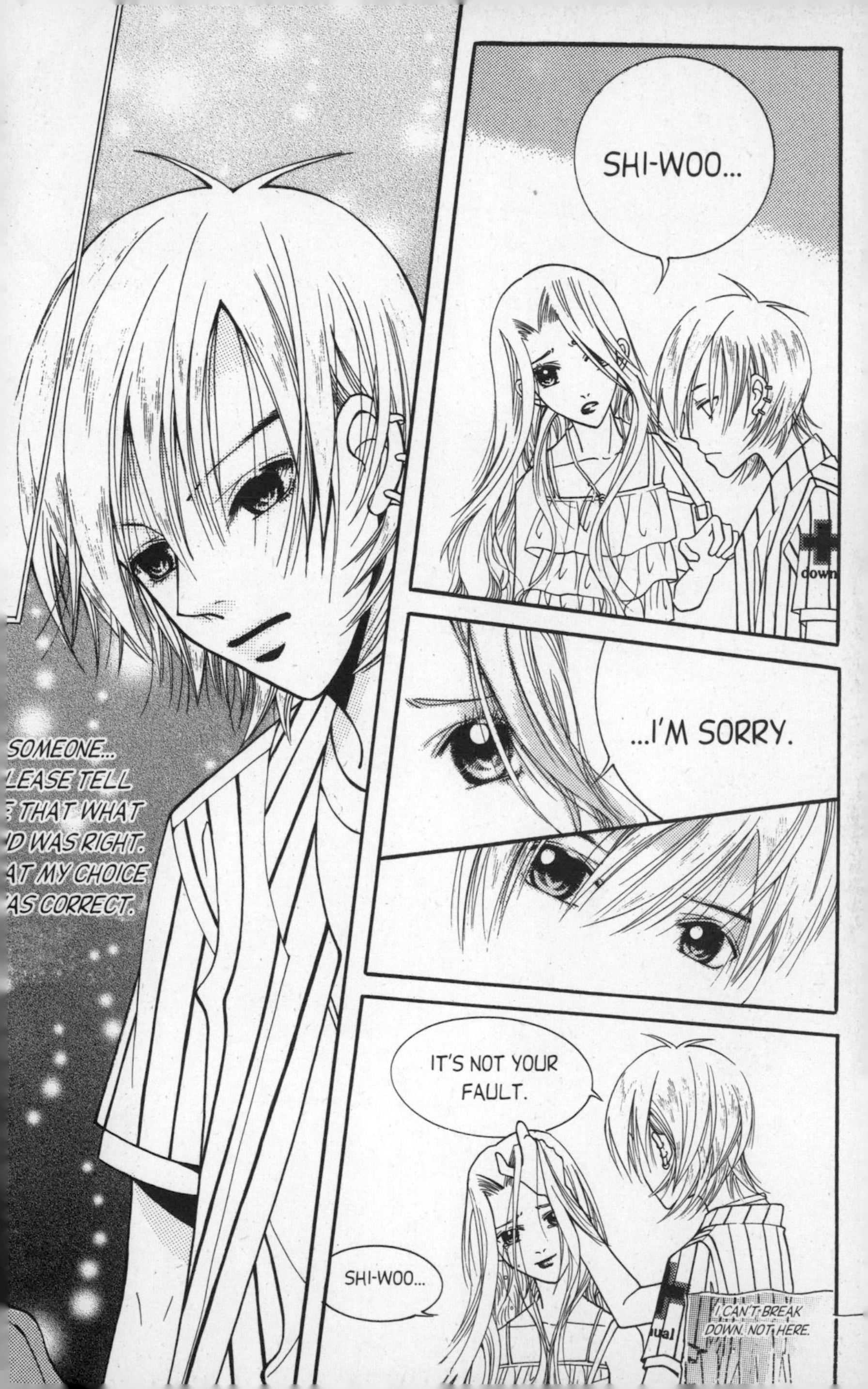
SOMEONE...
LEASE TELL
E THAT WHAT
D WAS RIGHT.
AT MY CHOICE
AS CORRECT.
SHI-WOO...
...I'M SORRY.
IT'S NOT YOUR FAULT.
SHI-WOO...
I CAN'T BREAK DOWN. NOT HERE.

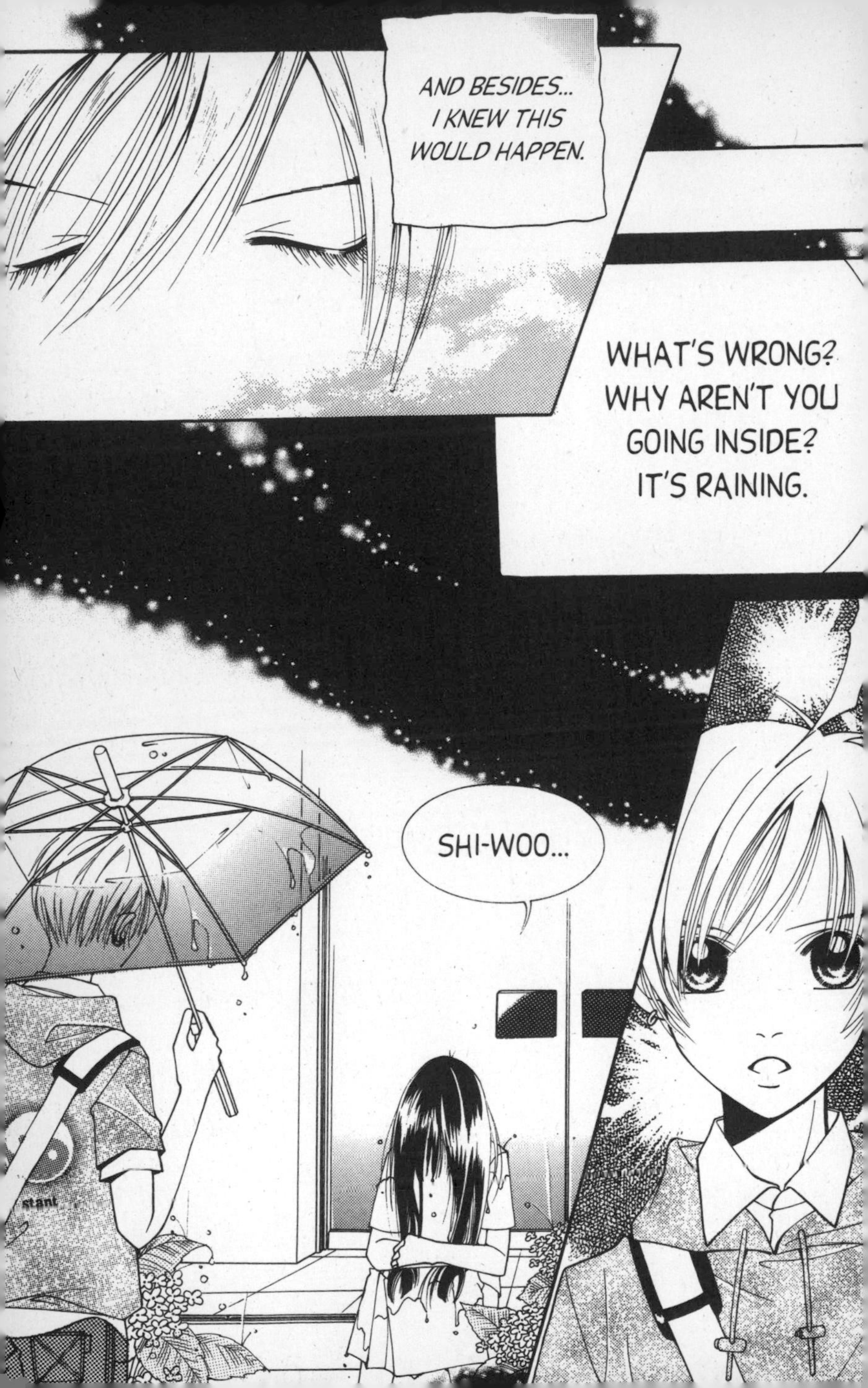
AND BESIDES... I KNEW THIS WOULD HAPPEN.
WHAT'S WRONG? WHY AREN'T YOU GOING INSIDE? IT'S RAINING.
SHI-WOO...

NE RAINY DAY, THREE YEARS AGO...
YOU HATE ME BECAUSE I BRING BAD LUCK, RIGHT?
...I HAD TO TAKE HER IN AS MY SISTER.

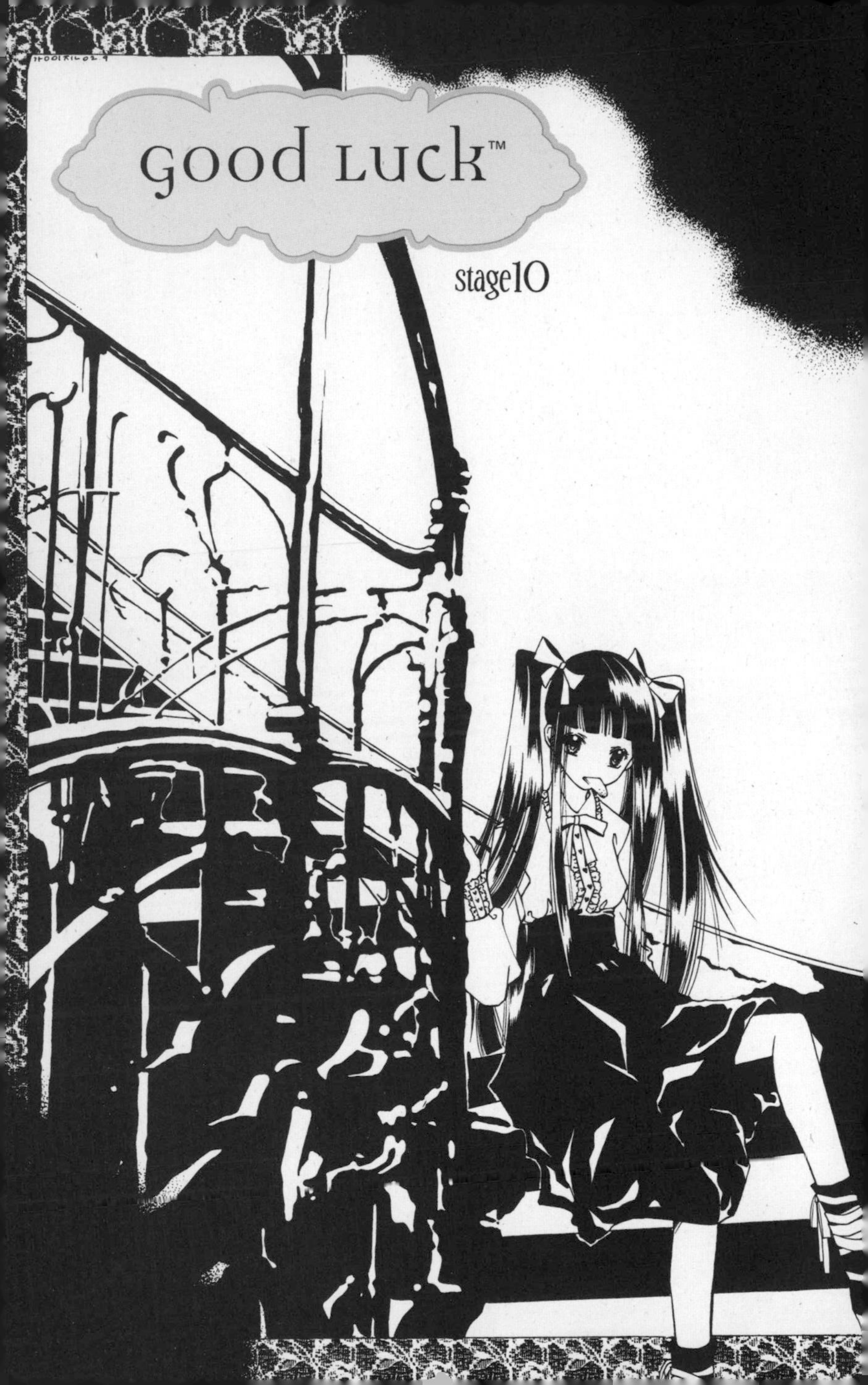
good luck™
stage10

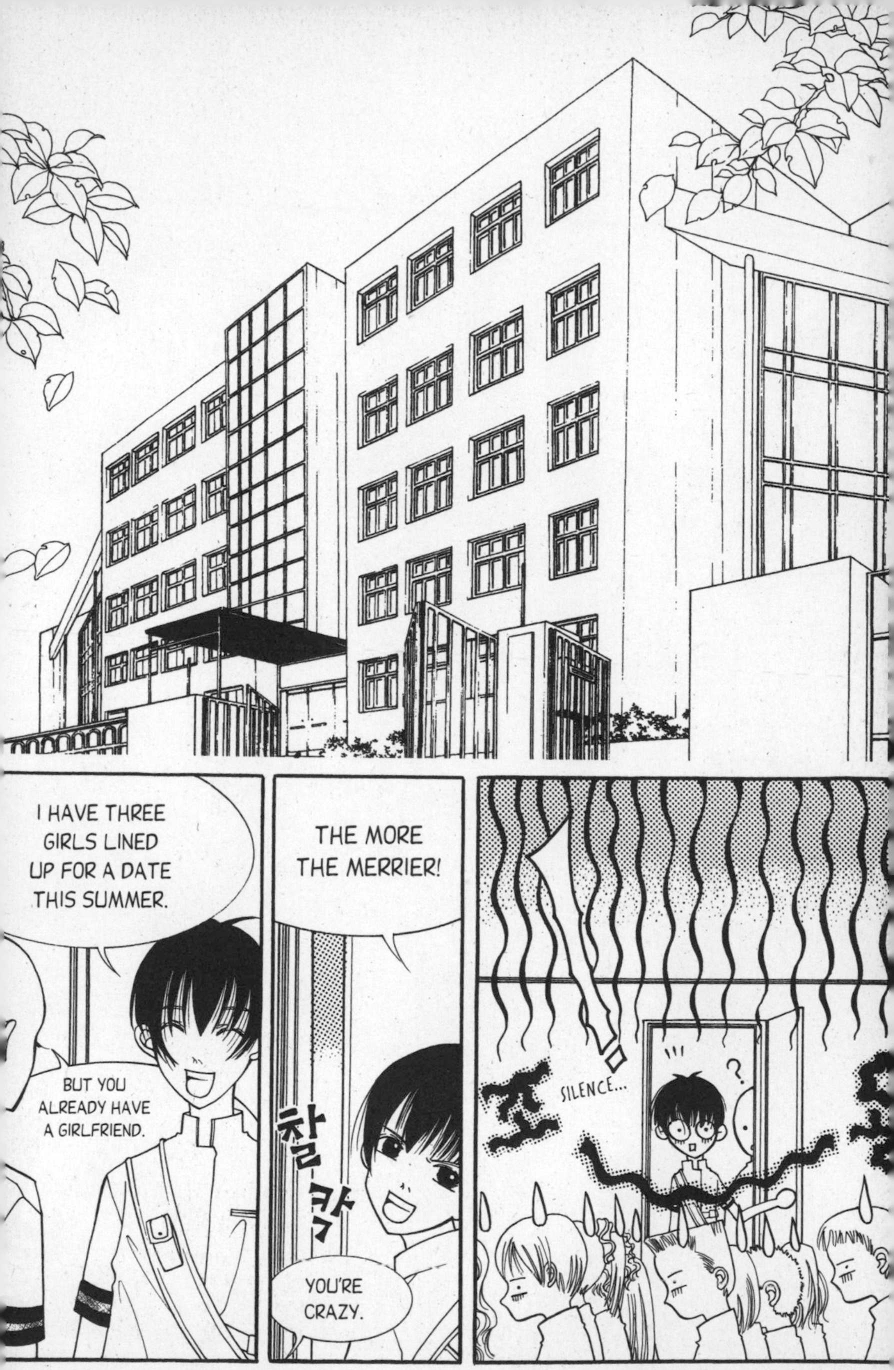
I HAVE THREE GIRLS LINED UP FOR A DATE THIS SUMMER.
BUT YOU ALREADY HAVE A GIRLFRIEND.
THE MORE THE MERRIER!
찰칵
YOU'RE CRAZY.
조
SILENCE...

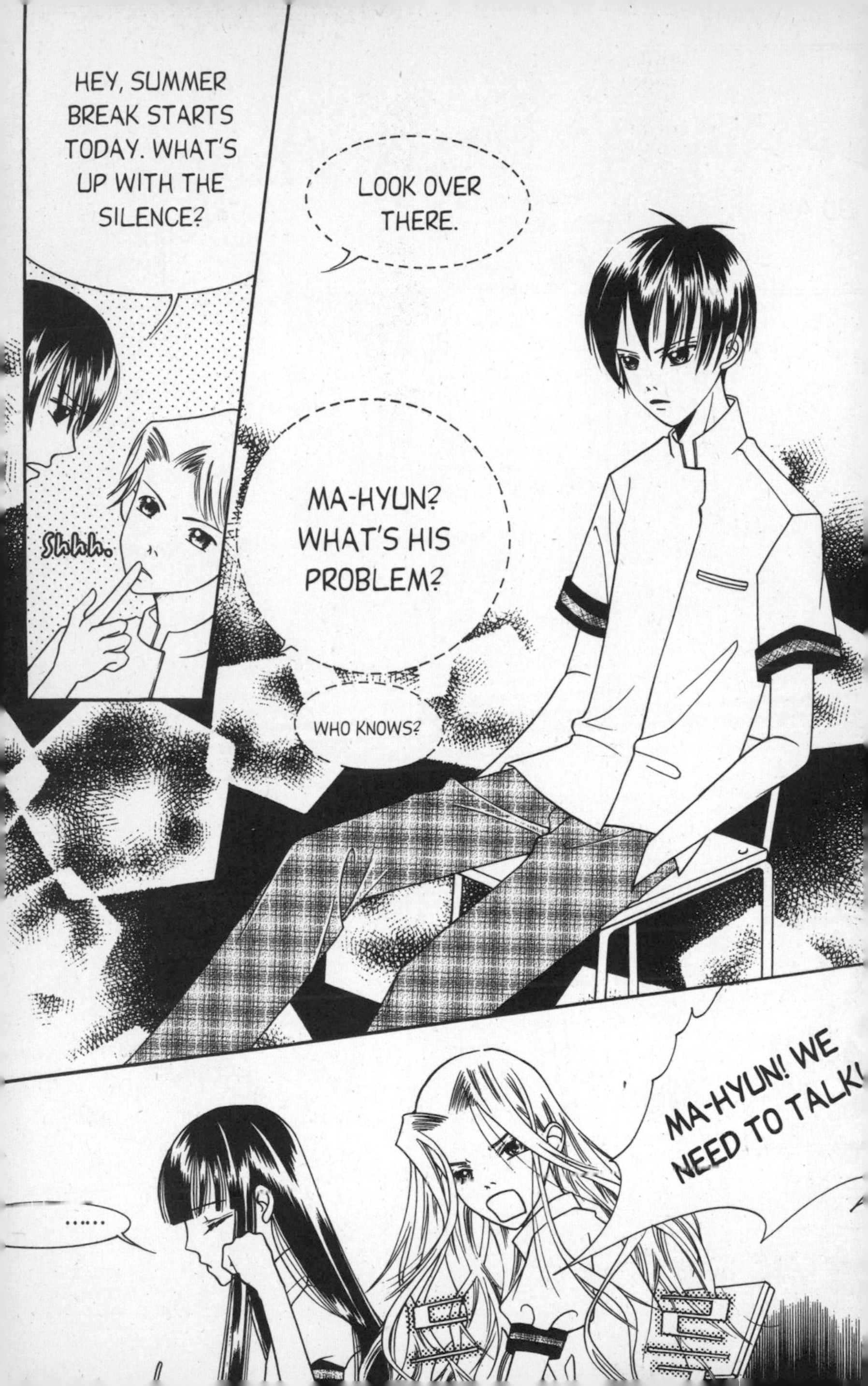
HEY, SUMMER BREAK STARTS TODAY. WHAT'S UP WITH THE SILENCE?
Shhh.
LOOK OVER THERE.
MA-HYUN? WHAT'S HIS PROBLEM?
WHO KNOWS?
......
MA-HYUN! WE NEED TO TALK!

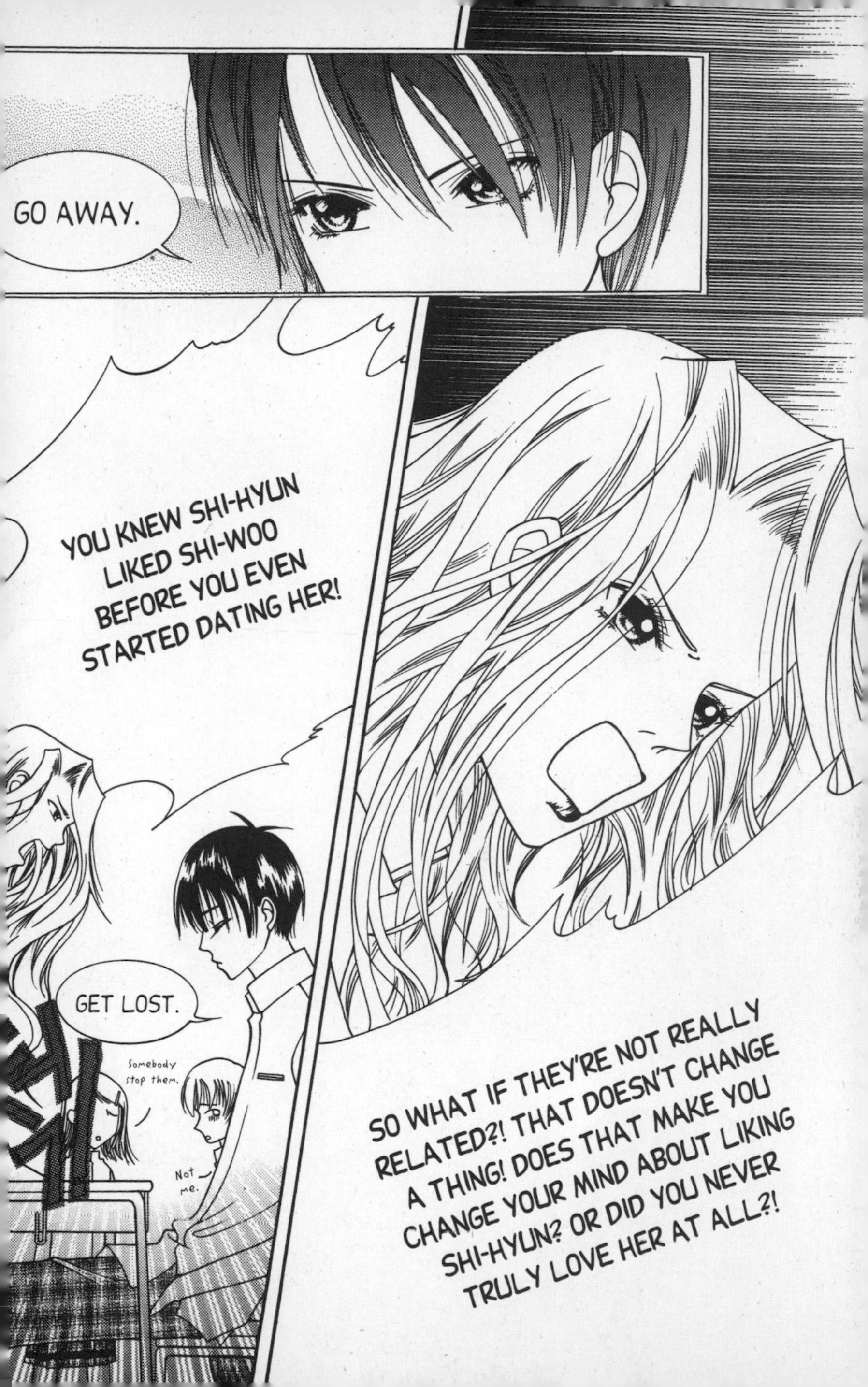
GO AWAY.
YOU KNEW SHI-HYUN LIKED SHI-WOO BEFORE YOU EVEN STARTED DATING HER!
GET LOST.
Somebody stop them.
Not me.
SO WHAT IF THEY'RE NOT REALLY RELATED?! THAT DOESN'T CHANGE A THING! DOES THAT MAKE YOU CHANGE YOUR MIND ABOUT LIKING SHI-HYUN? OR DID YOU NEVER TRULY LOVE HER AT ALL?!

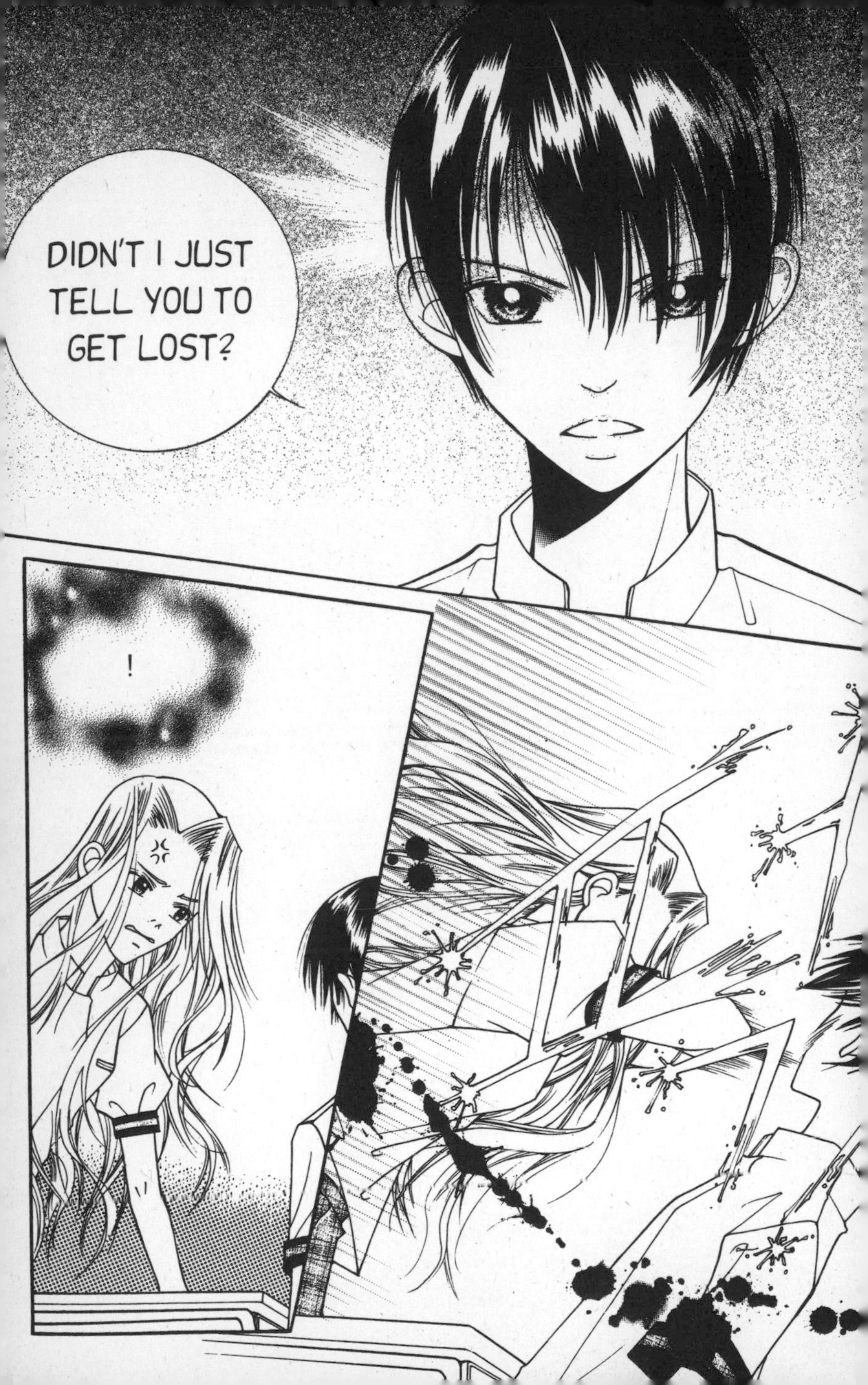
DIDN'T I JUST TELL YOU TO GET LOST?
!

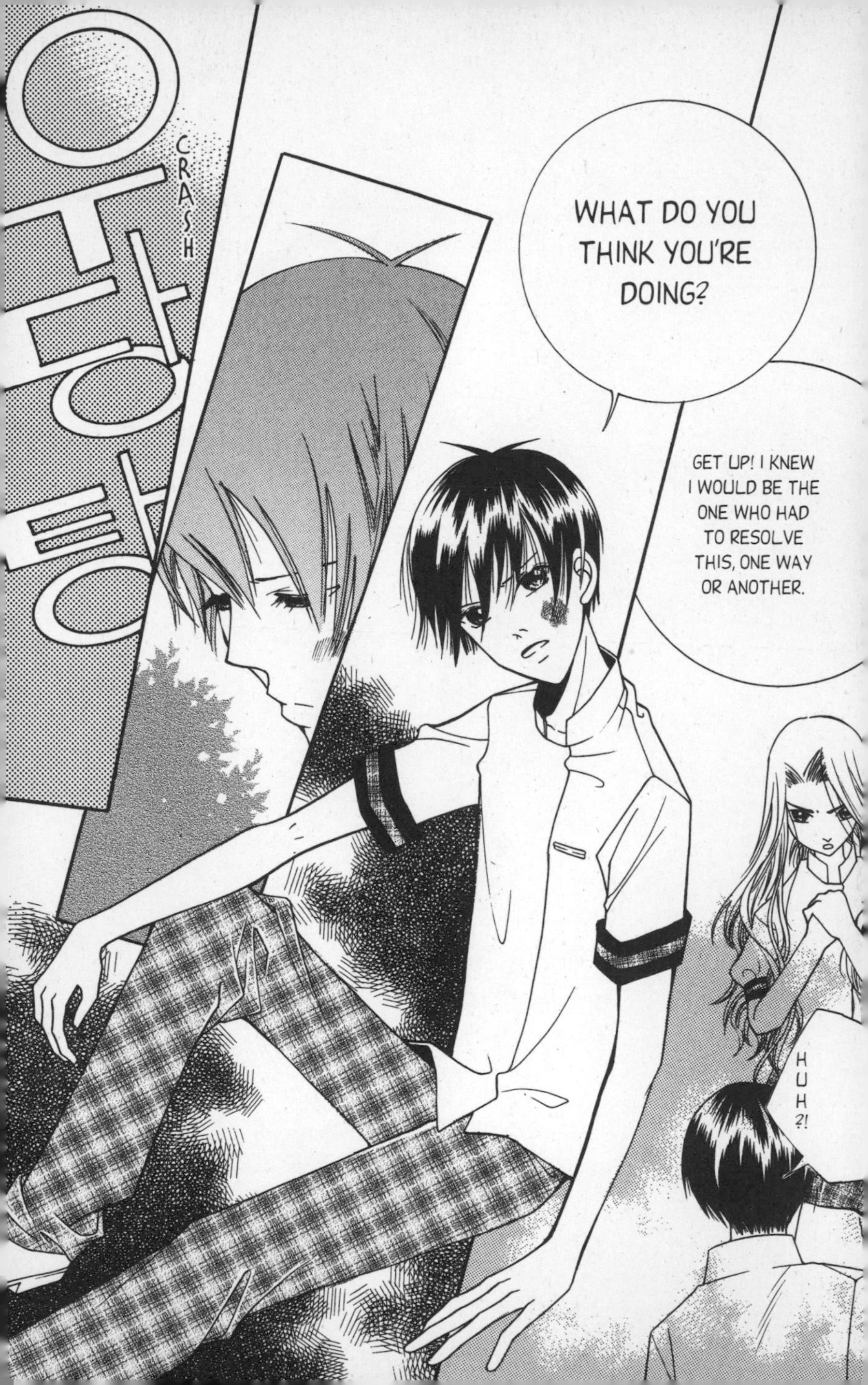
CRASH
WHAT DO YOU THINK YOU'RE DOING?
GET UP! I KNEW I WOULD BE THE ONE WHO HAD TO RESOLVE THIS, ONE WAY OR ANOTHER.
HUH?!

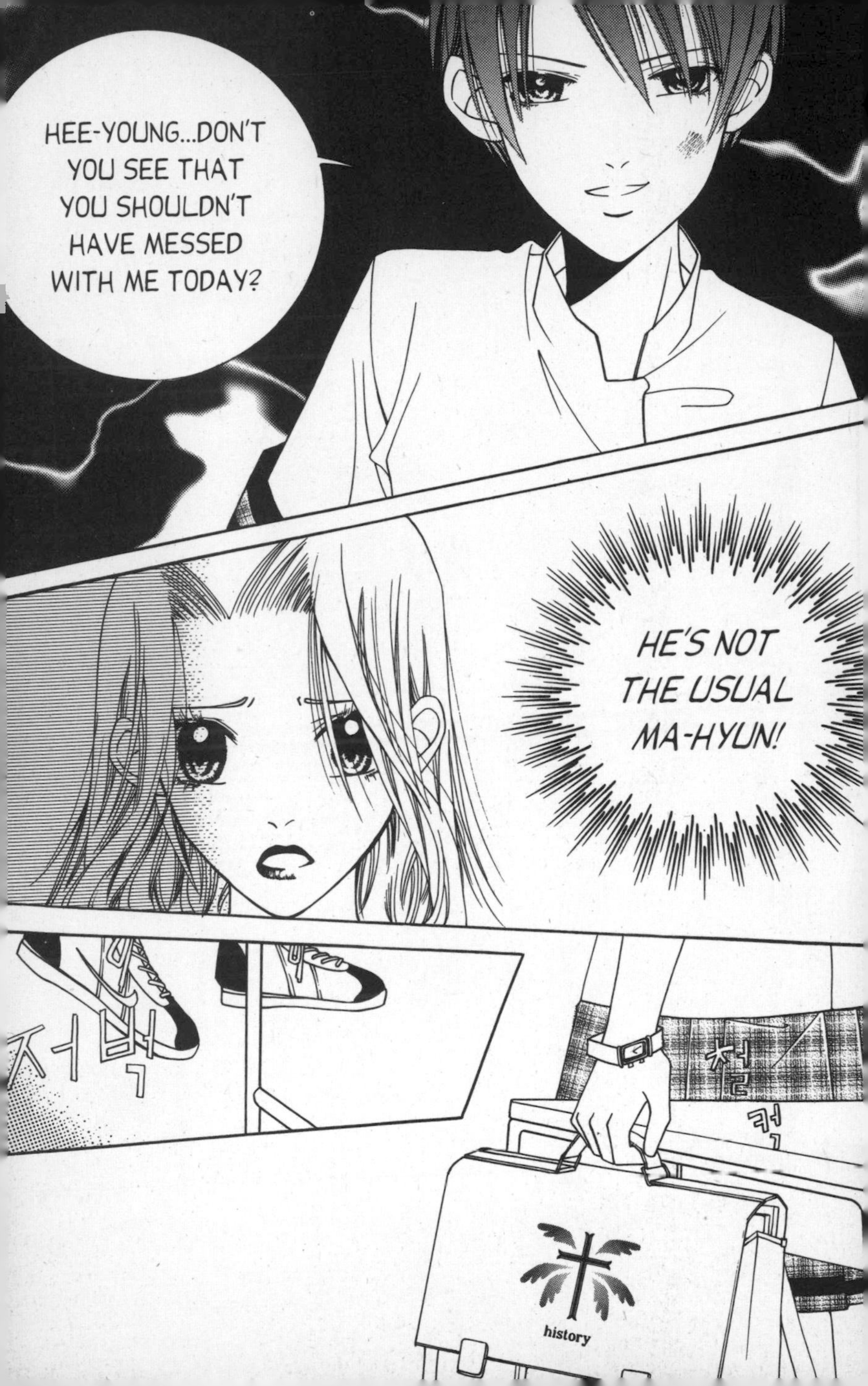
HEE-YOUNG...DON'T YOU SEE THAT YOU SHOULDN'T HAVE MESSED WITH ME TODAY?
HE'S NOT THE USUAL MA-HYUN!
저벅
철컥
history

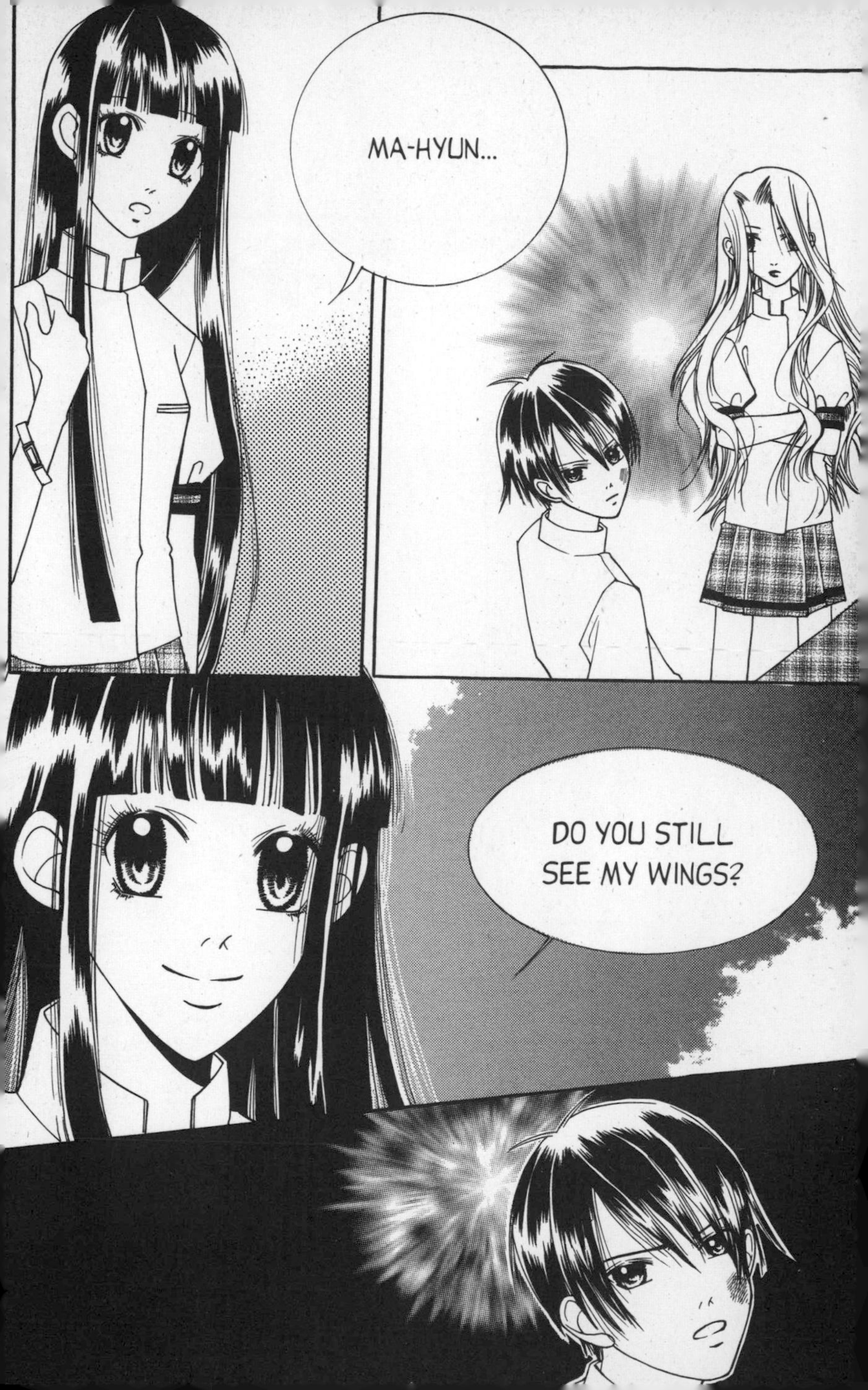
MA-HYUN...
DO YOU STILL SEE MY WINGS?

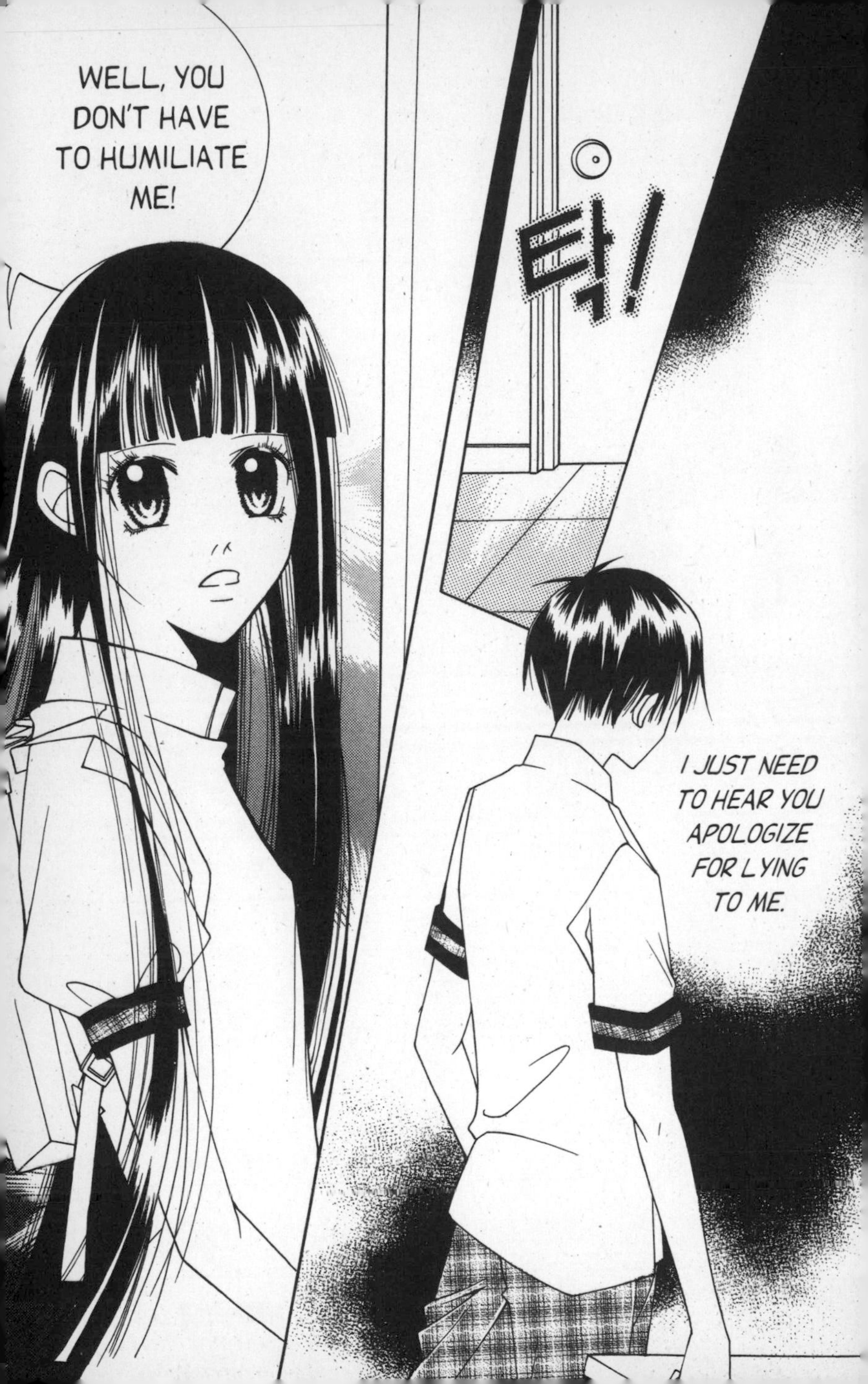
WELL, YOU DON'T HAVE TO HUMILIATE ME!
탁!
I JUST NEED TO HEAR YOU APOLOGIZE FOR LYING TO ME.

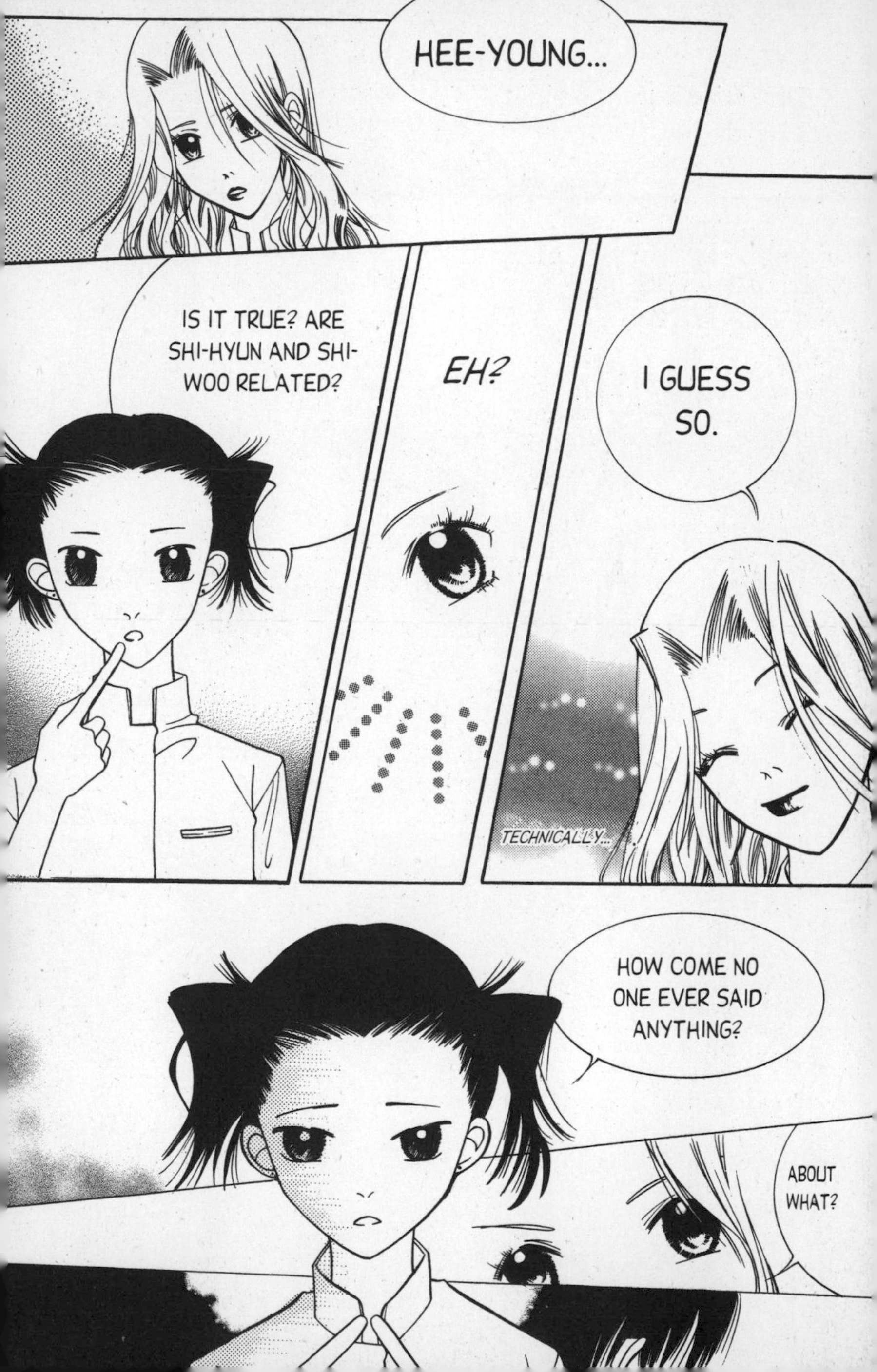
HEE-YOUNG...
IS IT TRUE? ARE SHI-HYUN AND SHI-WOO RELATED?
EH?
I GUESS SO.
TECHNICALLY...
HOW COME NO ONE EVER SAID ANYTHING?
ABOUT WHAT?

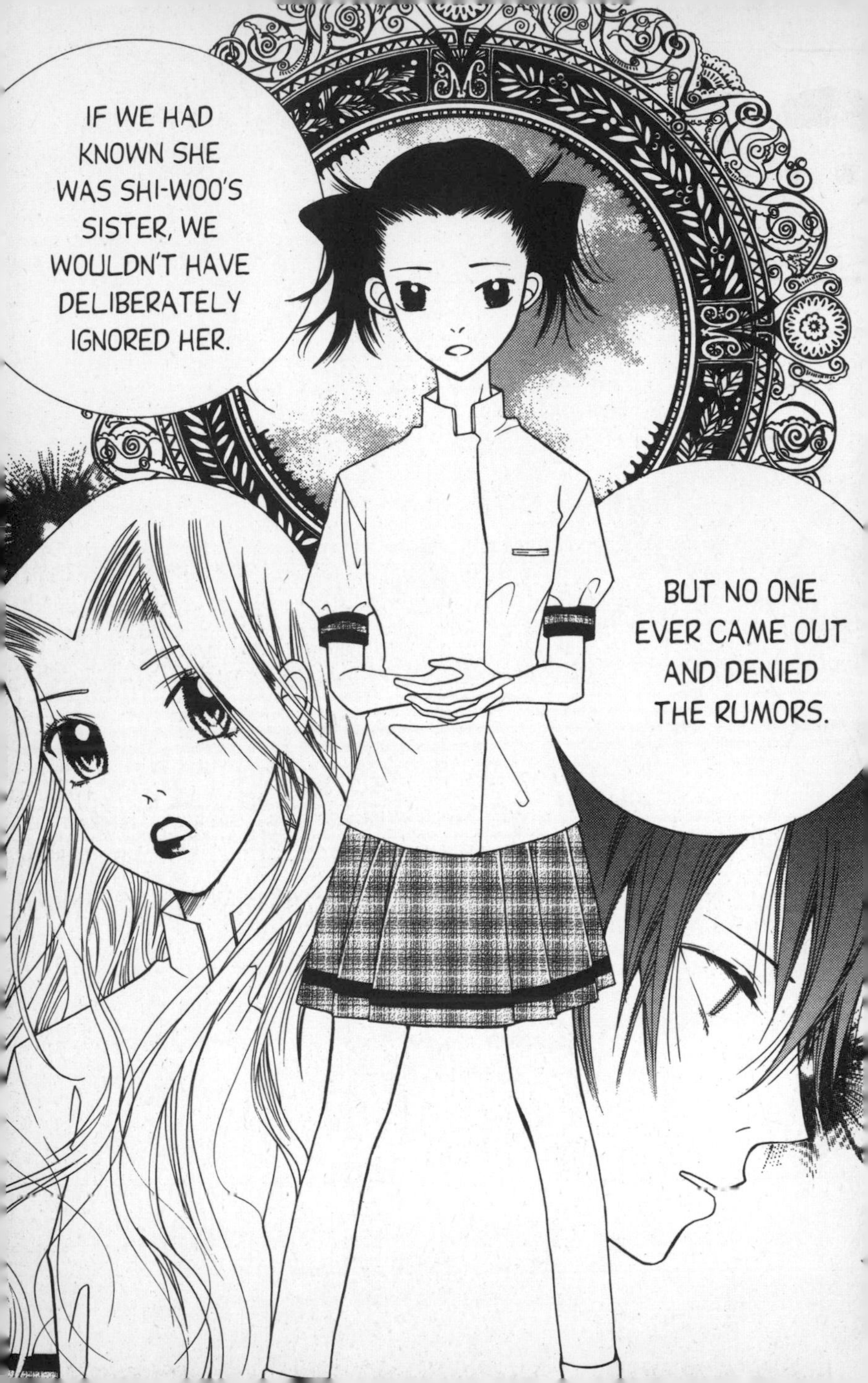
IF WE HAD KNOWN SHE WAS SHI-WOO'S SISTER, WE WOULDN'T HAVE DELIBERATELY IGNORED HER.
BUT NO ONE EVER CAME OUT AND DENIED THE RUMORS.

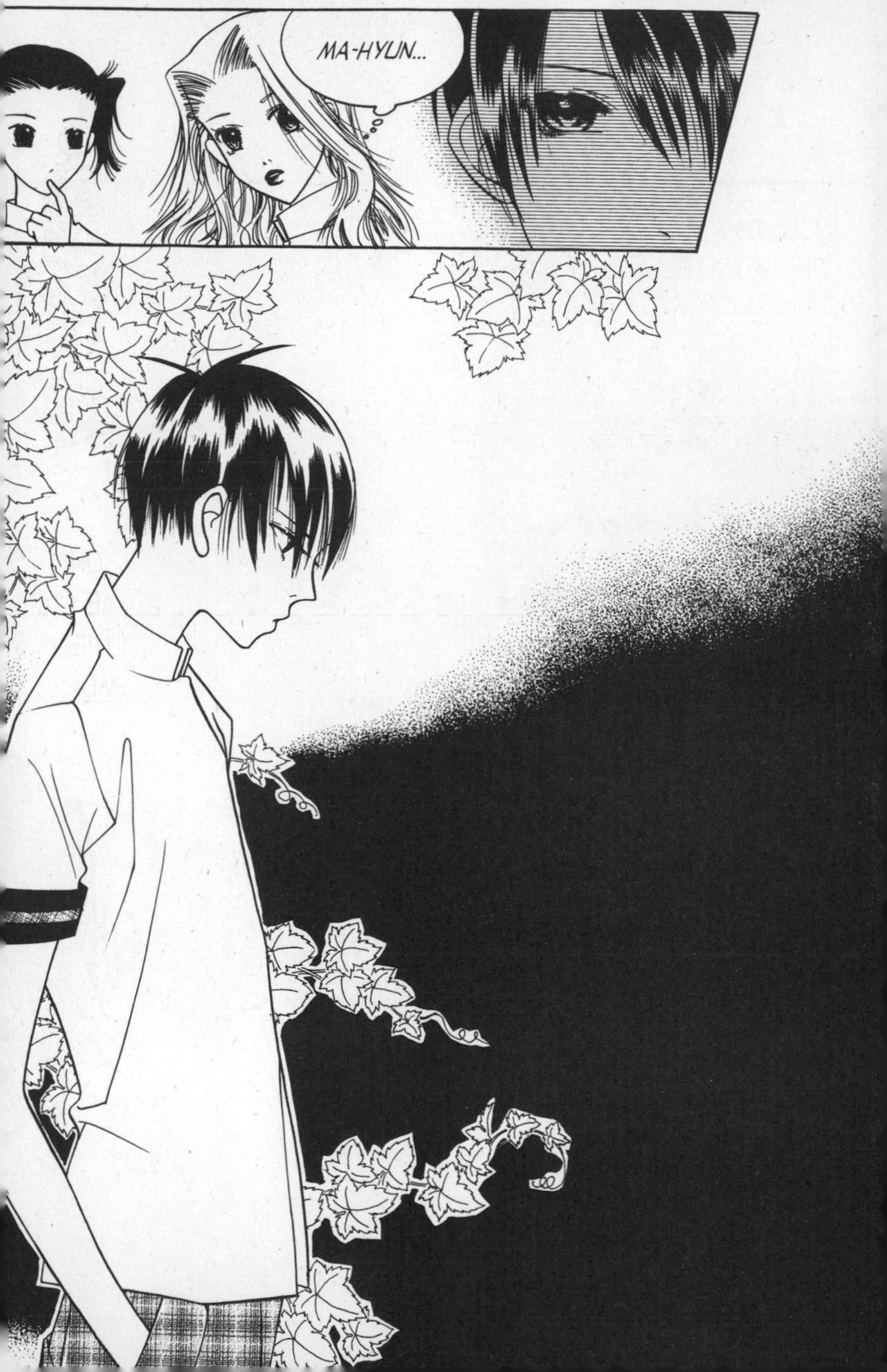
MA-HYUN...

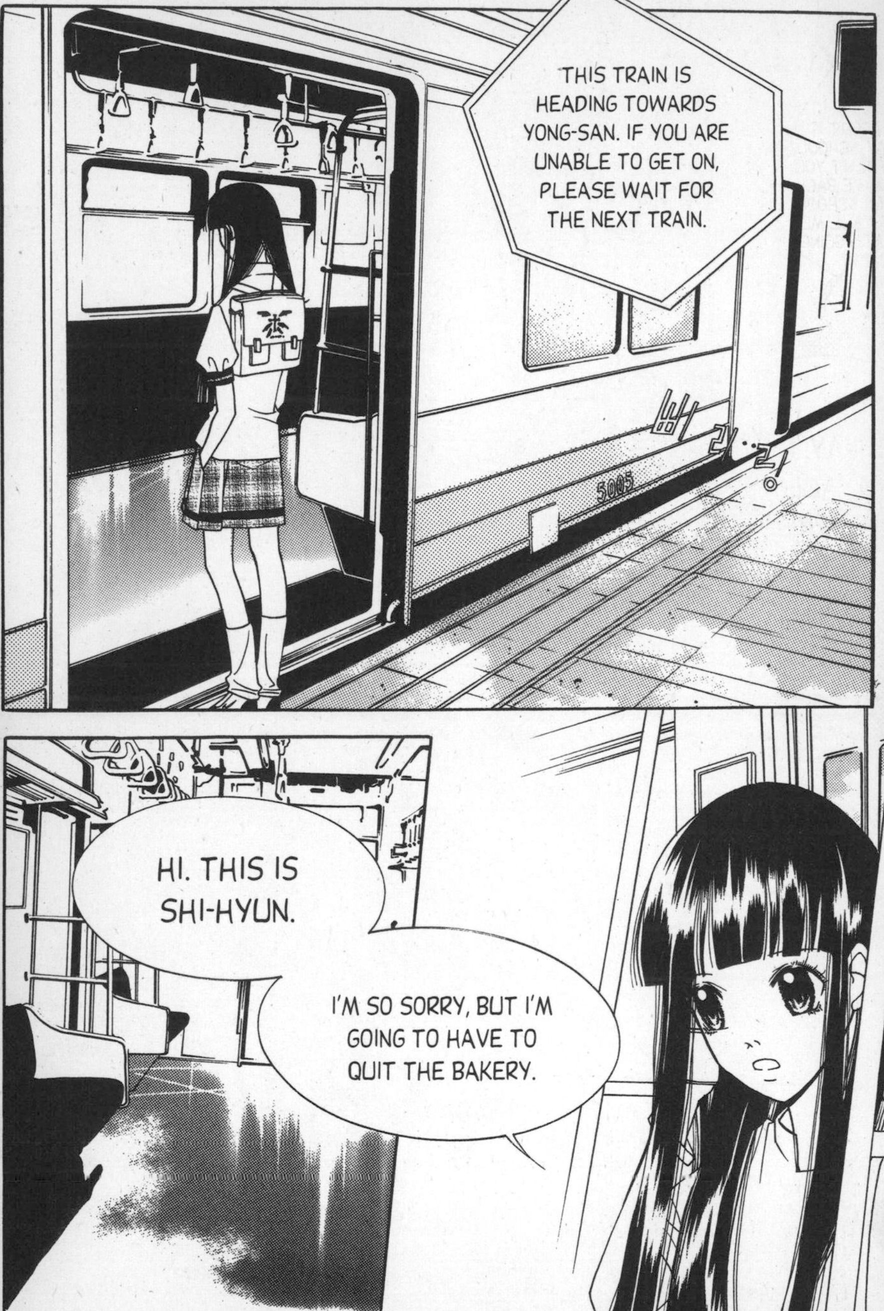
THIS TRAIN IS HEADING TOWARDS YONG-SAN. IF YOU ARE UNABLE TO GET ON, PLEASE WAIT FOR THE NEXT TRAIN.
5005
HI. THIS IS SHI-HYUN.
I'M SO SORRY, BUT I'M GOING TO HAVE TO QUIT THE BAKERY.

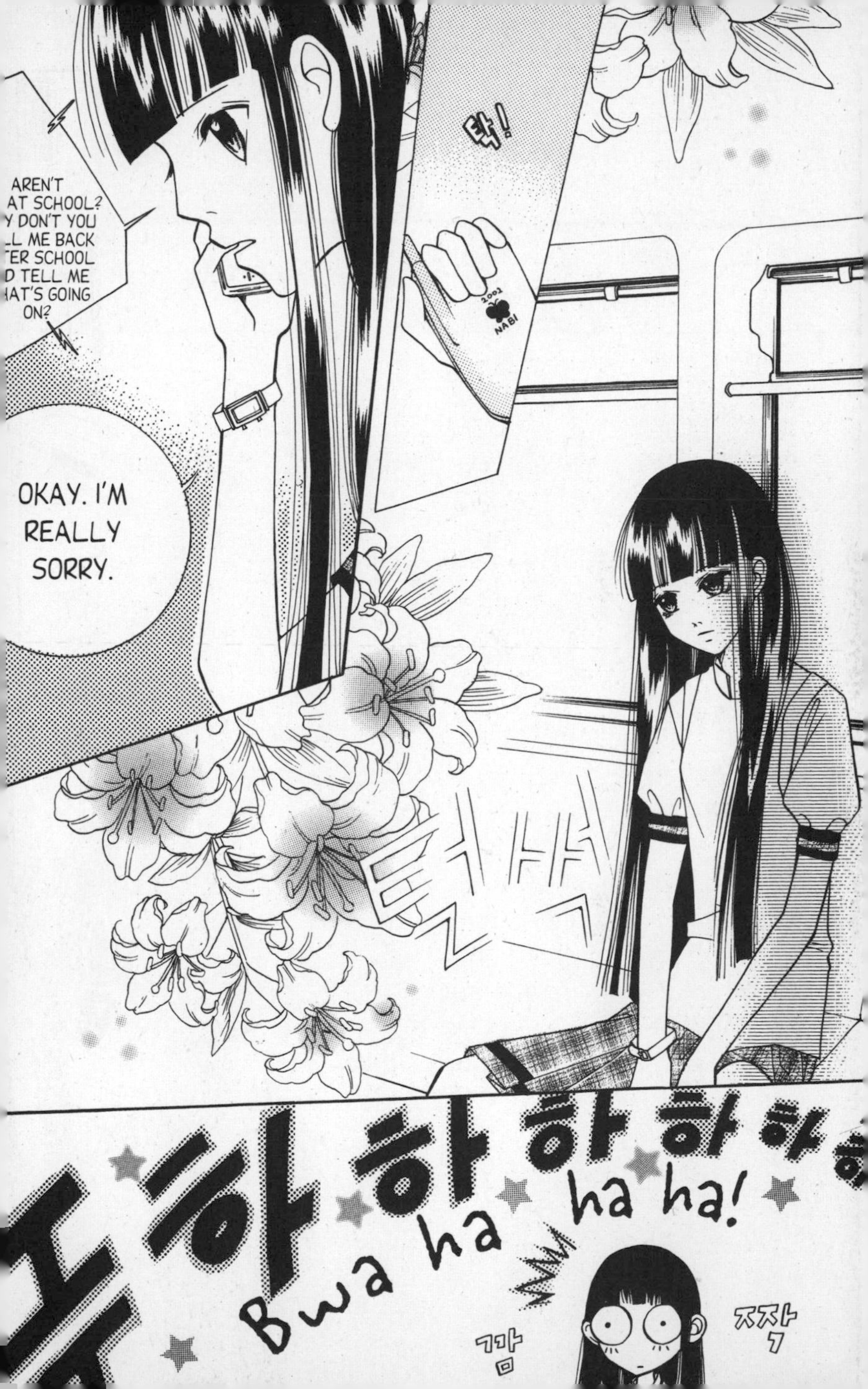
AREN'T
AT SCHOOL?
Y DON'T YOU
LL ME BACK
TER SCHOOL
D TELL ME
HAT'S GOING
ON?
탁!
OKAY. I'M REALLY SORRY.
Bwa ha ha ha!
끔

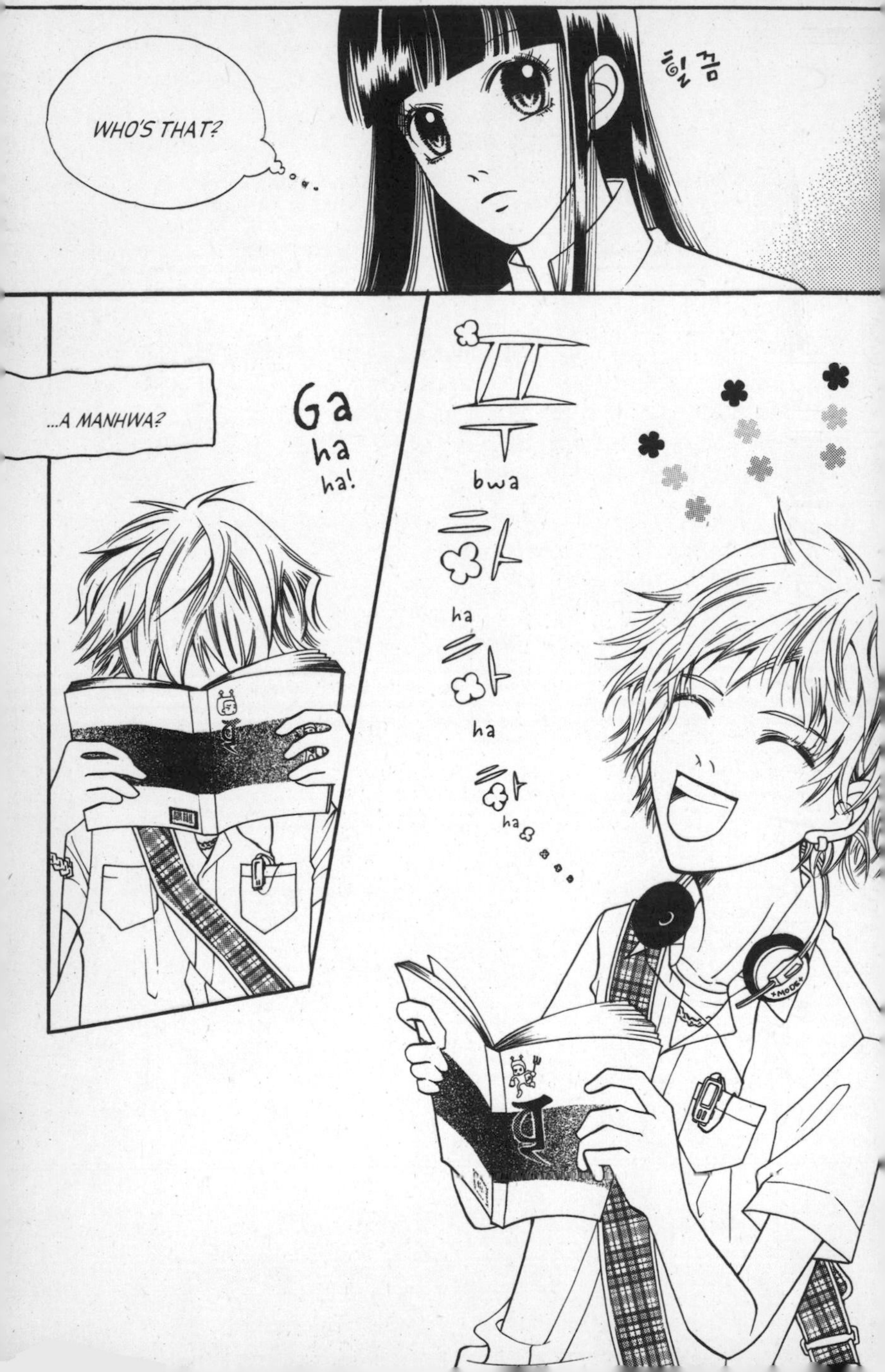
WHO'S THAT?
힐끔
...A MANHWA?
Ga ha ha!
푸
bwa
하
ha
하
ha
하
ha...

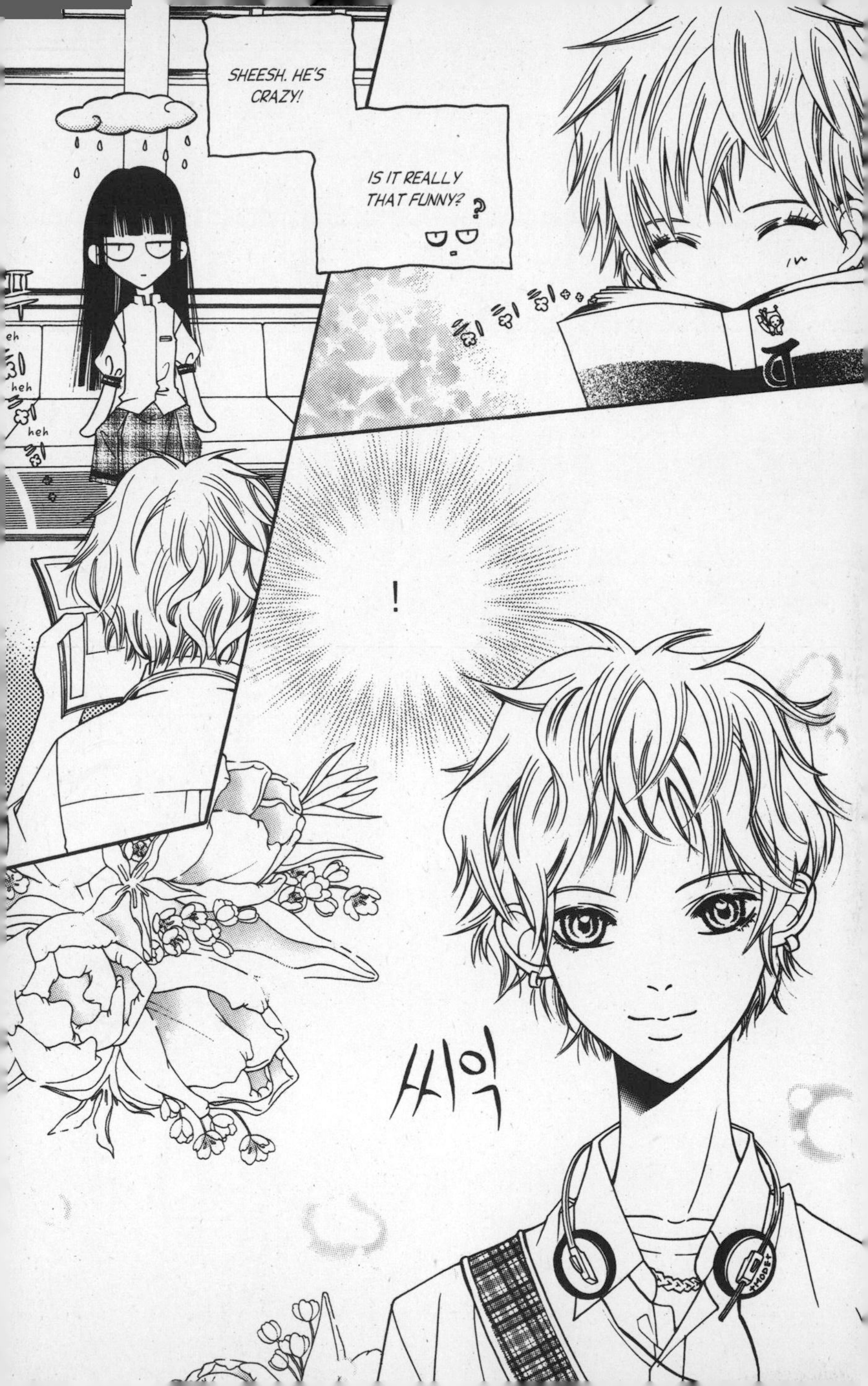

SHEESH. HE'S CRAZY!
IS IT REALLY THAT FUNNY?
heh
heh
heh
!
씨익

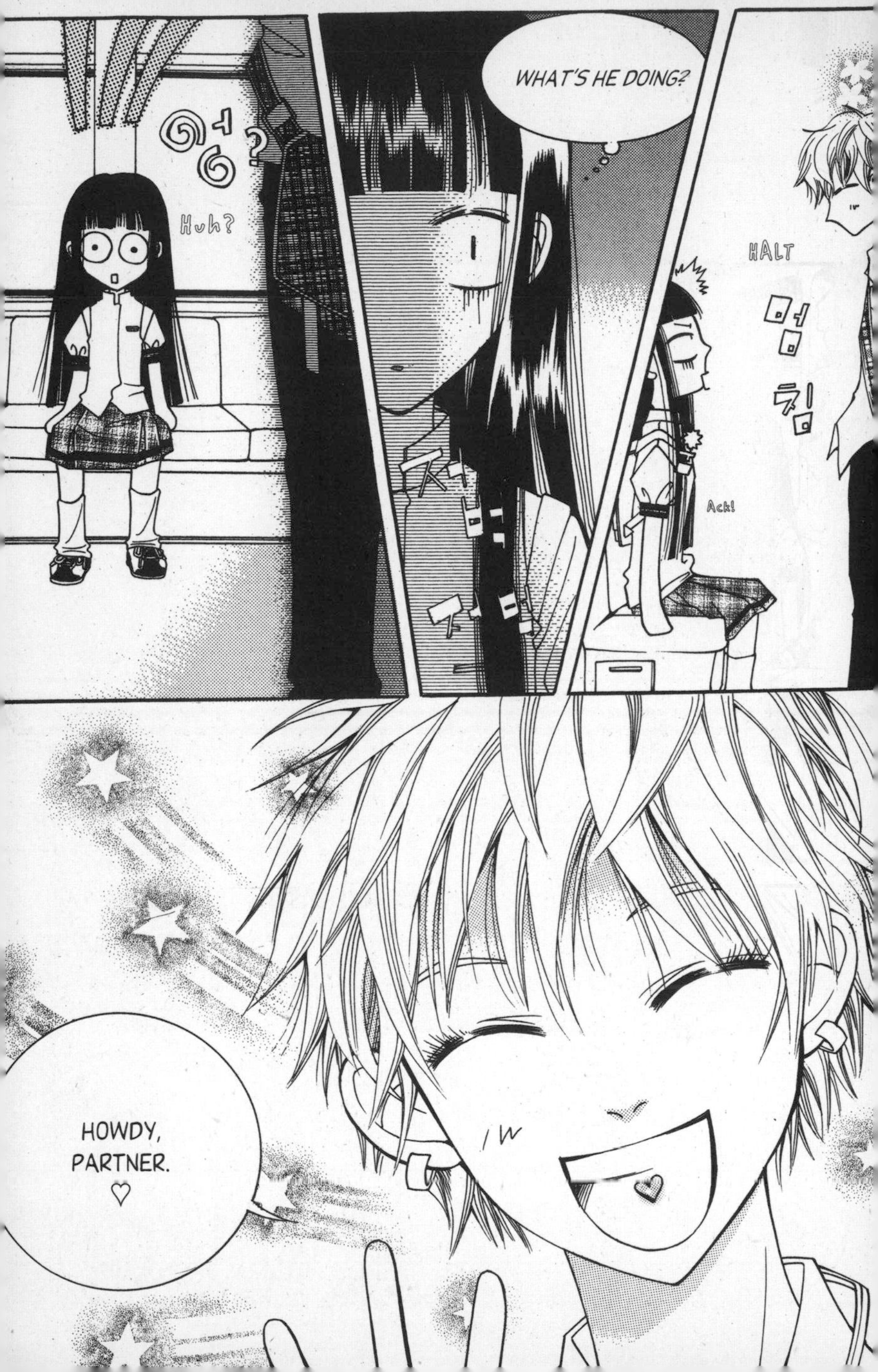
Huh?
WHAT'S HE DOING?
HALT
Ack!
HOWDY, PARTNER. ♡

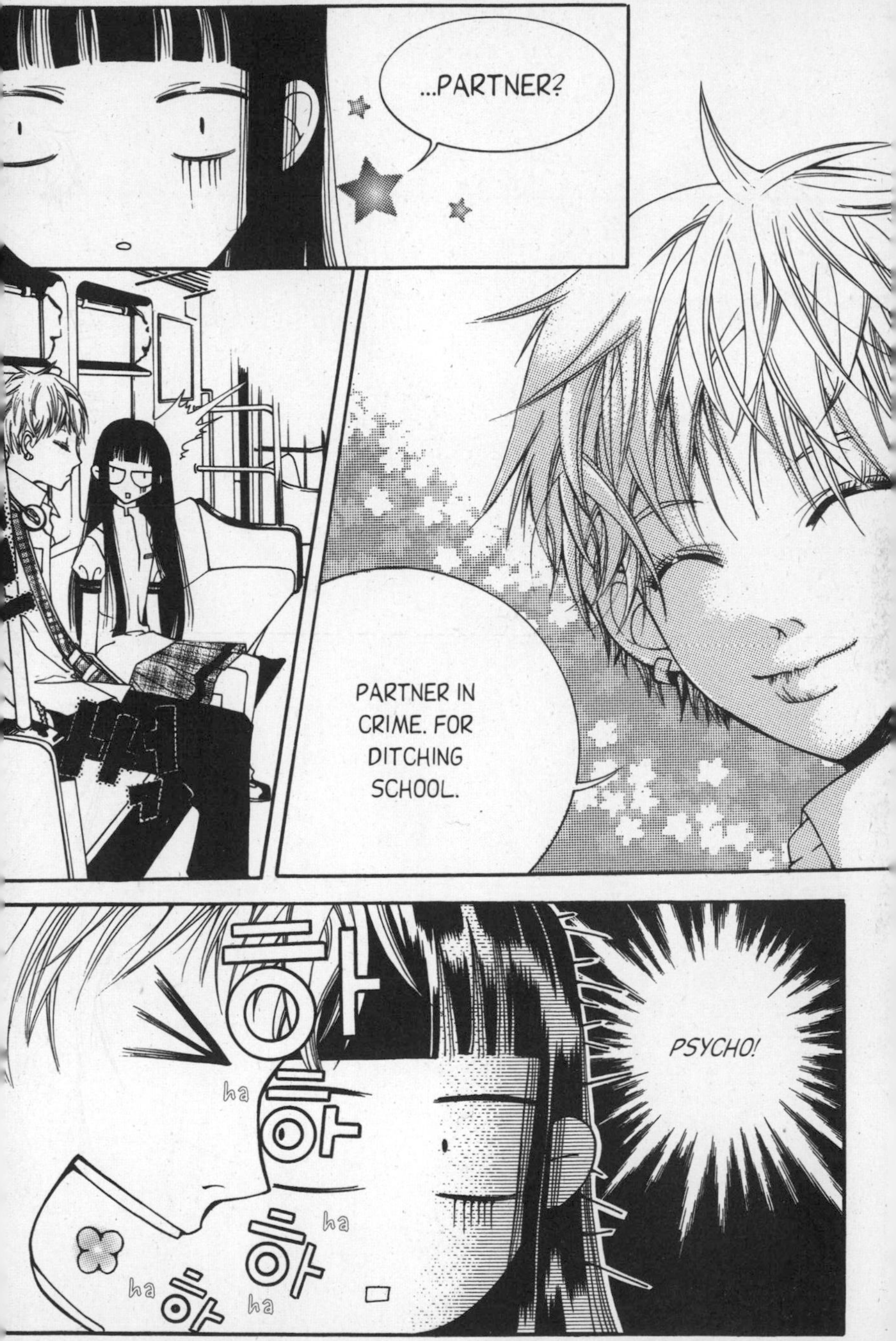
...PARTNER?
PARTNER IN CRIME. FOR DITCHING SCHOOL.
하
ha
하
ha
하
ha
하
ha
PSYCHO!

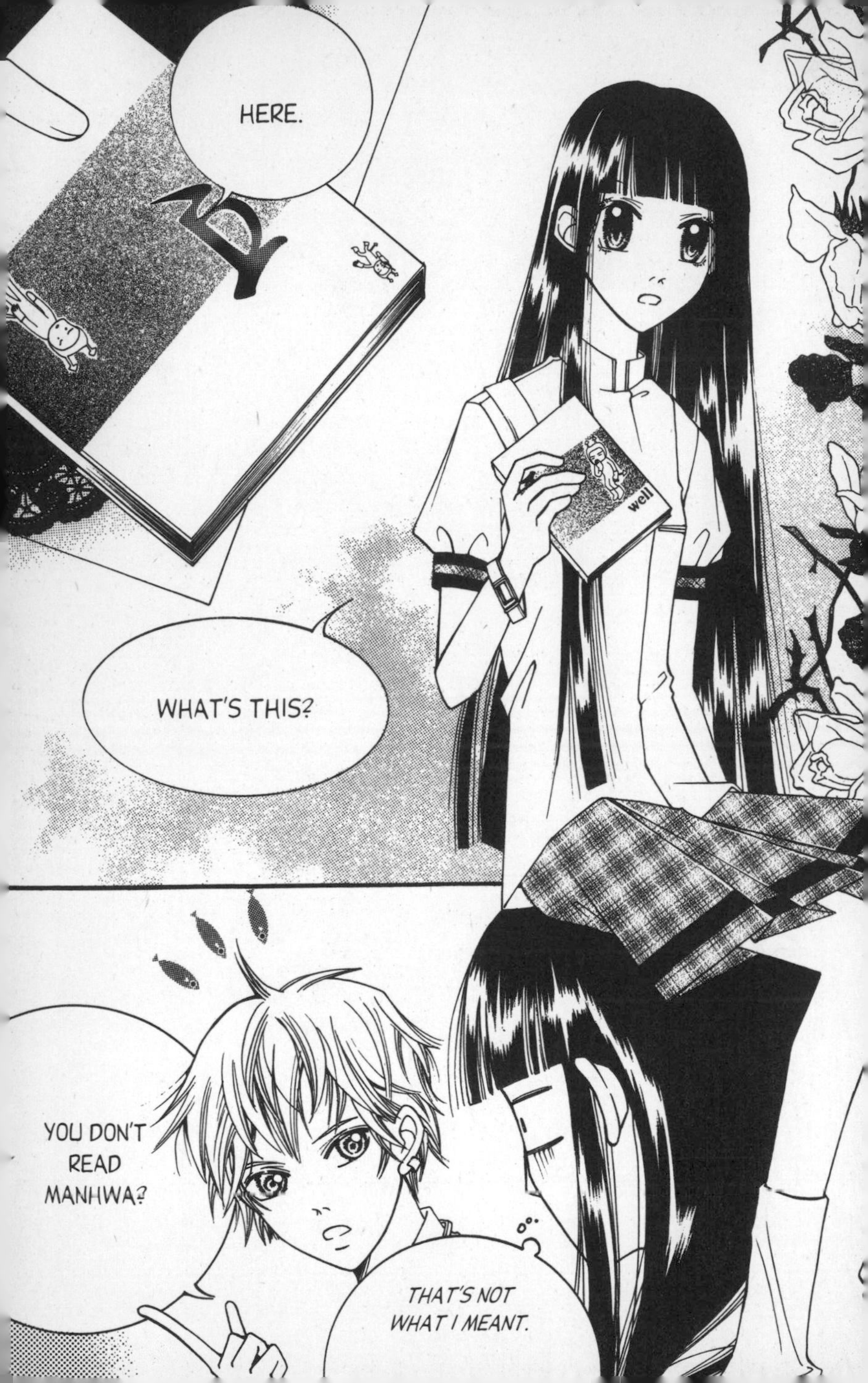
HERE.
WHAT'S THIS?
well
YOU DON'T READ MANHWA?
THAT'S NOT WHAT I MEANT.

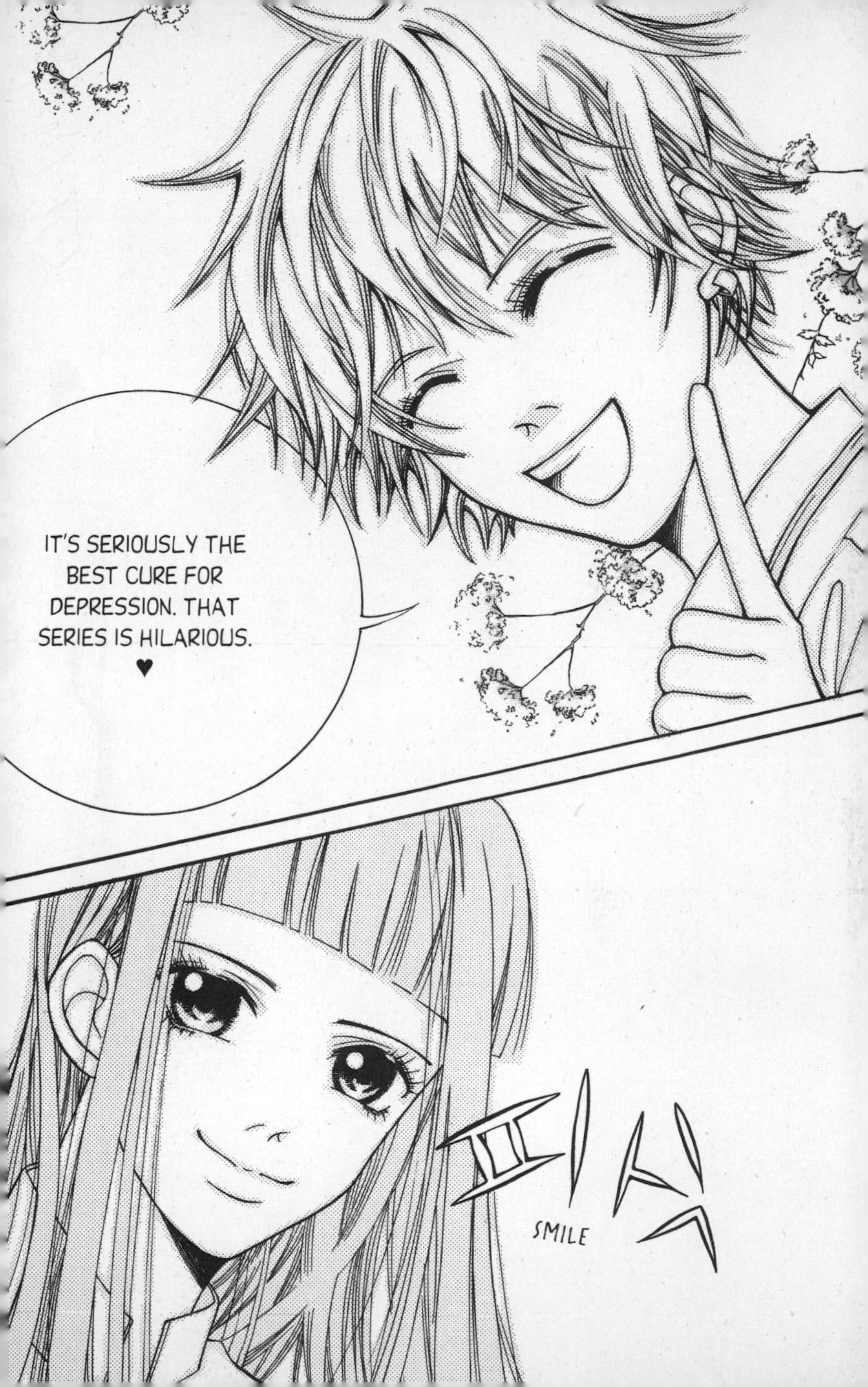
IT'S SERIOUSLY THE BEST CURE FOR DEPRESSION. THAT SERIES IS HILARIOUS. ♥
SMILE

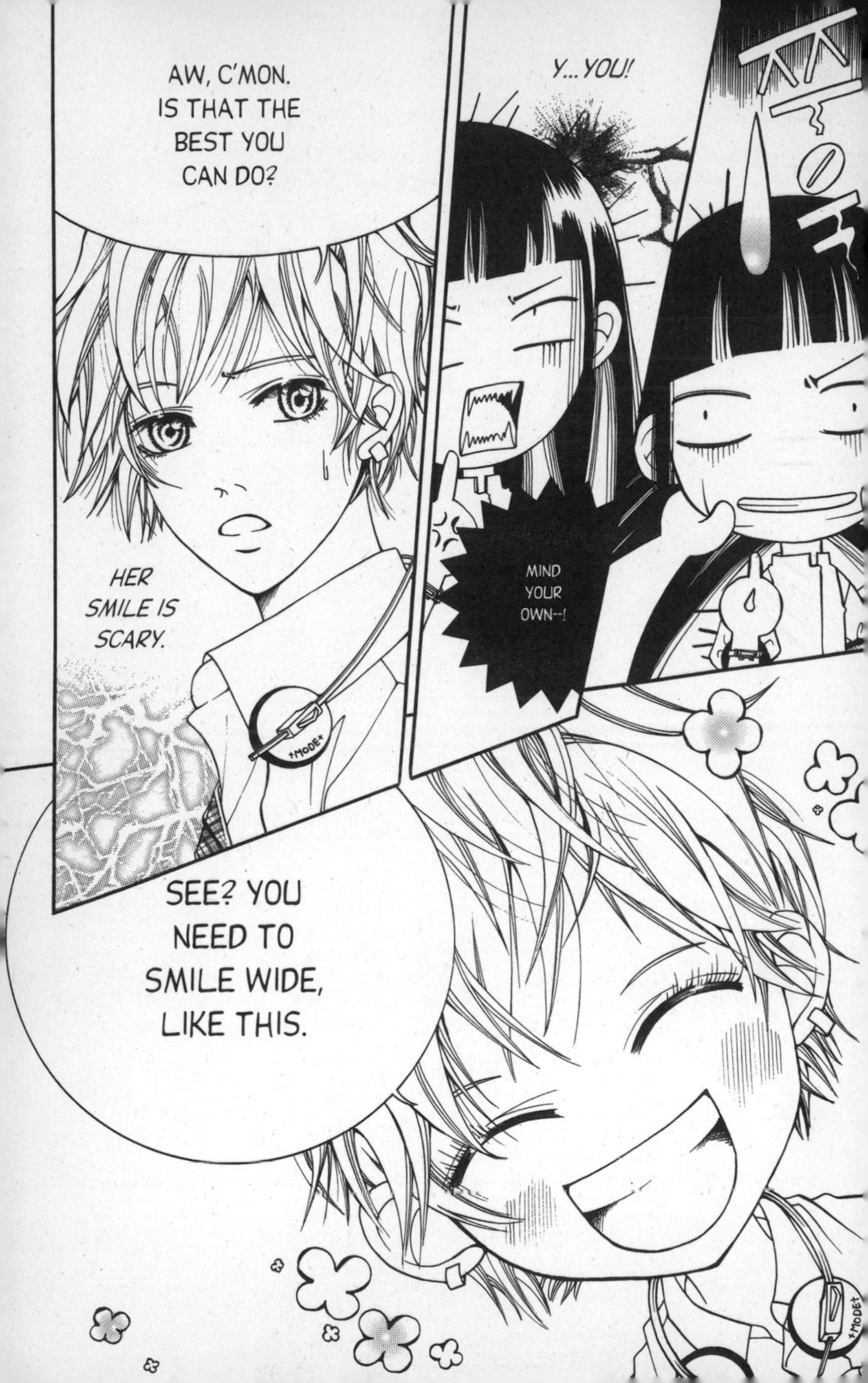
AW, C'MON. IS THAT THE BEST YOU CAN DO?
HER SMILE IS SCARY.
Y... YOU!
MIND YOUR OWN--!
SEE? YOU NEED TO SMILE WIDE, LIKE THIS.

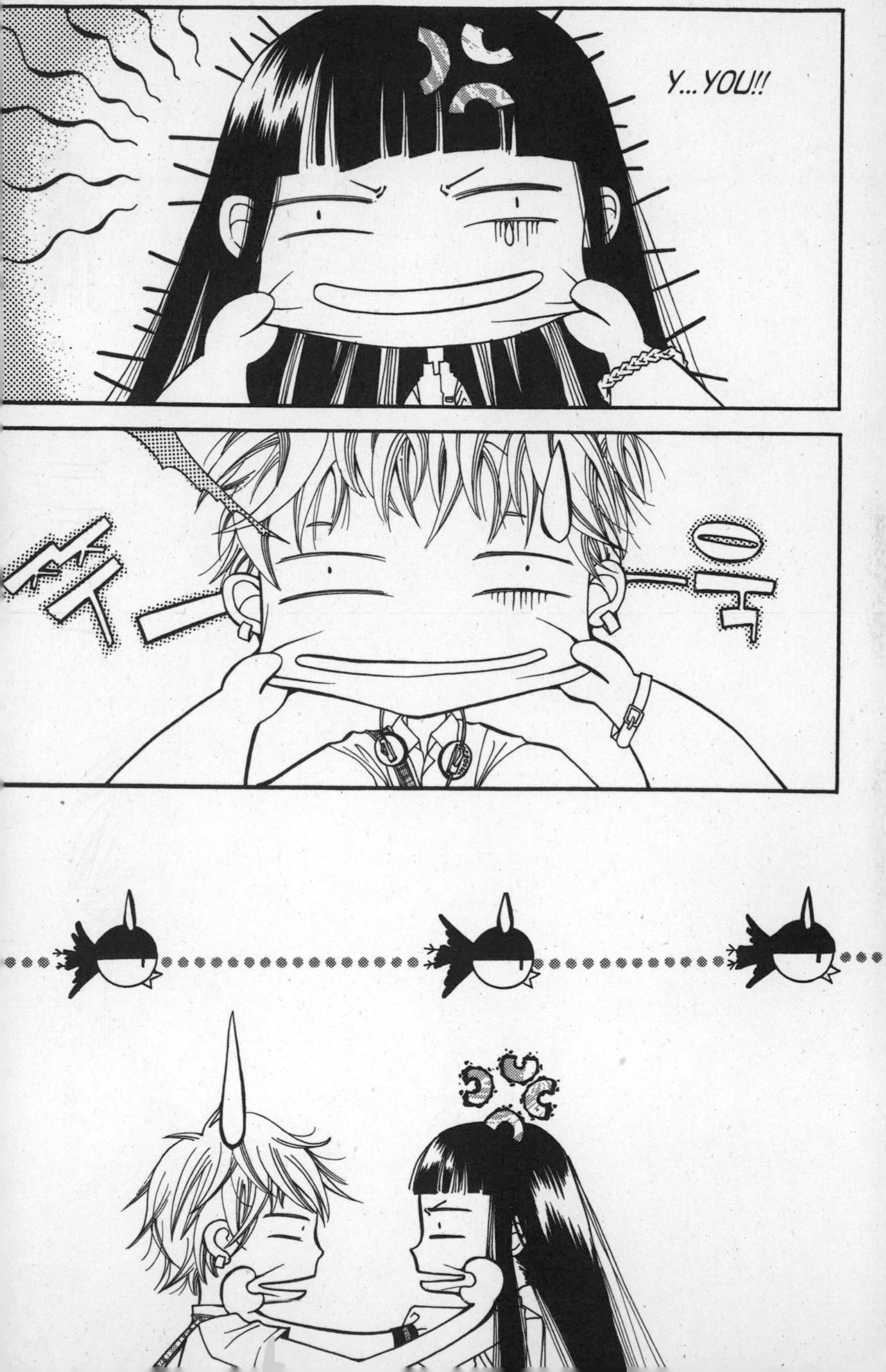
Y...YOU!!

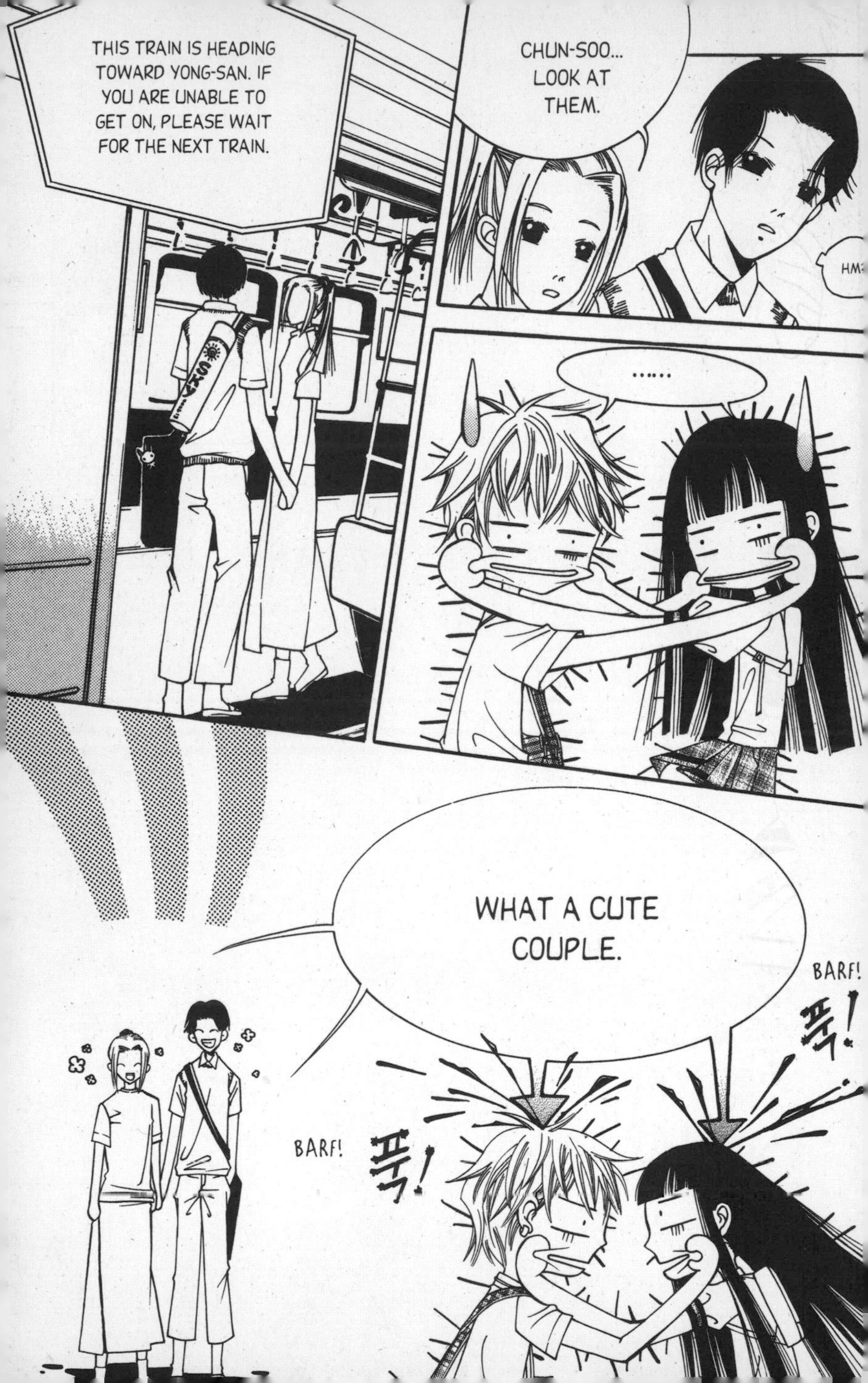
THIS TRAIN IS HEADING TOWARD YONG-SAN. IF YOU ARE UNABLE TO GET ON, PLEASE WAIT FOR THE NEXT TRAIN.
CHUN-SOO... LOOK AT THEM.
HM?
......
WHAT A CUTE COUPLE.
BARF!
푹!
BARF!
푹!

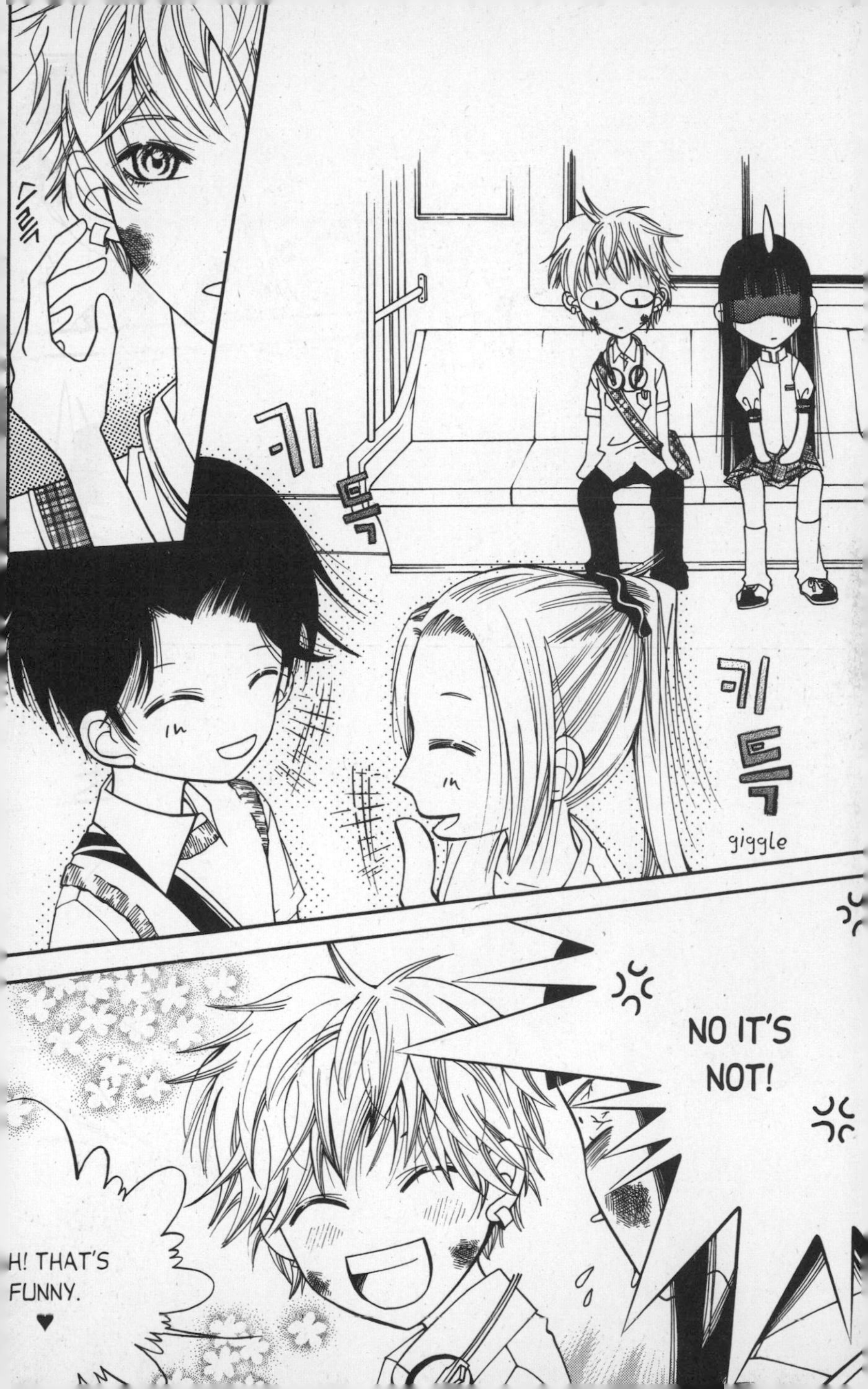
키득
키득
giggle
H! THAT'S FUNNY. ♥
NO IT'S NOT!

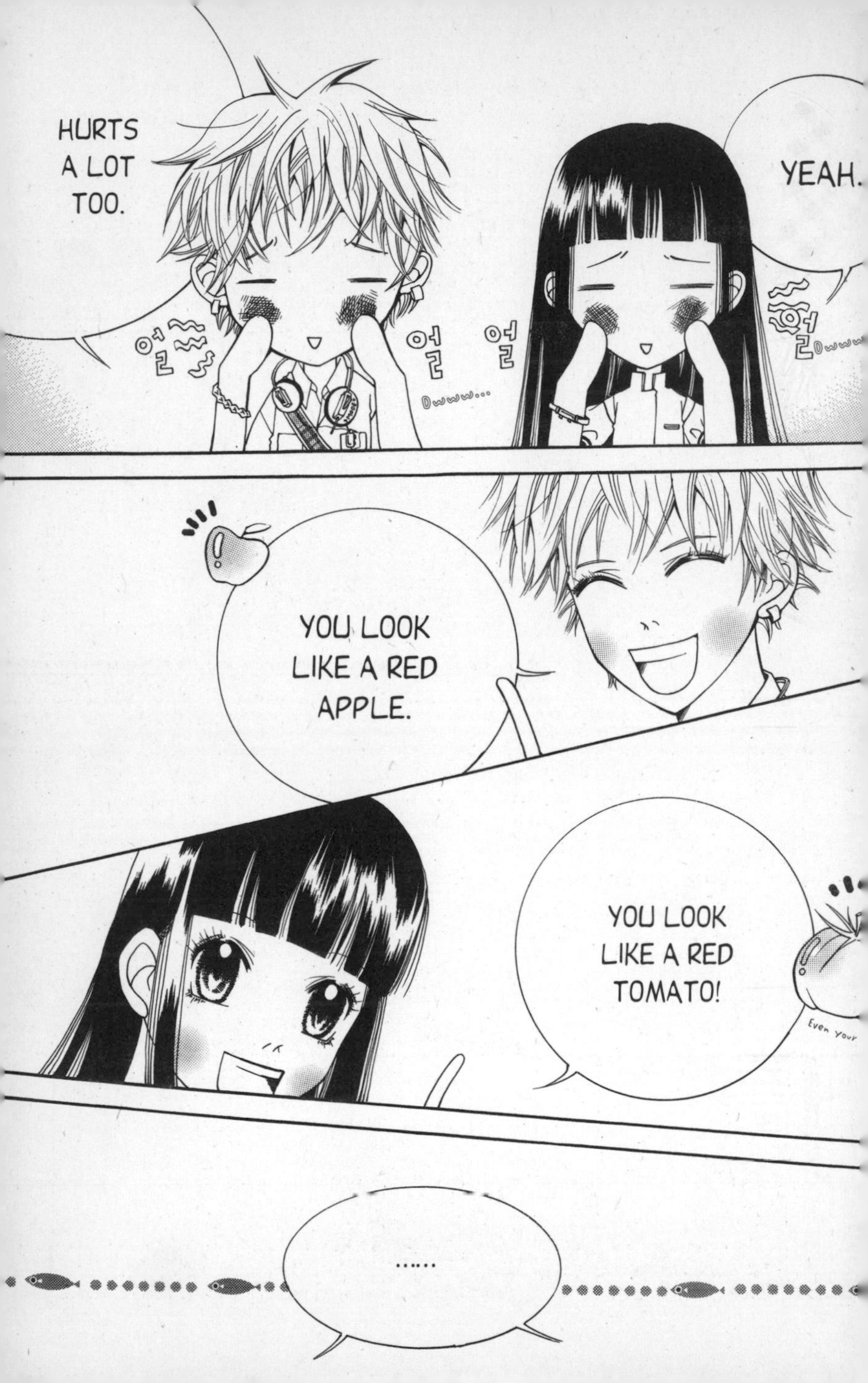
HURTS A LOT TOO.
YEAH.
얼~ 얼~ 얼 얼
얼 얼 Owww...
Owww...
YOU LOOK LIKE A RED APPLE.
YOU LOOK LIKE A RED TOMATO!
Even your
......

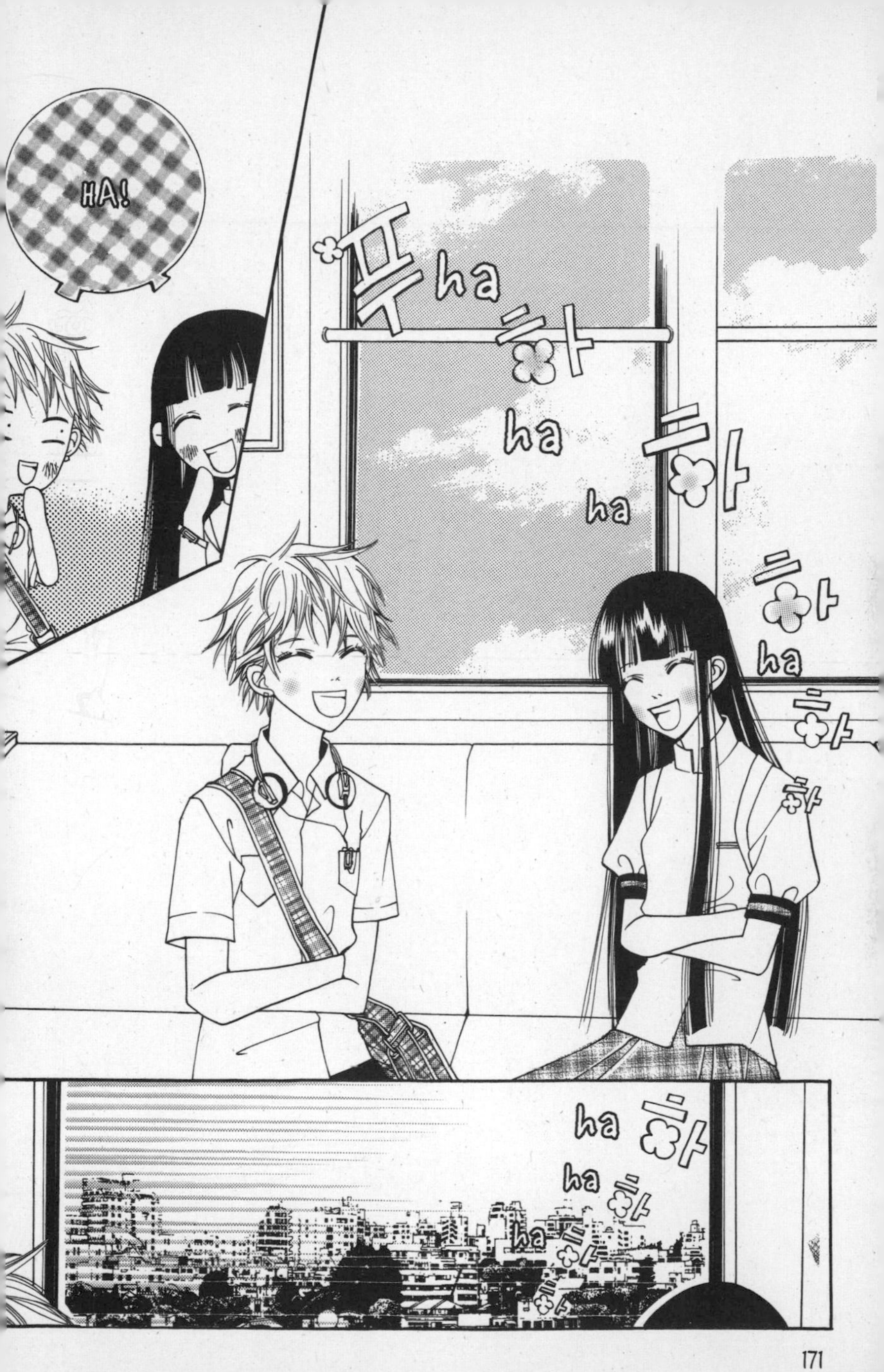
HA!
푸 ha
하
ha
하
ha
하
ha
하
하
ha 하
ha 하
ha 하
하

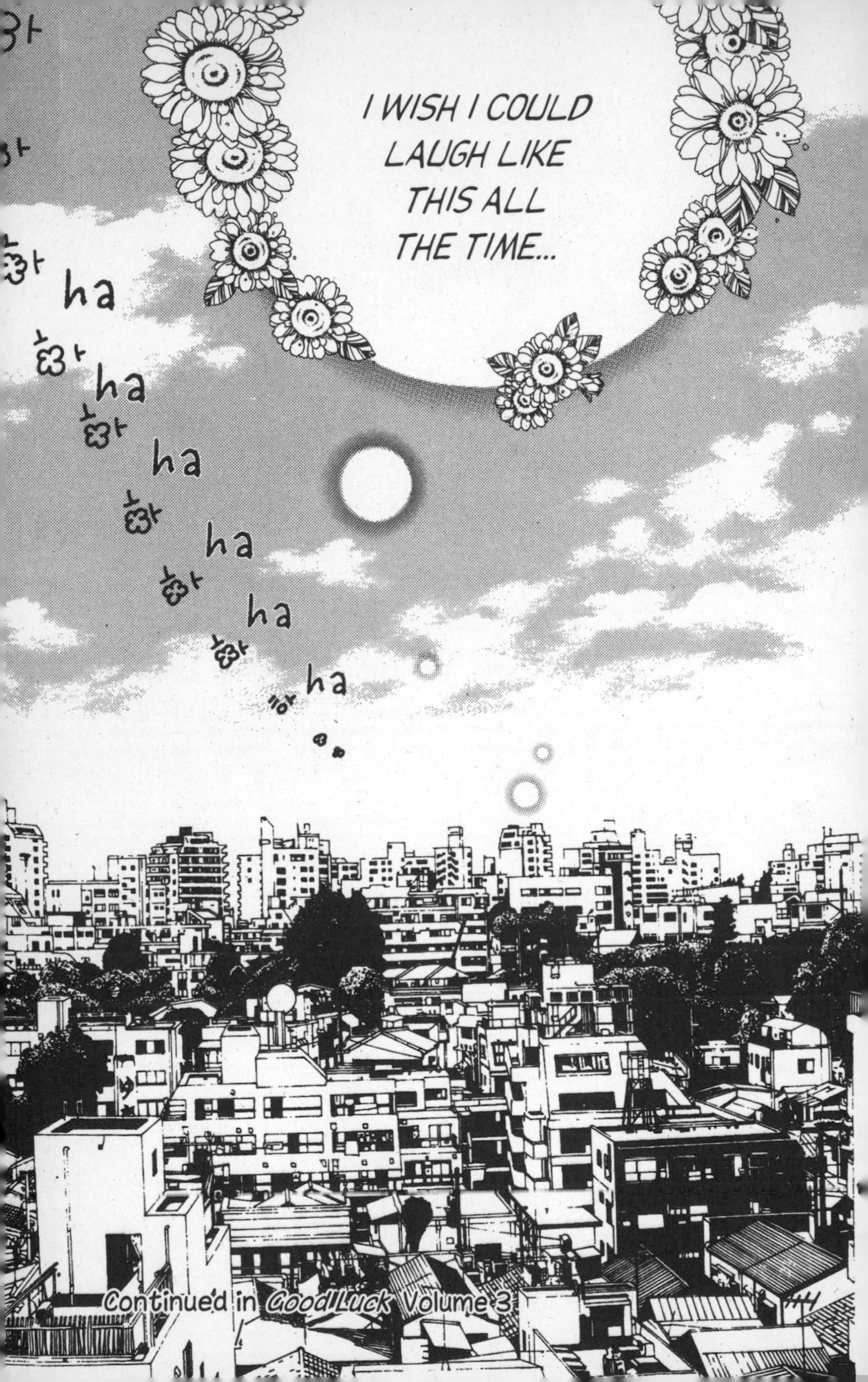
I WISH I COULD LAUGH LIKE THIS ALL THE TIME...
ha
ha
ha
ha
ha
ha
Continued in Good Luck Volume 3

Epilogue

But it's hard.

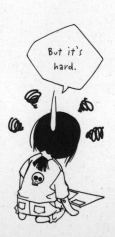

good luck™

good luck™
3

TOKYOPOP

E-JIN KANG

NEXT VOL. PREVIEW!

SHI-HYUN'S NEW FRIEND FROM THE TRAIN, DA-MIN, TURNS OUT TO BE EVEN MORE EXCITING THAN SHE THOUGHT. IN FACT, HE MIGHT JUST BE HER TICKET TO STARDOM! BUT WHAT WILL MA-HYUN AND SHI-WOO DO WHEN THEY FIND OUT? PREPARE FOR THE ULTIMATE LOVE QUADRANGLE IN THE NEXT VOLUME OF GOOD LUCK!